DANCE OF THE NOMAD

DANCE OF THE NOMAD

A Study of the Selected Notebooks of A. D. Hope

ANN McCULLOCH

THE AUSTRALIAN NATIONAL UNIVERSITY
E PRESS

Published by ANU E Press
The Australian National University
Canberra ACT 0200, Australia
Email: anuepress@anu.edu.au

This title is also available online at: http://epress.anu.edu.au/dance_nomad_citation.html

National Library of Australia Cataloguing-in-Publication Entry

    Author: McCulloch, A. M. (Ann Maree), 1949-
    Title: Dance of the nomad : a study of the selected notebooks of A.D. Hope / Ann McCulloch.
    ISBN: 9781921666902 (pbk.) 9781921666919 (eBook)
    Notes: Includes bibliographical references.
    Subjects: Hope, A. D. (Alec Derwent), 1907-2000--Criticism and interpretation.
           Hope, A. D. (Alec Derwent), 1907-2000--Notebooks, sketchbooks, etc.
    Dewey Number: A828.3

All rights reserved. No part of this publication may be reproduced, stored in a retrieval system or transmitted in any form or by any means, electronic, mechanical, photocopying or otherwise, without the prior permission of the publisher.

Cover design by Emily Brissenden

Cover: Professor A. D. Hope. 1991. L. Seselja. NL36907.
By permission of National Library of Australia.

This edition © 2010 ANU E Press
First edition © 2005 Pandanus Books

In memory of my parents
Ann and Kevin McDermott
and sister in law, Dina McDermott

LETTER TO ANN McCULLOCH

'This may well be rym doggerel', dear Ann
But the best I can manage in liquor so late
At night.
You asked me where I'd begin in your place. I can
Not answer that. But as a general case I might.

Drop the proviso, 'Supposing That I were you';
I find it impossible to think myself in your place
But in general almost any writer would do:
The problem is much the same in every case.
Where to begin? — No matter where you start,
You will find three persons in one at least,
All real,
All with different roots; How can you tell them
Apart
Each entwined as they are with the others
With whom you must deal?

So it doesn't much matter where you decide
To begin;
You cannot trace ends without encountering
Them all.
So the only advice I can give you is just
Dig in
Where you come on a light or a lead however
Small

And resist, if you can, the biographer's
natural urge
To tidy the subject up and deliver him neat.
Remember loose ends hang loose, won't mix
Or merge
But without them the portrait must always be incomplete.

And Negative Capability, don't forget that,
The thing that marks off a poet from other men!
If you forget what I wrote, wearing my other hat,
I suggest you read 'The Three Faces of Love' again.
But more important, and perhaps hardest of all,
What most biographers tend to ignore or dismiss
Are the random decisions, the cross-road choices
I call
My Otherwise Mountain. Its shape and importance is this:

We are shaped by our choices, even those that
We did not make
Or which were made for us, sometimes against
Our will.
Where pathways diverge, the ones that we did
Not take
Mostly forgotten, serve to determine us still.
So the Otherwise Mountain is a tremendous pile
Built of the choices whose ends are still unseen,
Peopled with ghostly shades, mile upon mile,
Ghosts of the countless persons we might
have been.
Would they have been more fortunate or less?
Looking back I can see pitfalls side-stepped,
Chances lost.
But mostly they keep their secrets. I cannot
Guess
Had I dared more or cared less to count the cost.

These are the things a biographer cannot
Know
Yet must somehow try to envisage and calculate.
Like those shadowy possible selves drifting
To and fro,
All they can do is ponder the problem and wait.

page ix
Dance of the Nomad

They wait for a moment when at last we shall
Meet
The only moment that gives me no choice at all,
The moment that makes me whole, all my
Acts complete
When I see the Otherwise Mountain crumble
And fall
And merge the things that I did with those
Undone
Since I am the product of everything that I
Rejected or chose to do in the long run
And I shall not reach it until I come
To die.

That is all I can do. It is you must record
And create.
From now on it is you must decide what you
Think about me.
I cannot contribute opinions or join in
Debate
But to check matters of fact of course I am free.
Good Luck to you!
Your amorphous
    Biographee!

A. D. Hope

ACKNOWLEDGEMENTS

Conversations as much as the writings of A. D. Hope have been the impetus of this book. I have learnt from colleagues, students, and respondents to conference papers who either initiated or participated in these conversations. Their questions and subsequent discussions were invaluable in my construction of an overview of Hope's thoughts whilst attempting to honour my pact with him that he was not 'to be delivered neat'. A special thank you is extended to Penelope Hope with whom I spent many wonderful hours. Early conversations with participants in the six documentary video programmes which formed an integral part of the research for this book were pivotal; my gratitude therefore extends to: Hilary Webster; Chris Wallace Crabbe; Bill Ramson; Bob Holden; Arthur Burns; David Brooks, Nicki Stasko, The poet, πό; George Watts; Harry Heseltine and to others who formed a significant part in the representation of this research: Adrian Murrell Barker and Francis Treacey. Particular thanks to Tony Hood and Rita Kryshkovski who, during this period, assisted me with the editing of the film script, and at critical times since, have proved to be valued listeners, questioners and friends.

The years of research at the National Library of Australia involved numerous trips from Melbourne to Canberra. I was fortunate that friends in Canberra not only took care of me on my visits but also often assisted me in my research inquiries. Bob and Rosemary Brissenden were crucial in this regard. Indeed it was through them that I gained the initial desire to pursue this work. I thank Sally Burns and Andrew Hope, who, during the years when Alec Hope was in their immediate care, always welcomed me into their home despite the inconvenience this must have caused. I will always be grateful to Mart Idnurm for the high quality of his close reading and analysis of Hope's notes on cosmology, and to Prillie Idnurm, whose wisdom extends into all areas of human endeavor, and served as one of my most insistent and valued questioners. I am also grateful to Gun Ringwood, who provided me with friendship, informed advice, accommodation and critical assessment at a moment's notice and my sister Joan Ritchie who wove into my Canberra visits welcomed meetings, lunches and general support.

Given the often illegible script of Hope's Notebooks I became reliant on a network of friends, family and colleagues who helped decipher the screed. They include: Aliki Pavlou; my sister Chris Chalmers; my children Kate and Alexander; my nephew William McDermott, Ron Vowles and my parents Ann and Kevin McDermott. Rai Sahib was not only an invaluable de-coder of the sometimes illegible script, but also of great assistance in word-processing early documents selected for the book. I also thank Caroline Williamson for her patient and meticulous work on the manuscripts. There were also others whose interest in my work sustained my perseverance: David Brooks, Kati Berenson, Helen Tebble, Justin Clemens, Peter Davis, Tim Megihan, Deborah Walker, John Forrest. Corin Spenser, and perhaps especially, Dameon Vesquez.

To particular friends and colleagues I owe a great debt. To Aliki Pavlou and Alan Woodruff for keeping my spirit alive during the later stages, rigorously checking corrections made, and assisting me in tracking down elusive information; to Adrian Alder, a doctoral research student at Deakin University, who gave considerable time, creative imagination and rigorous research skills to gathering source material for the construction of endnotes. Ron Goodrich and Paul Monaghan warrant thanks for the time each gave to translations from Latin. Ron Goodrich's assistance covered many areas; his perceptive and rigorous reading of the manuscript at crucial times provided a depth of wisdom, searching scholarship and creative thinking that enhanced the work.

I thank John Ritchie for his general support and, in particular, for suggesting that I submit this work to Pandanus Books. It has been a pleasure to work with the production editor, Justine Molony, whose dedication, enthusiasm and intelligence has played a large part in the realisation of this work

I wish to thank the officers from the National Library of Australia whose assistance has always been exact, friendly and persistent. Finally I am grateful to Deakin University for providing me with research leave at crucial times, both in the early years of research and in more recent times when final drafts were being written. My greatest debt goes to A. D. Hope who gave me not only the opportunity to have access to his work but who gave tirelessly of his time, wisdom and humour.

Ann McCulloch

CONTENTS

Letter to Ann McCulloch		viii
Acknowledgements		xi
Preface		xv
Overview and Argument: Mapping the Maze		xxi
I	A. D. Hope: Dance of a Nomad in Flight from the Doppelgänger	1
II	Negative Capability	35
III	Anti-Modernism	61
IV	Argument and Commentary on Critics and Writers	97
V	What is Art?	137
VI	Source of His Poetry	165
VII	A Sense of Detachment	187
VIII	Cosmology	219
IX	Wine, Women and Insectual Song	245
X	A Sense of Destiny	279
XI	The Dream-Team	303
XII	Argument by Analogy	333
Bibliography		357

PREFACE

A chance meeting with A. D. Hope in a lift in 1983 might be seen as a source of this work. At the time, I was studying for a PhD in Literature at the Australian National University, and Hope, although retired from academia, occupied an office in the A. D. Hope Building from which he conducted his vocation as a poet. A humorous exchange between us led to a lunch that became a weekly event for the next three years.

If I were to identify the nature of the intellectual rapport between us, I would characterise it in terms of our common experience of knowledge as provisional, subjective and ultimately elusive. On my part, I was drawn to Hope's view, implicit in his poetry and other writings, that art (poetry) was a superior force as a means for the creation of new being, of new values and as a guide for the conduct of our lives; and that it was no less trustworthy than the arguments of philosophy, the demonstration of science and the supposed 'certainties' of revelation. Indeed, I had found in Hope's poetry a metaphysics that drew from all of these areas yet simultaneously transformed into music. These meetings involved Hope telling me about his life, the philosophies that informed his poetry and his reading or asking me to read his poetry. Hope asked me to write his story and, in the early weeks of our conversations, he stressed the significance of his notebooks. It was not until 1986, when I received a Harold White Fellowship at the National Library of Australia, that I first came to read them.

It would be an understatement to say that I found the experience daunting. The range of Hope's knowledge seemed in those early years impossible to negotiate. It occurs to me now as I survey the final selections how influenced I might have been by the entries written in the first folder I opened. This folder was different from the notebooks in that it contained nine entries only, which had been written between 1955 and 1964. Some of them are dated by year instead of by month. They were loose-leafed, unlike the other notebooks, which were bound. The content of this folder tells a tale that I could come to understand only after the dozens of readings I gave the bound notebooks. They are also possibly the most 'personal' of Hope's entries. Applying the term 'personal' to any of Hope's writings is problematic, as when he does come to speak of himself in an emotional way it will invariably be about his role in this world as a poet and as a thinker.

His first entry, dated 11 September (1955?), deals with his love of the sea and is titled 'Eastern View'. Hope is holidaying by the sea and relishing the effects of lying naked in the sun. At night-time, watching the 'lights of home wink from the far end of the bay, and the waves crashing and sighing on the beach', he recalls his earliest memory of empathy with the sea when, as an eight-year-old, he had camped with his family at Swansea: 'I awoke to hear the sea sobbing mysteriously on the beach and found that I was crying. I had been crying in my sleep. I felt whole again — every tension relaxed. Finished a poem.' Hope concludes the entry with his resolution: 'I must always return to the sea.'

A week later (18 September), Hope writes about the possibility of writing a journal. The thoughts expressed in this entry explain why Hope in the end rejected the idea of writing one and why instead he decided in favour of writing what he preferred to call 'notebooks'. Hope writes that it is 'Probably impossible to keep a readable journal: something spontaneous and unpremeditated. But writing for me is always composition, the thinking out of what is to be said, the choice and rejection of forms and the intensive struggle of rival ideas. It is a habit hard to oppose — I don't know whether I want to oppose it … these habits of composition have been built up for poetry which is necessary. Another initial difficulty is that I have so much the habit of talking to myself that to write to myself seems as silly as writing letters to a friend one sees every day.' Hope goes on to debate the arguments against preserving his habits of composition: 'To leave a record of mind? Have I anything to say that I do not think better embodied in other forms? To leave a record of daily events, happenings, fears and disappointments — it is my general principle to cheat the gossip-mongers if I can — no letters, no memoirs, no biography — to leave simply the body of verse to speak for itself. To record the secret life? — Yes, if I could without leaving it to the gossips. To keep a record of the passing reflections, ideas and experiences, which I find so often that I have forgotten when I want to use them? I think this is the only real justification.'

Six months later (3 March 1956), James McAuley asked Hope at dinner whether he had ever thought of keeping a journal. Hope acknowledges in this third entry that the fact that McAuley asked and also intimated that he had begun one was 'probably part of the mysterious doppelgänger effect between us'.

In the fourth entry (26 September 1956), Hope records that he has an inclination not to read any more: 'a feeling that I have taken enough in, and that to take in more will be mere stuffing the over-fed beast of the mind.' This entry emphasises a choice Hope was plagued with until his retirement: between profession and vocation. When he wrote this entry he was adamant: 'by vocation I am a poet. The poet has had as much, perhaps more than he can profitably use and he needs the next ten years for himself.' It is the case, however, that Hope continued to read and engaged in many scholarly projects.

The entry that follows this (7 December 1957) relates to a comment made to Hope by Tasmanian poet Norma Davis. Hope writes that her comment — 'All your life you have been trying to write someone else's poems. Now it is time to write your own' — was the 'most perceptive and the most disturbing thing anyone has ever said to me'. His next entry is in March 1960 and was written when he heard that Norma Davis had killed herself. He wonders if, 'when she wrote to me three years ago asking for advice, comfort, help — it was difficult to know what, but she seemed in some desperation — I put her off with my own trouble — could I have helped? Would it have made a difference?' Hope had a Nietzschean attitude towards regret, believing that it served no purpose in life. In all my conversations with him, the only regret he ever expressed was in relation to Norma Davis, whose book of poetry he had reviewed negatively just before her death.

Hope's seventh entry (7 May 1960) concerns his fascination with the fact that he, as an adult, never expressed rage, particularly given his memories of himself as a small boy: 'I had an ungovernable temper. I was not an insatiable child but when anger was aroused it burst out in a fury that quite overwhelmed me.' He concludes that rather than this childish rage having atrophied, it was instead 'sealed away like a subterranean lake of unused rage'. He compares it with 'wine laid away in a cellar' that matures — waiting to be drawn from when he comes to write satirical works.

His eighth entry (June 1960) begins: 'I see colours differently with one eye than with the other. Which tells the truth?' This leads to a discussion on the subjective nature of sensual perception and the degree to which it offers different messages at different times, whether referring to the colour of wheat, or to how a woman appears when one is in love with her and when out of love with her. Similarly, he applies this to ideas, noting that in one moment he writes an idea down that has the utmost significance but when he returns to it later it is quite ordinary. This view of Hope's, in time, will lead to his views on 'negative capability' discussed in chapter two. His last entry (July 1960) involves Penelope, his wife, telling him of an overwhelming and growing passion to own a house of her own in a good suburb, as she says, 'to join the establishment'. Hope is not keen on the idea, disinclined as he is 'to own anything or to ally [himself] with any group at all, a time, moreover when my children [are] almost grown up, I see a chance at last to free myself from encumbrance and involvement. When I cease to be Dean of the Faculty next year, I plan to resign from all bodies and societies and perhaps in a year or two I could retire and write'. It would be another seven years before Hope resigned. At the time of his retirement, he was elected Professor Emeritus, and he occupied an office in the A. D. Hope building for 25 years. Nevertheless, this entry emphasises not only his determined commitment to his vocation as a poet but also his awareness of his lack of loyalty to ideas or institutions, his 'indisposition to belief and commitment to parties and customs'. Instead, Hope notes: 'To myself I seem to have gone through life like a gipsy — not rebelling or conforming, but making my way in considerable indifference to the concerns of those around me though I am interested and often sympathetic. Perhaps it would be better to say that I have lived in this country, this civilisation and this age like an anthropologist living for the time being with a native tribe, involved in the common life but not in any way committed to it. But from what country did I come and to whom do I make my report?'

Thirty years later Hope returned to this early entry and wrote the poem, *Visitant*, which appeared in his last book of poetry, *Orpheus* (1991). The last stanza reads:

>   *Now it is time to return,*
>   *I shall miss this world more than I thought.*
>   *All I came merely to learn*
>   *Holds me now with such love and concern,*
>   *To whom do I make my report?*

These entries, floating in a separate folder, and written prior to his decision to compile his thoughts in notebooks, tell a story of their own, covering as they do pivotal moments of reflection concerning his passions and buried rage; his sole recorded experience of regret; a rare expression of empathy experienced with his friend and fellow poet; his insistence that his vocation is one of a poet rather than a scholar; his curiosity at the way sensual perception, given its subjective nature, has an arbitrary relationship with 'truth'; the process that led him to writing his notebooks; and how, despite his empathy with the nomadic lifestyle of his mythical hero Odysseus and the writer Tolstoy, his decision at his wife's request to buy a home and settle ensured that his 'dance of the nomad' would be primarily one of the mind and spirit.

I have attempted to tell Hope's 'story' in many ways over the years: filmed interviews, six programs of filmed documentary, and other critical writings. It is my belief that the story of A. D. Hope is the story of an extraordinary mind and that this mind is contained in his notebooks and his poetry. I am aware that the selections I have made could be construed from another perspective; however, as stated above, this selection is one informed and shaped by that initial encounter with his 1955–1964 folder. And I was also guided by the conversations and interviews I had with Hope, and the weeks we spent discussing a number of the notebooks together. Nevertheless, although the writings belong to Hope, this selection is my own and it inevitably reflects an interpretation on my part. Apart from the sheer complexity and breadth of Hope's work, the other greatest obstacle in bringing this work to fruition was Hope's often illegible handwriting; some entries were excluded because it was simply impossible to decipher the script. In the end, it was because Hope's work resists categorisation that I drew on a Deleuzian mapping of thought, as explained in the next section, in preference to a structure that might suggest a concise, logical breakdown of his theoretical and aesthetic interests.

OVERVIEW AND ARGUMENT:
MAPPING THE MAZE

This book presents an argument. It is one that subverts slick categorising of a writer too readily represented as conservative, sexist and old-fashioned. The argument asks readers to enter into the Hope world, which is contradictory, nomadic and incessantly dedicated to the capacities of human beings to act, contemplate and create. It is not a world in which answers are anticipated but rather one in which they are nevertheless relentlessly pursued. It is said of Hope that he was stuck in old forms and was therefore unable to deal with himself as subject. This book argues an opposite view. The extent to which he experimented with ideas in the guise of another testifies to his philosophical conviction as a nomad.

The subject is Hope, the subject is world,[1] and the poem is the bridge that tenuously connects mind and matter. If this bridge is difficult to navigate it is because from the chasm below there comes the echo of the 'ghostly shades' of the people he might have been and the 'truths' that he almost had, which jostle for recognition in the music of his poetic form.

In selecting extracts for this compilation, I feel that, more than anything else, it has been Hope's 'detachment' that has fascinated me; and it informs each of the areas that I have selected in organising the material and presenting an argument of a kind. Don Juan, Faustus and Odysseus were also my 'guides' in that the obsessions, travels and philosophies of life of these mythological figures were influential in the development of Hope's poetic vision. Hope indicates in his notebooks that his obsession with Faustus 'must at one time have amounted to an identification'.[2] He notes with some humour that when he was in his twenties he had the idea of making a will in which he would lay it down that on his tombstone there would appear only his name, his dates and the first lines of the concluding chorus of Marlowe's play. He quotes:

> *Cut is the branch that might have*
> *grown full straight,*
> *And burned is Apollo's laurel bough*
> *That sometime grew within this learned man.*[3]

He recognised this as rather silly when older, yet confessed that he felt even closer to Faustus now: 'Marlowe's Faustus, not Goethe's, for whom I feel interest and admiration but no sense of kinship. Goethe has re-made him too much in his own image'; Hope reiterates constantly the need of a poet to be detached from the personal.

A. D. Hope is a very serious poet but he is also, a lot of the time, seriously funny. To miss his irony, his humour, his game playing, his detachment, his peculiar way of celebrating the joy and terror of human existence is to miss out on the music and magic of his dance with language. When I asked Hope where he thought I should begin in attempting to represent his work and his life, whether in film or in biographical commentaries,[4] he responded with a poem. The following two stanzas served to guide me:

> *Where to begin? — No matter where you start,*
> *You will find three persons in one at least, all real,*
> *All with different roots; How can you tell them apart*
> *Each entwined as they are with others with whom you must deal?*
>
> *And resist, if you can, the biographer's natural urge*
> *To tidy the subject up and deliver him neat.*
> *Remember loose ends hang loose, won't mix or merge,*
> *But without them the portrait must always be incomplete.*[5]

In an attempt to follow this advice, I have chosen chapter headings that I hope will be construed as the names of pathways in a maze, separate yet merging with each other. They attempt to map an intellectual life and the point of emergence of the art; yet equally they form frameworks in which it can be seen how precarious the connection is between the two. We are, Hope told me often, the result not only of the choices we made but of those we did not choose:

> *We are shaped by our choices, even those we did not make*
> *Or which were made for us, sometimes against our will.*

Where pathways diverge, the ones that we did not take
Mostly forgotten, serve to determine us still.[6]

Hope does see living as partly composed of blind choices, and he has noted that in looking back one sees that comparatively trivial choices have often determined one's course. I believe that he would like his notes to be read in this spirit. It is within the context of the maze that my selections from Hope's notebooks appear; a reader might choose any of the chapters as a starting point when negotiating the pathways.

Hope writes narratives with philosophical questions in poetic form. These questions often emerge from the most unlikely of sources. In the preface to a selection of his literary essays, Hope identifies with the Autolycus of *The Winter's Tale* who said of himself: 'My father named me Autolycus; who, being as I am, littered under Mercury, was likewise a snapper-up of unconsidered trifles.'[7] These 'trifles' that Hope becomes interested in form not only the content of his literary essays, but often the subject matter of his poems and his notebooks. The 'trifles' Hope refers to were 'snapped-up' because of 'an idle curiosity which led me into all sorts of corners and byways of literary history. Curiosity begat speculation and speculation in turn led to an attempt to solve a problem.'[8] It is characteristic of Hope to undermine himself as an expert in the fields he dares to enter; yet one is nevertheless overwhelmed by the knowledge that informs his writings. It is clear that despite his naming himself a 'rogue', albeit an entertaining one, his aim is to 'solve a problem' and to push knowledge beyond known frontiers as a means of discovering new ways of being and seeing.

As a poet, Hope recognises that human beings engage with the world as contemplators and people of action; these activities might well be subject matter for his poems. Yet, specifically as a poet, Hope is fascinated, perhaps even obsessed, with his view that beyond the ways of life of contemplation and action, there is a third way; and together the three comprise 'all the modes of man's existence'. Hope argues:

> The third way of life I should call the *creative* way. It is distinguished from the others in the same manner: by a distinct relation of man to the ends he proposes and desires and by a distinctive emotion which attends the pursuit and fruition of these ends. As the mark of the active way of life is to possess the objects of desire, and the mark of the

contemplative way of life is to enjoy the knowledge of the objects of desire, so the mark of the creative way of life is to bring new objects of desire into being. Those who have this gift or urge have it as Dante says, as bees have the instinct to make honey.[9]

During the extensive time I spent with Hope, in my attempt to make sense of what often appeared to me to be as a philosophy of contradictions, he referred me back to his essay *The Three Faces of Love* more than to any other. In reading my selections from Hope's notebooks, it would be wise to remember the significance he gave to this creative way of life; it haunts and invigorates his excursions into all those 'trifles' he hunts down in order to solve some related problem.

In creating 'new being', Hope ventures into worlds of mystery where moments of insight slip and shift and often resist ultimate illumination. He enters his 'stories' (drawn from mythology and socio-cultural activity) with philosophical questions (couched in an argument that relies on analogy) and he resists the 'quick fix' of the emotional and the confessional (wearing armour in his stance as the detached observer). Hope questions the habits of mind and heart that deliver metaphysical and phenomenological world views across time and cultures. There is an ebb and flow of belief against disbelief, engagement against detachment and form against content.

I decided to treat Hope's notebooks thematically, with entries selected under each theme, to be presented in chronological order. This method allows the reader to ascertain whether there have been changes, developments and breaks away from belief and disbelief entertained at different points in Hope's life. Hope's entire life and work was influenced by a philosophical propensity termed 'Negative Capability', which Hope first encountered when he read the letters of John Keats.[10] It must have been a rare moment of intellectual empathy for Hope, who recorded in his notebook in 1969 that his generation of poets and critics, given their obsessive need to write — as if a new method was necessarily a better method — might be better served if they employed a 'degree of negative capability' that would allow them to 'enter into all theories and all techniques, to test and taste with no irritable concern with rights and wrong, with mine and thine'.[11] It is not the case, however, that Keats provided Hope with formulae in which to couch his philosophies. Keats' writings about poetic processes, his view that 'memory should not be called knowledge', which might cause poets to be 'led away by custom', and his insight that poets can create from a variety of sources, from diverse areas of knowledge and experience in a 'beautiful circuiting',[12] are ones that testify to an elective affinity between the two poets.

Keats' explication of 'negative capability' represents the states of commonality experienced by poets whose poetry has a philosophical nexus. Neither Keats nor Hope were interested in developing theories, nor did either of them have an absorbing interest in public affairs or any aspirations to being the voice of their age. Although each can be described as having a philosophical mind, this does not mean that they were at all interested in creating new theoretical systems for poetry. Creating such theories was alien to their minds.

This lack of interest in theories, in constructing linked maxims posing as knowledge, is what defines them as poets guided in their creative process by the spirit of 'negative capability'. This perspectivism, however, involved paradoxes, which manifested themselves when the main ideas they shared were positioned against each other. Keats spoke of the value of 'disinterestedness', of fleeing from the need to construct one's identity in terms of what one knows, and of being able to live with 'uncertainties, mysteries, doubts'. He argued against an irritable need to extend our identities in terms of feeling certain about ideas or notions of 'truth' — in fact, he advocated a 'negating of one's own identity'. Hope's views on the necessary 'detachment' of a poet, and his disaffection with confessional poetry, work within Keats' world view. Nevertheless, an ego persists in another sense, and, as I have argued within the body of this work, Hope might not always be as 'detached' and 'disinterested' as he argues he should be.

Yet he has much in common with Keats' philosophy of entering into the imagined self of another; that is, to 'become' someone who might hold views that Hope himself does not. As Keats wrote, '[I can] abstract myself from my present being and take an interest in my future being [only] in the sense and manner in which I can go out of myself entirely and enter into the minds and feelings of others.'[13] Priority here is given to the imaginative process itself. It is as if the process of imagination, unleashed by acting out the world of others, is the identity of the poet. This hypothetical 'future being' is perhaps the one that discovers the means to represent in poetry that 'beauty is truth'. Truth here does not mean 'knowledge' but rather a reality disclosed by poetry. Keats, referring to Shakespeare's *King Lear*, writes:

> The reality disclosed may be distressing and even cruel to human nature. But the harmony with truth will remain, and even deepen, to the extent that the emerging reality is being instantly matched at every stage by the 'depth of speculation excited' — by the corresponding release and extensions, in other words, of human insight.

Keats, in pursuing examples of how this poetical insight might bring 'power and passion' to an object, speaks of the affinity of many senses in a kind of unison: 'There is a gusto in the colouring of Titian. Not only do his heads seem to think — his bodies seem to feel.' The poetic interest is in the 'interplay and coalescence of impressions', the fusion of 'both sensual and spiritual' or a moment captured in which the poet might be 'thinking of the past and future while speaking of the present'.

Keats and Hope agree that 'at any point [of constructing poetry] one point may serve as a fruitful beginning'. For Hope, as demonstrated in the chapter *Source of Poetry*, a poem might find its beginning in a dream, a conversation with a friend or a newspaper clipping; for Keats, man 'on a certain day may read a certain page of full poesy or distilled prose, and let him wander with it, and bring home to it, and prophesy upon it, and dream upon it … When Man has arrived at a certain ripeness in intellect any one grand and spiritual passage serves him as a starting post towards all "the two-and-thirty Palaces"'.[14]

Given Hope's tendency to enter many ideas, or the minds of others, or emulate or satirise a poem or poet, or rewrite a play or subvert the notion of 'truth' or concepts of 'normality' (whether dictated by axioms of science or morality), or to simply entertain a passing thought, it was impossible to order his notebooks in a logical, structured manner that would suggest a kind of answer to the questions one asks of Hope's work.

The arrangement of these selections, therefore, consists of a mapping of Hope's territory that conforms to the rhizomic model created by Deleuze and Guattari. As such, it resists the more rigid, ordered systems of thought and chronology. Instead, the 12 points of entry, designated as chapters, that follow this one — a first entry point into the mind of Hope — entail an implied analysis that has grown like the rhizome entwining disparate elements into its unmapped expansion.[15] I have created a map, but only with the recognition that it is one 'that must be produced, constructed [anew by each reader]. A map that is always detachable, connectable, reversible, modifiable, and has multiple entryways and exits and its own lines of flight'.[16] This rhizomic model is to be distinguished from more familiar models of knowledge that function like a tree, with an ordered root system below (logic, a priori knowledge, concepts of the norm) and branches radiating off a central trunk (resultant knowledge, universal truth) above. Deleuze and Guattari denominate this as an 'arborescent' or a 'tap-root' system. For them, a more powerful account of how knowledge develops can be suggested by those root systems known as rhizomes: there is no central node to which all connections refer, no fixed organisational structure, no hierarchical orderings. Place a potato in a dark cupboard for a length of time and the wild growth of labyrinthine roots entangling with each other and seemingly undirected by any overarching order will give a sense of the rhizome. Hope's notebooks are best represented rhizomically. His writings resist — indeed, part of their intent and virtue is that they resist — any rigid, easy, external structure of chronology and theme.

When making a decision about how to order the pathways, it was clear to me that, given the extent to which the themes impinge on each other, and yet the independence of each, there could not be any 'correct' order. My final choice has been to begin with Hope's philosophical preference for 'negative capability'. It is in the selections that focus on Hope's interest in cosmology, the dream-team and women, as the source of desire and poetic imagery, that his philosophical allegiance to 'negative capability' and his view that the most powerful form of argument is wrought by analogy are seen to be at play.

Categorising the selections from Hope's notebooks under themes is not to suggest that the concerns of one are not woven into the fabric of the selections elsewhere. I have ended with 'analogy' because it is Hope's preferred form of argument whether writing poetry, prose or plays — a form of argument that best meets the creative powers of 'negative creativity'. This created in my mind a circle, with no beginning or ending; instead there are entry points at any point on the circumference.

These 'entryways' and 'exits' are named with the following conceptual frameworks:

Negative Capability establishes the philosophical thrust of Hope's world view, emphasising the importance of treating all knowledge as provisional. Hope sees the poet as an actor who takes on a role and asks 'what if?' of imagined situations; only weaker, 'less healthy' minds, Hope argues, find themselves obsessed with 'coherence, control and whatever'. This means that we shouldn't be afraid of contradictions in Hope's work. On the contrary, one should anticipate that Hope will enter into different ideas, sometimes testing them, sometimes merely representing them, and sometimes satirising them.

Anti-Modernism records Hope's constant and relentless attack on modernism, particularly its emergence in poetry as 'free verse'. Hope's insistence that a poem is 'a creation of new being', that in communicating a philosophical idea it must do so in a musical form, possible only if the poem is crafted according to the rules of rhyme and metre, set him apart from many of his contemporaries. Hope's belief in the provisional nature of all knowledge, it would seem, does not include the question of form in poetic construction. Hope's position, though, is more complex than this contradiction might suggest. His distaste for what he saw as a lack of craft, a mere collection of poetic images without form, was not disconnected, in his view, from the modernist tendency to use the poem as a confessional, as a mere pouring forth of emotional feelings. This lack of control he saw as being related to the abandonment of rhyme and metre.

A Sense of Detachment might be read with interest when considering these views. Here there are representations of many sides of Hope's belief in being a detached spectator of life and a detached creator in his poems, and they hint at how these can, at times, reveal a personality in the act of concealing it. Nevertheless, from the early 1980s, it is clear that he feels, despite his avowal that the best poetry is distilled, crafted and 'disinterested', that he has lost the battle against the writers of free verse.

Argument and Commentary on Critics and Writers selectively represents Hope's dialogues with writers, thinkers and artists of his time, as well as those from the past who influenced his poetic vision.

What is Art? presents Hope's analysis of the criteria for great art. His views on 'genius' and the relationship between the poet and the voice of the narrator are explored.

Source of His Poetry outlines experiences from life, or ideas from other works, which Hope anticipates drawing on at a later period as the sources of poems.

Cosmology communicates Hope's excitement when confronted with scientific interpretations of the world. A half-hearted determinist, Hope enjoyed taking on the scientists — physicists, astronomers, biologists, etc. — often because of their inability to accept the provisional nature of knowledge. In the light of this, scientific concepts themselves are often a source of inspiration for his work, though simultaneously the subject matter of the poem might be dealing with further issues.

Wine, Women and Insectual Song selects from a vast range of material dealing with sexuality, and with Hope's passionate interest in women as muses, as writers and as subjects of his poetry. Central to his vision is his belief that women provide a way for him to access a distinctive metaphysical view of life. Sexuality, which for Hope is interchangeable with love, is the basis of much of Hope's poetry. His descriptions of the sexual behaviour of insects include unforgettable images of sensual beauty, which he draws from in many poems.

A Sense of Destiny consists of Hope's jottings about how he comes to see himself as a poet and how others have either attempted to cate-gorise him or simply to praise him.

The Dream-Team manifests the diversity of Hope's thoughts. There are more entries in the notebooks on his theory of dreams than on any other topic, and many of these seem to be dealing with all his poetic and personal preoccupations. Hope's theory is an alternative to Freud's, and throughout his notebooks he has recorded numerous dreams, delighting in how he, in his dreams, is taken over:

> *… by a throng*
> *of revellers and roisterers who proceed*
> *To invent whole theatres of improbable dreams.*[17]

Argument by Analogy dramatises the ways in which a philosophical argument can be represented via analogy. Hope believed that all great poems contained within their music an argument of some kind. He distrusted arguments based on the assumption that certain facts are fundamental, elemental and axiomatic and that, in knowledge, no other facts have to be brought into consonance with them; and he attributed this insight to the teaching he received from John Anderson as an undergraduate at the University of Sydney.[18] Hope's use of analogy as his preferred form of argument follows on from the removal of the dead hand of 19th-century rationalism, which had formed the earlier basis of his thinking. This chapter explores the gamut of his views on society, whether directed at social and individual mores, the processes of artistic creation or the impact of technology on our lives.

The 12 points of entry that characterise the 'structure' of this text are presented chronologically. The choice of pathways constitutes an argument of how Hope's view of himself and his work is a paradoxical one, hovering as it does between intention and realisation. Hope, of course, would concede that to be in charge of self, or the world one wishes to represent poetically, is an impossible task. The notebooks, however, show his struggle to control personal and aesthetic boundaries and a certain amusement at his failure to do so. Endemic to my selections, and the pathways down which they are accessed, is an implied argument that Hope's need to be detached was equally a source of his brilliance as well as an expression of his personal anguish.[19]

Notes

1. See J. Clemens and D. Pettman, *Avoiding the Subject: Media, Culture and the Object*, in which they argue that one can grasp the subject only by avoiding it — and necessarily in new, unprecedented, even unrecognisable ways. Hope's 'detachment', his insistence on traditional poetic forms, is his way of creating poems that enact subjectivity itself in the guise of avoiding or suppressing it. Clemens' and Pettman's treatment of the object highlights feedback loops between philosophy, technology and politics. In a surprisingly similar manner, Hope, in engaging in the precarious relationship between mind and world, sees his poems as 'objects' that nonetheless are loops between philosophy and art, which are generated within the creative process itself as it carves out constantly changing, always provisional, 'new being' in a state of 'becoming'.
2. Hope, A. D. Book XX, 1978, p. 149.
3. Ibid.
4. See McCulloch, *The Dance of Language: An Annotated Chronology, His Life, His Work, His Views*.
5. See poem addressed to Ann McCulloch in its entirety in McCulloch, 'A Lecture: Given on the Eve of A. D. Hope's Eightieth Birthday', pp. 12–13.
6. Ibid.
7. See Hope, *The Pack of Autolycus*, p. v.
8. Ibid.
9. Hope, 'The Three Faces of Love', in *The Cave and the Spring*, p. 24.
10. Geoffrey Cumberlege (ed.), *Letters of John Keats*, Selected by Frederick Page.
11. Hope, Book X, 1969, p. 91.
12. See *Letters of John Keats*, letter 48, To John Hamilton Reynolds, pp. 78–81.
13. Walter Jackson Bate, 'Negative Capability' in *Keats: A Collection of Critical Essays*, p. 64.
14. The 32 'places of delight' of the Buddhist doctrine. Quoted in *Letters of John Keats*, p. 78.
15. See Deleuze and Guattari, *A Thousand Plateaus*, p. 21, where a rhizome is described as different from the 'arborescent type ... Unlike the tree, the rhizome is an antigenealogy. It is a short-term memory, or antimemory. The rhizome operates by variation, expansion, conquest, capture, offshoots. Unlike the graphic arts, drawing, or photography, unlike tracings, the rhizome pertains to a map'.
16. Ibid.
17. Hope, *Orpheus*, p. 17.
18. Hope, Book VII, 1964, p. 118.
19. See, in particular, poems written by Hope when dealing with living in an Australian landscape.

I

A. D. HOPE: DANCE OF A NOMAD IN FLIGHT FROM THE DOPPELGÄNGER

THE NATURE OF THE DANCE

A Most Astonishing Thing

A most astonishing thing
Seventy years have I lived;
…

Seventy years have I lived
No ragged beggar-man,
Seventy years have I lived
Seventy years man and boy,
And never have I danced for joy.

(W. B. Yeats, *Imitated from the Japanese*)

But I have! all of my 75 years I recall breaking into an involuntary, solitary dance — though it happens only at long intervals. Only a few days ago I surprised myself at it.

I often see young children do it and it looks involuntary too and certainly is the outward and visible sign of joy. I had always thought it a common habit but perhaps not. I am surprised that Yeats was so far even from the impulse towards it, that he had to catch the idea from a Japanese poem.

In my experience, the phrase 'dance for joy' is not exact. The dance and the joy are one thing — which is why I call it involuntary. They are outer and inner manifestations of the one state of being.[1]

26–X–1982

When I was selecting entries from A. D. Hope's notebooks, there were certain comments Hope had made to me that merged together and became a preoccupation: 'Do not deliver me neat'; 'Laughter is a very serious business'; 'Poetry is a dance of language'; writing poetry is 'the creation of new being'. The notebooks themselves emerge as the most intricate of dances, a dance of images that never ends; it is a dance with rhythmical gestures that infiltrate lightly, ironically and always musically towards the lands of mind, space, desire and the unknown. Readers of Hope's writings are also 'led on a dance', if for a moment there is an anticipation of categorising his thoughts into any system.

The notebooks provide an intellectual background to his writings as a poet, playwright and critic. His stature as a poet is intimately related to his capacity to see his work and the work of other poets and philosophers and thinkers as part of a general human activity: a continuing philosophical attempt to see human beings as part of the totality of the universe. This perspective permeates everything he writes as a poet, critic and commentator. Hope sees men and women as thinking beings and creative beings, as part of a very complex yet mostly comprehensible universe, and this awareness reveals itself and gives strength to very simple poems and to quite complex ones. Each poem he wrote appears in the notebooks at the time it was created. The philosophical preoccupations recorded at that time are, however, not necessarily connected with the poem; it is more often the case that the source of the poem will be found in notes written a decade or so earlier. Hope himself believed that the reason that he decided to keep a journal was in the end a practical one: to keep a record of passing reflections that were often forgotten when he wanted to use them.

Bob Brissenden, arguably the closest of Hope's friends,[2] has pointed out:

> There are complexities he doesn't cope with that are evident in the work of other writers and thinkers. It is old fashioned, it is structured, but it is always the expression of a creative intelligence of considerable stature and it is this which gives an intellectual foundation to his writings. When one compares him with almost all other Australian poets, even Australian writers, what becomes apparent, I think, is that the mind which is part of what produces Alec Hope's poetry is just rather more distinguished than most other literary minds in Australia. It has a rigour and toughness and imaginative quality and sympathy and a concern with metaphysical issues which just does not exist elsewhere. By elsewhere, I mean in the writings of other poets.[3]

The notebooks do not provide a means of interpreting Hope's art. His poems stand by themselves, complete unto themselves. They do, however (to use Auden's phrase), explain 'the peculiar flavour of the verbal dishes'.

In selecting from approximately three-quarters of a million words, which Hope wrote in his notebooks from 1950 until the death of his wife, Penelope, in 1988, it was this 'peculiar flavour of the verbal dish' that most interested me. This was the beginning of being led by Hope and his writings on a dance that was more often than not daunting rather than merry. Despite his scholarly engagement with metaphysics, mythology, psychology and cultural movements, and despite his antagonism towards aspects of modernism and his fierce views on the need for the poet's personal detachment when entering into an argument of a poem, there is always an element of play and disinterested contemplation of the world in his work.

The notebooks provide a context for this paradoxical poet who is equally engaged and disengaged, playful and serious, defiantly absent from his poems, yet present despite himself. In 1985 Hope wrote in a poem titled *Memento Mori* of 'the body's decrease of power ... the ultimate indications of old age':

> *Please God, I shall be spared that other drift*
> *Towards the collapse of mind that haunted Swift*
> *Seen as a cold eye masked his mortal rage.*[4]

Unusually for Hope this poem brings into the subject area, perhaps, the poet's own immediate experience of life. It dares to look over the side of an abyss, though characteristically it will only peer and then withdraw. It ends by speaking of finding the courage to tell a friend of these fears, rather than confronting them directly:

> *'I shall die like that tree;' he said, 'the top*
> *Perishes first. Before I meet my end*
> *My mind will go. I know I shall die mad.'*
>
> *And knowing that nothing he could do would stop*
> *It happening, he took courage to tell his friend.*
> *The horror and the courage were all he had.*

Whether the voice belongs to Swift or Hope is left ambiguous. The areas of Hope's life that he wishes to make known exist in his notebooks and his poems. A doppelgänger of his own lurks in the background, referring not only to the death that we all know we must meet, but to one he might have felt lay within the creative process itself if he attempted to reveal or expose his inner self. Indeed, in his notebooks, when flirting with the notion of writing an autobiography, he writes:

> I would write it as a travel book under the title A *Visit to Earth*: it would involve no pose or artifice, since I have always felt that detachment travellers feel, no matter how well they know and feel at home in their countries they visit. No matter how immersed in the life of a foreign country they may become, their first impressions are always from the outside looking in — and that has been my attitude to the world I live in and still is.
>
> (8.1.79)[5]

This 'detachment' that Hope is drawn to discuss as a poet, as an observer of life, and as a man of action living in a personal world, is further complicated by his role as an Australian poet. It is a complication that arises because of his refusal to deal primarily, in the subject matter of his poetry, with what some of his contemporaries would prefer to designate as specifically Australian material.

AUSTRALIA IN THE BONES

Hope made a substantial contribution in the 1960s, along with Tom Inglis Moore, to the establishment of Australian literature as a subject of study within the university. It was frequently suggested, however, that he was really a European poet writing in Australia rather than an Australian poet writing about Australia. Hope insisted in his creative and critical writing that Australian literature had to be part of world literature, and it had to be judged accordingly. Furthermore, he believed that his 'Australianness' was bred in the bone. He pointed out on a number of occasions that no matter what he wrote or how he wrote it there could be no escape from the intense memories of his Australian childhood. He understood that the relationship between Australian culture and that of Britain, in the first instance, but also other European countries, is an essential part of our history.

Hope's intense interest in Australian literature is represented throughout this book, whether in his dialogues with writers or when he is discussing the emergence of 'free verse'. During the 1980s, Hope felt that he had lost the battle with poets who preferred this form. In *The Mermaid in the Zodiac*, he expresses his sense of defeat with direct reference to Australian fauna. He asks the question:

> *I wonder among what poets I shall be found,*
> *Shall I be sorted with the goats or with the sheep?*

He notes that:

> *I will have no truck with the scribblers of my time*
> *Who try to pass off their chopped-up prose as verse.*

And he concludes that:

> *I expect I shall stand, looking rather out of place,*
> *Between the mouth-organs and the didgeridoos;*
> *Not a sheep in sight, but a goat with a puzzled face*
> *Among all those Kangaroos.*[6]

A number of Hope's poems did, in fact, draw directly from Australia; and, ironically, it is in these instances that he has chosen to break his own rules on being detached. Hope's poems *Australia, Ascent into Hell, Country Places, Beyond Khancoban* and *The Drifting Continent* all invoke the Australian landscape; and each of these poems engages the 'I' of Hope's persona. Are they inside or outside Hope's philosophical vision, which denies 'personism' and mostly excludes references to the physical geography of Australia? Or do they enact the breaking apart of subjectivity, with the physical, the spiritual and the psychological collapsing into each other and producing a new subjectivity, which seeks to 'step into unknown spaces' in order to discover 'new countries of the mind'?[7] Perhaps they enact the thinking of Deleuze and Guattari that 'writing has nothing to do with signifying, but with land surveying, map-making, even of countries yet to come'.[8]

In *Beyond Khancoban*, the narrator, who, given the autobiographical nature of the poem, one might safely assume to be Hope, negotiates a land whose 'hills', 'valleys', still 'great mountains' are 'Feasted with music of which', Hope maintains within the poem, he is 'not aware'. It is a landscape lost in thought, composed of winding roads and rises that elicit a music not known until now, and Hope turns 'its world into music' as he drives. From the perspective of the moving car, the trees are dancing, not 'out there' but 'in the mind', though Hope insists that the mind is also entering into the dance, making this 'land' conscious:

> *In our minds is it able to enter the dance;*
> *Moved by our music things learn themselves and rejoice.*
> *I would count it worth while to spend life for this single glance,*
> *To have made them conscious in me, to have lent them my voice.*[9]

The poem ends with Hope arriving on the Monaro, the place of his birth, 'where a mind began'. He claims that place as his own, the spot to which he returns, 'from which long ago I was made, / Cooma, and wonder whether it made me or not / … But here the Monaro claims me; I recognize / … the place where a mind began …'.[10] The land, identity and mind fuse in this poem while Hope tells a story of the part he plays in capturing music and thought from the land. The space of the land he has re-territorialised as the nomadic mind tests the relevance of his birthplace to the voice that emerges from it. The philosophy endemic to this nomadic mind is expressed in his poem *The Nomads*.

NOMADOLOGY

The Nomads

Men in cities, men busy everywhere
Live by a faith that roads lead to some end:
Home, pleasure, a goal attained, a lover, a friend
If it were not so, they say, we must despair.

But not the nomads, they never think this way;
Wherever they chance to stop, the roads go on,
To nowhere, to anywhere. For them the one
Despair is a fixed roof, a permanent stay.

Theirs are different natures. They see the things we see;
The words are the same — they look with different eyes.
I would not call them more human or less wise,
Nor think them less happy, more justified than we.

They are simply other: they give and they forgive.
But do not ask for anything in return,
Learn only what they have no need to unlearn,
Clutch at no rights, claim no prerogative.

When I ask my friend the nomad: 'Would you agree
I have made my mark in the world?', he answers: 'why,
Yes, you have made something of your life; but I
Prefer to find out what life will make of me.'

I speak of love. He laughs, saying: 'Friend, you have won
That treasure to hold and keep; but love for me
Is a wayward lightning, a chance felicity,
An ungrasped gateway opening on the unknown.'

I talk of his life, the endless, empty miles,
The trivial monotony of the wanderer's way.
He asks, have I lived by the joy of the single day?
I talk then of death, but he looks at me and smiles,

Saying, 'Ah, but you live so rooted in time, you see.
You have never experienced an absolute moment, my friend.
Death is not the beginning of anything, nor the end
But, as each instant lived for itself must be,
That pure, that limitless 'now', Eternity.'

1975[11]

Hope would like, I think, to cast himself as a kind of nomad of the mind. In his notebooks, he speaks with evident pleasure of these nomads. They are people who find it impossible to settle down within any system, in any country of belief, though the advantages of settlement and the power that comes from the corporate ownership and organisation of ideas might be obvious to them. Instead they wander from place to place, learning the language of the settled inhabitants, and often taking on the colour of their civilisation and perhaps contributing something here and there. But they remain fundamentally untouched and untamed. They are not scorners, critics or sceptics, nor are they indifferent or agnostic. They are simply without the urge or the instinct to take root which is common to most minds. Because of their lack of interest in acquiring property in ideas, they are born thieves and plunderers of the settled lands, where they might even settle for brief periods. But something always drives them back to the desert. They have their own legends and songs for which the city-dwellers may develop a craze. The nomads understand themselves in another sense, the sense of being too much at one with the whole world to identify themselves with any single part of it. They rarely meet. They do not form societies or alliances, and yet in a mysterious way they are in touch with all the other members of their curious tribe. When two of them do meet casually, they recognise each other at once and the bystanders suddenly hear the guttural language of the wilderness, the speech of people who do not sleep under roofs and whose words never echo back from enclosing walls. It is the forgotten primitive speech of men without possessions, vested interests and family ties, a tongue which is therefore safe from and even inept for argument or persuasion. For Hope, this is the language of poetry.[12]

AREAS OF WITHDRAWAL AND ANTAGONISM

There are four areas of either withdrawal or antagonism that form a large part of Hope's poetic vision. These concern an avoidance of direct reference firstly to the landscape of his homeland, and secondly to stories and memories of his childhood. These, he maintains, are deep sources of his poetry from which he draws incessantly, but are not manifest in any literal sense in his poetry. Hope dramatises, thirdly, a certain detachment from the notion that the personal emotional life be invoked directly in the final production of a poem; and, fourthly, he asserts without qualification the necessity of a poem being in verse form. The nomadology of his philosophies in seeming contradiction to these four areas combines with them and creates a particular kind of subjectivity that lies buried in his productions. Each of these qualities of his art remains itself. Hope's poetics therefore consist of rules to be followed on one hand, but, on the other, his 'nomadology' and his philosophy of 'negative capability' involve an opposition towards larger rules that dictate unquestioning compliance with moral, political, social and scientific axioms. The forms imposed by the poet code and decode space, but the negative capability of Hope's philosophy, partially manifest in his poem *The Nomads*, proceeds altogether differently.

NEGATIVE CAPABILITY: CONNECTIONS WITH NOMADOLOGY

In his notebooks, Hope writes extensively about his particular brand of nomadology. His adaptation of Keats' 'negative capability' informs all his poems. He sees himself as entering into ideas and beliefs as an actor to see where they might lead him,[13] but not — and he is emphatic about this — to confirm a truth about them. He propounds his view that knowledge is provisional and that there is no way of building permanent beliefs, that values are made by people and that even a notion such as the relativity of values is unprovable; what people think and say are parts of nature and not separate from it.[14] He points out that there is no such thing as a 'normal' person and yet how curious it is that 'most social, moral and other types of value theory are built on the supposition, and most literature takes it for granted'.[15] Hope queries the laws of science and, in discussing the fallacy of Eddington's Net, suggests it might be implicit in all our thinking;[16] he points out the extent to which we have had to limit and formalise our perceptions to exclude certain perfectly natural forces and types of operation, which could have led to alternative methods of perception and communication — a specialisation observable almost everywhere in nature. He writes of how he never loses his awareness of the narrowness of our bases of knowledge of the world and the way that what we are aware of gets in the way of what we are totally unaware of,[17] an idea expressed in his poem A Swallow in the House, in which the swallow becomes the human being, who, searching in the dark for answers, for a way out of failed systems, falls stunned to the ground after crashing against glass. He writes:

> *Something left out, not to be reckoned with,*
> *Not conceived by science or adumbrated in myth;*
> *Something of which he is totally unaware*
> *As the swallow of its undreamt nightmare, solid air.*[18]

NOMADIC COSMOLOGY

Hope often prefaces his writings on cosmology with statements of his ignorance in these areas; but this does not stop him exploring ideas that he thinks at times to be foolish and contradictory. Hope's pact with negative capability allows his mind to wander dramatically. In keeping all systems of belief suspended (which he applies to scientific axioms as well as to those pertaining to systems of morality and social strictures), the imagination is able to touch an 'actuality' that is held in suspension between all the forms of the possible; 'the known' always ready to dissolve into the ocean of the unlimited. All breakthroughs in theories, Hope insists, are replaceable and in turn are replaced by new paradigms of thought. The process is repeatable and unlimited.

Hope's suspiciousness towards scientific hypotheses predates, for example, Kuhn's work on the shifting nature of scientific paradigms.[19] As early as the 1950s, Hope wrote in his notebooks that it had taken him a long time to perceive what he now saw to be a blind spot of what he once called the scientific attitude, but which now he was more inclined to call 'scientificism', that is, 'the tendency to limit thinking by habits of mind it sets up'.[20] This was a significant breakthrough for Hope, who had been brought up in the discipline of empiricism and had previously defended it against the idealism and rationalism that preceded it. The notebooks record his consequent journeys into many areas of science and into many dialogues with scientific writers who, in Hope's view, use inappropriate or incorrect language that confuses their audience rather than enlightens it.

RHIZOMIC TERRITORIES: SCHIZOPHRENIC AND PARANOIAC

Hope deals with the passions and thought. His interest is in whether they cause or are affected by social feelings, moral feelings, fear, love, religious awe and ecstasy, hate, greed, lust, anger, pride and mastery. His nomadology takes him to other lands of mythology, biblical stories and cosmology, where he plunders and reinvents ideas without thought of settling in one place. He translates poems from one language to another and one recalls his thoughts in *Western Elegies: V: The Tongues*:

> *For the man who knows only one speech is an ox in a paradise orchard,*
> *Munching on grass and ignoring the fruits of delectable flavour*
> *That ripen upon its boughs and depend from the vines that adorn it.*
> *The man who has only one tongue lives forever alone on an island*
> *Shut in on himself by conventions he is only dimly aware of,*
> *Like a beast whose mind is fenced by the narrow extent of its instincts.*[21]

Hope's favourite means of dramatising these passions of thought, feelings and languages is in poetry, which in his view gives the whole frame of things, whether stated explicitly or implied.

In a Deleuzian sense, Hope is concerned (at least with regard to the content of his poems) with the outside, with perspectivism,[22] with 'multiplicities', which are 'defined by means of the outside: by the abstract line, the line of flight or of deterritorialisation following which they change nature by being connected with others'[23] and with 'the unthought, the exterior, the surface, the simulacrum, the fold, [that which] resists assimilation, [that which] remains foreign even within a presumed identity'.[24] Hope's philosophy, inherent in his art, falls within the range of what Deleuze and Guattari refer to as schizophrenic and might therefore escape the affects of bourgeois repression. Hope's refusal to align himself with any political persuasion as well as his rejection of the Freudian model is relevant here; his intellectual capacity to break down barriers, to engage in multiplicity, becoming, flowing, and to engage with partial objects, fragments of experience, memory and feeling, which might be linked in chance and unexpected ways, might characterise his work as a rhizome as defined by Deleuze. The opposite pole to the schizophrenic one is that of the paranoiac. The paranoiac pole is marked by its unifying ways, its procedures, and its search for order, similarity and wholeness, and it assumes an identity and completeness of objects and selves within conforming constraints and recognised limits. At the paranoiac pole there is an incessant pressure to 'territorialise', to make out and maintain the directions of desire. I refer now to those two areas of Hope's work, discussed earlier, that might be construed as paranoiac: his insistence on the superiority of traditional verse form; and his antipathy towards poetry in which the poet treats the poem as a confessional wherein personal feelings and belief systems can be identified. He believes that poetry more than any other art most encapsulates the 'being' of existence and that only poetry written in traditional rhyming verse structures embodies the nature, rhythm and music of life. In the second instance, he holds fast to the view that a poet has no 'identity', a view he has adopted from Keats' rejection of the romantic view of the poet:

> A poet is the most unpoetical of anything in existence; because he has no identity — he is continually in, for — and filling some other Body — The Sun, the Moon, the Sea and Men and Women who are creatures of impulse are poetical and have about them an unchangeable attribute — the poet has none; no identity — he is certainly the most unpoetical of all God's creatures.[25]

Hope's 'rule' that a poet should not use the poem to express personal grief is 'paranoiac', but his practice of being an actor, who enters an idea or an emotion in a poem, not as himself, but as many, is 'schizophrenic'. Deleuze and Guattari, when introducing their text 'Rhizome', take a similar stance, calling themselves 'many' rather than two separate individuals: 'Not to arrive at the point where it's no longer of any importance whether one says I or not. We are no longer ourselves. Each will know his own. We have been helped, inspired, multiplied.'[26] A question persists. Is Hope's detachment schizophrenic or paranoiac? Is it intellectual or emotional?

DETACHMENT AND ANTI-MODERNISM

Hope's detachment reflects his lifelong belief for his poetry 'to test and taste with no irritable concern with right and wrong', yet it seems at odds with his irritation towards confessional poets and those who choose to write in free verse. The latter Hope sees as the enemies of art in that they undermine the only structure which, he believes, extends human consciousness, which captures the music of existence and grapples with the mystery of being. Nevertheless, this coding of his own space within a poem combines with his rhizomic territories in a way that offers up a simultaneous revelation and concealment. Hope, the nomad thinker, propounds that no system can provide an answer, yet Hope, the 'paranoiac' craftsman, dictates that no poem that works outside the system of traditional verse structures can grapple with the mystery of being. The dialectic is set, one in which repression and expression of desire is enacted. The paranoiac tendency in Hope's work eludes binary oppositions by a constant dialectic of repression and expression of desire. These oppositions recombine through the art of his irony, which allows the myth of his detachment to remain unjudged and uncategorised. The subject for Hope is not at the centre but on the periphery, with no fixed identity, forever decentred, defined by the states through which it passes. The form of his poems, the verse form, may be a 'striated' space, but it is a space in which the nomadic mind, usually more at home in 'smooth' space, finds his music.[27]

Given Hope's views, it is not difficult to understand his non-literal rendering of his personal life and the geography of his homeland. He maintains that they emerge in his choice of language, image and story — always the most insistent and sacred of sources. The 'land' and snatches of personal experience from life or dreams, in so much as they are incorporated into a collectivity of motifs, are not to be understood as one part of a tripartite division between the realm of reality, the realm of representation or representivity, and the realm of subjectivity. The 'space' of the physical and/or psychological landscape is traversed in an excursion towards the construction of 'desire' and/or thought. Hope characterises this as 'the creation of being'; it is not bounded or comprehended via oppositions of inner/outer and subject/object. The geography of his poetry is physical, spiritual and psychological, 'aspects' that collapse into each other breaking apart a subjectivity while seeking a dimension beyond purely physical boundaries.

It is fascinating to note that the two poems — *Ascent into Hell* and *Australia* — that do draw directly from Australia's landscape are those that touch on, albeit in a rhizomic manner, aspects of Hope's personal life. In *Australia*, the geography of 'drab green and desolate grey' and 'rivers of waters' that drown among 'inland sands' sets up a geography of the mind. This is a country he saw as empty of 'songs, architecture, history'. It was a place in which her five cities, like five teeming sores, drained her of her substance, and yet it was the place that he chose to return to:

> *Yet there are some like me turn gladly home*
> *From the lush jungle of modern thought, to find*
> *The Arabian desert of the human mind,*
> *Hoping, if still from the deserts the prophets come.*[28]

If Hope is one of those prophets from the 'Arabian desert of the human mind', negotiating smooth spaces within his nomadology, he does so by creating striated spaces, or at least by entering into models of thought to recreate new spaces. *Ascent into Hell* is indeed a daring poem, dealing as it does with incidents in his childhood that led to recurring adult nightmares and to a pathway back in time.

Guattari notes that psychological theories provide a multiplicity of and assemblages of subjectivation: 'None of them, whether fantasmatic, delirious or theoretical can be said to express an objective knowledge of the psyche.'[29] Hope would agree with this and, like Guattari, rejects the Freudian dualistic rendition of consciousness and unconsciousness and all 'the manichean oppositions correlative to Oedipal triangulation and to the castration complex.'[30] Hope's contempt for Freudian analysis is first seen in his poem *The Return from the Freudian Islands*. Hope disliked a theory that he saw as responsible for explaining away the fears, repressions and misguided passions reductively, bringing, in his mind, the poet to a place where there was nothing but '… A faint, dry sound / As first a poet buttoned on his skin'.[31] This contempt took on another guise in the poem Private Dick, in which the protagonist is Dick, a private investigator but unmistakably a Freudian analyst. No one is safe from Private Dick:

> *Take to Art; set up your easel — landscape painting is just clean fun,*
> *Free from the dingiest moral measles — Ah, now he's got you on the run:*
> *Private Dick leans over your shoulder, breathes hot peppermint down*
>   *your neck:*
> *Call that a tree? That's a Phallic Symbol! Boy, is that psyche of*
>   *yours a wreck!*[32]

Within the story of the poem, Dick, at death, is condemned to perdition and takes on his next client, Nick himself: 'Back they go through the psychic tangles, the dreams he dreamed and the beds he wet / The games he played with his sisters' bangles, the nice little snake he kept as a pet.' Dick, however, is no match for Nick, who is able to cancel Dick's file with a simple trick: 'The final triumph of mind over matter.' Hope needs to escape from his work being analysed along Freudian lines. Perhaps Hope's decision to create his own theory of dreams was simply his trick of asserting his mind over his 'matter', which would so easily slip under the Freudian gaze.

THE DREAM-TEAM

In Hope's own conception of the unconscious, it is fertilised by his 'dream-team', an army of helpers who in his dreams inhabit a more schizophrenic unconscious, one that Guattari would agree was 'liberated from familial shackles, turned more towards actual praxis than towards fixations on, and regressions to the past. An unconscious of flux and of abstract machines rather than an unconscious of structure and language.'[33]

A reading of Hope's *On the Night Shift*[34] informs us of the team's activities. They move in when 'the body is put to bed' and 'The oceanic rhythm of sleep draws on'. The brain is taken over by a throng of 'revellers and roisterers who proceed / To invent whole theatres of improbable dreams'. These revellers rewrite Hope's scripts, they invoke the 'envious Doubles who haunt' his looking glass, they parody his worries of the day; they show him 'marvellous landscapes, prospects of sky and sea, / Reminders that living is an act of joy'; they scribble verse, give lectures, plan whole novels; they tease Hope and give him powers that real life denies him; they are the helpers on whom he depends. Hope maintains that without his dream-team his part as the poet would falter and become flat and tame, but that, without him, the craftsman, 'the wild surreal play of his unconscious' would result in 'formless inconsequence'. The dreams are there for the poet 'to tap creative energy from a host of clues'. His point is that half the process by which poems grow is something that not even their authors understand, but that they nevertheless 'do give themselves away'. This admission that authors 'do give themselves away' is not elaborated on or explained in the poem. It suggests though that no matter how a poet might wish to conceal, he will inevitably reveal aspects of himself.

Hope's notebooks rarely include personal experiences from his childhood. It is fascinating to realise that the ones he has recorded appear in his poem *Ascent into Hell*[35] and that the story he tells is set within the Australian landscape of his childhood. The poem begins with Hope, the self-acknowledged narrator, noting that he looks in his dreams for answers. The poem dramatises the conscious poet who talks of the dreams he has had as an adult that include childhood experiences, and memories of dreams he had as a child, as well as the events of his life that might have given rise to them. The poet draws on these clues in order to celebrate the mystery of imagined beginnings, looking forward for ascents, moving forward towards finding the lost soul of the past, present and future. The dreams of his unconscious, both of the 'I' of the present and the 'he' of the past, are turned towards the praxis of poetry-making, creations of being, rather than towards emergent narratives that focus on fixations or regressions.

The landscape of Hope's childhood home in Tasmania figures predominantly, although glimpsed only momentarily in *Ascent into Hell* as a realm of reality. But just at the point at which we might see 'the landlocked valley and the river', 'the poplars' and 'the gum trees', we're told that the very geographic formations 'make distance an emotion'. He revisits the landscape, which in itself is unchanged, but it is seen as always growing within him as his search among the old dreams and memories extends his territories of the present. The poet, as in *The Drifting Continent*,[36] sustains a detachment, in that he is reflecting on his role as a creator. The poet creates music about himself as a dreamer, as a son, as an adult negotiating the child still within him; he knows that in entering the receding country of his past and present he fears an abyss but also ascends towards seeing before him new constructions of himself as a lost one. The physicality of the land is touched and met by the mind, 'deterritorialising' settled notions regarding the relationship between the unconscious and conscious modes of thought and being.

ABSENCES I: POLITICAL ENGAGEMENT

It is instructive to note 'absences' in Hope's notebooks. He might have believed that his omissions and evasions were covered by his adoption of 'negative capability'. 'Don't deliver me neat' is his fervent plea to those who wish to tell his story. Yet when one examines the overall pattern of Hope's notebooks one is led to suspect that his belief and non-belief have a certain neatness of intention.

One evident omission in the notebooks is any reference to political allegiance other than a few entries expressing his lack of interest in it. Hope lists social activities that he admits to being prejudiced against, and one of these is 'Politics'. He maintains that the healthiest, happiest and most creative minds should not be constricted by any ideological creed.

In the spirit of 'negative capability', Hope did not align himself with any political party or preferences. References to politics throughout his notebooks are sparse, and when included, are chosen as justifications for his prejudice towards politics. He expresses the notion of the impossibility of having faith in an ideology represented in a government in favour of an alternative one instituted in another form of government. In an entry entitled 'Violence and Lies',[37] he quotes from Solzhenitsyn's 1970 Nobel Prize lecture:

> … violence does not and cannot exist on its own. It is inextricably bound up with the lie. The link between them is fundamental and entirely natural and organic: violence has nothing to cover itself with except the lie, and the lie has no way of maintaining itself except by violence. At the time of its birth, violence operates openly and is even proud of itself. But no sooner has it affirmed and established itself than it feels the air around it growing thinner

and cannot continue to exist without surrounding itself with a smoke-screen of lies ... Violence does not always and of necessity come right out and throttle you: more often than not it simply demands of its subjects that they subscribe to the lie or participate in it.

Hope finds this comment 'profoundly true'. He writes:

> ... the depressing thing is that every party, every government and every form of political institution I can recall has at one time or another used this combination of violence and the lie to maintain itself. Totalitarian and police-states have done it so grossly and on such a scale that we overlook the instances of the same thing in democracies. If one were a Tolstoyan one would say that it is an inevitable concomitant of government. Power breeds opposition, opposition breeds violence; violence breeds the lie. Too simple perhaps, but a very usual pattern.

Hope qualifies his view to the extent of commenting that in his age 'truth' has never been subjected to such skilful and powerful attack and that it triumphs and still continues to triumph or at least to manifest itself.[38] It is not clear here what Hope means by truth but what is clear is his belief that 'truth', whatever that might be, exists in an arena outside politics.

Hope remained disengaged during some of the most crucial debates of the 20th century. Thinkers engaged in, for example, demonstrations against the Vietnam War during the 1960s and 1970s were disappointed that someone with such enormous gifts did not involve himself in social and political debates. Hope's Olympian detachment in political matters and his valorisation of traditional forms in poetry have led him to be categorised as conservative, as lacking in political knowledge, or, worse, as uncaring. Nevertheless, his refusal to participate in political demonstrations against the war angered many. Bob Brissenden, after viewing the filmed interview I did with Hope about his detachment from taking a political stand, made some illuminating comments that represented how people on the left, including colleagues and friends, responded to him at this time:

… Alec and politics … Alec is a bit disingenuous in his comments about politics. It is true, I think, that he was in some sense a political innocent. He had a generally, or he has a generally conservative leaning. His most enduring friendships were with people like James McAuley and Leonie Kramer, who were certainly conservative figures. He was, or he is, non-ideological. I think he distrusts rigid systems. His innate scepticism prevented him from ever publicly committing himself to political positions. If one were to make a criticism of his political stance, I think I'd say he confused conservatism in literary matters with conservatism in political matters.

The period in which writers were most strongly asked to commit themselves politically was when the Vietnam War was at its height. There were very many people in Australia who felt unhappy about the Vietnam War … very many writers, and there were public statements about it and about Australia's involvement in Vietnam. The import of most of these statements was really that by being involved in it we weren't really helping the Vietnamese. Alec was approached for his support, for this stance, a number of times, and he refused to commit himself one way or the other on the grounds that he didn't really know enough about it. Finally he did agree to participate in one of the big readings, public readings, organised by people who opposed Australia's involvement in Vietnam. He read a poem which was partly a translation of the comment on a Greek epitaph for the Spartans who fell fighting the Persians. It had a general application in a war they knew nothing much about. It was subsequently chosen as the title for an anthology of writing by people objecting to the Vietnam situation. It was an important commitment on his part, I think, and I don't think he really does himself justice in his remarks about this involvement in the interview.[39]

ABSENCES II: AUTOBIOGRAPHY

Hope's notebooks do not provide personal commentaries on his life, his family, friends or responses to the events of daily life. Although most of the people he has known are mentioned, references to them are in terms of his poetry, his criticisms and his philosophies. Antipathies and sympathies tend to be expressed in terms of whether they as writers commit the crime of modernism; daily adventures and personal contacts are recorded only to the extent that such experiences lead to a poetic or philosophical notion. Hope works overtime in warding off interpretations of his personal life, whether through Freudian analysis or in the search for causal relationships between the life and the poem. Hope does all that he can to correct misinterpretations, even to the extent of correcting the idea that the 'Derwent' in his name is a reference to his Tasmanian origin, and that he was named after the river. Instead one is informed: 'according to my mother, I was named after Derwent Street in Redfern, Sydney — a slum street in which my father rather oddly chose to propose to her while she was picking her way through a series of unsavoury puddles.'[40]

Hope goes on to say that his father denied this and that Hope was unable to find a Derwent Street in Redfern, though there is one in Glebe, another suburb of Sydney. His correction of the Tasmanian river suggestion leads us away from factual error and towards other possibilities. The entry ends with Hope's characteristic humour and his inevitable irony: 'What pleases me is that [the] name is Celtic, *dwrgent*, meaning "clear water" even if I was named after a street full of muddy pools.'[41]

Hope has indicated that his relationship with his mother was a most significant and creative one.[42] References to her throughout the notebooks are sparse. When she appears she does so in relation to her role as the nurturer of Hope's talents. Florence Hope was trained to be a concert pianist. Marriage and motherhood made the non-realisation of this dream one of Hope's preoccupations. In one of his entries concerning the antics of the dream-team he records a dream in which he is being toyed with by this ambitious group: 'They tried to produce me as the author of a full-scale piano concerto.' He is relieved to find that his mother is seated next to him and that she will be able to perform the piece. The dream continues with the performance not being able to go ahead because of all kinds of mix-ups with the orchestra. There is no performance. On waking, Hope recognises the failure as being: 'the result of someone in the team realising that in spite of the elaborate score there was in fact no concerto and the dream-team [was] as unable to present the actual music as I was to read it.'[43]

In a later entry titled 'John Field',[44] Hope reconstructs a dream in which music by John Field is being played. In his reconstruction Hope offers reasons for the elements of the dream, noting that although the music in the dream did not sound like John Field, the presence of his name on the music sheets might relate to his memory of his mother playing nocturnes to him when he was a boy. This dream also involves the audience being handed out pages of a poem. It seems that his dream-team in a number of instances presents to the dreamer an interface and convergence of music, mother and poetry.

Penelope, A. D. Hope's wife, also is an absence from the notebooks, except on two occasions. Under the heading of 'The Great Wave', Hope records a dream of Penelope's:

> After listening with horror to a lecture by Arthur Burns on the subject of the next world war, Penelope had the following dream and wrote it down when she woke: 'I dreamt last night of an enormous wave towering up against the sky with threatening teeth of foam, a battle on its crest, and a dark hungry shadow in its curve. I thought: It's coming, it's coming, and I saw the world drowned — the birds in their nests and darting among the trees. The trees falling and their branches broken and hurled away. The fruit swirling in the water. Houses and electric wires. The open screaming mouths swept every way. And I heard the noises. And then the wave was under me lifting me and moving on. And there was the beautiful earth beyond, unharmed, innocent and as if no wave had passed.'
>
> She had been very upset by what she took to be the inhuman calculations of power politics and the total disregard of humanity and 'people' in Arthur's discussion of the probabilities and possibilities in the present world situation — though I knew that Arthur is in fact deeply concerned with this. The dream, so vivid and so momentous, seems to have come as a message of reassurance. Where from?[45]

Penelope Hope was also a writer. One of her books, *Long Ago is Far Away*,[46] gives accounts of the early exploration and settlement of the Papuan Gulf area. Penelope tried to keep out of Hope's literary world,[47] and was self-contained within her own — her writing, her artistic interests, her family and her friends. Hope was grateful that Penelope preferred to exist outside his literary circles, and that she understood his decision not to discuss any of his poems with anyone, including her, until they were completed. He notes that Penelope understood his nature, that he was more self-absorbed than she. Hope conceded that he did not always behave very well: 'I do remember somewhere half way through, I was behaving badly and she said, "If you go on like that I'll have to leave you." And I said, "You couldn't do that; I couldn't live with anybody but you." I remembered this just after she died; I got so used to the combo, that it was only [with] the shock of losing her that I realised how close we were getting to be at the time … how special we were to each other …'[48]

Penelope Hope was one of the most gracious, dignified, compassionate, intelligent and beautiful people I have met in my life. In first meeting Penelope, I had intended to ask her many questions about her life with Alec, her views on his work and her perceptions of him generally. I'm not sure when I decided against this or if the decision was ever a conscious one. Instead, I enjoyed Penelope's company, listening to her stories of her life and responding to her broad interests in the arts and her insights into human nature. If she spoke of Alec Hope it was in this context. She clearly loved him intensely. It was also evident that a great deal of patience was necessary on her part in being the spouse of this famous and celebrated man. Not only was he self-absorbed by nature, but his work, whether at the university or attending conferences or the hours spent writing in his notebooks and writing his poems in his study at night, meant that the work entailed in bringing up their three children fell on Penelope's shoulders. Coupled with this was the parade of friends, colleagues, disciples and students taking up space that might have been hers. Hope's fascination with women and their fascination for him, whether on a personal level or due to his fame, was an arena that required great tolerance. Penelope said to me once, somewhat facetiously, when we were discussing this, that 'all women should shoot themselves at 40'. The dignity, good humour and intelligence with which Penelope hosted numerous dinner parties for Hope's followers, visiting writers from overseas and friends were instructive.

Hope mentions Penelope only in relation to times they were travelling together and their relationship with their daughter Emily. Emily appears in the notebooks. For example, when Hope visited Melbourne and was met by her at the station. Emily also appears in a few of his dreams. She was an artist, a painter and a silversmith, as well as a writer.[49] Penelope was deeply interested and involved in Emily's art. On occasion they would work together, Penelope polishing the stones that Emily set in her jewellery and sculptures. Emily contracted cancer in her late thirties and died in 1979. An entry in the notebooks entitled 'Revenants?' records the following:

> After Emily's death last August Penelope and I, comparing notes found that we both had had [a] very strong impression of her active presence particularly during the sorting and packing of her effects and her works of art. Feelings of being directed or opposed in what we were doing or in choices we were about to make. I, in particular felt strong resistance to my preserving all the drawings until I 'replied' that I was sure I was unable to judge what to leave or destroy and intended to get further and more expert advice. Penelope suffered from a strong almost hallucinatory feeling that Emily was trying to 'take her with her' as she felt it — something she had also had to combat in the few months before E died.
>
> Judy Campbell has recently told me of an extremely strong impression, after David's death, of his actual presence and a similar participation in her task of sorting and making decisions about the disposal of his papers.[50] Even stranger was the fact that she has suddenly taken to writing poems — though she has never done this before. These poems come quite involuntarily, sometimes two or three in a bunch, and she feels impelled to write them down as though from dictation. She has showed me several. They are on themes similar to those of David's later poems, close to his style and vocabulary, though rougher and less metrically controlled. The first of them appeared to be a poem by David addressed to her.
>
> It is very odd. But it can also be dangerous. Emily's loss of the use of her right arm was a greater tragedy to her

as an artist. When she had with infinite courage and effort, taught her left arm to take over and to write, draw and paint — though she could no longer do silver-work, enameling and sculpture — and then the left arm began to fail she indicated that she had nothing to live for. But she felt that I did not really *know* what it was like. I suppose I was too calm and cheerful, but it was a deliberate attempt to keep her going and to support Penelope who, near the end was very close to collapse.

On the 19th February, Emily's birthday, she was naturally much in my mind. As I went out to the street in the dark to put out waste-papers for collection the next day, I fell heavily going up the asphalt incline to the curb. My impression was of a stumble and then of my feet being hurled from under me as I fell back on my right side crushing my right arm under me. For the next twelve hours — indeed the next three days I was not only in fairly severe pain as Emily had been but my right arm was quite useless and I began to realise what it had been like for her.

With the build-up of a sense of presences just mentioned I suffered from a superstitious idea that she might have deliberately engineered the accident to this end. Common sense won in the end. I went back next day and observed the hole in the asphalt in which I had obviously caught the toe of my sandal. Moreover I reflected that Emily was incapable of inflicting such an injury. But it shows how easily one can slip into superstitious beliefs and take an emotional impression for actual evidence.[50]

Hope's last book of poetry, *Orpheus* (1991), opens with a tribute to Penelope, who died in 1988. In the poem Trees, he recalls sitting with Penelope and watching the trees in their garden. But now, in the act of writing the poem, he surmises that the trees he experiences alone 'remember her' within their foliage. In *Drifting Continent*, it is the people who become the ciphers and the land the enduring drifting essence; in Trees, it is the foliage that contains the music and the mind. Subject and object merge and recombine in Hope's constant 'reterritorialising' of new continents of the mind, of space, and of the powers that come with searching for new knowledge.

Penelope and Alec's twin sons, Geoffrey and Andrew, do not appear in the notebooks. Hope did, however, discuss their work and interests in conversations. There is an entry relating to Geoffrey's son, James. Hope saw in this child a remarkable response to music, which takes the form of a dance. Hope enjoyed classical music and he records an evening during which he watched James respond to Bach's *No. 5 Brandenburg* concerto:

> As the music broke into the room with its vigorous rhythm, the child was suddenly quite transformed. He began to clap and beat time to the rhythms, his face lit up and he seemed to be inside the music and to understand it as though it was a familiar language. He caught my eye with a sudden intelligence and seemed to invite me to take part, which I did. Finally he got down onto the floor and invented a sort of dance sitting and turning.[51]

Hope had stopped writing in his notebooks by the time that another grandson, Alexander, was born. Alexander is the son of Andrew and his partner Sally Burns, both of whom cared for Hope for a number of years after Penelope's death. On my last visit to Alec's home, before he moved into a nursing home, I watched him sitting on the verandah, in the midwinter sun, overlooking a large leafy garden in Forrest, Canberra, watched over by his then two-year-old grandson. The little boy followed me around for the day, as I poked my way through manuscripts, and spoke in what can only be described as the poetic mode. 'The sun is biting me,' he announced when the clouds parted and the sun hit him through the glass. 'Put this hat upon your head,' he suggested, handing me a hat that looked as if it had been made by gypsies. Alec watched him and smiled, but the smiles were coming less frequently now; no longer interested in his writing and reading, he mostly sat and thought in the secret room of his mind.

CONCLUDING THOUGHTS

Hope's visions are almost always ironic. His irony tends to underscore a fierceness to his satirical approach, which, according to Judith Wright, entailed a 'half-hysterical cocktail-party wit' and which in his earlier reviews and poems had a 'particular note of angry wit'. 'Polemic,' Wright writes, 'can be admirable; Hope has not always been so.' Wright argues further that, 'From a satirist, he has turned himself into a poet and a poet with a vision of the world that is compelling and highly organized.'[52] Wright in this essay focuses on what she sees as Hope's dualistic view of the world and it is clear that she believes that the narrator in his earlier poems was self-conscious. The notebooks, however, indicate that Hope saw himself as a satirist throughout his life and that he was always detached from the voice of the poem. I intimated earlier that the story he thinks he is telling in the notebooks has a kind of neatness of intention, but it might not be exactly the one he hopes to render. When Wright believes that Hope is the voice in his earlier poems she believes this takes away from his art. She sees his poems as confessional. She cites *Observation Car* as an example of a poem in which Hope has misjudged his listeners: 'Either we want to be amused, or we are interested in the private self-analysis of the poet; we cannot attend to both in the space of the one poem.'[53] Hope argues in his notebooks that he is an actor who enters an argument of a poem and that the voice is not his. I argue that there are poems in which the ironic voice is unmistakably Hope's but that this does not take away from their compelling beauty and 'truth'. Nevertheless, it does mean that I have not accepted that Hope's views of himself as a spectator, somewhat detached from the workings of the world at a personal level, is always the case in his poetry. I would, however, argue that the simultaneous revealment and concealment at the heart of his work is complicated by the 'discursive mode'[54] — his preferred form of argument, which has a satirical edge. I do not agree with Wright that he withdraws from satire or that a poem cannot deal simultaneously both with self-analysis as a poet, which entails the use of the personal, and with universal questions dealing with the role of poetry. Instead, I contend that his satire is made more ambiguous and less polemical by his irony. It is a 'complication' in that Hope deals explicitly with his role as a poet, a lover, a friend and an arbiter of taste and that his ironic stance teases his audience with the questions: Is this the poet speaking about himself or is it the poet speaking for all young poets attempting to resolve the relationship between the life and the art (*Observation Car*),[55] and, later in his life, for all old poets about to die (*Old Poet*)?[56] If the poems have a universal application do they then sustain Hope's preferred detachment? When Hope does draw on autobiographical material in his poems, it is most likely that he is dealing with an emotional source that feeds the content of his poetry and his role as a poet that will have universal application to the proper purpose of poetry, and that this will form an argument that is not personal or confessional. Similarly, when he sharpens his satiric wit he is most likely targeting forces that impede the survival of what he believes to be the highest form of poetry. The ironic edge that persists subverts what might be perceived as 'personal' and might also be Hope consciously or unconsciously giving ironic attention to his belief systems and lack of them. 'Let humour be my epitaph,' Hope said to me often. Hope nevertheless is clear about the purpose of satire. He believes it targets evil, incoherence and folly in society, which, according to Hope, are not only connected but 'rely and depend on one another'. When satire strikes, 'it weakens and shakes the forces that corrupt the heart and destroy poetry'. Hope recognises that satire has always been 'regarded with suspicion', and that unlike epic poetry, tragedy, dancing and singing, it has 'no acknowledged muse'.[57] His omissions in relation to political questions will tend to be judged by a reader's ideological stance. Hope would argue, however, that you cannot be an activist and a poet — that is, a poet cannot be told to write a poem that serves a political purpose. If satire is targeted at 'evil' in society, then, in accordance with Hope's antipathy towards poetry used as a political weapon, it follows that his satire will not be directed at political atrocities. Hope reserves his critical eye for modernity whether that be, for example, marriage (*The Brides*), mass culture (*Standardisation*), tourism (*A Letter from Rome*), psychoanalysis (*Private Dick*) or the role of the poet (*Observation Car*). These evils of modernity, in Hope's view, stifle creativity and impoverish and corrupt the poetic forms.

Hope's refusal to own the voice in his poems in a personal autobiographical sense is further complicated in his adaptation of the spirit of 'negative capability'. To discuss this, I am drawing on his note-taking in relation first to the voice in a poem; second, his contempt for free verse and other similar expressions of modernism in the arts; and thirdly, the rather strained personal detachment he has towards his life and the people with whom he shared this life. In response to Yeats 'The intellect of man is forced to choose / Perfection of the life, or of the work',[58] Hope notes, in 1979, that the perfection of the poet's gift in his work might require him to remain chaotic as a character. The poet should have no character and is continually informing and filling some other body. Perfection of the life in these circumstances is almost impossible in the ordinary sense. And yet, he adds, as a life to live it is perhaps perfect. In another entry, he writes:

> The sort of person who devotes himself to objects and people, is distinctively different as a rule from the sort of person who devotes himself to activities and processes. I can more easily imagine myself dying for a cause or giving up everything else for art or knowledge than for any persons, however dear or any possession however splendid or beautiful.[59]

It seems that if Hope has a cause, it is a quest for knowledge, a quest for the perfection of the poetic expression of it. In consequence, the enemies are those who destroy the vessel, the container of the wisdom, the story and the new knowledge that comes with the creation of new being. Writers of free verse are the enemies because they undermine the only structure that he believes extends human consciousness, that captures the music of existence and enters and grapples with the mystery of being. It becomes evident that one of the horrors that free verse has accommodated is the poet writing about his or her personal experiences. His comments on Sylvia Plath, however, tell us perhaps as much about his own fears, hinted at in *Memento Mori,* as they might about Plath. He writes:

> Why do I dislike her poetry so much? I feel that I am being infected with something at once bright, competent in an artificial way, nervously aware, modish and very sick. I feel as though I were having a nervous breakdown by proxy — but a nervous breakdown somehow contrived and deliberately and fashionably arranged — a self-conscious 'poetical' imitation of a nervous breakdown — all those smartly effective, sequentially incoherent images — the witty, too witty paranoia — the tenderly exploited broken heart — the exhibitionist anguish — sick, sick, ah sick! Even the last poems [*Winter Trees*] have this feeling of display of her modish psychosis about them, of keeping an artistically touched up self-inflicted wound open for exhibition until the photographers arrive from *Vogue*.[60]

Whatever one's views are on Plath, this entry disturbs me in what it might say about Hope. One might accept the intelligence and even the philosophical explanations that hold up the ideas that the poet has no character, that he or she should enter a poem as an actor asking 'what if?' of a situation. Certainly, Hope has written extraordinary, beautiful, profound and passionate poems within this framework. But is it the case that a poem written in traditional verse structures is more likely than free verse to hide, neglect or avoid exploration of personal anguish?

It seems to me that Hope's character and his personal plight do on occasion break through the mask. There are revelations of a personal kind, though his irony tends to conceal them at a moment of potential exposure. It's not that he refuses to comment on his views in a poem, but more that, at points at which he might collapse into a form of anguish or further exploration of pain, there is a pulling back, a fear perhaps that might lurk around that photographer from *Vogue*. He maintains that in poetry, or in real life, once you make the test not 'what a thing is, but how important it is to you, you are on the path to the trivial and the trumped up'.[61] His aversion to the personal and the subjective is even supported by his dream-team, which he sees as inspiring agents. He recognises them as the resources of the imagination but he notes that they are weak on management. Their taste is often appalling and their powers of integration nil. Their thoughts are half-truths. Consequently, the dreams of which Hope cannot make sense of himself become of great interest to those approaching Hope's work from a Freudian perspective. Hope would have nothing but contempt for such an approach, and would merely repeat with conviction that great poetry demands impersonality, that all poetry containing the 'I' is limited (despite his own use of it), and that poetry without the craft and detachment of the poet fails as poetry.

In earlier years, Hope thought Jung's theory of archetypal images to be as 'misleading as Freud's mumbo-jumbo — that a work of art is no more than the underlying to which he reduced it'.[62] Hope, however, came to recognise in Jung's writings the answer to Freud's cross-reduction of works of art to their alleged underlying symbolic expression of repressed fears and desires, his fallacy of confusing results with their causes. Hope identifies specifically with an excerpt from Jung in which he argues that art is not a disease: a work of art is not a human being, but is something supra-personal. It is a thing, a personality, hence it cannot be judged by personal criteria. Indeed, the special significance of a true work of art resides in the fact that it has escaped from the limitations of the personal and has soared beyond the personal concerns of its creator.[63] It is nevertheless the case that Hope, in his art, has produced a subjectivity of a kind. Its 'processual creativity', to borrow a phrase from Guattari,[64] might reflect a stifled desire and/or fear as well as achieving a certain disinterestedness. Interpreting what these fears and desires are within the context of Hope's ironic vision is of course another matter. Hope believes it is a travesty to exploit love and grief in poetry. The rule is, it seems, 'don't exploit your own feelings', which might or might not be translated as 'don't give yourself away'.

We are left with the poems. Do they tell us about the man? Is there revelation despite concealment? Whatever one might think about his argument for the detachment of the poet, it is clear that his argument is not only an intellectual and imaginative one; it is also a deeply personal one from which he flees in terror — maybe from 'those doubles that haunt him in the glass'.

There is a dream that Hope jotted into his notebooks. It characterises a nomad of the mind and space whose poetry is understood in its dynamism, by its becoming, and by its variability in which the self or identity is on the periphery, defined by the states through which it passes, whether that be the smooth and/or striated space of the mind, the land and that 'processual creativity' produced by desire. In the dream, the human being is equated with the poet's imagination:

> There was this image. It was that of a human, specifically the poet's imagination being like a swan coasting on the surface of the world-mind and continually casting down its thoughts into the deep blue below. But the blue was that of the sky and the real swan was swimming on the inside of the surface of the sphere and was mirrored on the outside by his reflected image, while the song in which his thoughts were embodied sank outwards into the endless depth. It had a peculiar significance which now escapes me, though the vividness of the image remains unimpaired. As I recall, the swan itself was white, but its mirror image was a pale gold or biscuit coloured against the intense blue of the sky.[65]

In Hope's final book of poetry, he writes in *Visitant*[66] that he feels that the world has left him behind, bred as he was to a different law, and coming from a distant shore 'to watch, to appraise, to divine'. The last few stanzas bid his readers farewell and end with an entreaty of a kind:

> *Yet much that I saw became dear;*
> *Some few were close to my heart;*
> *Although it was perfectly clear*
> *I was stranger here*
> *Standing aloof and apart.*
>
> *Now it is time to return,*
> *I shall miss this world more than I thought,*
> *All I came merely to learn*
> *Holds me now with love and concern,*
> *To whom do I make my report?*[67]

Perhaps Hope's art of ironic detachment is something all cultures need — a spectator who views a web, and leaves his own, woven as much by argument and analogy as by myth, music and traditional verse structures. This silken tapestry, left for us to admire and seek ways of entering the centre of its mystification, is designed to celebrate the passions of mind and heart. Whether we choose to find there hidden expressions of grief, despair and loneliness, or if we attempt to rip away the masks and expose the doppelgänger that haunted Hope's looking glass, we might find good copy for 'the *Vogue* photographers', but not, in Hope's view, the meaning of his poems.

Notes

1. Hope, Book XXII, 1982, pp. 109–10
2. Robert Francis Brissenden, poet, critic and novelist, and reader in English at The Australian National University until his retirement in 1988, was a colleague of Hope's. Hope referred to him in an interview as 'my closest friend' and one 'who most understood my poetry'.
3. McCulloch, 'Interview with Bob Brissenden', Canberra, May 1990.
4. Hope, *Orpheus*, p. 56.
5. Hope, Book XX, 1979, p. 160.
6. Hope, *Orpheus*, p. 42.
7. Hope, *Selected Poems*, p. 13,
8. Deleuze and Guattari, *On the Line*, p . 5 .
9. Hope, *Selected Poems*, p. 184.
10. Ibid; This poem can be seen as autobiographical; Hope was born in Cooma, New South Wales.
11. Hope, Book XVIII, 1975, pp. 3–5.
12. Hope, Book VI, 1960, p. 40.
13. Hope, Book X, 1969, p. 93.
14. Ibid., p. 91.
15. Hope, Book IX, 1967, pp. 66–7.
16. Hope, Book XIV, pp. 36–9. Also see Chapter Two of this text for Hope's explanation of what is meant by Eddington's Net.
17. Hope, Book XXI, 1979, pp. 10–11.
18. Hope, *Orpheus*, p . 3 3
19. See Kuhn, *The Structures of Scientific Revolutions*, in which Kuhn demonstrates across time how a scientific theory is accepted for a period as a determining paradigm of 'truth' and how scientific communities agree to replace this paradigm with another: 'Paradigms gain their status because they are more successful than their competitors in solving a few problems that the group of practitioners have come to recognize as acute' (p. 23).
20. Hope, Book IV, 1952–58, p. 62.
21. Hope, *Orpheus*, p . 1 2 .
22. This term is used in the Nietzschean sense. See Solomon and Higgins, *Reading Nietzsche*, pp. 9, 63: 'Central to Nietzsche's middle works is the idea, and the style of perspectivism. Unlike most philosophers, who argue directly for the truth of a single idea or system, Nietzsche argues for a plurality of perspectives, a plurality of "truths", if you like, with none of them the true one'; 'many views and values are possible and indeed appropriate for different people'.
23. Deleuze and Guattari, 'Introduction: Rhizome', p. 16.
24. See Grosz, *Space, Time and Perversion*, pp. 131–2, where she analyses the thoughts of Deleuze and Guattari in a way that sheds further light on how Hope, in his writings, has pre-empted their thinking. Of particular interest is her insight that Deleuze does not attempt 'to abandon binarized thought or replace it with an alternative; binarized categories, rather, are played off against each other, they are rendered molecular, global and analysed in their molar particularities, so that the

possibilities of their reconnections, their realignment in different "systems" is established. So it is not as if the outside or the exterior must remain eternally counterposed to an interiority that it contains: rather the outside is the transmutability of the inside.'

25 Keats, quoted in Hope, 'The Reputation of Karoline Von Günderrode', p. 75.
26 Deleuze and Guattari, *On the Line*, p. 1.
27 'Striated space' is a term used by Deleuze and Guattari, and is placed in opposition to, though not always separate from, 'smooth space'. See *A Thousand Plateaus*, '1440: The Smooth and the Striated', pp. 474–500, in which these writers examine the terms in relation to a. the technological model; b. the musical model; c. maritime model; d. the mathematical model; e. the physical model; and f. the aesthetic model: nomad art. In discussing these models, the writers characterise 'smooth space' as nomadic and 'striated space' as sedentary. The former in geographical metaphor can be seen in a desert or the sea, the latter in a city or a woven texture in which a striated space is 'necessarily delimited, closed on at least one side: the fabric can be infinite in length but not in width, which is determined by the frame of the warp; the necessity of a back and forth motion implies a closed space' (p. 474).
28 Hope, *Collected Poems: 1930–1965*, pp. 31–3.
29 Guattari, *Chaosmosis: an ethico-aesthetic paradigm*, p. 11.
30 Ibid., p. 12.
31 Hope, *Poems*, pp. 115–17.
32 Hope, *A. D. Hope*, pp. 8–11.
33 Guattari, *Chaosmosis*, p. 11.
34 Hope, *Orpheus*, pp. 17–21.
35 Hope, *Collected Poems: 1930–1965*, pp. 31–3.
36 Hope, *Selected Poems*, pp. 186–90.
37 Hope, Book XVIII, 1975, pp. 86–7.
38 Ibid.
39 McCulloch, 'Interview with Bob Brissenden'.
40 Hope, Book XVIII, 1975, p. 96.
41 Ibid.
42 McCulloch, 'Interviews with Hope: 1985–1994'.
43 Hope, Book XXI, 1979–82, pp. 32–3.
44 Ibid., pp. 156–7.
45 Ibid., pp. 58–9.
46 Penelope Hope, *Long Ago is Far Away*. This book is based on a collection of records of people who happened to come to the rivers that flow into the Gulf of Papua; from the visit of the Fly up until 1929 when government influence appeared to have been established and the world depression was thwarting those who had helped to develop the country by European standards.
47 McCulloch, Conversations with Penelope Hope, 1986–88.
48 See McCulloch, *A. D. Hope The Dance of Language*.
49 See Emily Hope, *The Queen of the Nagus*, as an example of her work. This beautiful book comprises a story written by Emily, who explores the

possibilities in the event that women are accepted as equal partners to men, and is illustrated by paintings she did when she was in Nepal.
50 Hope, Book XXI, 1980, pp. 73–6.
51 Hope, Book XXII, 1982, pp. 116–17.
52 Wright, 'A. D. Hope', pp. 80–1.
53 Ibid., p. 82.
54 See Hope's essay 'The Discursive Mode', p. 9, in which he argues that 'The first step in intelligent regeneration of the soil of poetry may well be to re-establish the discursive mode, in particular to restore the practice of formal satire'.
55 Hope, 'Observation Car', *Selected Poems*, pp. 5–7, which ends with a sense of anxiety that his original plans to be 'the Eater of Time, a poet and not that sly / Anus of mind the historian' have been curtailed. He argues that 'It was so simple and plain / To live by the sole, insatiable influx of the eye. / But something went wrong with the plan: I am still on the train.'
56 See Hope, 'Old Poet', *Orpheus*, p. 38: 'What are these young girls doing / Crowding at my gate … They are gathered to the dancing, / To dance your dance of death.'
57 Hope, 'The Satiric Muse', p. 61.
58 See Yeats, 'The Choice', The Collected Poems, p. 278.
59 Hope, Book XX, 1978, p. 39.
60 Hope, Book XX, 1979, p. 51.
61 Ibid.
62 Hope, Book XXI, 1981, pp. 176–9.
63 See Jung, 'On the Revelation of Psychosis', p. 71.
64 Guattari, Chaosmosis, p. 13.
65 Hope, Book XXI, 1979, p. 2.
66 Hope, Orpheus, p. 43.
67 Ibid.

II

NEGATIVE CAPABILITY

'The New Men' will be people with an immense store of negative capability, taking a provisional world for granted and not asking for permanent assurances or faiths anchored in fixed systems ... I believe I am such myself and thanks to a great indifference to what other people think I have been a happy man most of my life.[1]

Introduction

Hope was naturally drawn towards the concept of 'negative capability'; it provided him with an unlimited environment in which he could taste, test and explore the vagaries of human existence. Life was to be a continual celebration of 'being' and 'becoming', lived with a sense of irony and Nietzschean perspectivism.[2]

    Hope, as a young poet, acknowledged that the creative life was as significant in human existence as a life of action or a life of contemplation. The poet was most rich if he/she was continually open to a field of forces unhampered by the privilege of one epistemological, logical or metaphysical set of values. It was the face behind the mask and beyond the strictures of codes and 'truths' that he was most intent on bringing into his metaphorical field. Hope feared that what we know often gets in the way of what we might learn, and that such a perspective requires a joyful embrace of all hypothetical explanations of the world.

As a creator, Hope, the poet, was amused by the way most people around him thought. Having understood all stories from life as metaphors, whether embodied in gods, cosmological theories or moral axioms, he, in the spirit of 'negative capability', enjoyed finding the flaw in the argument that had foolishly promised a truth of some kind. It would not be far-fetched to conceive of Hope like Nietzsche's Zarathustra: a wanderer, a nomad, a homeless creator laughing at certainties yet inspired by the way metaphor is active in gathering its strength in a continual process of displacement and transference. This does not, however, make him unaware that the passing of some beliefs is a great loss to the human spirit. Entries in his notebooks cite, for example, the belief in the eternal life of the soul, a rich source of metaphor and story that once played a fruitful role in the creative life.

Hope's perspectivism, his insistence on the shifting nature of all paradigms of thought, whether sociological, moral or scientific, fuels his representation of people as active, contemplative and creative beings.

THE THREE FACES OF LOVE

L'animo, ch'è creato ad amor presto,
Ad ogni cosa è mobile che piace,
Tosto che dal piacere è desto.
Vostra apprensira da esser verace
Tragge intenzione, e dentro a voi la spiega,
Si che l'animo ad essa volger face …
Poi come il foco movesi in altura
per la sua forma, ch'è nata a salire …[3]

— Purgatorio XVIII, II, 19–33.

This suggests another way in which we could make a clear distinction between the contemplative emotions and the active, without necessarily accepting the scholastic and Aristotelian psychology. For it is true that every object can be both an object in itself or the original of an object in the mind with which the mind connects it. It is true that there is a pleasure in the thought or sight of an object of desire which accompanies the first movement to attain it and another and different pleasure of attainment, fruition and contentment. Now the object may be pursued and enjoyed in itself and this is active life. But we may also enjoy the object of thought, imagination or memory or the object itself as though it were an object of thought, in itself: as there is no need to do anything in order to attain the image which is there without effort and sometimes without volition; the pleasure is different from those concerned in active pursuit of the original object: this is contemplative life. But if from the objects of contemplation we are moved to create further objects in the world by music, painting, poems dances and so on, then a third sort of pleasure arises — that which is out-going not intaking, expressive not possessive and the end of which is another pleasure: that of contemplation again: this is creative life. The objects of creative life, once created, become, of course, objects of the first two sorts and only creative life is life *sui generis*. Thus, where the scholastic distinction sees only two kinds of activity, I would think there should be three. And so the mind can desire in three ways and find three kinds of satisfaction of its desires. I should, in Thomistic or Aristotelian terms, describe these as the three aspects or modes of Love in human minds and hearts. St Thomas might agree that the third, as more like the divine nature, is the highest. But of course he makes a sharp distinction between Divine and human creation.

— Book VI, 1959, pp. 4–5.

'PARADISE LOST'

It all depends on the subordinate position of Eve … 'He for God only, she for God in him' … Without this, is there any reason why Satan should not have decided to tempt Adam first? Suppose Adam to have succumbed to flattery of his understanding only a little less crude than that to which Eve succumbs; suppose, as well, that he tries to tempt Eve to eat the apple too and that she, already pregnant and weighing the risk of Adam's life against that of her unborn child, quite naturally refuses. This would be to tamper with the original story but not much more than Milton has already tampered with it. But how would the fall of Adam look then, poor thing? And how would the great poem look, even supposing Eve not to be pregnant at the time, had she refused, let us say for fear of the consequences and not from genuine obedience, to eat the apple. As a good wife she would continue to live with Adam, whom she loved in any case. In due course she became pregnant. But what of original sin? What part in Adam's fall would his children then have had? Theological myths have to be very carefully arranged if they are to carry any conviction. You cannot have a great epic called 'Paradise Half-Lost'.

— Book VI, 1959, p. 26.

RELATIVE MORALS

If the natural history of morals were to reveal that what is considered moral or immoral in any society, reflects the needs and desires of that society at a certain stage of its existence, then one would expect certain moral views to outlast their usefulness. In a society living more or less at subsistence level gluttony is obviously a crime and a sin because it is equivalent to murdering or starving other people. And for the same reason infanticide may be a moral duty. But in a society with an excess or a sufficiency of food gluttony is a venial fault that affects the individual only and [is] condemned no more severely than personal vanity — not pleasant but not important. Many primitive societies approve or condone homosexuality. 'Christian societies' count it a sin. But a society, threatened with over-population might well make it a virtue, as medieval Christianity made chastity a virtue. In a complex society based on ownership as a source of power and position, theft, envy and greed are obviously bound to be major sins, but a simple society living easily without any sentiment for prestige based on goods would have no reason to consider these 'deadly sins' as more than bad manners. It is difficult to imagine a society in which murder and wrath would not be crime and sin respectively, since they are always disruptive — nor one in which love and kindness would not be virtues.

There seems at any rate to be a confusion in most collections of virtues and vices, sins and laudable acts, between acts and states which are deleterious or beneficial in themselves to the agent, and those which are indifferent to the agent but deleterious or beneficial to society. Dishonesty and cruelty corrupt the agent and harm others.

But eating and drinking and fucking seem only to harm the agent if carried to excess, or intermitted altogether. Their social effects vary according to the circumstances. But there is nothing inherently corrupting or destructive in any of them.

— Book VI, 1960, pp. 71–2.

MEMENTO MORI

The fact that each of us must die, that science can provide no discovery to prevent it, social legislation no protection or alleviation, that each of us must face one disaster that cannot be shared or sold or outwitted is the last protection against a protected and sheltered comfort which increasingly the race takes to be its natural condition. This is the last bulwark against the triviality and frivolity of mind that complete safety and comfort tend to bring with them. There is a sense in which the abolition of death would be the negation of life.

A time may well come in which most of the material problems of man's life on earth will be overcome and each will be assured of comfort and security from the cradle to the grave. Men's minds will be led to consider death as their last serious problem. There will arise a poetry of death, a philosophy of death and even a cult of death unlike anything of the sort before, though several societies have had such cults.

— Book VI, 1960, p. 89.

'THE SOUL SECURED I'

The Soul, secur'd in her existence, smiles
at the drawn dagger, and defies its point
The stars shall fade away, the sun himself
Grow dim with age and Nature sink in years;
but then shalt flourish in immortal youth
unhurt amid the war of elements
the wrecks of matter, and the crush of worlds.

— Cato: V.I.

A great change has come over things since these noble lines were written. For the great mass of people engaged by the practical life and absorbed by it, an after-life was probably a holding concern, something to be secured in this world but to be attended to when it came along. For those engaged in the intellectual life, a world in which a few intellectuals believe or even entertain the notion of the immortal soul makes a great difference to their intellectual pursuits. This is not so much a matter of belief or lack of belief in an immortal soul, but a result of the fact that through ancient philosophy and Christian theology, the soul was regarded as the seat and agent of all the rational and intellectual powers of man. A thinking animal, fallible and ephemeral is a very different thing from a permanent intellectual creature temporarily attached to its animal and only partly dependent on it for the operation and success of its rational powers. The older belief may have been in error, but if so, it is an example of those fruitful errors which made for a noble conception of human life and gave the intellectual life a superior dignity and appeal. The decline of regard for the contemplative life in our world is in part due to this and the loss of this regard is severe and may be fatal in the long run.

— Book VIII, 1961, pp. 2–3.

OPAQUE GLASS

Ingenious devices for letting in the light without allowing you to see out, such as modern techniques provide — eg., glass brick walls, crinkle-glass, sanded glass and so on — remind me very much of most present-day forms of education.

— Book VII, 1961, p. 4.

FAITH AND CERTAINTY

In the quarrel between a materialist and a religious view of the world, each side is apt to claim certainty for its side and to point out how much the other depends on unprovable and even unwarranted hypotheses. The type of mind which can be content to recognise the hypotheses on both sides without demanding certainty in either seems comparatively rare. A continual exercise of suspended judgement on matters which admit of no proof seems almost impossible to most temperaments and an attempt to keep it up seems to produce a corruption of intellectual fibre or a relapse into indifference. To such minds the contemplation of the limits of human knowledge is gruesome. They must opt for one of the alternatives and compensate with the emotional 'certainty' of a faith for the intellectual certainty which the facts deny them. The exceptional minds are marked out by joy, the exhilaration with which they are able to contemplate the hypothetical nature of all explanations of the world.

— Book VII, 1961, p. 128.

THE ENLIGHTENMENT

One important result of the Enlightenment and all its continuations has been to demonstrate that if you remove the bases of their superstitions, people will simply invent others for themselves often more harmful for wearing an appearance of science or rational structure which blinds the believers to the false premises. This has happened so often since the eighteenth century, and in so many departments of knowledge, and so many spheres of action, that it suggests that superstition is necessary to men and societies, that it at least supplies a need for which no substitute has yet been found.

But it may also suggest that what science calls superstitions, fallible as their ideas may prove to be, supply spurious answers to real questions which science is too limited by its own presuppositions — dare one say, its own superstitions to consider the force of. The failure of the Enlightenment was to deny the reality of the questions along with that of the answers.

— Book VIII, 1964, p. 19.

PANTHEON

I am so used, by the attitude of my age and upbringing, to thinking of any god as a doubtful concept and many gods as mere absurdity that it comes as a surprise travelling in the Peloponnese to feel the gods near, quite natural and exercising their numinous force. On the bus from Argos to Olympia across the Arcadian plateau, it came as no surprise to recognise the bus-driver as Pan, whom he very closely resembled both in features and bearing. Not even the fact that he stopped the bus to say a prayer at a wayside shrine as we began our descent towards Olympia destroyed the illusion, since so many Christian shrines are on the spot occupied by a pagan before them. The little nun who showed us round at Agia Moni [Zoodochos Pigi][4] the ancient well and spring of Hera, where she renewed her virginity annually, now the Virgin Mary's spring, kept crossing herself all the time she stood with us. I put out my hand to touch the water but found myself impelled to desist with a powerful feeling of sacrilege.

In the same way, it was not merely a series of thunderstorms at Olympia, marking the end of the autumn and the beginning of the rains, but a sense of Zeus the Thunderer, himself — as though the thunder had taken on a personal note never heard before.

On the spot, it is not only natural, but quite easy to believe in a Pantheon of gods and to find the notion of a single 'monolithic', abstract deity contradictory and unsatisfactory. In the desert of Arabia it might be the other way about. Certainly if one is going to give assent to the possibility of supernatural beings at all — or perhaps superhuman would be a better word, it is the 'naturalness' of the Greek Pantheon that wins assent — then there seems no reason to stop at one. Theology knows nothing of Occam's Razor,[5] since it is an area of speculation in which the critical words 'praeter necessitaten' have no relevance and perhaps no meaning.

— Hydra 1965
— Book VIII, 1965, pp. 140–1.

PRIVATE AND PUBLIC

Classification, grouping things together as similar in some respect or similar in the way we feel about them, is sometimes quite conscious and explicit and it requires an explicit effort to free oneself from an arbitrary prejudice when such a classification happens to be baseless, eg., classing fornication with murder, social standing or lack of it with worth or ability, whales with fish and so on.

Sometimes we do not classify at all but behave as though we did, and the explicit statement of the group and its members can be illuminating or at any rate entertaining.

For example, there are certain activities which we habitually perform in public with no sense of unease or incongruity; others which are not so and which, if we have to do them in public, make us uncomfortable at the least and so acutely shamed or mortified at the most, that we may be willing to go to any lengths to avoid them, like poor Virginie in the shipwreck or Margaret Fuller for that matter, if anyone doubts the truth of Bernardin de St Pierre's fiction.[6] The list of private activities differs from society to society, from age to age and from class to class in the same society, but in my own it makes a curious but very real 'group': pissing, shitting, making love, copulating, sleeping, bathing, praying, writing (especially poetry), going naked ... there are a few others, but few: almost any society will have still others and omit some of these. Some for example pray in public, some have no objection to nakedness or making love in public. In fact the actual nature of the act does not matter very much. It is the way it is regarded or the conditions under which it can be carried on — writing and praying need to be uninterrupted as other forms of art or of worship do not.

It is interesting that writing is distinguished in this way from all the other arts. It is the only one that *cannot* be practised in public.

— Book IX, 1965, pp. 3–4.

THE MIRRORS 1965–68

If I make the lashes dark
And the eyes more bright
And the lips more scarlet
Or ask if all be right
From mirror after mirror,
No vanity's displayed:
I'm looking for the face I had
Before the world was made.

W. B. Yeats: A Woman Young and Old[7]

It is much the same for a poet as for the woman or the actor. It is what Yeats called the 'Mask', what Keats called the operation of negative capability — essentially a means of looking into a mirror to find something *other* than oneself, which is to become oneself for the time of creation.

— Book IX, 1966, pp. 138–9.

PROTECTIVE COLOURING

Reading Montherlant's Le Chaos et La Nuit, it occurs to me how apt we are to see types like his Celestino as aberrations from a normal human make up. It is this that makes him absurd and delightfully monstrous. In the book he is treated, too, as *Spanish* and, therefore, from a French point of view, racially and inherently monstrous. But of course he is nothing of the sort: he is an example of Congreve's idea of a 'humorous' character. An extreme case of what we are all like more or less. He pursues his humour, he is stupid, he cuts himself off from his surroundings and so loses the protective colouring that most social animals learn to adopt. I find it easier in a foreign country like this to see that for all my enjoyment of Celestino, I am probably as much a grotesque if they could know me as we are allowed to know Celestino, to the Puerto Ricans and negroes with whom I am surrounded in West Side New York.

The great thing about the interpolated tales in *Don Quixote* is the way they bring out the 'relative' nature of social values, in class, in race, in country and epoch. Each has its normal men, but the norms are of such a kind that there is no normal norm; there is no normal society, and since no man exists outside a society, there is no 'normal man'. Yet most social, moral and other types of value theory are built on the supposition. Most literature takes it for granted.

— New York, June 1967
— Book IX, 1967, pp. 66–7.

NEW MEN

Another possibility would not be the usual speculative emergence of some kind of *Übermensch* or the development of hitherto unknown kinds of mental power, but simply the fading out of certain limiting conditions which prevent men as they are living in the world as it is.

The greatest problem is that morally, socially, artistically we are brought up and adapted to deal with a world of a definite and definable kind. In the past if a new world view came into being it was as definite as the old one; doubt could exist only as to which was the *true* one. We are all fundamentally Big-Endians or Little-Endians.[8] But now we live in a world which offers us a choice of possible cosmologies and keeps on changing the choice so fast that we have no time to build a permanent belief on any. The same is true of biology, psychology, social theory, ethics. All our knowledge is provisional and we are trying to live by 'permanent' or 'reliable' beliefs and principles in what is and from now on promises to be a purely 'provisional' world. The New Men will be people with an immense store of negative capability, taking a provisional world for granted and not asking for permanent assurances or faiths anchored in fixed systems.

I meet such people from time to time. Often they are unhappy because the 'fixed believers' who form the majority have persuaded them that they are irresponsible or defective, when in fact they are the most healthy and whole of men. I believe I am such myself and thanks to a great indifference to what other people think I have been a happy man most of my life.

— Book X, 1968, pp. 19–20.

DEFECT VERSUS ILLUSION

I

In the debate between Science and Religion, the general assumption is that religion has the worst of it because it cannot produce any testable 'facts'. It cannot devise any social or controlled experiment to decide between the two points of view.

Neither of course can science, but science is not on the defensive, believes it has no onus of proof and has accumulated a pretty pile of evidence for its point of view … or so it thinks. Those who believe in God have, they say, 'experience' of God but they cannot produce this experience to be tested and they have no means of proving that it is not an illusion, as their opponents claim it to be. But neither can their opponents prove that it is not a power or a sense that not everyone possesses, like colour vision for example, and that it is they who are 'defective' not the others who are deluded.

II

One could regard the extreme mystic experience and the hunger and incompleteness of these types of mind as a perfectly normal but terminal unit in a human series of which the other terminal unit is the happy solipsist, the person to whom this is an imperfect and unsatisfactory world because of the plurality of beings in it, whose ideal is the opposite of union with God, the self contemplation of his single self in an empty universe. Both yearn for and can adumbrate or suggest an experience which is ineffable.

Each, perhaps is aiming at the same consummation, imperfectly understood, but setting off in the opposite direction from the other.

I must stay where I am, but I must try to follow those journeys in imagination.

— Book X, 1968, pp. 54–5.

NATURAL LAW

'There is nothing either good or bad but thinking makes it so.'

'Beauty is in the eye of the beholder', etc. etc. It is interesting that this should so often be taken as incompatible with natural law (in ethics), the reality of beauty (in esthetics), even the objective reality of values in economics. There is certainly much to be said for such views and it is impossible to prove them wrong. But if we accept them we have not proved the unreality, the relativity or the illusory nature of values — was this the existentialist fallacy perhaps? — we have simply said that values are man-made, as cities and ivilizations and the music of Bach and Beethoven are man-made. The mistake arises perhaps from the view that man, and what he thinks and does are not a part of nature, the view that opposes the natural to the artificial.

— Book X, 1969, p. 91.

NEGATIVE CAPABILITY

What Keats has said on this subject seems to me of the first importance, but it deals only or perhaps primarily with the poet's relations with his world and time.

There is another way of looking at the same idea which considers the poet's relations with his art. A great deal of the time of my generation has gone into endless discussion of the 'true nature' of poetry, the superiority of one technique to another, the stimulating business of revolution and heresy hunting, and in particular the obsession with 'originality' and novelty to a point where it seemed obvious to many that a new method was necessarily a better method.

A degree of negative capability in the writer which allows him to enter into all theories and all techniques, to test and taste with no irritable concern with right and wrong, with mine and thine, might be what is badly needed.

— Williamstown, Mass., 1969
— Book X, 1969, p. 93.

EDDINGTON'S NET

> *Apart from these two pure numbers [the 'fine structure constant' and the ratio of the masses of electrons and protons] the subject [of physics] in his day appeared to be almost closed. Eddington produced the intellectually stimulating idea that the whole of physics might possibly be analogous to the activities of an ichthyologist ... who devoted a long and distinguished scientific career to the discovery of the basic biological law which bears his name. The law states that 'no fish are less than two inches long'. The ichthyologist never realised that his law was nothing but a reflection of the size of the mesh of the net in which he caught specimens for his study.*
>
> P. T. Matthews: *The Nuclear Apple*, p. 23.

Matthews goes on to make fun of Eddington and concludes that 'there seems no justification nowadays [1971] for the view that the whole content of physics is determined by the techniques which define its boundaries — that nothing comes out which has not implicitly been put in'.

This is rather puzzling. The framing of an hypothesis, the evolution of a new technique to test this hypothesis, is of course implicitly putting in what we expect to come out. There is no other method of procedure, as the author seems to imply there is. What Eddington's Parable of the Net is meant to do is to keep the theorist and the experimenter aware of the 'Fallacy of the Net' implicit in our thinking. It is no different from the advances in mathematics or logic due, in the last few years, to study of the way the techniques of these sciences tend to define their boundaries.

But there are great areas of human thinking to which the Fallacy of the Net still needs to be applied and in particular to 'reticulation' imposed on us by the span of consciousness. We have become well aware in the last half-century of the sorts of events possible below the minimum threshold, but those which may be concealed from us above the maximum are still in unknown territory. The limitations of the nets thrown into the ocean of Being by the senses [have] been partly explored (as have some missed by the senses altogether, eg., those parts of the electro-magnetic series outside colour and warmth) and their capacities enlarged by instruments, but those imposed by the brain itself are only beginning to be surmised. Once the idea takes hold one cannot stop. It applies to every area of knowledge, of awareness, of introspection or of social intercourse. We can see ourselves as savages on an atoll trying to make a world picture on the basis of the flotsam and jetsam of the shoreline. Eddington's Net becomes the basis of a new world-view.

Eddington's Net applies, of course, to the formulation of his own parable. Because the nets used by his scientist are small, as the reticulations of the net are definite, it excludes fishes larger than the net can take as well as letting those too small to be taken escape. Eddington's preoccupations limited the scope of his parable. Moreover his 'scientific' approach excluded a parable that would have taken in the poetry of earth as well as its measurements.

— Ballina, 24–IX–72
— Book XIV, 1972, pp. 36–9,

FINAL CAUSE

I wonder whether it has occurred to anyone that the idea of God may be one towards which the universe is working rather than that from which it arises, a Final Cause rather than a Prime Mover.

Immediately on asking this silly question I take the trouble to find out and find it a fairly constant preoccupation of philosophers and theologians though they are not usually raising the idea as such. It comes into some forms of Pantheism.

— Book XII, 1971–2, pp. 96–7.

I expect it has. Everything has been thought of before, but there may be a new way of putting this one, that would make it practically a new idea.

Could analysis of history and biology suggest what sort of a God we are in fact in [the] process of evolving?

Could any survey of colonial animals have predicted even one of the possible forms of multi-cellular animals? I imagine not even the lowliest, let alone the most advanced.

Evolution is one science, like cosmology, in which prediction is not a result of accredited theory. Not even the most experienced specialist in a set of related species can predict which way the cat will jump next to evolve a new one.

But he *can* describe the ways in which it *tends to happen* and prepare us for the unexpected.

If in the past man has been busy making God in his own image, it must be remembered that he is only just beginning to learn to shape and control his *own* image. When he learns about that, religion may take a quite unexpected turn. So far it has been the other way about. Men's image of God has been anthropomorphic — even the most abstract and rational ones — and the image of God thus formed has limited his power to advance in finding new images of *man*. What might not be possible if we were to realise that we were the active partners in the adventure of the Divine?

THE GHOST IN THE MACHINE

What worries me about the claims sometimes made that modern physicists have not only abandoned determinism but dispensed with logic in their operations and theories is that however much this may apply to the objects of their investigations, it obviously does not apply to the *way* they investigate and reason. Their experiments assume a determinism, a cause-effect regularity in the way they set them up, record and deduce the results, which they deny to the results themselves. They argue by common logic that their results can only be explained in terms that call common logic [into] question.

Until this anomaly is cleared up it is pointless for supporters of extra-sensory perception or psycho-kinesis to claim support from modern particle physics. It is the old fallacy of *ignotum per ignotius*. I remember talking to Sir John Ecclesix about Newton's hint in the last edition of the *Principia* which was taken up by early psychologists of the Hartley School. They set to work on a sort of psychological physics on the theory of a sort of mental atoms to be called vibratuncle, if I remember the term correctly. It was the first attempt at a scientific approach to what is now called para-psychology and it failed because nobody could find or demonstrate a vibratuncle. Eccles rather thought he could and that he could demonstrate it interacting with an atom.

This arises from reading Koestler's messy little book *The Roots of Coincidence*, the motto of which might well be 'Once a journalist, always a journalist', that is to say a man who tries to argue in an expert field with only superficial knowledge (eg., what I am now doing).

It seems to me that the whole of Koestler's argument by analogy is on the wrong track. A better line might well be along the lines that to deal with the world around [us], we have had to limit and formalise our perceptions to exclude certain perfectly natural forces and types of operation which could have been alternative methods of perception and communication — a specialisation observable almost everywhere in nature. There is no *need* in fact to appeal to the analogy of physics, even if the analogy could be demonstrated.

(Use for The Abdiel Appendix)[10]
— Book XV, 1973, pp. 16–18.

MORE THOUGHTS ON ECONOMICS OF TIME

[See Notebook XII, 1971, pp. 8–12: London, 1971, Economics of Space and Time]

The economics of Time gives each of us a roughly equivalent capital which cannot be bartered or exchanged. This gives the economics of time a stability which the economics of space, of goods and possessions and money does not have. But it *is* subject to inflation of a sort. Those religions which preach a life after death or before birth, or which promise both in the form of a soul continually reborn in other bodies, affect the value of our time holdings in much the same way as the wildest inflation of a currency system.

— Book XIX, 1976, p. 2.

ALL THINGS BRIGHT AND BEAUTIFUL

Cecil Alexander's hymn was a great favourite of mine as a child and there was a special magic in the image:

> *The purple-headed mountain*
> *The river running by*

which it still has for me. I don't think I noticed the illogical optimism of the idea that all the bright and beautiful things were God's handiwork while nothing was said about the darker side of his creation. And I was quite ready to accept the social theory of

> *The rich man in his castle*
> *The poor man at his gate,*
> *God made them high or lowly*
> *And ordered their estate.*

Of course I took it in the sense the author intended: God was on the side of the landed gentry — his attitude to riches acquired by trade or manufacture was not considered. However in some ways it now seems to me a witless production and though I still sing it with pleasure I have altered the text to suit myself.

> *All things bright and beautiful*
> *All creatures great and small,*
> *All things wise and wonderful,*
> *The Lord God made them all,*
> *etc.*

To be followed by

> *All things dark and dreadful,*
> *Beasts that live by blood*
> *All monsters and disasters*
> *Of Famine, Plague or Flood,*
> *Shark and snake and spider*
> *And every deadly pest,*
> *The good Lord God, remember,*
> *He made them with the rest.*

I should like to think that Cecil Alexander could hear me.

— 17–1–1976
— Book XIX, 1976, pp. 4–5.

CELESTIAL LIGHT

Wordsworth's

> *There was a time when meadow, grove and stream*
> *To me did seem*
> *Apparelled in celestial light*[11]

is usually not taken literally. It is assumed that the illumination was in Wordsworth himself and not an actual light — an *extra* light — on the landscape itself. Wordsworth encourages this notion with the clumsy 'to me did seem', as though in recollection he doubts that he actually saw it. He reinforces it later in the ode when he confesses that this no longer happens to him: 'where is it now, the glory …?' etc. But it occurs to me that we *can* take him quite literally and that it [is] an experience shared by many other people — a sudden or momentary experience with some; involuntary with some; with others almost a permanent state and one that can at any rate be called up at will. The similar reports of people under the influence of particular drugs, such as mescalin might suggest that the effect is an illusion due to some abnormal physiological condition. On the other hand, recent experiments on people who see 'auras' and/or a halo of some force round living matter, which can be photographed and seen as a shifting and vibrating pattern of light in such photographs, might suggest that it is an effect external to the observer. Traherne's 'orient and immortal wheat' comes to mind and many other reports. I have experienced it myself at times — usually only briefly — as an effect of a light added to the ordinary light of the sun or of lamps and differentiated from such light by an intense 'stasis' and a feeling that it emanates from the objects observed.

— Carlton, 1976
— Book XIX, 1976, pp. 84–5.

OBJECTIVE STUPIDITY

In the years that I had to deal with various kinds of 'objective tests' in which one has to choose between various preferred answers, my objection to every sort except those testing minutiae of information was always the same: the candidate was not asked to think anything out for himself. The tests were only of that lower sort of intelligence which can judge between alternative solutions to a problem. The higher sort of intelligence which is required for judging the problem itself and devising one's own possible solutions was never called into play. The candidate more intelligent, creative or critical than his examiners had no chance to display his real quality (someone like the young mathematician Abel, for example). It seemed to me an adequate method of testing only servile or second-rate minds. When I visited the research centre in this sort of examining near Princeton in 1958 and spent a day with the specialists on their admittedly very sophisticated 'objective tests' for ability in English, I could not get them to admit that their tests still suffered from this major defect. In fact, when they claimed that their methods were being adopted by college after college and that soon all tertiary education would go over to the system, I refrained from saying that it seemed a good way to make the country safe for mediocrity.

Today in a foolish spy thriller by a man who otherwise shows all the gifts of a novelist, *Billion Dollar Brain* by Len Deighton, I came across the perfect description of the system. The hero, after taking one of these tests, remarks: 'We were then given a simple exam which consisted of crossing out stupid answers in order to leave the least stupid one.'[12]

That of course is the whole point. The answer preferred may in fact not be stupid at all, but because the examinee has not arrived at it for himself he has answered stupidly and if there is a better alternative (as there so often is if one has time to think about it), which he could have given, he has been reduced to the level of the moderately bright dullard.

In order to limit the possible 'right' answers, the deviser of the test has to exclude from his mind all other possible ways of looking at the problem than the one he chooses. He has to eliminate imagination, and suppress his more subtle habits of manipulating and recognising the innate ambiguity of language. He has to ignore the difference that 'context' makes to a question or a statement and to do this is forced to choose only run-of-the-mill contexts implying his own culture and epoch. In other words, he has to impose dullness on himself in order to frame his tests.

At a deeper level the subject touches on the most important division of human beings one from another, those who operate *within* a system of experience or ideas or values which work well enough and with which they are content; for them in theory at least, 'objective tests' are feasible — and those who are constantly aware of the limitations of the systems which for practical reasons we are all compelled to work with, those again for whom creation of new ideas or values is their constant preoccupation.

For such people the whole notion of inventing an objective test is absurd, since those who frame the questions do not know what to ask, and even if they did, cannot tell beforehand which answers will be right or wrong. I cannot at the moment put my finger on the point, but this note seems to be worth considering for *The New Cratylus*.

— Mysore, 15–1–77
— Book XIX, 1977, pp. 125–8.

SI SILEAT

I have just come across Elizabeth Fry's [then Elizabeth Gurney] description of hearing a woman of the Quaker persuasion, Deborah Darby preach when she was staying at the house of her cousin Priscilla Gurney in Wales: Elizabeth was then about nineteen:

> I think my feelings that night, at Deborah Darby's, were the most exalted I ever remember. I, in a manner, was one of the beginners of the Meeting; suddenly my mind felt clothed with light, as with a garment, and I felt silenced before God; I cried with the heavenly feeling of humility and repentance. Then when I was in this awful state, there were two sermons preached ... But that silence, which first took possession of my mind exceeded all the rest.[13]

I am irresistably reminded of St Augustine's last conversation with his mother at Ostia, a passage in the *Confessions*[14] which is never far from my mind and not always or even usually in a religious context. The older I grow the more often I am convinced of the narrowness of the bases of knowledge of the world and the way what we are aware of gets in the way of what we are totally unaware of. I have a great yeaning for that 'si silent omnino'.

— Book XXI, 1979, pp. 11–12.

'TOUT SAVOIR.'

'Tout savoir, c'est tout pardonner' has been very much an attitude of mind in this generation and as a means of liberalising manners and getting rid of absurd prejudice it has something to be said for it.

But on the debit side it has much nonsense to answer for. It has too often led to the view that if we know all the circumstances that lead to crime, cruelty or folly, those who commit acts of these kinds, have nothing to answer for. They are victims of the way things are or of their own unfortunate natures. It is a view that denies man responsibility and makes nonsense of his moral nature. The most deliberate and calculating acts of wickedness, cruelty, dishonesty and neglect dissolve in this bath of social and psychological explanation. They cannot be blamed or indeed punished.

— Book XXI, 1980, p. 120.

DARWIN AND MILTON

I learn from the editor of Darwin's *Journals of the Voyage of the Beagle* that the only works of literature which accompanied him on the whole voyage were the Old Testament and Milton's poems.[15]

The mind reels at the thought of the one attempt to justify the ways of God to man, as the constant companion of the man who was really responsible for turning Milton's system out of doors. I am even more surprised to learn that Darwin began the voyage in the firm belief in 'special creation' and the intention of becoming a country parson of the Church of England. No doubt it was the devil who put all those Galapagos finches in his path. It is to be seen as the Second Fall of Man.

— 25–3–1981
— Book XXI, 1981, p. 189.

POLITICS AND LOGOS

The Right is often wrong but it has a true function;
The Left is sometimes right but with odious unction
That the Right is on the way out, the Left is here to stay,
Unaware that it will be the Right of a later day
We need both their visions and their gift for the absurd
To keep our insight active and to activate the Word.

— Book XXII, 1981, p. 46.

Notes

1. Hope, Book X, 1968, pp. 19–20.
2. Hope's philosophical view throughout his notebooks and his poetry coincides with Nietzschean perspectivism which is one that sees all theories as interpretations, that knowledge is provisional in a state of continual becoming and which denies the notion of absolute truth.
3. This quotation is from *Purgatorio*, Canto XVIII, ll. 19ff., in which Dante's typically medieval doctrine of love and the three stages by which it passes into action is given expression (ll. 22–4, 28–33). See John Ciardo, who translates the segment as follows:

    The soul, being created prone to love
    is drawn at once to all that pleases it, as
    soon as pleasure summons it to move.
    From that which really is, your apprehension.

4. The place where the ancient well and spring of Hera once was is now occupied by a monastery, Agai Moni (Holy Monastery), which is situated north-west of the village of Diakofti, 30 kilometres from Kythera. It was built in 1840 and dedicated to Our Lord the Saviour. Tradition claims that the monastery's holy icon was found in the bushes by a shepherd in 1759. It is said that Theodoros Kolokotronis prayed here for a successful outcome to the Greek Revolution. To thank the Lord, he helped renovate the monastery in 1822.
5. See Honderich (ed.), *The Oxford Companion to Philosophy*, p. 633, where McCord Adams' definition of Ockham's Razor is quoted as: 'A methodological principle dictating a bias towards simplicity in theory construction, where the parameters of simplicity vary from kinds of entity to the number of presupposed axioms to characteristics of curves drawn between data points.' Although found in Aristotle, it became associated with William Ockham because it captures the spirit of his philosophical conclusions.
6. Jacques Henri Bernardin de Saint-Pierre, a follower of Rousseau, wrote the novel *Paul and Virginie* in 1787; it was a poetic romance of virtuous love in which the heroine, Virginie, shows restraint in the manner desciibed by Hope. Margaret Fuller (1810–51), a poet, editor, translator, literary critic and author of the classic feminist tract *Women in the Nineteenth Century*, describes in the latter the degrees to which women would go to ensure an invisibility as regards to their private bodily functions.
7. See Yeats, 'Before the World was Made', *The Collected Poems*, p. 308.
8. See Swift, *Gulliver's Travels*, in which the expressions 'Big Endians' and 'Little Endians' were first coined. Swift's 'Big Endians' were exiled from Mildendo, the metropolis, for refusing to break eggs at the smaller end (Part 1, Chapter 4, pp. 55–60). Today the term refers to any conflict over trivial differences adhered to with religious zeal.
9. See Hutchinson, *Dictionary of Ideas*, p. 161, in which John Eccles, born in 1903, is described as an Australian physiologist who shared with Alan Hodgkin and Andrew Huxley the 1963 Nobel Prize for Medicine for work on conduction in the central nervous system. In some of his later works, he argued that the mind has an existence independent of the brain.

10 The Abdiel Appendix finds its source in Milton's I, 'The Argument', Book V, when Abdiel, a Seraph, opposes those who wish to rebel against their God. Hope had plans to write a work titled 'The Abdiel Appendix'. He writes about this project: 'The Abdiel Appendix purports to be some notes on Earth and the human race written for his own amusement by an archangel charged with a survey of planets and their occupants in a section of the universe. I have sketched out this vast enterprise but written no part of it and shall not live long enough now.' See Book IX, 1973, pp. 118–24.

11 See Wordsworth, 'Intimations of Immortality from Reflections of Early Childhood', Stanza I, lines 1 to 4, *The Norton Anthology of Poetry*, p. 551.

12 See Deighton, *Billion Dollar Brain*, p. 153. Hope's favourite reading matter was detective stories and spy-thrillers, when not engaged in scholarly pursuits.

13 Elizabeth Fry (born Gurney), 1780–1845, was an English Quaker philanthropist. She formed an association for the improvement of conditions for female prisoners in 1817 and worked with her brother Joseph Gurney (1788–1847) on a 1819 report on prison reform.

14 See St Augustine, *Confessions*, Chap. IX: 25, where he speaks with his mother as she is dying. Augustine refers to a silence that exists beyond the senses and intellect. He speaks of when his conversation with his mother 'did gradually pass through all corporal things … we soared higher yet by inward musing, and discoursing, and admiring Thy works; and we came to our own minds, and went beyond them … We were saying, then, if to any man the tumult of the flesh were silenced — silenced the phantasies of earth, waters, and air — silenced, too, the poles; yea, the very soul be silenced to herself, and go beyond herself by not thinking of herself — silenced fancies and imaginary revelations, every tongue, and every sign, and whatsoever exists by passing away, since, if any could hearken …' Hope's yearning for 'si sileat omnino' is for this kind of silence that exists beyond thought and sensual experience and which provides a space where the 'unknowable' exists and, he implies, might be experienced.

15 See Moorehead, *Darwin and the Beagle*, p. 39, where he notes: 'There was a round of farewells with Charles coaching up to London and Cambridge and back to Shrewsbury to make his final arrangements. Books he must have: Humboldt, Milton and the Bible, Lysell's first volume of *Principles of Geology* (a parting gift from Henslow), just off the press …'

III

ANTI-MODERNISM

Introduction

Hope's antagonism towards free verse reaches passionate proportions. It is the one area of his thought that brings out the poet's personality, despite his views on the need to suppress personality when creating a poem. He is a poet who, outside the poem, happily acknowledges the mask he wears, being as an actor entering a situation, an emotion or a particular belief, testing them while he creates something new. On all other issues he appears tranquil and assured, but it seems he has an engagement here that defies his stated preference for detachment.

Current theory would not be sympathetic to Hope's view that free verse cannot be termed poetry. Nevertheless, current theory cannot on its own terms eradicate any perspective as defunct. Much of Hope's argument outlined in *The New Cratylus* relies on his view that poetry has a unique access to a musical realm through rhyming and rhythmic schemes. Of course, there are all kinds of music and there are many ideological, cultural and aesthetic reasons why free verse emerged when and how it did. Hope is impatient and irritated by any show of enthusiasm or support for experimental art, rapping over the knuckles any favourite poet or critic of his — Chris Wallace-Crabbe, for example — who dared to explore the territory with a scholarly or artistic eye.

Many entries in the notebooks oppose modernist stratagems and preoccupations; Hope felt that an obsessional quest to record the personal, the confessional and the immediate was eradicating the music and craft endemic to traditional verse forms. Perhaps, he argues, there is an unnecessary conflict between those who wish only to remember and those who in wishing to foretell attempt, too aggressively, to forget.

Hope's role as an anti-modernist applies primarily to his antagonism to the practice of free verse. It does not signify that he was not a modern poet. Vincent Buckley points out that Hope was 'in an intriguing and unconventional sense a modern poet ... Other poets, English and Irish, expressed admiration of his power. His forms intrigued them; they were forms which, while drafting rules for formality, spoke very directly of their concerns, of which they had quite a breadth; they were direct to the reader, they created an utterance, they enforced their central concerns with lateral perceptions ... [and] they intrigued the reader with the newness of the old'.[1]

Hope saw the modernists as becoming increasingly obsessed with representing the processes of other functions of other arts, appropriating and commenting but not creating something new. Nevertheless, the philosophies and metaphysical views that Hope channelled into his art stemmed from modernist preoccupations. As a modernist poet and philosopher, his art entailed a reconfiguring of ancient mythology and biblical stories, a subversion of Newtonian concepts of time, a distrust of systems of knowledge that attempted to represent any long-term truth, and a production of a unique kind of subjectivication, which, although in flight from the personal, dealt with the alienation, isolation, grief and despair involved in living in a secular age. Nevertheless, when Hope explores what is lost when modernist writers ignore the stories buried in old myths (whether Greek or European) and suggests that writers might return to them in the future, he has not foreseen that these myths in being sterotypically white 'male' ones would be seen as lacking a wider application in a world that has learnt well the lessons and insights that have emerged from post-colonial, feminist and queer theory.

One can accept Hope's arguments against free verse on their own terms, even if one is opposed to them. His craft as a poet, the seductive nature of his vast subject matter and the sheer beauty of his imagery and structure ensure that what he has to say about poetry and its construction deserves to be heard. It is, nevertheless, difficult to accept his views on modern painting and music. His severe criticism of some modern painting (never specified) does not seem to stem from a position of knowledge, tending in its delivery to be fed by taste and misinformed rage rather than from the vantage point of someone educated in this area. Although it can be conceded that there exist examples of modern poetry and modern painting that warrant disapproval, given that Hope does not refer directly to specific modern paintings, it is difficult to assess his condemnations. Hope writes: 'What disturbs me, I think, with poetry and painting is that I have always held that the arts properly explore and create new values, yet these writers and painters often seem not to be creating anything.'[2] Hope's anti-modernist position is a complex one, in the intellectual integrity that feeds it and in the rage it engenders in him.

DE-CREATION OF VALUES I

Reading a good deal of 'modern' poetry and looking at 'modern' painting I find myself moved and irritated, responding and repelled. 'Modern' music produces no effect except a desire to stop listening so that it is not in question. What disturbs me, I think, with poetry and painting is that I have always held that the arts properly explore and create new modes of experience and in the process create new values, yet these writers and painters often seem not to be creating anything any more than they re-create the other function of the arts.

What they do produce could best be described as morbid growths on the healthy body. We ought to have a word for another process or gift: the Decreative Talents, talents which operate like cancers and have the same sort of relation to healthy creation as a cancer or a tumour has to healthy and normal cell-growth.

If one were to follow up this analogy one might suggest that one feature of a cancerous growth is that it is a community of cells out of control or touch with the rest of the cell-community and its organisation. Sometimes the rebels are harmless and produce warts or benign tumours, at others they prove destructive to the whole body.

There might be a point in looking at some art 'movements' in this way. They are nearly all marked by a withdrawal from ordinary society, the creation of a society of artists, who begin by despising the tastes and views of the society around them, and end by losing touch with 'ordinary men' altogether.

In our society the poets represent the benign cancer, a meaningless but harmless mass of cells, an effusion and vast effloration of images and feelings, stimulations of sensibility of no use or interest to living minds. Painting has imposed itself on our society, it is fashionable, revered, studied and propagated; it represents the malignant cancer.

The decreative arts of course protect themselves by a cunning mimicry of the creative ones, and it is difficult to attack them without being accused of attacking art in general.

— Book VIII, 1964, pp. 4–5.

DON GIOVANNI

One thing lost to modern literature is the fertilising convention of certain themes or legends which writers take up again and again as the Greek dramatists took up the legendary themes of tragedy or as medieval story-tellers worked and reworked the themes of their predecessors. Such a convention has many uses and advantages. It provides the literary tradition itself with a common set of themes continually fruitful and stimulating of new genius, gives it homogeneity and provides it with norms and standards of achievement. It provides and keeps alive certain archetypal images and ideas which are fertilising to the imaginative energies of the grown man as the archetypal stories of childhood are in establishing common patterns and figures of the general mind; it gives to genius a field already worked and enriched for a fresh creation, which has already evident a body of great work in which a new creation is ready to grow and it provides a challenge that tests and raises the powers of genius; more important, a subject of this sort is inexhaustible. Far from tending to become worked out or exhausted by repeated treatment, it exhibits the depth and range of imagination, a profundity that is often lost when literature continually seeks to exploit only new themes and in consequence is never forced to explore them to the depths, to meditate on their ultimate significance.

Modern European tradition has tended to return to classical legend or to work over old forms while finding new legends. Its one continuing source of repeated treatment has been the Christian legend and this has had its importance, though it has been a minor one. The Bible was unfortunately too sacred a text for a secular imagination to work freely upon. Since 1400 AD, few of the universal legends have arisen and few have taken root to be treated and reworked by men of genius in successive generations. The only examples I can think of are the romances of chivalry treated by Cervantes, by Pulci, Boccaccio and Ariosto and by Spenser. Had Milton followed his earlier impulse he might have given us another example instead of *Paradise Lost*. But these like classic and Christian themes are not in themselves the product of modern European Civilisation. They have been taken over from another time or race. The Faust legend and the Don Juan legend are almost the only ones that have taken root and been the inspiration of successive generations of genius. Both are universal themes deeply rooted in the form of our civilisation and both are still fertile and unexhausted.

Apart from the innumerable lesser writers who have attempted the theme with more or less success and with more or less insight, the legend of Don Juan, has been illuminated and re-treated by a succession of genuises who have penetrated its tremendous and slightly absurd mystery and built up for future time the test and challenge to new creative genius. Terco, de Molina, Molière, Mozart, Da Ponte, Byron, Pushkin. There is a study to be done here which would illuminate much that is dark to and a challenge to the present age.

— Book IV, 1955, pp. 71–3.

THE NEW CRITICISM

In so far as the New Criticism, so-called, now becoming popular in America has anything to recommend it, it is simply a return to the old *texte expliqué* of classical teaching. In so far as it is theoretic and pretentious, it is like a man who will not be able to tell you whether a girl or a rose is beautiful until he has studied them under a microscope [See *Meanjin*, No. 1, 1957]. The concern of the critic is with beauty and if beauty resides in minute particulars, as Blake averred, it is also true that minute particulars do not in themselves make beauty. But I gather that the new critics reject the word, beauty, as the new deists solve their problems by ignoring the word God.

It is valuable in asking that criticism be concerned only with the poem as a [Ding an Sich], not with the poem as biography, social or literary history. But it becomes absurd when it ignores what biography, history and literary history have to tell us about the poem — as absurd as a man who tried to read a foreign language without using a dictionary for the words he did not know.

— Book V, 1957–58, p. 16.

REMEMBERERS AND FORELOOKERS

The Rememberers know only the past and tend to think themselves worse than their ancestors. What the Forelookers tell them about the future seems to them loathsome and barely comprehensible. At the same time they are ashamed of themselves and their attachment to the past, for it seems to imply a lack of imagination, enterprise, daring and freedom. They call themselves the Slaves of Time and justify themselves as the conservers of tradition. But they cannot help themselves. It is their nature and without this food they wither and decay.

The Forelookers are in love with the future and spend happy lives disagreeing with one another's prophecies and predictions. They despise the past and are embarrassed to have to acknowledge their debt to it and their connexion with it, as a man might be if he had to carry his own placenta about with him, still attached by the umbilical cord. They are proud of their emancipation and consider themselves aggressive creative, and free.

To the Assessors who visit this country from time to time for their instruction and amusement, it seems that the two races are equally deluded about themselves. The limited power of the Rememberers to forecast the processes of the future and their comparative indifference to change and progress, leaves them in fact much more free to choose than the Forelookers who have made a science of prediction and find themselves bound in every choice by foreknowledge of the outcome. And the Rememberers are the really creative and imaginative party for a similar reason. Not only is the substance of their minds richer with the traditional stores of past time, but the very frame and pressure of their minds conduces them to let ideas grow naturally, to develop towards ends not in themselves at first foreseen or even predictable, whereas the Forelookers by their very habit of mind are for the most part incapable of this. They propose an end and work towards it most efficiently. But because they are trained to eschew dream and fantasy in the interest of accurate prediction, they never create anything. They produce very ingenious variations and developments of what already exists but can never produce anything new except by accident. The two races embarrass each other for this reason. The Rememberers find the Forelookers not only sterile and superficial but destructive. They can do nothing against their incomprehension of what the Rememberers call the real nature of man and the real values of the world. As the Forelookers are so often the planners, the activists, the collectors of power, they regard them as extremely dangerous. The Forelookers would like to despise and ignore the Rememberers, but in fact they are unable to leave them out of account. This is because they constantly find that their predictions are upset and deranged by the contribution of the Rememberers to the changing patterns of society. And because this contribution is truly creative and therefore unpredictable, it completely baffles the powers of the Forelookers. They attempt to meet this by getting control of the processes of education in such a way as to stultify the gifts of the Rememberers, by encouraging 'progressive' substitutes for the traditional arts and customs. But the substitutes lack charm and vitality to such an extent that people are always apt to revolt and return to the true bread of life — even members of their own race are apt to be seduced.

— Book VI, 1960, pp. 59–61.

THE HISTORICAL SENSE I

This is not quite the same as a sense of history. The present age is probably superior to any preceding age in its sense of history. It knows more about the past; it knows it more fully and accurately; it is better able to avoid anachronisms of thought, of feeling and hence of interpretation. It is less apt to make comparative judgements of value, to consider itself self-evidently better or worse, in terms of the things that make human life worthwhile, than some other age or civilisation.

But if it has a better sense of history, I cannot see that it is better equipped with what I call historical sense: the awareness of the limitations on its own bases of judgement. It sees itself as an end product. It sees the past as what gives meaning to the present, but it also sees the past as having existed in order to give meaning to the present, and it does not think of itself in the same way in respect of the future. A man who judges his parents in terms of what they have done for *him*, ignoring or discounting what they did for themselves, a man who judges his children in terms of how they affect him, may be said to lack the historical sense.

— Book VIII, 1965, p. 42.

DE-CREATION OF VALUES II

There is something to add to the remarks on the difficulty of distinguishing the De-creative arts from the truly creative. It is not simply a matter of mimicry but of our inability to foresee and therefore to see the present in terms of the future rather than of the past. I find myself bored and repelled by most so-called 'abstract' painting and sculpture, which seems to me monotonous, meaningless, pretentious and arbitrary. But no doubt there were people like me who felt the same about the first attempts to produce pure music, music enjoyed for the 'abstract' pattern of sounds alone, unassociated with words of a song or chant or the traditional movements of a miming or a sacred dance. One can imagine them judging the idea by the efforts of musicians not yet habituated to think in pure musical 'forms' and still fumbling to free themselves from the literary or ritual or choreographic associations of some musical phrases, perhaps of the whole resources of music as it then was. These critics could have no conception of what might emerge as Bach, Mozart, Beethoven or Vitoria evolved new forms and perfected them.

On the other hand the fact that the argument will not in any case apply in literature may make us cautious in accepting the view that the same argument as applies in the case of music can apply in that of painting or sculpture. There is a difference for example, in the case of poetry, which is fatal to the analogy. Poetry cannot be 'freed' from ideas, words, expression because its material is just that. To 'free it', as some of the pure-poetry fanatics have tried to do, is to extinguish it. The real analogy is that of freeing poetry from its associations with music, dance and drama. This has already been done and poetry is now as 'pure' an art as music. But painting and sculpture have never been mixed arts in this sense. They have sometimes been constrained by religious or hieratical conventions, but soon freed themselves. Their 'literary' themes do not impose restrictions on the pictorial forms even in historical painting and the representation of forms is essential to these arts since they are bound to create forms of their own if they abandon those existing in nature. The analogy with music is inexact since the forms of language or dance are *not* musical forms, the forms of nature *are* pictorial forms just as much as those invented by the artist.

— Book VIII, 1965, pp. 70–2.

POETRY AND THE UNREAL

What seems to us unreal in experience from time to time may do so because the events are so strange and improbable, so unfamiliar or fantastic or because we ourselves have that curious feeling that even familiar things for some reason have become unreal, remote or utterly indifferent to us. In either case we are able to see that if this state of affairs persists too long it ceases to have its effect. Indeed the unreal can only appear so if we have a strong hold on reality, just as the unusual can only impress us as such if we are accustomed to something else that we regard as normal. The reverse, of course, is not true. We do not recognise the real by the unreal, the usual by the abnormal.

One problem for poets today is that their product is outside the ordinary range of experience. The poets themselves feel this and when they are conscious of it as well, they must envy the writers of [those] ages and places when poetry was a part of daily life and there was no conscious feeling of unreal, unnatural or abnormal activity in producing it.

— Book VIII, 1965, p. 84.

DRACULA

Re-reading *Dracula* here in Athens for lack of anything else to read, and remembering it as a rather tawdry, sensational and sentimental piece of nonsense, I find myself thinking of it now as a most impressive structure under the Victorian and novelettish treatment. Like *Frankenstein*, it is a crude masterpiece, a 'primitive' in the sense that certain untrained painters are 'primitives', and having a strange force behind the 'illiterate' technique — Stoker of course was only relatively illiterate, he was not a creative genius, any more than was Mary Shelley. Both were educated in the ordinary literary sense. Both *Frankenstein* and *Dracula* have demonstrated their quality in spite of their crudeness. This is the rare and exciting quality of bringing into being an archetypal figure of the general imagination: something that transcends literature and the merely literary imagination.

They could have been figures and myths like those of Faust and Don Juan, had they not come too late. Faust and Don Juan were able to profit by the fact that the old tradition was still in force, the tradition of successive generations of writers, especially writers of genius, treating the same myth, drawing out of it all its imaginative riches and extending its meaning till it embraced and illuminated the world. But by the time Mary Shelley and Bram Stoker came to write, this tradition was dead, except in the academic way that produced *Atalanta in Calydon*[3] and Joyce's *Ulysses*. So, in spite of their tremendous hold on popular imagination, in spite of the sign this would have given to earlier writers of the rich store of material lying there, they have remained the Ur-Hamlets, the El Burlador de Sevilla's[4] of great works and master-treatments never to be written while the modern delusions about 'originality' continue.

Perhaps the tradition is not quite dead. The Wagnerian operas *Ulysses*, *Mourning Becomes Electra* and so on are signs that while in a shamefaced way and trying to pretend to [be] something else, some of the best creative minds feel the necessity and the waste of offered riches. Sooner or later writers may return unashamedly to treat the great themes over and over again, and the bow of Ulysses, in this sense, will sort out the men from the boys.

It would be interesting to set these four, Don Juan, Faust, Frankenstein and Dracula against a corresponding four from Greek imagination — with the Greeks there were so many that it would [be] a random choice: Heracles, Orestes, Theseus, Oedipus would do — and to see what conclusions could be drawn.

The four *Zoas* as Popular Heroes!

Book VIII, 1965, pp. 156–8.

CONSPICUOUS CONSUMPTION

I keep meeting local American poets, Robert Lowell, Stanley Kunitz, William Smith, Richard Wilbur, John Ashbery, Adrienne Rich, etc., and I get some of their verse and read it when I have met them and remember the name. I find it very like the verse written in Australia, but with a feeling of being a little more, and more luxuriously, occasional, as though produced for an audience who could afford a better product and could equally afford to throw it away when they had used it once.

My first thought was that this reminds me of something going on all over the world and that perhaps one sees better in America, where people are not afraid to follow their noses, what really is going on: the natural and perhaps quite unconscious response to a civilization increasingly given over to the idea of using and discarding: highly finished and acceptable products, but products not really meant to last and indeed often designed to be replaced by 'the next year's model'.

My second thought was: why not? It is well known that language is a very perishable product, particularly on the side of its emotional habits. With all the help of a literary tradition, supported by education, much of the poetry of the past perishes in a way that pictures or music do not, or do to a lesser degree. The other arts present us with direct sensual material, poetry only with code and symbol capable for a time, and while poet and audience share a common set of habits and experiences, of transferring the dance from one mind to others. But a new set of habits, a new fashion, other corps of taste can intervene to cripple the old code. We often get surprising results from Chaucer or Milton or Pope, but we should not deceive ourselves. They are not always those the poems were written for and the effects we get from Homer or the *Rig-Veda* are probably even more remote from those intended by their authors. They are now artifacts of a kind that would have surprised their original audience. They are often mere effects of time, of the loss of old and the addition of new contexts of history.

What may be happening on a larger scale than we think is that a quite serious but ephemeral poetry is replacing or at any rate invading the field of poetry traditionally written to last. The conditions of the small cultural group, the tribe or culture held together by a single tradition and set of values, which favours a 'permanent' poetry, are less and less possible in the amorphous great societies of today. It is not really that poets imitate manufacturers, but the same forces act on both in different ways. You can say if you like that poetry becomes a sort of journalism, in that, however well he writes no journalist expects what he writes to have any permanency. It might be better to say that poetry has begun to move into the range of arts like dancing and cooking. No cook expects his cake to be eaten twice. All cooking is occasional and so is most modern poetry.

— Book IX, 1967, pp. 68–70.

DEATH IN THE CELL

'The cell itself is surrounded by a cell-membrane. About 75Å thick, this is more than a mere boundary and is seen to contain three layers. It is believed to be composed of two layers of protein each 20Å across, enclosing a fat (lipid) layer of 35Å. This characteristic structure is seen with the same dimensions in all cells and has been termed the unit membrane. It forms a permeable but highly selective barrier for the cell, which can distinguish various chemical molecules and atoms, rapidly passing and concentrating some, while excluding others. The loss of this property is perhaps the most characteristic indication of cell death.'

Royston Clowes: *The Structure of Life*, p. 24.

This (the last sentence) is equally true of multicellular organisms and perhaps truest of all in the world of taste and ideas. What seems to be happening in the arts at present is a breakdown of the selective process which we vaguely call taste. Useless and even lethal elements are let in, amounts are not regulated, necessary and useful substances are excluded; the organisation on which the mind depends for the practice and enjoyment of specific kinds of art is starved, distorted and finally dies. A mind so ruined cannot regenerate itself though the man continues to live and to go through the motions of attending exhibitions, reading books, learning concepts. All real discrimination is lost and he can be imposed on by any sterile or poisonous fabulum: pop art, noise-machines, or the elaborate verbalisations that often pass for poems today.

Perhaps the most interesting thought is that it illuminates the metaphysical notion of death, or rather the 'point of death' as the moment when discrimination ceases, whether it is still possible or not.

— Book IX, 1965–68, pp. 81–2.

THE 'DIALOGUE OF ONE'

One inevitably spends so much of one's life writing for an audience — in the case of poetry, largely an imaginary audience — that one gets out of the way of thinking of the alternative: writing as a sort of talking to oneself — or rather of 'pure talking', as it were: no holds barred, no reservations, no translations, no need to compromise in any way. In literature I can think of no examples. Those that come to mind, the eccentrics, the cranks, the beatniks, the pure expression boys are just the reverse: people who have given up and let themselves run loose, but always with a public in view — a kind of exhibitionism: come and watch my pure ego perform!

It is in things like the later paintings of Goya, the last quartets of Beethoven and in his Goldberg and Diabelli Variations,[5] that I feel I am observing an artist using his art to talk to himself about things beyond social communication at all.

— 12–VII–71
— Book XII, 1971, p. 98.

THE FLIGHT FROM CHARACTER

It would surely be one of the interests of the future to consider the flight from character which has marked my age. I remember some rather suspect argument from McDougall in my youth on the distinction of character and personality.[6] But the distinction stands even if the reasons were shaky. Personality is related to character in something the same way that the total physical body is related to the bone-structure. In the past education put the stress on character, in the last hundred years it has shifted to an emphasis in developing the personality, the individual *persona*. What no one seems to have noticed is that the educators have used the psychology of their day as a means of eroding the idea of character altogether. Soon we may have the means to produce a charming skin with nothing to hang it on.

— Book XV, 1973, p. 37.

MORE ANSWERS

Dante and Virgil give Mr T. S. Eliot a Straight Talking To[7]

On the bare cornice of Hell's seventh crater
We met a shade who said his name was Tom,
After that saint men call the Dubitator.

He would not say what country he was from,
But claimed a major poet among the living
And minor prophet of the wrath to come

Had been his lot. Then, not without misgiving
This Thomas Stearns was questioned by my master
About his life and works, till he, perceiving

What poets we were and where we found him, cast a
Dismal eye on that infernal ground,
Admitting he had been a poetaster.

'And yet,' said he, 'on earth my verse was crowned
With Laurel which this air below has blasted.
Tell me, you glorious pair, whose names resound

'Through time, whose mighty poems have outlasted
The empires that they celebrated, say
Why were my life-long efforts largely wasted?

'By what misfortune did I go astray
In middle life — though one of you came through it,
In that same wood where he, too, lost his way?'

Then Vergil turned to me and said, 'Although it
Is now too late for him to mend the matter,
Should we not succour this unhappy poet?'

'Poet born or made? — I rather think the latter —
He was a banker, now he needs a broker.
He has his death — we do not need to flatter,

'But, in the hand Fate dealt him, find the joker.'
Then I to him: 'Do you remember, brother,
A poem of yours that touched me once, East Coker?

'If I recall, in that, somewhere or other,
You made a humble and sincere confession,
But called your native tongue a false step-mother.

'Could you repeat it to us here in session,
We shall speak truth, with pity as we can,
Though mercy makes no part in our profession.'

'Yes, truth untempered to a truthful man.
From men in whom the truth was proved and tried!
Speak on! Winnow my wheat and bolt my bran!

'This is what in those bad last years' I cried:
'So here I am, in the middle way, having had twenty years —
Twenty years largely wasted, the years of l'entre deux —
Trying to learn to use words, and every attempt
is a wholly new start, a different kind of failure.
Because one has only learned to get the better of words
For the thing one no longer has to say, or the way in which
One is no longer disposed to say it. And so each venture
Is a new beginning, a raid on the inarticulate
With shabby equipment always deteriorating
In the general mess of imprecision of feeling,
Undisciplined squads of emotion. And what there is to conquer
By strength and submission, has already been discovered
Once or twice, or several times, by men whom one cannot hope
To emulate ...'

He broke off, weeping then, and while we waited
Stale airs swirled round us from the nether pit,
Till he, his passion some degree abated,

Resumed: 'In the same poem, I admit,
I called the old poetic forms of verse
For our new modern talents quite unfit,

'Yet owned and I went farther and fared worse:
That was a way of putting it — not very satisfactorily:
A periphrasic study in a worn-out poetic fashion,
Leaving one still with the intolerable wrestle
With words and meaning. The poetry does not matter.

The poetry does not matter! The thing was said,
I thought my master caught his breath in token
Of anger or impatience, but instead

He gazed at our poor shade when he had spoken
In wonder and in pity; then began:
'Was this then verse I heard, so lame, so broken

'That none could tell its measure or make it scan?
Words obey him alone who leads them dancing,
Not him who works to your drill-sergeant plan.'

'You cannot hope to call forth their entrancing
Hid music, nor breathe life into their clay
Until the word of metre sets them glancing,

'Gleaming with light on their celestial way.
Your melancholy half-prose was a venture
Doomed from the start: What more is there to say?'

He paused as though the sill of further censure
Tempted him on; then, smiling turned to me:
'Dante, who shares with you this misadventure

'Of the dark wood and the lost way, will be
A safer guide.' And I to him in wonder
No less than Virgil's, cried: 'What fallacy

'Or misconception did you labour under,
Misguided man? Real poets never "try
to use words", as you put it; your first blunder

'Was treating them like slaves or tools. The high
Art that we serve begins with Love and patience
To learn to let the words use us. They fly

'Like leaves from autumn gales, your machinations
To "get the better of them", trick, compel.
Your next fault was to take poetic fashions

'As your concern at all; a sense of smell
Is all a poet needs against decay;
The naked muse, the native tongue rebel

'When poets tell them what to wear each day.
Old forms are not outmoded by new speech,
Nor next year's fruit by roots in yesterday.

'What language was this that you could not reach,
So transitory, so ephemeral?
And what truth was it, so worthwhile to teach

'One day, the next day not worth saying at all?
Journalists plan such perishable wares,
But poets should not beat the beck and call

'Of trivial word-flux and such current affairs
As a year's commerce renders out of date.
Truth ignores fashion and Beauty never cares.

'Your worst fault was to underestimate
Your own gift, or deny it altogether:
Poets do not "raid the inarticulate";

'They waken sleeping images, untether
The captive truths and lead them towards the light,
Break time's hard frost and foster growing weather.

'To fertilize the mothering womb aright
Their task: not that mechanical construction
Implied in your description of your plight,

'Your poem — factory geared for mass-production
Your barracks built to regiment raw squads
Of feelings — drilled for conquest? Or destruction?

'Such language, friend, reveals you quite at odds
With all true poets know themselves to be:
Earth's living talismans, the sacred rods

'That strike her rock and set its waters free.
I marvel at the cause of your affliction,
For I, at least, unlike my guide here, see

'In you a poet by instinct and conviction;
A poet ruined, but a poet born.'

He left us with a kind of valediction
And faded on the blowing of a horn.

Dante's sermon is meant to echo the views on poetry and its language of the author of *De Vilgari Eloquentia* but only in a general way — not by direct reference — except theory of the 'permanent language'.

I hope the echo of Eliot in the last two lines will not be taken unkindly: it is meant as a tribute to one of Eliot's real poems — the section II of *Little Gidding* where he catches so well the movement of Dante's terja rima — [without the rima].

— Book XV, 1974, pp. 144–52.

A DEFINITION OF POETRY

Mark O'Connor[8] has just brought me [a] new definition of poetry by one of the new generation, Stewart Garret: 'Poetry: A group of words artfully arranged to bore the reader.'

This was meant, in part at least, as a joke; but it is a sinister joke and not altogether a joke. When large numbers of people are not able to respond to poetry because the habits of response, the traditional sensibility to this use of words have been lost, poetry must be just that to the disinherited. And the process has been largely the work of poets themselves in the last half century of reckless exploitation and experiments, in several generations of contempt for the poetic tradition and deliberate rejection of the past. Talking to high-school children, as I often do, I am always finding numbers of them genuinely puzzled by what seem to them meaningless exercises in verbalisation.

— Book XVI, 1974, p. 29.

INVITATION TO A RESURRECTION

Nobody any more bursts out singing;
Words never dance to a song.
Verse, which once went soaring, winging,
Shambles and shuffles along.
No poet sings any more;
The Muses have all gone arty;
The free-verse voice is a bore;
The voice of a cocktail party.

Nobody any more speaks the word
Once uttered, to outlast time;
Jargon and journalese are preferred;
Nobody bothers with rhyme.
But who quotes the poets today,
Those blind mouths leading the blind
And nothing at all they say
Has power to enchant the mind.

Who in any case cares to read them?
Do they read one another, perhaps?
Is it the thought that people don't need them
Makes them such sociable chaps?

'Let's start an anthology, Max,[9]
— With a cultural grant it's easy —
We'll scratch one another's backs
And publish sludge for the sleazy.

'Let's bury Song in our "concrete" coffin,
Abolish rhyme, rhythm and grace;
Let's be avant-garde once too often
And find ourselves out of the race.'
It's happened quite often before:
When young Turks have had their fling,
They find they're not young any more.
Since free-verse voice is a bore,
The voice of street-corner whore,
Will anyone join me and sing?

— Book XVIII, 1975, pp. 36–7.

THE EROSION OF LANGUAGE

The totally unnecessary change to the metric system of measures has not only impoverished the language, it will shortly be seen to have damaged the existing monuments of art. Already I feel self-conscious about using the word 'miles' in poetry, whereas the new alternative, with its pedantic, scientific, technological echoes, its entire lack of the overtones of the ordinary word, is quite impossible:

'How many kilometres to Babylon?
Three score and ten.
Can I get there by candle-light?
Aye, and back again.

No it will not do at all!

> 'He that compelleth thee to go a Kilometre with him, go with him twain.'

Even less.

Or Robert Frost: 'And kilometres to go before I sleep.' No, a thousand times no!

The damage works in two ways: (1) the useful, meaningful, old and also contemporary word is uprooted and there is nothing to take its place, for the purposes of poetry; (2) the word so lost becomes 'literary' and then archaic so that poems of the past in which it is used in a quite straightforward way now aquire an old-world, perhaps precious, overtone which quite alters their effect — as though Frost had written self-consciously: 'And leagues to go before I sleep.'

— Forrest Lodge, 26–III–76
— Book XIX, 1976, pp. 42–3.

CONVERSION OF CHAOS

Reading Peter Steele's thesis on Swift, I come across an enchanting remark about Tennyson attributed to Carlyle:

> 'Alfred is always carrying a bit of chaos around with him and turning it into cosmos.'[10]

It is of course what all poets worth the name do all the time, but I am glad it was said about Tennyson. Gerard Hopkins' prattle about Tennyson's 'Parnassian' has damaged him — as though Tennyson wrote mechanically or mindlessly, or was a victim of his own habitual eloquence.

But it seems an unlikely remark for Carlyle to have made.

Reading this a few weeks later it occurs to me that a good description of many modern poets would be: 'He is always carrying a bit of the cosmos with him and turning it into chaos.'

— Book XIX, 1976, p. 45.

THE POETRY EXPLOSION

As the populations of the world get bigger, we find ourselves less and less able to see the inevitable result in poetry, as, indeed, in all the arts. The enormous inflated tribe is no longer cohesive, no longer shares a common social background or a common tradition; the resources of the language became impoverished and its vocabulary inflated and etiolated at the same time; the decline in sensibility since the seventeenth century which Eliott noticed was more probably an impoverishment of the means of expression and a coarsening of the possibilities of response.

One would have expected a general failing of interest in poetry and in a sense this is so: a smaller and smaller proportion of the great tribe read, write or in any way participate in poetry, but the enormous growth of numbers and the ease of publication mean that the land carries more poets to square mile than ever before; and most of them are concerned with trivialities and [are] such bad craftsmen that their tedious productions have no inherent interest. The next step is to mend this state of affairs by organising the poetry industry, by advertising and by reinforcing feeble verse and lack of inspiration by mutual admiration societies, awards and prizes, conferences and poetry festivals and other cultural orgies. One becomes a poet not by creating a thing of light and beauty but by becoming a ticket-holding member of a poetry group or society which is able to publish the effusions of its members, whatever their quality by getting a cultural grant from the public purse.

This week I have received two notices through the mail which reflect this state of affairs. One is an invitation to allow my particulars to appear in a reference work called *Men of Distinction* — no, *Men of Achievement*. As a poet I am to be flattered by appearing with generals, statesmen, scientists and actors who have made a name for themselves. As anyone eligible to appear in these pages is already likely to have his name in a variety of *Who's Who* type of publications, it is clear that *Men of Achievement* is [a] pure vanity publication. As far as poets are concerned it is a simple promotion stunt.

The other notice concerns a publication called *The Poet's Yearbook 1976*. The blurb reads:

The only comprehensive survey of present [day] poetry activities in Great Britain and Ireland. 316 poetry publishers with latest titles (844 works of poetry and 250 books about poetry and poets). 20 record companies. Index of published authors. 146 poetry magazines and 71 others which publish poetry. 101 local poetry groups in all parts of the country. 137 poetry awards, fellowships and money-making opportunities for poets. Details of grants available to both poets and publishers ... articles on the selection of markets etc, etc.

And with all this commercial hubbub of 'present day poetry activities', to reflect that since the death of Yeats England has been without a single outstanding poet and that in the swarming undergrowth: 'The sound is forced, the notes are few'!

The busy, social, commercial activity is just as evident in this country. It is strange to people of my generation for whom poetry was a solitary and private occupation.

— 6–II–76
NB: Used in my speech at Monash University 19–V–1976.
— Book XIX, 1976, pp. 25–8.

BUILT IN OBSOLESCENCE

I had expected that 'free verse' would have a limited span of life but it seems to be on the increase everywhere. In the last few months the new editors of *Meanjin* and *Quadrant*[11] have published nothing else, the Canadian magazines have long been taken over by its flabby shuffle. The dance of language seems to have been forgotten. Those who practice it are growing older and none of the young care to learn the craft properly. They prefer the easy way. Because *anyone* can write free verse and no one can write it well for long. Its formlessness defeats even the best talents. I find this depressing, but this morning I was cheered by a new thought. The habit in the manufacturing world of ensuring that its products will wear out in a reasonable time and have to be replaced by new models seems to me to be precisely what a majority of poets now writing seem to be doing. Free verse is admirable for their purpose; it may catch attention for the moment but because it has no form it is not easy to recall. It is not memorable or to be valued for itself and soon crumbles. Because most of it is about little personal observations of no abiding interest, its triviality tends to the same result. And so does the immense over-production — another point in which poetry is in line with gadget manufacture.

Bad poetry is depressing in itself but there is no need to be depressed about it as an historical event. It carries within itself its own principle of built-in obsolescence.

> *Another Age shall see the golden Ear*
> *In brown the Slope and nod on the Parterre,*
> *Deep Harvests hide their rotting contraband,*
> *And laughing Ceres re-assume the land.*[12]

6–VII–1970
— Book XX, 1977, pp. 15–16.

WORD INTERPLAY

I am writing a note about Randolph Stow's poems and intent on the problem of the date of his 'The Ship Becalmed'.[13] I write that 'it is in regular stanza form, metre and style of the poems in his verse volume', instead of 'in his first volume'. The substitution, occurring quite unconsciously, is just the sort of thing the Dream Team is always apt to do. At times, as here, one suspects a kind of intentional pun (I was going on to remark that Stow in the first book of poems which he later referred to as 'juvenilia' had showed a remarkable command of the traditional techniques of verse, for so young a poet and that his later loosened-up, semi-free verse was often not nearly so effective). In other cases it seems to have no perceptible object and to be a purely mechanical slip or confusion.

16–VIII–77
— Book XX, 1977–79, p. 22.

THOMAS GRAY ON MODERN ART

Some frail memorial still erected nigh
with uncouth rhymes and shapeless sculpture decked
Implores the passing tribute of a sigh[14]

Of course if Gray had been given a foresight of present day verse and painting or sculpture, it is unlikely that he would have paid it exactly that tribute. It is more likely to have been a cry of dismay and incredulity. The sigh is left to us who have to accept these monsters as an accomplished fact.

— Book XX, 1977, p. 48.

NEWS ITEM: THE SAVAGE BEAST

'Moscow, Sunday, AAP-Reuter — A wolf that had been worrying sheep at a State farm near Minsky is behind bars in Leningrad Zoo, because of its fondness for tango music, Tass reports.

Shepherds were playing tango records for their own amusement and the wolf became so enraptured [that] it was easily caught.'

Canberra Times, 9–IV–79.

Hm!
But I do recall that John Burton[15] when he left politics and farmed at Weetangera told me that he found his cows gave more milk if music was played to them during the milking and that the yield while they listened to Mozart was far ahead of that for any other composer. That for pop-music and jazz was the lowest. It is possible that the legend of the dolphins ravished by the sounds of Orion's harp has a basis of fact. Dr Lilley[16] does not seem to have tested dolphins for this but he has suggested that we might impress the 'singing' humpback and sperm whales by letting them hear a symphony orchestra adapted to their own range of sound.

Journalists are apt to garble news they do not get at first hand and to make up such cock-and-bull stories when news is in short supply, but I hope the story of the wolf is true and that Leningrad Zoo has arranged tango programs for him (or her).

— Book XXI, March, 1979, pp. 5–6.

ON BLAKE'S PROPHETIC BOOKS

'When this verse was first dictated to me, I considered it a monotonous cadence like that used by Milton and Shakespeare and all writers of English Blank Verse ... But I soon found that in the mouth of a true orator such monotony was not only awkward, but as much a bondage as rhyme itself. I therefore hope to have produced a variety in every line, both of cadence and number of syllables ... etc.'

(*Jerusalem*, 'To the Public')

'I am not ashamed, afraid or averse to tell you what ought to be told: That I am under the direction of Messengers from Heaven, Daily and Nightly ...'

(Letter to Thomas Butts, 1802, during the composition of *Jerusalem*.)

Memory of these two passages and of the dreary result, for the most part, of the combination of angelic dictation with Blake's perverse theory of poetic rhythm led me suddenly to the following:

How could the angels of Apocalypse
Dictate such dull lines for a poet's lips?
Not fluent enough in English, I suppose,
They thought he wrote in prose.

— Book XXI, 1980, pp. 77–8.

TESTING, TESTING

In this selection Hope has taken a poem by Auden and transposed it into what he sees might be a typical 'free verse' representation of the content of Auden's poem.

Dear, though the night is gone,
Its dream still haunts to-day,
That brought us to a room
Cavernous, lofty as
A railway terminus,
And crowded in that gloom
Were beds, and we in one
In a far corner lay.

Our whisper woke no clocks,
We kissed and I was glad
At everything you did,
Indifferent to those
Who sat with hostile eyes
In pairs on every bed,
Arms round each other's neck,
Inert and vaguely sad.

O but what worm of guilt
Or what malignant doubt
Am I the victim of,
That you then, unabashed,
Did what I never wished,
Confessed another love;
And I, submissive, felt
Unwanted and went out?

Let this evening go by, now,
My love — yet the dream still shafes away at
What has brought us together, here in this room
High as a cave and mute
As the last cold station
In that night lined with criss-crossed beds.
We lie on the one
Set furtherest apart.

Our whispers don't push at time:
We kiss, I'm delighted
With everything you do,
Even though the others alongside me
Are watching from their beds
With hate in their eyes
And slack, exhausted hands.

Where's the sin, what's the mistake,
The uneasiness flooded with regret
That makes me the victim
When quickly, not hesitating, you accomplish
What I'd never consent to?
Softly you tell me
You've taken someone else
And, full of sadness, I feel myself
The odd man out, and quickly leave.

— Book XXI, 1980, pp. 95–6.

THE DEATH OF CRITICISM

Reading an essay, 'The Experimental Artist' by Christopher Wallace-Crabbe[17] I find myself disturbed by his indifference to craftmanship. When he went to America, he who was a craftsman-like poet, seems to have absorbed some of the current heresies. At any rate he returned writing sloppy and verbose 'free verse'. The essay opens with a pose of impartiality:

> Over the past century ... the association of art with the cutting edge of experience has had a remarkably good innings. The experimental arts are respectable and prestigious. At the same time 'craftsmanship' and 'skill' are terms that have suffered badly: neither writer nor painter nor composer is much flattered by being acclaimed for mastery of his craft; it is his vision or his sensibility that matters ...

It soons becomes clear, however, that he subscribes to this view that vision and sensibility can be conveyed without skill and craft, and that even down-right bad writing does not matter. A few pages on the remarks of Norman Mailer whom he hails as '"the greatest experimental writer on the job today"… One of the things that makes Mailer so refreshing is the fact that he, like Lawrence, is constantly reaching out into lurid or vulgar prose styles', and of Mailer's novel *Marilyn*: 'Uneven and often plain bad as the book is, it is at best a daring and delicate experiment in a new manner'.

Come on, Chris! You used to have a reasonably good literary judgement. To say that 'craftmanship' and 'skill' are no longer terms of praise in the arts is not simply to note an interesting historical change. It is to say that there has been a general lowering of critical standards and a corruption of public taste. To say that Mailer, and D. H. Lawrence before him, constantly lapse into lurid or vulgar prose styles is simply to say that they are bad writers and to call such bad writing refreshing is to say that the critic has abandoned any basis of judgement and is totally confused. He knows it is bad writing and in the same sentence he is trying to plead the opposite. To say that *Marilyn* is uneven and often plain bad should be the end of the matter. It is a bad book and that is that and as an experiment in a new manner it is seen to have failed. The fact that you detect 'great tenderness' in the author's attitude is irrelevant. Nothing excuses bad writing and the attempt to argue that this bad writing was the only way for the new experiment to succeed reveals the muddle-headed critic and the muddle-headed novelist alike.

I am reminded of T. S. Eliot (another of Wallace-Crabbe's heroes) in his candid confession of failure in 'East Coker', which ends with the statement: 'The poetry does not matter!'

God in Heaven!

— Book XXI, 1980, pp. 115–18.

'SHORED AGAINST MY RUINS'

My stand against most of the current trends in poetry seems to me a hopeless rear-guard action bound in the long run to fail. But I have just noticed a remark by Allen Tate, quoted from a review and printed on the back of the dust-cover of *New Poems* in 1968 (Viking Press Edition):

The poetry of sensibility which has dominated verse in English since the Pound-Eliot revolution is declining; and it is likely that the poetry of statement, such as Hope has reviewed and mastered, will dominate the second half of the century.

If I could believe that I should be happy. Perhaps the tide is turning but the turn is so slow that it is imperceptible. Already it is 1980 and the poetry of sensibility is still in full flood.
— Book XXI, 1980, p. 121.

EXODUS 17, 1–7

'Lord, just one word
A word in your ear:
Your Chosen People, Lord;
There's Trouble, I fear.'

'Don't bother me, prophet;
I left them in your hand,
Out of Egypt and off it
Right to the Promised Land.'

'Lord, in these deserts they
Say they're misled:
"In Egypt anyway
At least we had bread."

'Here in your wilderness
They cry: "We thirst!"
There's no water, I confess.
I fear the worst!'

'These Children of Israel,
They grumble, they belly-ache.
Show me where to dig a well,
Lord, for heaven's sake!'

'Leave them to me, man;
Just do as I say.
I've thought up a plan,
A fine joke to play.

'They don't trust my covenant;
They don't trust you.
I'll teach them government.
Watch what I do!

'To Hovels lead on,
The great dry crag;
Say there's water in the stone;
Man, it's in the bag!'

'But this has got to work, Lord.
If it fails to do,
They'll put me to the sword.
I'll be just an ex-Jew.'

'It's all fixed, Moses;
Don't be such a kike!
Man moves but God disposes.
Strike, Moses, strike!'

Moses raised his rod;
Tapped that stony face,
Calling on his God
To save the Chosen Race.

Who would have thought a
Thing could go so wrong?
Instead of clear water,
Out gushed turbid song.

Raucous from the rock
Rock Music broke.
The People stood in shock
At God's little joke.

The People then went mad;
They stomped and they roared.
Moses groaned out loud:
'Watcha doin?, Lord?

'It's days now since most
Drank even one drop.
Lord, they'll all be lost
If this doesn't stop.'

'Take it easy, man,
And roll with the punch.
From Beersheba to Dan
I'm through with this bunch.'

'They murmur, they rebel;
They grumble, they grouch;
Twelve tribes of Israel
Is twenty tribes too much.'

'Tell it not in G'ceth
Nor in Ashkelon,
But, Moses, write my wrath
On tablets of stone;

'And when you lead the few
Who survive this day,
Should the Children rubbish you
As such Children may,

'Don't forget, Moses;
Moses, don't you grieve!
We've always got Rock Music
Tucked up our sleeve.'

Partly written to get my detestation of so-called Rock Music off my chest and partly by an incident in Joseph Furphy's The Buln Buln and the Brolga.[18] I considered a chorus stanza:

*Deadly Rock Music
Could anything be worse?
Rock Music, Rock Music,
God's final curse!*

But feel it would weaken the ballad structure.

— Book XXII, 1981, pp. 40–4.

DIABELLI VARIATIONS

Listening to these once again I am struck with the idea that Beethoven is not, as I always thought, taking someone else's musical idea and using it as a composition of his own, but that he is using it as an experiment: something there arouses the idea of a work to which this can lead him, a work totally his own. I have no idea whether Beethoven found what he was apparently looking for in his long search — why did he continue to 33, for God's sake? Beethoven could have foreseen at that age what the very naive idea of Diabelli could lead to. But he was obviously looking towards something beyond any development or continuation of the Diabelli theme: a break-through into a new creative masterpiece of his own, something out of this world and out of his own musical world such as we all dream of. I am at this moment listening to that section where the piano utters only single and quite separate bass notes, as though the composer was pausing, listening and waiting for what-might-come-what-perhaps never came or for this is not a genuine variation one theme.

I am led to reflect how often poets in reading their fellows, perhaps unconsciously, do the same thing (like these *Diabelli Variations*). They do not as they imagine repeat to themselves beloved and envied lines for their own satisfaction. What they are really doing is looking for a secret or, even more important, an egress for a spirit already caught in the web of too many others doing the same thing.

For this reason perhaps I read my contemporaries less and less — and with a sense of guilt when I do, 'What doest thou here Elijah?'

I need the release but I need even more to be released from what releases me. But I know I am a child of my age and that the new grows a bit of the old by a natural process. It is not achieved, as my generation believed, by a revolutionary process which jettisons the old completely — or tries to.

The *Diabelli Variations* are also nearly over and Ludwig is back on his hand of one note at a time while he waits for the 'true voice'. It doesn't come and he uses his expertise to keep going to the end. He gets lots of ideas — but not what he was obviously looking for. He ends up weaving an obvious gown to his own cleverness, which is what the *Diabelli Variations* have always been praised for. But, success or failure, is not this the quest on which all poets, all artists are really engaged. Who can answer that question? We only know that it draws us on in spite of everything.

It is this that makes most contemporary criticism out-of-date before it is even uttered. We have passed them by even before they started speaking.

What we have left them for their learned judgements is the dry chrysalis case from which the butterfly has emerged.

— Book XXII, 1982, pp. 95–8.

Notes

1. Buckley, 'Ease and the Vernacular: Notes on A. D. Hope', p. 48.
2. See Hope, Book VIII, 1964–1965, pp. 4–5.
3. See Swinburne, 'Atalanta in Calydon' (1865): a drama written in the classical Greek form, with choruses, notably the hymn to Artemis.
4. See 'Spanish Literature', Brittanica '' CD 2000, 1994–98, *Encyclopaedia Britannica*, Inc., where El Burlador de Seville is a fictitious character who is the symbol of libertinism. Originating in popular legend, he was first given literary personality in the tragic drama *El Burlador de Seville* (1630; *The Seducer of Seville*), attributed to the Spanish dramatist Tirso de Molina. Through Tirso's tragedy, Don Juan became a universal character, as familiar as Don Quixote, Hamlet and Faust. Subsequently, he became the hero-villain of plays, novels and poems; his legend was assured enduring popularity through Mozart's opera *Don Giovanni* (1787).
5. Hope is incorrect here in attributing the Goldberg variations to Beethoven. The composer of the Goldberg Variations was J. S. Bach.
6. William McDougall was a psychologist. From 1898, McDougall held lectureships at Cambridge (St John's College) and Oxford (Corpus Christi College) and was appointed Professor of Psychology at Harvard (1920–28). McDougall 'was a leading critic of the rising tide of behaviourism within psychology. He abhorred its simple-minded materialism and empiricism that would for half a century set aside most of human nature as unsuitable for scientific study'. McDougall believed that behaviourism neglected 'the innate instinctual, purpose-providing systems'. He was antagonistic towards 'confronting behaviourism by means of the banal experiments that were eventually to constitute so much of the twentieth-century academic psychology'. Hope, who was qualified as a psychologist, in this notebook reference is most probably referring to the text: William Mc Dougall, *Character and the Conduct of Life*, Methuen, London, 1927.
7. This poem was published in Hope, *A Book of Answers*, pp. 89–92, with 'HOME TRUTHS FROM ABROAD or Dante and Virgil answer Mr. T. S. Eliot'.
8. Mark O'Connor has written plays and short stories but is best known as an award-winning poet. O'Connor was a close friend of A. D. Hope. See Wilde, Hooton & Andrews, *The Oxford Companion to Australian Literature*, pp. 528–9, where he is referred to as 'A sensitive and accurate observer of nature …' and further: 'A proponent of phonetically-accurate spelling, he writes a rhythmic verse that is well suited to oral delivery.'
9. The reference here to 'Max' is most likely to Max Harris, who as co-editor of *Angry Penguins*, was victim to the 'The Em Malley Hoax'. Two Australian poets, Harold Stewart and James McAuley, who, like Hope, were in opposition to free verse, created the poet Ern Malley and wrote a collection of poems in free verse. The failure of Harris and his co-editors to detect the hoax had negative ramifications on the cause of modernism at that time.
10. See Steele, Peter, Jonathan Swift: Preacher and Jester, PhD, Melbourne University, September, 1975, p. 254. See further Steele, Peter, *Jonathan Swift: Preacher and Jester*, Clarendon Press, Melbourne, 1978, p. 200, where Steele writes, 'Carlyle is reported to have said of Tennyson, "Arthur is always carrying a bit of chaos around with him and turning it into cosmos"'. Steele writes, 'Something like this

is Swift's intention, though Swift's "bit of chaos" seems to have been rather more refractory than Tennyson's. The world in upheaval is summoned however temporarily and provisionally, into the harmonies of prose …' Steele then quotes a passage from Swift's *Remarks Upon Tindall's 'Rights of the Christian Church'.*

11 In the mid-1970s until the early 1980s the new editors of *Meanjin* and *Quadrant* were respectively Jim Davidson (1974–82) and Judith Brett (1982) (*Meanjin*) and Peter Coleman, Elwyn Lynn and H.W.Arndt (*Quadrant*).

12 Pope, *Epistle IV*, to Richard Boyle, Earl of Burlington, line 173–6.

13 Stow has written three collection of poems: *Act One* (1957); *Outrider* (1962); *A Counterfeit Silence* (1969), and *Randolph Stow Reads from His Own Work* (1974) Hope mentions 'Dr Lilley' as a source of information here but does not provide a relevant reference. Such a reference has not surfaced in research. Wallace-Crabbe, *The Experimental Artist*, p. Joseph Furphy's *The Buln-Buln and the Brolga*, is a long story that originally formed part of *Such is Life* (1903); it was deleted during the revision of *Such is Life* and was first published in 1948.

14 Gray, *Elegy Written in a Country Church-Yard*, stanza 20.

15 John Burton was a diplomat in foreign affairs during World War II.

16 See Robert Biegler, 'Begging in Cephalopods?' www.dal.ca/-ceph/T.C.P./octopanrep.html, Dalhousie University, accessed 15/8/02, who makes reference to Dr John Lilley in the context of discussing sign-tracking (the use of pleasant and unpleasant stimuli to elicit particular behaviour in animals, birds and mammals); he notes that Dr Lilley, in the 1960s, believed that dolphins exceeded the normal expectations of 'animal' behaviour. Lilley believed that dolphins had their own language. Experiments constructed to prove this were not conclusive at this time.

17 Wallace-Crabbe, 'The Experimental Artist'. This article that Hope has attributed to Chris Wallace-Crabbe has not surfaced despite numerous attempts to track it down. Wallace-Crabbe has only a vague recollection of such an article that he may have written but was unable to provide the bibliographical reference.

18 Joseph Furphy's *The Buln Buln and the Brolga*, is a long story that originally formed part of *Such is Life* (1903); it was deleted during the revision of *Such is Life* and was first published in 1948.

IV

ARGUMENT AND COMMENTARY ON CRITICS AND WRITERS

The notebooks record with humour, impartial argument and sometimes with passionate fury Hope's views on the art and/or the disease of criticism. His distaste for free verse and its associated side effects is expressed through analogies with other disciplines or by drawing on modes of operation of social structures. Within these large frameworks, Hope takes on writers, critics, poets and artists who have dared to stray into the 'enemy' camp.

Hope does not hold back when he comes across fraudulent research, incoherence and vanity among celebrated writers and critics. Robert Graves, Yvor Winters and F. R. Leavis are some of the writers who are recipients of Hope's scorn.

This section also communicates the extent to which Hope was amused, informed or titillated by what he terms 'literary gossip'. I have also chosen to include in this chapter samples of his commitment to poets, writers, thinkers, artists and friends who he believed had made his life richer.

TRAVEL NOTES 1958

(a) After a year spent in visiting the great universities and the great libraries of the English-speaking world I find myself more and more oppressed by the bulk and weight of studies which appear no longer to be determined by what there is to study but by the number of those who teach and study and the need to publish [a] as means of advancement or mere maintenance and subsistence.

The study of literature, in my life-time, has changed from an ancillary service, conscious that its life and its purpose were secondary and to some extent parasitic, into a great industry using literature as its raw material and concerned to find enough of this material to provide for the starving and multiplying hordes of research workers. The study of literature no longer means the study of poems and plays, romances and essays, but the study of hundreds of books about each work of literature — a jungle of secondary growth that bids fair to strangle the primary growth. More and more writers are taking refuge in this world.

The poet-on-campus, the novelist or poet who earns his regular living as a lecturer or professor in the department of English, the teacher of creative writing are perhaps all symptoms of a transformation taking place in our time, such that in a hundred years the academic institutions will train writers, control and exploit literature in its own way and to its own ends. The 'free' writer will be as much of an anomaly and a curiosity, as the owner of a cottage factory. The change will be similar to that by which a hunting society becomes a herding and pastoralist society. Writers will be 'bred for milk' or 'bred for beef'. Fantastic as it sounds it seems to me quite possible and perhaps to have already begun to happen.

(b) I find myself wondering how long the human mind can stand the loss of its old faculty, of oblivion. Former civilizations preserved as much of the past as they needed or desired. For the first time in the course of time it has been possible and thought desirable for a civilization to document and study itself. To forget nothing and to preserve everything even the voices and appearance of the past. The effect is like that of a body unable to eliminate its waste. What one gets in the end is not a civilization at all but a mass of corrupting customs, costive minds and suffocating hearts. Meanwhile the fields denied the waste and dung, grow sterile too.

— Book V, 1958, p. 83–4.

WHY NOT TRY IT?

Critics often go on as though esthetic beliefs and artistic practices were subject to a moral order, as though there were a universal church of art and they were the watchdogs against the wickedness of the heretics. And the heretics go on as though they had discovered, and alone discovered, the secret of the good life, concealed from all time to be revealed to them alone at last. But this is not so. The theories of art, like their practice, are still almost completely empirical. Certain practices 'work', certain practices do not. That is all we know for sure. And even what we think we are sure of can be overturned by someone who finds a way to succeed where others have tried and failed to make it work. There is no deccalogue and no categorical imperative in these matters.

A great deal of criticism consists of the arbitrary and indeed unconscious elevation of local tribal customs to the status of eternal and universal verities. And those who reject the customs and taboos of the tribe are just as bad. They believe themselves the recipients of a divine moral revelation.

— Book VI, 1960, p. 69.

SONNET TO A BROTHER POET

A man of letters, Hippolyte Babou,
— God help us, but there's something in a name!
A Man of Taste, a Critic of some fame,
Once dammed your Fleurs du Mal in a review.

Alas, poor Pooh-Bah! Poor Baboon-Babou,
He was so confident, so sure the game
Was his by right, it almost seems a shame
Time should have left him weltering in the pooh.

But oh, to see the charlatan, the hack,
These self-appointed police of taste and style
Proved wrong, to watch the hollow judgement crack,
Ridicule shrivel that smug, Olympian calm,
Brings poets, when they meet, once in a while,
What belly-laughs, what recompense, what balm!

— Hydra 1965

I don't know where I got the idea. I thought Professor Schmidt's little book, but it's not there and it's not true! Babou praised the *Fleurs du Mal* and defended Baudelaire, though on feeble grounds. See notebook IX — where I try to wriggle out of the gaffe!

— Book VIII, 1964, p. 152.

LITERARY GOSSIP I

I am not much of an admirer of the chit-chat school and think the collection of trivial anecdotes about famous people is often disgusting rather than amusing or interesting. Yet my heart warms to Aubrey and his:

> How these curiosities would be quite forgott, did not such idle fellowes as I am putt them down.
>
> *Brief Lives*: Venetia Digby

I set down here while I remember them — a few bits of gossip about writers and others:

Tennyson: Mrs Stewart Murray, of Sulton Verrey near Warminster, in 1929 told me that when she was a young girl she was at a luncheon at which Tennyson was present. She was nervous about doing the right thing and when her host, who was carving said: 'How do you like your mutton, Miss Cust, thick or thin?' She hesitated, not knowing what to say and then answered, 'O, thin please!' — To her unutterable confusion Tennyon's voice came booming down the table: 'Only *Fools* like their mutton cut thin!'

Aubrey Beardsley: Miss Matilda Talbot of Lacock Abbey, Wilts. told me this about the same time: 'I used to know Aubrey Beardsley when I was young and we were friends. I once asked him: 'Aubrey, why do you draw such horrible subjects?' He said: 'I have dreadful nightmares which oppress me for days after. If I draw them I find they do not worry me.'

Christopher Brennan: The students who heard him used to say of Brennan that he delighted to embarrass the women in his classes, they thought on purpose, by lecturing on Kant, which he pronounced with the K very hard and the German 'a' very forcefully produced. So that he appeared constantly to be saying things like, 'You must pay more attention to Cunt gentlemen', 'Cunt is absolutely fundamental to an understanding of Romantic German literature', 'We must not press Cunt too far', 'Cunt will satisfy us where Schlegel merely stimulates', etc. Whether this was true or not I do not know, I think it was Arthur Pelham who told me.

When I was in my early twenties I heard all sorts of stories about this — to us young men — fabulous character from students of his. I have forgotten most of them, which is one reason why I write these details now. One was the story of a fellow-student who called to see C. J. B. in his room at the university one evening, knocked and had no answer so tried the door which opened and he went in. Chris was sitting in his chair weeping. On the gas bracket (or on the table in front of him) was a pair of women's garters. The student went away and closed the door without speaking. It was the day a dear friend — rumour said his mistress — had been knocked down and killed in the street. Chris had been to see the body and brought away the garters.

One day a year or so before he died, I was drinking in Adams Hotel in Sydney — the gorgeous Nineties Bar — with Ralph Piddington son of Mr Justice Piddington.[1] Ralph said something about Chris Brennan and at my reply asked in surprise: 'Have you never met him?' I said that I had never even seen him. 'Well we must go and see him at once,' said Ralph, 'he's drinking himself downhill very fast now and won't last much longer. You must hear him talk, if he still can.'

We hired one of the horse-cabs that still plied in Sydney and went to Kings Cross where Ralph said we would be sure to find him in the lounge bar of the Mansions Hotel. And so we did, but he was sitting at a table so sodden that we could not get more than a grunt or two and some incoherent muttering from him. After a while I got up and went into the lavatory and while I was standing at the pissoir Chris lumbered up beside me. I had finished my business and, taking a pencil from my pocket I wrote on the wall in front of us a line of verse from a Pompeian wall inscription:

> MULTO MELIUS QUAM GLABER
> FUTUITER CUNNUS PILOSSUS.[2]

(This turns out to be wrong, but it was the way I recalled it.) Chris looked at it for a moment, took the pencil out of my hand, and as

I remember, wrote some further lines, then talked clearly and interestingly about Latin accentual verse and we returned to Ralph. I was pleased and thought I might hear him talk, but after a minute or two he relapsed into his stupor. Still I am glad I did meet him and have sometimes thought of making a poem on the meeting. I am glad too that it was the 'cunnus pilossus' that brought us together.

Mary Gilmore: I never met her either. But one night just after my return from Oxford I talked to a group called The Henry Lawson Society, which at that time seemed to consist partly of schoolteachers and others interested in Australian writing and partly of old mates of Henry Lawson and their mates. With an accent that must have shocked them, and with what I now remember as a condescending manner, I explained just why Henry Kendall, my subject, was no poet and would not survive in the literary history of the future. My audience was appalled and hurt and then rather hostile as the discussion that followed got under way. Finally someone asked me: well who would you call a *good* Australian poet? I mentioned Brennan and my audience then [began] to decry Brennan. An elderly woman with a striking appearance was sitting in the middle row and had not taken any part in the dog-fight. Suddenly she got to her feet and in a surprisingly powerful voice said: 'This young man is quite right. Brennan was the Thunder and the Lighting!' She said some other things I wish I could now remember and left before the end of the meeting. I learned that it was Mary Gilmore.

Henry Lawson: John Le Gay Brereton[3] talked to me a good deal about Lawson when I was a student of his. As far as I can now remember the way he told it, it went like this:

> When I was a boy studying at the university my father lent me the gate keeper's cottage where I could study undisturbed. At that time I had made friends with Henry Lawson and he often visited me at night. I would be at my books and there would be a tap on the window and there would be Henry:
>
> 'Is the coast clear, Jack?' I would say that it was. 'I've got a sugar-bag with a few bottles in it planted down by the gate. It is all right to come in?' I would open up and we would settle down to talk. Many people thought Henry quite uneducated in those days but he used to get me to talk about my university studies and get me to get him books from the university library

and lend him things from my own books. He read a good deal more in English writers than some people think.

When Henry and I were in New Zealand we walked for several days along the railway line. We were too hard up to take the train. Several times we spent the night at gangers' camps and there was usually a bit to drink and a lot of singing and yarning round the camp-fire at night. A lot of the gangers were Maoris and the Maori girls and women would come and sit round the fire with us with their knees up to rest their arms on. They wore no pants and the whole of their what-nots was visible in the fire light. Some of them were extremely handsome and Henry was very susceptible and I had a lot of trouble keeping him in control. I guessed that we would be in real trouble with the Maoris if Henry with a few drinks in started making up to their women. But I got him through safely. [I think Brereton may have been telling this as something he had heard from Lawson's companion.]

Henry and I used to drink in a little wine shop near the bottom of George Street in Sydney. It was kept by an old German and his wife. One afternoon we had been sitting for an hour or so talking and drinking and we were both a little far gone. Henry got up to go out the back for the needs of nature and after a minute or so I followed him. I was just in time to see the following scene: in the passage was a sink (or it may have been a tub) in which the German had been blending some white wine of the type we had been drinking. There was Henry pissing cheerfully into the fluid, which, in his condition, he took to be what he was looking for. At the other end of the passage was the German's wife with her mouth open for the shriek which followed at once. I grabbed Henry and dragged him out and without giving him time to do up his fly we took to our heels. On consultation later we decided that the Germans were frugal folk, unlikely to waste the wine, which, as far as they knew, might not have been polluted — so for this and other reasons we decided to find another place to drink for the next few months. When we went back the incident had apparently been forgotten.

Not edifying perhaps — but if we are grateful to Aubrey for the story of Sir Walter Raleigh and the Maid of Honour in Windsor Great Park and the other story of Mary Pembroke and the stallions,[4] these fragments may also earn their keep one day.

— Book IX, 1965, pp. 21–8.

A WORD FOR THE CRITICS

No, let the righteous rather thwart
And friendly smite my cheek,
I would not then retort,
But be resigned and meek.
But let not what they gave for balm
Increase my raging smart;
Nay, I will pray my psalm
Against their hand and heart.
Let such false judges as commend
Their harsh precarious prose,
This my song attend,
Which in sweet measure flows.

— Christopher Smart: Psalm CX/I

Their harsh precarious prose! What a treasure of a phrase, for solace and for use!

— Book IX, 1965, p. 34.

THE USE OF CRITICISM

There is a good deal to be said for Aristotle's notion of this in *The Politics*: that great works need criticism because they are so inexhaustibly rich; each generation, each period of taste finds in them things which the limitations of other times hid from them. So in the end the work emerges fully 'realised' in its wholeness and its detail.

But there is another side to it. Criticism is so much commoner than creation and so much criticism is misinterpretation or blurs the exact detail and flattens the clear harmonies, that the original work tends in time to become obscured and distorted by the mass of irrelevant ideas about it. So each generation repudiating the last is able to clear the jungle from the great monument for a moment, before it begins to cover it again with its own irrelevancy.

The study of criticism, as opposed to the study of literature, then becomes necessary in order to be able to sterilise and clear so that the great work can stand alone in its naked strength.

Book IX, 1966, p. 50.

ROBERT GRAVES

I admire Graves and except for his recent verse, like his solid, well carpentered poems. (His earlier ones whereas those later ones where the spurious white goddess replaces the genuine muse can only be described in Daisy Ashford's immortal phrase: Piffle before the wind!)[5] Yet I cannot forgive him the nasty attack on W. B. Yeats in *These Be Your Gods, O Israel* — nasty and dishonest. When he was in Australia lately I deliberately avoided meeting him because I did not trust myself not to start a fight. I went off camping to Freycinet Peninsula and walked and met possums and kangaroos and bandicoots instead. Jim McAuley who had arranged a dinner for me to meet Graves thought it a peculiar choice.

— Book IX, 1968, p. 101.

REPLY TO A CRITIC

Why *should* I keep up with the times? If the times don't like it,
Let *them* change direction and try to catch up with me.

— Book IX, 1967, p. 109.

THE CRITICS

The poet, a devoted cook
Prepared us this delicious book:
His critic's works, there is no question.
Are the by-products of digestion.

(1934)

And speaking as one of them in each case.

(1974)
— Book IX, 1968.

LITERARY GOSSIP II

C. P. Snow: When I was writing *Poor Charley's Dream*, Derry Jeffares[6] came to stay with me after attending a conference in Brisbane. I asked him if he knew Snow and he said he did. I asked: 'What is he like?' 'Oh he's a kind man and able enough,' said Derry, 'but incredibly vain. When Leavis made his attack on him be broke down completely, wept and stormed and got drunk for nights on end.' I don't know how reliable my Irish friend may have been, but I felt better about teasing Snow after that. Anyone who could take Leavis so seriously must have been bogus.

About this time Dorothy Green[7] came back from seeing Martin Boyd[8] in Rome. He told her, in passing that was really about or based on Barbara Bainton.

— Book IX, 1968, p. 160.

REFLECTIONS ON RETIREMENT

The first few months of my retirement, I now realise, have been very like the first few months of a man who has lived on the edge of poverty and suddenly comes into a fortune. There is the same battle between fixed habits of management of one's resources and the impulse to spend in a reckless and unlimited spree; there's the realisation that must come to many suddenly made rich: that they are not educated to the enjoyment and use of wealth, and the same tendency to fall back on an over indulgence in the sorts of pleasures possible to a poor man: instead of learning Greek and the piano, I spend more time sitting at the same old office desk, opening my mail and sorting my files.

I remember the retired and wealthy grazier I saw when I took Hiramatsu to Grenfell. His sons had taken over his properties and, according to the secretary of the local club, he came into town early each day and spent his whole day playing the poker machines. The most dreary and pointless of all forms of gambling. As he had so much money, there was not even the excitement of risking everything or the gratification of winning a sum that would mean anything to him. In the same way, after years of temporal penury, with a fortune in time on my hands, I am surprised at the temptation to fritter it away at meaningless and mechanical occupations. It is exactly the opposite of what I had expected.

— July 1969
— Book X, 1969, p. 148.

F. R. LEAVIS

After making fun of him and his disciples for as many years, I finally met Leavis for two periods of half an hour each in York this year. I had built up for myself the picture of a large, arrogant overbearing person and was taken aback on meeting him to find him a small, thin, bald little man with a fussy, nervous manner, apparently a victim of uncontrollable logorrhea. He did not stop talking at all. Brockbank and I attempted to steer the monologue when he got onto something interesting by asking questions or interjecting an occasional remark but without effect. He talked only of literature on the first occasion and much of what he said was interesting and entertaining but he appeared unable to keep to a topic or develop it, slipping from book to book and from author to author, as though at the mercy of some kind of 'free association' — accounts of a lecture he gave later in London, allegedly on Wordsworth who served him simply as a point of departure, confirmed this impression. His tone of voice and his manner were excited and compulsive, as the monologues of some schizophrenics are — something suggestive of manic excitement. One had the impression of the great critical machine running loose and out of control. On the second occasion we were alone, the tone and the manner were the same but he talked obsessively about his lecture engagements and the way the postal strike had upset these. Yet there was nothing incoherent in the monologue. The opinions were clear and to the point; he quoted from the texts appositely and amusingly. Several remarks about Johnson and Pope I should like to have recorded but they were quickly lost in the constant and constantly veering stream of opinion. He obviously had not the slightest idea who I was — why should he? — and I felt rather embarrassed by the fact that next day I was to hold him up to public ridicule by reading *Dunciad Minor* to the undergraduates and their teachers, particularly as he was being so unguarded and affable. But I thought of his perverse attacks on Milton and Fielding and Scott and his wilful persecution of young men who differed from him or were students of his academic opponents at Cambridge, and hardened my heart.

Stephen Spender, to whom I talked a week or so later in London, told me a story of his being invited to read his poetry at Downing College and his dismay when he arrived to find that Leavis had heard of the arrangements shortly before and had simply vetoed the reading. 'Spender shall *not* appear in this college.' I thought of the literary gangsterism by which Leavis maintained himself. But I could not help feeling sorry for the little old man. I found myself wishing that in his person he could have been a more satisfactory monster.

Leavis's attack on Milton's verse reminds me of a man who, having habituated himself to the sounds of a brook, complains of the ocean that its music is heavy and monotonous.

— 29–IV–71

Perhaps the most interesting thing about this meeting with Leavis was the experience of confronting a mind operating only on a 'literary' level — nothing above or below the world of books — a shape of the complete monomania that art always tends to become.

— 1–V–71

— Book XII, 1971.

MYSTIQUES

In a dream last night, I put an end to a long discussion, now forgotten, by saying: 'The University of Chicago invented Economics in order to provide a *mystique* for the barren techniques of Commerce.' This profound absurdity crushed the complex arguments of my companions and I woke feeling pleased with myself as though I had really hit on an important truth.

Although the remark was quite silly in itself, it is true, I think, that we do often invent 'theories' of subjects to dignify and perhaps condone techniques and practices which are either indefensible or need no justification, and these then become the subjects of unnecessary specialist study at university level, when they could be safely left to the study of practical ways and means in polytechnics. Economics as a whole may be a respectable study, but Business Principles, Cookery or Public Speaking are not. I am half-inclined to say that Literary Criticism is another [of] these practical arts which are below the level of intellectual theory, in that it has no theoretical 'principles', and that when I. A. Richards remarked that 2,000 years of theorising since Aristotle had established nothing, he was near to seeing the truth of the matter. Certainly his attempt to establish it on a new basis by using the methods of empirical science has not had much success, and neither has Northrop Frye's even more strenuous approach. Criticism remains an essentially banausic art.

— 26–IV–71
— Book XII, 1971, pp. 50–1.

DUNCIAD MINOR

What I ought to have said about the title in my preface is that it is not only described as *Minor* in deference to its great predecessor, but because that was about poets and this is about a minor sort of literary men, critics — bad writers are a disaster; bad critics are only a nuisance.

— Book XIV, 1972, p. 58.

YVOR WINTERS

For no reason I suddenly begin thinking of Yvor Winters[9] this morning while I was shaving. In the fall of 1958 Penelope and I spent a fortnight to three weeks staying with Judy and Evan Jones at Palo Alto in California, while I visited Leland Stanford University and the Institute of Advanced Studies on the hills above the university. During this time I met Yvor Winters, persuaded him to let me attend some of his lectures on the English poets and spent an evening at his house where as I remember, we talked about South American Spanish poets, breeding Airedales and how to deal with gophers.

I came to California with a high regard for Winters as a poet and as a critic though I had not read much of his critical writing. He was at the time supposed to be conducting a highly successful 'school for poets', and from what I saw and heard this was the case as long as the young men had the force of character to resist the powerful pressure of Winters' own personality. And he had great charm and magnetism with this personal force. But his lectures were unbelievable in their dogmatic scrappiness. At this stage of his career he seemed to have completely revalued the whole corpus of English poetry and dismissed most of it as worthless. His students found it engaging, amusing and exasperating, because reputations rose and fell from week to week. One of them told me that Yvor had reduced the worthwhile poets in English to five, one of whom was always Winters and three of whom were former pupils of his, while the fourth would be changed weekly and might be a poet no one had ever heard of. I have no doubt that this was a deliberately absurd legend, but it had a good deal to back it up. Winters remained interesting, just and penetrating in many of his comments on poetry. There was always the feeling for larger issues and magnanimous opinion that marked his earlier criticism, but what one noticed more was a sort of irresponsible crankiness about most of his judgements. It was as though the machine was operating [at] full strength but had lost its rudder or governor — or, to put it another way, that the continual exercise of fine distinctions, the exercise of a more and more refined scrutiny had resulted in a collapse of the mechanisms of discrimination, so that when applied they gave quite random answers, though the principles of judgement remained sound enough. I cannot help making a comparison with Leavis when I met him later, apparently suffering from a similar collapse. It may be commoner than we think for powerful minds, operating on fragile systems of good and bad and continually forced to refine, to collapse in the end into a sort of critical anarchy.

On the subject of breeding Airedales, on the contrary, Winters was knowledgeable and interesting and, on keeping gophers out of one's lawn, fantastic: the method was simple, a rocking chair on the porch or stoop flanked on one side by a table provided with beer, on the other a pile of handy-sized fire-wood billets. One had only to sit drinking beer and watching the lawn surface; when the turf began to bulge a well-aimed billet would take the gopher on the nose as it emerged.

— 30–VII–73
— Book XV, 1973, pp. 55–8.

MORE ANSWERS

ROBERT GRAVES AND W. B. YEATS

Malice begets malice, of course and I was maliciously pleased to find that Graves in his scurrilous attack on Yeats (*These Be Your Gods, O Israel*) in the Clark Lectures had fallen flat in a passage where he lectures Yeats on not reading Macrobius properly before quoting him. Which is precisely what Graves himself was doing at that moment, taking one of the poems in *A Woman Young and Old* as being the poet in person talking to a young bride about his homosexual pleasures. A more grotesque misreading could hardly be imagined. So that I composed the following with considerable satisfaction.

The Spectre of W. B. Yeats to Robert Graves

My bones are stowed; my sleep is sound;
I know I lie in Irish ground;
What wretch, then, conjures me to come
Like Samuel's spirit from the tomb
And wakes the dead and turns the sod,
To learn he has been cursed by God

You, Robert Graves, by Hare and Burke,
Why all this corpse and coffin work?
To be dug up in France and laid
Forever in Ben Bulben's shade
Is all an Irish poet craves:
He has no need of other 'graves'.
But speak, poor wizard, tell me true,
What was it could have prompted you
To stab dead poets in the back
With this mean-spirited attack?
Was it fierce envy, settled hate
Or a mere itch to demonstrate
To Cambridge dons and Cambridge dames
Your faculty for calling names?
What spurious goddess sent you down
From Sinai to play the clown
And make the undergraduates laugh
By proving me their Golden Calf
And smash the Tables of the Law
To raise a general guffaw?

And tell me, Robert, was it wise
To tilt at signs and mysteries,
My symbols, seances and spells
While warlock Graves, in cap and bells,
Trumped up from folk-lore's bones and rags
White goddesses and triple hags?
Did you not recollect a knack
In pots to call the kettle black?
Nor, throwing stones at mine, reflect
Your glass-house likelier to be wrecked?
For mine was honest nonsense, yours
Mad mumpsimus with Nancy's drawers.

Next, who appointed you, I ask,
To take up your fellow bards to task,
Pontificate upon the times
And tell your peers to mend their rhymes,
Inventing rules to prove us wrong

About the finer points of song?
Or was your study to annoy
And prove yourself a warty boy
And with the jaw-bone of an ass,
Like Samson, slay the poets en masse?
But these are trifles: I'll be brief
And turn to your attack-in-chief,
That poem you laboured to discredit,
While showing that you had not read it —
Come, Mr Graves, now don't be vexed,
But pay attention to the text.

Peruse your commentary! You note,
In the first sentence you misquote.
(Unless incumbent of a chair
In Cambridge, one must have a care.)
You then, deliberately no doubt,
Turning my syntax inside out,
Insinuate me to have been —
With a fine nose for the obscene
And cocksure critical aplomb —
A Sodomite and a Peeping Tom.
Query; how could you think so? Answer:
You'd only read the second stanza
And, in your atrabilious rage,
Neglected to turn back the page.
Had you done so, and read the title,
You might have learned — the point is vital
To one of your profound acumen —
The lines were spoken by a woman!

Fie, Robert fie! Were these the ways
To add fresh laurels to your bays
And prove yourself a man of parts
Before a Faculty of Arts?

Robert, I have you on the hip!
Now will you prate of scholarship
And raise false witness from the dead
To teach us what Macrobius said?

Take my advice: in future learn
To read a text you mean to spurn,
And look more closely at the letters,
Before you criticise your betters.

— Book XV, 1974, pp. 153–7.

JABBERWOCK BITES THE DUST OR ROBERT GRAVES AND EDWARD FITZGERALD

When Graves came to Australia, I helped to arrange his tour but refused to hear his translation of Omar Khayyam or to meet him because of his beastly Judas-work on W. B. Yeats. But I was not particularly impressed by specimens of his translations from what he claimed to be the genuine Omar: a poet ought, I thought, to have brought some poetry out of the original. Perhaps Fitzgerald, who did, was spurious, but it hardly seemed an improvement to produce a translation that was as flat as a board, however 'faithful'.

Now from the library, hard on the heels of one another, I gather Graves' and Omar Ali-Shah's translation and commentary on the *Rubaiyyat* and Ali Dashti's *In Search of Omar Khayyam* in L. P. Elwell-Sutton's translation from the Persian, and it gives me great pleasure to find that Graves, in fact, has fallen flat on his face at last. His introduction abounds in statements like: 'Fitzgerald's *Rubaiyyat* ... is now for its length, the most frequent source of modern English dictionaries of familiar quotations and a true *mumpsimus*', which introduces a piece of literary grossness and bad manners about poor Fitzgerald almost as bad as his treatment of Yeats in *These Be Your Gods* ... This pseudo-Persian scholar makes hay with the whole previous tradition of Persian scholarship. It is a wild, arrogant rant, taken as a whole, and despite a number of shrewd points in the argument, it has the smell of an ill-informed amateur-enthusiast about it. I am in no position to judge, but my prejudice against Graves makes me delighted to read L. P. Elwell-Sutton's introduction to Ali Dashti's book. After a scholarly account of the history of Omar Khayyam studies in East and West, and an account of Edward Heron Allen's investigation of Fitzgerald's relation to his sources for his *Rubaiyyat* (1899), he writes:

> In a detailed analysis of Fitzgeralds poem he [Heron Allen] listed against each stanza the original Persian quatrains that he thought must have inspired the paraphrase, and came to the conclusion that, while virtually no stanza of Fitzgerald's was an exact translation of a Khayyamic quatrain, nevertheless 97 of the 101 could be traced back to one, or combinations of more than one, of Khayyam's originals and that only 4 owed their origin to two other Persian poets, Attar and Hafez.'[10]

Graves's claim to have given the authentic Omar to the world, freed from the travesty of Fitzgerald and the imperfections of the Bodleian and other manuscripts and their spurious accretions, rests on the conviction that his collaborator Omar Ali-Shah had produced (or at least had access[ed] it — Ali-Shah in fact was unable to produce either the MS or a transcript or a photocopy when challenged to do so by sceptical specialists) a nearly contemporary MS which had been in the possession of his family in Afghanistan since 'shortly after Khayyam's death'. Such a claim, if substantiated, would indeed have put the whole vexed question on a new footing, since none of the extant manuscripts are said to be earlier than the fifteenth century and the earliest is in fact the Bodleian MS used by Fitzgerald, of which Graves is so contemptuous and which was among the ones used by Ed Heron Allen in testing Fitzgerald's use of his sources. Hear now the judgement on these false witnesses Graves and Ali-Shah: (Elwell-Sutton loquitur) 'Another unlikely offshoot of Fitzgerald's work was the appearance in 1967 of a new translation of 111 Khayyamic quatrains which was in fact a versification of the quatrains collected and translated by Edward Heron Allen in his search for the sources of Fitzgerald's poem, as described above. This new version would probably not have attracted very much attention but for two circumstances: firstly, that the final metrical version was the work of the well-known English poet Robert Graves, and secondly that both he and his Bristol-born, Anglo-Indian collaborator Omar Ali-Shah claimed that the translation, so far from being based on Heron Allen's book, was made from a manuscript "of uncontradictable authority" dated 1153 and still extant in the Hindu Kush region of Afghanistan. *The Times* reviewer, Major J. C. E. Bowen, was the first to question the origin of the translation on the grounds that it seemed remarkably similar to Fitzgerald's poem [*The Times*, 11 November 1967] and he was quickly followed by others whose suspicions were strengthened by the authors' failure to produce the original manuscript. ... It is sufficient to say that the virtual identity of the sequence of quatrains in Graves's version with that of the arbitrary and personal selection in Heron Allen's notes, the inclusion of verses obviously not composed by Khayyam, like the one traditionally said to have been recited by Khayyam's ghost to his mother and the appearance of two quatrains each of which is a conflation of two separate and independent half-quatrains, are features that could not have appeared in an authentic twelfth-century manuscript.'

It is fair to Graves to suspect that he could not have been stupid or dishonest enough to have connived at the fraud. But he seems to have been the victim of an elaborate confidence trick, and after his scornful abuse of Fitzgerald's ignorance and carelessness it is a perfect case of the biter bit, to find that what he took for the genuine Omar Khayyam was not even Fitzgerald's original, but an arbitrary set of texts used to test Fitzgerald and so modelled on Fitzgerald's poem itself. (And when he falls, he falls like Lucifer!)

Few of the ironies of scholarship have given me more pleasure than this.

Willy Yeats is avenged too!

Ah, frabjous day!

— February 1973
— Book XIV, 1973 pp. 89–95.

OUT OF HIS MOUTH: D. H. LAWRENCE

How I loathe ordinariness! How from my soul I abhor nice simple people, with their eternal price-list!

Letter to Aldous Huxley, c. August 1928

This belongs to the same stance and to the same period of his life as *Kangaroo*. How Lawrence gives himself away, his vanity and spite, his bolstering up an empty and irritable self-esteem, not by any positive achievement or talent, but by deriding his fellow men.

And at what price Lawrence's own price-list in which the salt of the earth is thrown out to be trampled under [the] foot of a self-promoter and a sham prophet. The quotation is picked up from a book entitled *D. H. Lawrence, Novelist, Poet, Prophet* edited by Stephen Spender, 1973.

Lawrence's arrogance is only matched by his pretentiousness and his power to impose on second rate minds (like Spender).

— Book XVIII, 1975, p. 88.

GOSSIP: NORMAN LINDSAY

Douglas Stewart in his pleasant book about Lindsay (p. 169) mentions my visit with Leonie Kramer to see Norman at Springwood. I thought I had described the visit but apparently not. Lindsay had written to me three or four years earlier, a generous and appreciative letter about my poems and had invited me to come and see him if I were ever in Springwood. I replied that several members of my family were there and I would gladly come over next time I went to see them. However some time passed and on my visits to Springwood there never seemed to be any spare time.

Then when I agreed to write a preface to Norman Lindsay's *Pen Drawings* for Angus & Robertson, after I had viewed the drawings at their George Street premises, Douglas suggested that he and Margaret should take me for the day to Springwood to meet Norman and talk about the pencil drawings. I agreed and Leonie was included in the party, I think because I was staying with her at the time and she was a friend of the Stewarts and had met Norman a few months before.

We set out from St Ives in Douglas's car and took the back road through Richmond over the Nepean and up through the bush to Springwood. It must have been late in 1968 or early in 1969.

Douglas had laid down the plan of campaign before we left: 'We'll take food and arrive just before lunch,' he said, 'give Norman time for a rest in the afternoon and leave after afternoon tea. He loves visits but he's very old and very frail. In fact he may not last much longer and it's not fair to tire him out.'

I was amused at the sequel to these pious intentions. As the car entered the Lindsays' drive and swung round to the back of the house, Douglas said, 'There he is!' and I saw a small figure in white with white hair, standing in the kitchen door waving and obviously talking nineteen to the dozen though we were still well out of earshot. He led us in and the frail old nonagenarian seemed to bounce rather [than] walk. While Margaret and Leonie cleared the kitchen of some dreadful half-eaten pie covered with mould, replaced it with food they had brought up and prepared lunch, I had a hilarious and delighted conversation with Norman about everything in the world except the drawings to which indeed only passing reference was made. Norman talked with great animation all through lunch though he appeared neither to eat nor drink himself. As soon as lunch was over he took me through most of the house, the ship-model room, the etching room and so on, darting about like a fish and talking mainly about his plans to outwit Rose in her opposition to his giving away all his pictures. 'What use have I for money, at my age?' It did not seem to occur to him that perhaps his family might have *some* use for the stuff. I thought of poor Sophie trying to head the old Tolstoy off from beggaring his family. In Norman however there was none of the gloomy moralising that bedevilled Tolstoy. He simply wanted to give — and perhaps to have the pleasure of getting his own way against Rose: 'I've found the way to do it,' he said with a chuckle. 'Rose can stop me selling the things but she can't legally stop me giving them away.'

Norman having spent his presumptive napping-time in skipping round the house, Douglas intimated that he had to feed his cats, birds and other dependants and took Leonie and me round the gallery, formerly a billiard room, where all the major oil-paintings were hung. By this time evening was coming on. Norman returned and we were talked into staying for an evening meal, but on condition we left immediately after.

In the event of course, the four of us got away about eleven o'clock at night, completely exhausted while Norman apparently as fresh as a daisy waved us off from the kitchen door, talking till we were out of earshot once more.

The only frail thing about him, as I said to Leonie, was his appearance. Physically there seemed nothing much inside the loose clothes. He looked as though one could have picked him up with one hand.

Not long after, of course, he died, though he did see the advance copy of the pencil drawings. He was very pleased with my preface and selected the best, in his opinion, of the originals, a drawing of Rita,[11] to be given to me. So I become a sort of accomplice in his mischievous game of outwitting the 'model wife'.

— Nov. 1975
— Book VIII, 1975, pp. 79–84.

TIME SPAN

(See an earlier note on the same subject which I had forgotten — Notebook XII, p. 58.)

James McAuley a few years ago remarked that my poems were often not in contemporary English, that I used a lot of 'literary' words and, even more often, turns of syntax that one would not use in conversation today. He was quite right, but I had forgotten it until Arthur Philips,[12] the hero of my *Dunciad*, asked me during questions after a reading of poetry, why I so often indulged in 'pastiche'. Jim's remark was neutral: he did not think my practice poor or affected, though his surprise was plainly tinged by the contemporary habit of writing in contemporary, even colloquial style. Arthur's question seemed to be tinged with malice and who shall blame him? Not I!

My own view is that a poet should take all language for his province if he wishes. I am as much at home in the language of the past four hundred years as in the language of today — more so in some respects since much of the language of today, especially that used by social scientists and journalists and the dissident young and politicians seems to me so distasteful that I do not care to be at home in it. All the English, and especially all the literary English used since Chaucer is so familiar to me that it seems contemporary enough to use in a poem. And sometimes it is more fun or more appropriate to write in the language of another period than in that of today. My time span of 'the present' seems to be wider than that of some others.

The thing that makes pastiche boring or artificial is not the *fact* of writing in [the] style of another period or another person, but in its being no more than that, a clever imitation without a life or force of its own. This is, or borders on, parody — though parody if well done

can be fun, can be beautiful and have the enchanting quality of wit —
but the effect roughly described as pastiche, when mastered is a proper
technique of writing. It is no more a criticism to say that such writing
is pastiche than it is to say that a good actor succeeds in entering into
and presenting the life of the person whose part he is playing.

The reproach hanging about the word 'pastiche' is all part of the
absurd theory that has been with us in one form or another ever since
the Romantics, that poetry is 'self-expression', that a poem is a confession or an involuntary ejaculation of some kind. If that were so, one
could see the point of the reproach — but of course it is a false and
perverse view.

The chief thing is to move easily and with assurance in one's
territory of language. Its range and extent do not matter, provided one
has made it one's own.

— Book XIX, 1976, pp. 98–100.

THE FLUTE-PLAYER

Here, alone, in Hobart for Jim McAuley's funeral, wondering whether I should have come, but feeling he would have liked me to be here. The season is bitter in spite of spring; the great mountain under whose image I went to school, hidden in driving rain and cloud; I get into my motel and find on the wall, instead of the usual *schmalz*, a very good reproduction of the player on the double flute from one of the Etruscan tombs, the young man in gay clothes, striding forward through spring foliage, his very large hands and feet seeming to emphasise the delicacy of the unheard music and the neck and back — flying fingers of the preceding figure in the procession seeming to beckon him on. An extraordinary impression! Look up the whole scene when I get back to Canberra.

— 17–X–76
— Book XIX, 1976, p. 101.

JAMES McAULEY

I

Last night I woke in some agitation from a dream in which I was present at the burial — I did not go on to the interment after the service in the cathedral in Hobart. In the dream the service was being held in a Protestant cathedral which seemed all wrong but there was a Catholic priest officiating. He was on a sort of balcony high up on the wall of the nave and the coffin was visible not quite pushed into a deep niche in [the] wall beside him. It was clear that Jim was being buried in the wall of the cathedral and that the niche would then be covered by a memorial plaque of which there were several already in place on the wall.

I woke up in protest saying: but he ought to have [been] buried in the earth — that is what he wanted and what his religion prescribes.

— 5–XI–1976
— Book XIX, 1976, p. 103.

II

It occurs to me that I should record a few things about J. McAuley, that other people are unlikely to know. I have recorded elsewhere our first meeting and he in *Quadrant* has denied it. Perhaps he is right: as he said to me in a letter, he too is unsure and memory plays odd tricks with us. But as far as I can be sure of memory itself, I have a clear and vivid recollection of the following.

When he left the university after failing to get a first class for his MA (a fact which angered him as he regarded his readers and judges as [being] in every way inferior to him, and was convinced that he had done a first class job), he took various teaching positions, at private schools misleadingly called Great Public Schools. When the Second World War broke out the head-master of one of these institutions summoned his younger masters and said that of course they would all be enlisting but the school would restore their jobs when they returned. This was McAuley's account and he was affronted by this method of being bullied into the army. As he was out of employment he came to live with us for a while before he went into the army by the ordinary process of conscription. It was then that we got to know each other well and explored each other's minds.

We lived in the old sandstone house now demolished, belonging to Woolwich Dock and looking over the harbour to Cockatoo Island and McAuley's visit was the occasion of many others of the group of young people he associated with — Oliver Sommerville, Ron Dunlop, Donald Horne, Bill Pritchett among them ...[13]

I recall that he was an uneasy sleeper. He had the room next to ours upstairs in the Woolwich House and would often wake us with the most frightful screams and outcries. The first time I rushed in and found him standing on the floor staring, struggling and shouting. He seemed to be fast asleep and in the morning had no recollection. Thereafter we ignored these nightmares as best we could.

At this time Jim's politics were well to the left, though I don't think he was ever a communist or a fellow-traveller. I have vivid memories of the musical entertainment he and John Reed (?) put on about the beginning of the war.[14] It was lively and amusing and violently against the Menzies government. The police were always trying to close it down on the pretext that it was charging for admission but Jim and his friends could pick out a copper in any disguise and insist that it was a free show. Though donations were welcome.

— Book XIX, 1976, pp. 103–6.

III

I should record that curious thing we both noticed in the days when we wrote fairly often to each other and met more often than in later years. Either Jim or I would mention a book we had been reading, an idea that had struck us, a poem we were working at or had finished, only to find that the other had been doing almost precisely the same thing or thinking along almost the same lines. It was as though some mental link was operating or some parallel line of growth was keeping us on the same course. I do not remember that this continued much after Jim went to Tasmania as Reader in Poetry. I wish now that I had kept a record of this 'doppelgänger' effect, but it was all in our letters and his to me were mostly destroyed in the fire that burned down University College with all my books and papers in 1952.

— Book XIX, 1976, p. 109.

IV

SOME REMARKS RECALLED

On his susceptibility, I think, to the attacks of reviewers: 'I pretend to be indifferent but actually I am just a mass of mince-meat.'
On Milton's critics, especially F. R. Leavis: 'Those who attack him usually end by levelling at their own deficiencies.'
On one of his sons (about 2 years): 'That child is composed almost entirely of Peanut Butter!'
On adultery (after conversion): 'A married man who sleeps with other women is just a shit!' (Which did not prevent him from remarking about such an exploit of his own: 'I was just stropping my tool.')
Reconstructed from memory of a letter about 1937 or '38: 'My idea of a poem is one that should obey all the laws of rhyme, of metre, of syntax and of logic and be able at the same time to display the perfect ease and grace best summed up in Horace's phrase *lucidus ordo*.'[15] (This catches the sense, not his actual words.)

— Book XIX, 1976, p. 109–11.

V

We were pretty much in agreement on most things connected with poetry, though an earlier admiration for the Augustans which involved seeing ourselves as guardians of the classic values 'in these last years of the Romantic Storm' was one from which Jim later broke away (when he turned to Spenser). He then wrote saying he could no longer 'feel' the Augustans and that they had taken poetry on an arid course. He seemed to have reverted to Matthew Arnold's untenable nonsense about prose and reason, which saddened me as I had regarded him as [a] champion of the view that Pope's verse was instinct with the highest of the passions, intellectual and moral fervour. He still had a good word to say for Dryden but I suspected, on perhaps inadequate grounds — *Letter to John Dryden* — more for Dryden's Catholic position than his poetry. *Letter to John Dryden* I did not like and thought a decline in taste and judgement. I paid no attention to it because all his life Jim had been subject to 'conversions' to various systems of ideas and before he could work his way through and out the other side, he would be filled with reforming zeal. I said nothing to him but published soon after my *Lambkin: A Fable*, which he disliked, so he probably got the point. The only other point on which I think we differed sharply was in our estimate of Christopher Brennan as a poet. I made a point of refuting him in a series of lectures in Hobart (revised and reprinted in *Native Companions*) and Jim sat in the front row of the audience grinning cheerfully as I made my points. Such things, for example his theory that my poetry was basically 'gnostic', did not disturb our friendship.

For many years we used, when either of us had finished a poem to send a copy to the other. We rarely discussed the poem at any length but each would comment on what we called 'soft spots' in image, rhythm, diction or idea — or else we would simply put a light cross in pencil in the margin opposite lines we felt needed to be looked at again. I don't know whether Jim found this useful, but I did. At some time after the war, I am not sure when, we gave up the habit. I think each of us by then felt confident enough in his own judgement.

Once, not long before we stopped exchanging poems he sent one called *The Muse*, to which I felt impelled to write an answering poem based on the same scheme and treatment. I sent it to him with an apology — I should have hated anyone to do the same thing to a poem of mine. It seemed to give him a shock, but he wrote back saying that he thought it was a quite legitimate thing to have done.

I think he realized that it was, in a sense, a special case: his poem was a statement of his attitude to poetry and what it meant for him and mine was in effect an answer saying, yes it is the same in general for me, but see too what the difference is. Perhaps I should not have published mine. He did not seem to mind, but then we never discussed each other's poetry when we met, though we often talked about poetry. I, at any rate always felt that there was a deep agreement and mutual support that needed no discussion and was indifferent to minor points of disagreement. I felt at one with him on these matters in a way I never have with any other person.

The last poem of mine that I sent him for comment was, I think, *Letter from Rome*. He praised it but took exception to the lines about pictures of the Annunciation enough to daunt the whole collective Midwives' Fellowship. (Writing Bombay. I can't recall the exact quotation.) I don't think the objection was literary. He did not hold with facetiousness on this subject.

The poem of mine he showed the most enthusiasm for (to me at least) was *The Death of the Bird*.

— Book XIX, 1976, p. 144–48.

VI

While he was at the Staff College at Middle Head in Sydney and after he had been offered and had refused the principalship — whether officially or not I do not know — after Alf Conlon[16] resigned — he wrote to me asking if I could help to get him back into a university, teaching English. I was then head of the English Department at Canberra and answered that I thought with his reputation he would have no trouble but that he might have to take a temporary drop in salary owing to his lack of higher degrees and university teaching experience. He replied that he could not afford, with his growing family, to take a senior lectureship which I, too cautiously perhaps, thought [was] what he would probably have to settle for. But not long after Murray Todd,[17] who had left me to take the Chair of English at Hobart, wrote saying that he had been trying to think of ways to restore the standing of that unhappy university (after the Orr Case) and that the Vice-Chancellor had agreed to his suggestion of a Readership in Poetry. Did I think Jim McAuley would be interested in an invitation, as they did not wish it to be an advertised 'job'? This was the perfect answer and for a couple of years Jim was perfectly happy writing poetry, reading and meeting a few students. But his passion for engagement in affairs did not leave him. He became interested in the archdiocese presided over by Gillian (Guilford) Young[18] whom I had known and admired in Canberra and with whom Jim brought me together so that we became friends — or I hope I may say so — he continued work for the DLP and was as immersed in politics as he had been in NSW. He began to study Law — I have no doubt there were many other things. I wrote to him about it, worrying that he was wasting his chance to get back to poetry and he answered, correctly analysing his own nature, that his poetry, however 'pure' it might seem, was a product of his engagement in practical affairs or at least dependent on them. I believed him.

When Murray Todd died, one of us wrote to the other, I forget which, and I was not surprised that Jim, after some struggle with himself, decided to apply for the Chair. I was on the selection committee and, to my surprise, found the others rather inclined to Ted Stokes[19] than Jim. I think my vigorous lobbying of Ian Maxwell,[20] the other external consultant, got Jim the chair in which he behaved so brilliantly and from which he did so much for the university. I felt Murray's approval in this though I admired Stokes and was sorry that he missed.

But my real concern and my happiness, as I now realise, was that, in a sense, I had got Jim to my own island, my own boyhood home and that he took to it at once and finally, just as his conversion to the Catholic Church proved final. Years later when he began to show restlessness, about the time when a second chair was created in Canberra and I hoped to lure him to join me there, he thought it over and wrote saying that Tasmania had claimed him and that was where he would stay.

He went at things professionally and with a poet's imagination, and naturally soon knew more about the animals and birds — he had practised bird-watching for years — the insects and plants of the island than I had ever done. It comes out in his last book about the sea and shore north of Swansea. Only once did I manage to tell him anything. I had been staying with him in Hobart and he took me and the children for a picnic into some country behind Mount Wellington to show me a strange new bird that had recently appeared. I recognised it as the sacred ibis which on its century-long migration from Egypt had reached the Lachlan Swamp in New South Wales some years before. When the swamps began to dry up in the Fifties the ibis began to migrate again and I had woken up one morning to find an army of them moving through Canberra. Now we stood and watched them at the end of their long journey.

— Book XIX, 1976, p. 148–53.

VII

I was twice surprised to see him composing a poem and I have no idea whether this was his ordinary method. The first time was when he was living with us in Woolwich and I recall his sitting in a chair in the living room totally absorbed so that he seemed unaware of what was going on around him.

The other time was on the same visit to Hobart I have mentioned. It was almost unbelievable. The four boys then all under ten were romping in the room making an indescribable din in the half-hour before dinner, the radio was blaring, the telephone kept ringing and Jim to whom I had been talking said: 'Just a minute!' as an idea occurred to him, took out a notebook and pen from his coat and began to write. I could see it was a poem. The noise continued at full blast and finally Norma called him to the telephone. He did not hear so she enlisted me. I went up to him and spoke and then shouted in his ear. He did not even stir. I told Norma to ask the caller to ring again and sat down. After about twenty minutes Jim came back into the world and handed me the finished poem of three or four stanzas with only two erasures. It is now one of his best-known lyrics — though I have unfortunately forgotten just which one. It particularly impressed *me*, for whom the slightest noise of voices, particularly children's voices makes concentration, let alone composition quite impossible.

— Book XIX, 1976, pp. 154–55.

IN MEMORIAM: J. P. M. 1976

Sleep sound here, brother, by your tranquil bay!
What can the tongue we both served now express
Other than this? All that is left to say
is loss and emptiness;

Empty as ocean stretches toward the pole
Beyond this island which you loved, my friend,
This island where at last you reached your goal
Of Landfall at Land's-end;

The island which your lucid poet's eye
Made living verse: wildflower and sedge and tree
And creatures of its bushland, beach and sky
Took root in poetry,

Until a world to which your poet's mouth
Gave being and utterance, country of the heart,
Land of the Holy Spirit in the South
Became its counterpart.

It was my island too, my boyhood's home
My 'land of similes', from all you gave,
This I hold close and cherish, as I come
To your untimely grave.

Where the great mount's apocalyptic beast
Now guards your bones and watches from the height,
Fixing his lion gaze towards the east
For the return of light,

Standing on this last promontory of time,
I match our spirits, the laggard and the swift;
Though we shared much beside the gift of rhyme,
Yours was the surer gift.

Your lamp trimmed, full of oil, you went before,
Early to taste the Bridegroom's feast of song;
Wait for me, friend, till I too reach that door;
I shall not keep you long.

— Jaipur, 9–1–1977
— Book VIII, 1977, pp. 117–19.

THE SCAFFOLD-MAKERS

After attending last year's literary conference and this year's in New Delhi — not to mention the literary corroboree at the Adelaide Festival 1976, I begin to form an image of works of literature almost totally obscured by a sort of critical scaffolding erected around them and I wonder whether it would not be better to let the untrained eye take a view of the building alone and unobstructed even at some loss from even the most illuminating of elucidators.

Of course I know that most of this discussion of literary questions is totally unnecessary; it is part of a parasitic industry. What I really wonder at is the fact that having been immersed so long as a professional in the industry I have not totally succumbed to accepting it as necessary and right. After all, what my *Dunciad Minor* was a protest against, was simply the excesses of the critical industry.

It has taken this abysmal series of international discussions to bring me up sharply against the fact that none of it is necessary and most of it is of no use to man or beast.

What started this off, I think was being taken to see an historic mosque which could only be viewed through a forest of wooden scaffolding as it was under repair.

— New Delhi, 4–V–1977
— Book XIX, 1977, p. 112.

POET AND CRITIC

I see that in the list of those attending the Delhi Conference I am referred to as 'Poet and Critic — as also in some publications of the *Who's Who* type. I should of course prefer to be listed simply as poet, though it may be that, like my enemy T. S. Eliot, the irony of history will see that the criticism outlives the poetry. I dare say that if Jesus Christ were alive today the *Who's Who* would list him as 'Prophet and Carpenter'!

— 18–I–1977
— Book XIX, 1977, p. 129.

JOHNSON'S MILTON

But original deficience cannot be supplied. The want of human interest is always felt. *Paradise Lost* is one of the books the reader lays down and forgets to take up again. None ever wished it longer than it is. Its perusal is a duty rather than a pleasure. We read Milton for instruction, retire harassed and overburdened and look elsewhere for recreation, we desert our master and seek for companions."

— Life of Milton

This reminds me of Jim McAuley's remark to me: 'Those who criticize the defects of Milton more often level at their own.' The last sentence in this passage should be taken with the first. The 'original deficience' to which Johnson was subject was his terror of solitude, his constant need of companionships. It was impossible for him to conceive the type of mind which longs for the solace of privacy, the attitude of mind which prompted Leonardo's note: *Quando tu sei solo, tu sei tutto tuo.* Imlac in *Rasselas*[21] cannot conceive any reason for the gaiety of everyone in Cairo society but that of attempting to emulate what they believe to be the happiness of others and hoping briefly to share in it. He tells the prince:

> In the assembly where you passed the last night, there appeared such spriteliness of air, and volatility of fancy, as might have suited beings of an higher order, formed to inhabit serener regions inaccessible to care or sorrow: yet, believe me prince, there was not one who did not dread the moment when solitude should deliver him to the tyranny of reflection.[22]

This struck me most forcibly because so often in the same circumstances, even though I am enjoying myself, there comes a point when I long for 'the moment when solitude should deliver me to the *pleasure* of reflection'.

This limitation of nature made it impossible for him to enjoy *Paradise Lost* or to understand Milton past a certain point. And I reflect that Johnson would not have understood me, or rather, that I find it difficult to understand the things he says about Milton's poem. All my reactions are so completely the other way about from his.

After that day on the shooting-range at Long Bay when I absconded from the regiment and lay for long hours in the bushes reading *Paradise Lost* totally enchanted with its music and its sweep of vision, a whole new world of poetic experience, it is incomprehensible that Johnson should, or indeed could have plodded through the whole poem as a chore, a duty and a harassment. It is true, I never wished the poem longer but that is because its length is so right, so adequate for the treatment of the theme. It never occurs to me to go to the poem for 'instruction' in Johnson's sense of the word: ie., for moral experience and a conspectus of human society, human history and the system of the universe. Fascinating as it is to be informed of Milton's views on these matters and deeply as he allows me to enter the poetry of his majestic conception, I only 'suspend belief'.

Perhaps the most surprising defect in Johnson's reading of the poem is his charge that it lacks human interest. Adam and Eve are a little too formal in their modes of domestic address, but they are human and delightful in their actions and feelings. The spirits, as Johnson observes, cannot be represented in human form. But what a variety of human form it is! Who can read through the debate in Hell and not find himself back in a professorial board meeting, a political debate or a council of military tacticians? God and the Messiah are partial failures. Pope was right: Verse And God the Father turns a school divine.

But Johnson appears simply deaf or colour-blind to all this. I recall André Gide's comments on reading Johnson — somewhere in his later journals — he found it a puzzle that the English could have so high an opinion of so dull and limited a writer. But Gide had his own side of intellectual and emotional crassness — who has not?

— 22–11–80
— Book XXI, 1980, pp. 65–9.

HONEST IAGO

Reading Jane Adamson on *Othello* I am struck first of all by the proper critical modesty with which she approaches the play. The way that she assumes that Shakespeare knew what he was about and that a critic's business is to try [to] find out before he condemns or puts his own construction on characters or plot — unlike, for example, Dr Leavis — she is particularly good on mistaken or inadequate interpretations of the character of Iago and his part in the theme of the play as a whole.

But the real problem with Iago is not critical assessment or moral analysis, but theatrical impact. The audience, who are in the know, as the people in the play are not, find it hard to credit that the other people on the stage cannot only credit Iago's 'honesty' but believe they observe it, that it is self-evident. The spectators cannot help feeling that the persons on stage must be idiots. This is all very well for Roderigo — he *is* an idiot, but it reflects on Othello, Desdemona and Cassio as well, who are all supposed to know Iago well. If they are stupid, they can hardly be tragic — pathetic at best. It is true, as Jane

Adamson, says that they all have reasons for deceiving themselves, but the point remains that Iago being a moral moron, having no conception of honour or integrity, gives a very poor imitation of it, a travesty that persons of real integrity and nobility of mind ought to have seen through very quickly. One cannot object to Othello falling into 'honest Iago's' trap once his emotions begin to cloud his judgement, shatter his trust and destroy his power to weigh evidence. But how did he ever come to think Iago 'honest' in the first place?

— Book XXII, 1981, pp. 9–10.

THE 'NOVEL OF IDEAS'

I have just come across the perfect comment on this department of literature. Carl Sagan, writing about the inadequacies of much Science Fiction says of Larry Niven's *Neutron Star*: 'We are asked too much. In a novel of ideas, the ideas have to work.' (*Broca's Brain*, p. 173.)

I wish I had thought of this when I dissected D. H. Lawrence's shoddy 'thought-adventure', *Kangaroo*. If the article is ever reprinted I must remember to quote Sagan as an epigraph.

It would of course apply to a much greater work like *Anna Karenina* but this illustrates another point. The ideas on which A. K. is supposed to depend are pretty shoddy too and they 'don't work'. But if one ignores them the book stands up in its own right. One does not have to accept Milton's theology in order to accept *Paradise Lost* as a *poem*. One does not, again, have to reject Mary Shelley's *Frankenstein* because its biology is out-dated to the point of absurdity. Its fable of human ingenuity and the dangers that that ingenuity may involve is not touched by the ignorance of particular scientific facts. One could say that Lawrence's almost total ignorance of political theories like Marxism and Fascism do not matter much. It is his own theory which fails him. It is so incoherent that one cannot say whether the 'ideas work' or not. As ideas they have no relevance to the real world. They belong to a private mythology of their author.

— Book XXII, 1981, pp. 17–18.

THOMAS HARDY'S POEMS

Yesterday I asked Jane Adamson what she was working on and she said she was looking into Hardy's poems to confirm a theory she had about them and would like to talk about her ideas.

As I have not read Hardy for half a century and could not recall any single poem except one of the *Satires of Circumstance*, I took down the volume before I slept in order to refresh my memory. I remember that when I read him I did not like his handling of verse; it seemed to me clumsy and gritty. But now I was appalled at his lack of ear, his clumsy inversions, his too obvious and often far-fetched rhymes dragged in and distorting the flow, the flatness of the language, nonetheless laced with tawdry poetical turns of phrase and sentimental clichés and above all by the sheer banality of the situations. It seems to me deliberate too.

— Book XXII, 1982, p. 75.

Notes

1. In 1912, it was decreed by Parliament that the workload of the High Court required seven justices to the Bench instead of five. Justice Piddington was appointed to the High Court Bench in 1913 but resigned one month later due to criticism centred on his abilities as a lawyer.
2. See Hope, *Chance Encounters*, p. 57, where he tranlates this: 'A hairy cunt fucks much better than a plucked one.' Hope also provides the following information: Roman prostitutes used to pluck their pubic hair thinking to make themselves more attractive.
3. John Le Gay Brereton (1871–1933) had a long association with Sydney University as a student, librarian and finally professor of English literature. His scholarship is evident in his work *Elizabethan Drama* (1948). He also wrote lyric poetry and two collections of essays, one of which told anecdotal stories connected with Christopher Brennan and Henry Lawson.
4. See Hope, *A Late Picking*, pp. 30–40, for the poem *The Countess of Pembroke's Dream*, which finds its source in Aubrey's story of Mary Pembroke and the stallions. The poem was published five years after this story was mentioned in his notebooks.
5. See Graves' controversial work *The White Goddess: A Historical Grammar of Poetic Myth*, which argues the existence of an all-important religion, originating in a remote past but continuing into the Christian era, based on the worship of a goddess; also see Hope, 'Professional Standards in Criticism: Yeats and Graves', in *A Book of Answers*, pp. 81–3, where Hope outlines the circumstances of Graves' attack on Yeats and why he was moved to 'answer' Graves from what he imagined would have been Yeats' perspective.
6. Norman Jeffares, Irish literary scholar and expert on Yeats.
7. Dorothy Green, (nee Auchterlonie) 1915–91, poet and literary critic, was an expert in Australian literature and was a close friend and colleague of Hope's at the Australian National University.
8. Martin Boyd (1893–1972) spent his childhood in Australia and was educated in Melbourne. His first three novels were published under the pen name Martin Mills. Although he used Australian characters in his novels, they were usually set entirely in England.
9. Yvor Winters (1900–68), an American poet, critic and academic at Stanford University whose attacks on such contemporary literary idols as T. S. Eliot and Henry James aroused much controversy. His collected poems were published in 1952. His last critical work, *Forms of Discovery: Critical and Historical Essays on the Forms of the Short Poem*, appeared in 1967.
10. The Persian poet Farid al-Din Muhammad ibn Ibrahim Attar (1145?–1221?) was a believer in Sufism, a form of Islamic mysticism. His most celebrated work was *Mantiq al-Tayr* (*The Conference of the Birds*), a poem consisting of 4,600 couplets. The poem uses allegory to illustrate the Sufi doctrine of union between the human and the divine.
11. This drawing was on the wall of Hope's office until the late 1980s in the A. D. Hope Building at The Australian National University.

12 A. A. Phillips was educated at Melbourne University and Oxford University. Phillips received attention in 1950 with his article 'The Cultural Cringe' in *Meanjin*, in which he is critical of Australians' tendency to be servile in the face of European culture. His book *The Australian Tradition* (1958), which consisted of a selection of his critical articles from *Meanjin* and *Overland*, established him as one of Australia's leading critics. He edited several books and wrote a critical work: *Henry Lawson* (1970). A. A. Phillips is the object of Hope's satire in *Dunciad Minor* (1970)

13 Oliver Sommerville was a Sydney poet contributing to journals such as *Arna* and *Hermes*. He was known as being politically and personally eccentric and for his impact on the life of the University of Sydney. Donald Horne was educated at the University of Sydney, worked as a reporter, editor and writer of numerous books. *The Lucky Country* (1964), a critique of Australian society, launched him into literary prominence. In 1972, he changed his political allegiance from a conservative one to one in which he became an ardent supporter of the Labor Party. Bill Pritchett was a senior public servant in the Defence Department.

14 John Reed (1901–81), although trained as a lawyer, became the President of the Contemporary Art Society, Melbourne, and founder and director of the Museum of Modern Art and Design of Australia in Melbourne. He, along with his wife Sunday, was one of the most influential proponents of modernism in Australian art. He was a prominent member of the Angry Penguins group and joint editor and publisher of *Angry Penguins*.

15 Translation of '*Lucidus ordo*', dependent on context, could range from 'path of illumination' to 'bright array'.

16 Alf Conlon was principal of the Staff College at Middle Head in Sydney.

17 Murray Todd was a colleague of Hope's; they taught together at Canberra University College. Hope dedicated his *A Book of Answers* to Todd, who died soon after taking the position of Chair of English at the University of Tasmania.

18 Gillian Guilford Young was the Archbishop of Tasmania during the 1960's.

19 Ted Stokes presumably was an academic in 1976; it has not been possible to secure any further information about him.

20 Ian Maxwell was a colleague of Hope's at Melbourne University.

21 Translation: When you are alone, then you are most yourself.

22 Rasselas (1759) was Johnson's only long fiction (originally published as *The Prince of Abyssinia: A Tale*). The tale explores and exposes the futility of the pursuit of happiness. Prince Rasselas, weary of life, escapes with his sister and the widely travelled poet Imlac, from the Happy Valley where they all are dissatisfied, to experience the world and make a thoughtful choice of life. Yet their journey is filled with disappointment and disillusion. They examine the lives of men in a wide range of occupations and modes of life in both urban and rural settings — rulers and shepherds, philosophers, scholars, astronomers, and a hermit. Johnson satirises the wish-fulfilling daydreams in which all indulge. His major characters resolve to substitute the 'choice of eternity' for the 'choice of life', and to return to Abyssinia (but not to Happy Valley) on their circular journey.

V

WHAT IS ART?

A. D. Hope, in his poetry and his criticism, is fascinated with the contemporary state of the arts. His favoured form of analysis is the use of analogy. The subsequent speculative arguments present varied modes of measuring and identifying the extent to which art has been corrupted by ideas and techniques of some modernist practitioners and critics. Although his interests extend to the visual and the musical, his prime focus is poetry, which he understands as 'a contemplative and creative activity concerned to bring into being a new order of nature and to maintain it'.[1]

In his earlier writings, there is much discussion on what marks a genius — a term that, in current times, has lost favour. Contemporary thought debunks the idea of 'the genius', which is now seen to belong to the obsolete canon that privileged white males of European descent. Hope believed, for example, that women could not achieve genius status while writing within an essentially male language. He discusses the manner in which a 'genius is creative in a genuine sense, and that the masterpieces of art constitute in themselves a new order of nature'.[2] Art at the highest level, he maintains, should achieve 'a new integration of vision, consciousness, awareness, revelation, [and] beauty'.[3] It is for that reason that he speaks of it as inspired and almost supernatural though necessarily human.

The question 'What is art?' involves querying also what it means to be an artist. He is bemused by what he sees as an expectation among young poets that they should have 'a "career" in poetry as though they were engineers or civil servants'.[4] Central to his inquiry into what constitutes a great work of art and the possible conditions that need to exist for an artist to create such work is his belief that theorising gets in the way of art. Nevertheless, poetry, he believes, has a metaphysical force because it has a power to present things 'under the aspect of eternity'[5] and acts as a 'forerunner and discoverer to philosophy proper', rendering perhaps an 'explorer's journal from where philosophy follows to make the maps'.[6] He argues throughout the notebooks that the 'sharp metrical and syntactical form of verse' might be limited in ways in which prose is not, but it is this limitation that gives it a brilliance of a kind denied to prose. And so, Hope writes, 'I am always running head on against the limitations of language and of imagination, but when a poem has emerged, has been struggled with and is now at last a finished object, it hardly ever seems to me to be an unachieved grasp at an unattainable or partly glimpsed idea. It is what it is: something new in the world, an achievement of something at one time, only half-glimpsed.'[7]

THE PHYSIO-CHEMICAL CLOCK

Children have sexual organs and sexual feelings and desires as I very well remember I have had from the age of five years or so. They are capable of falling deeply in love as I did at the age of eight, a passion of great intensity. During this period of life they engage in sexual play when taboos and prohibitions of their elders do not stop them. I only enjoyed the fantasies of sexual play. But until puberty they are, of course, unable to enter into the full use of their sexual powers or the full realization of what they can already to some degree fore-imagine. At a later stage of life, varying with each person, he or she loses these powers, while retaining full power to imagine, to recall and often to desire an experience no longer actually possible.

Is it absurd to suppose that the same may be true of other mental, spiritual and physical powers? Is there not a period of life before which creative energy and imagination are present but in a puerile form so that all that is possible to their possessor is a sort of creative play; and that there is a further period of life in which all that is possible is a more or less lively recall of past creative experience? Is this sort of thing perhaps true of the proper exercise of all gifts? Has each talent its own special ripening, adolescence, maturity and senility fixed by a physiological clock?

Mozart?
Pascal?
Rimbard?
Minou Drouet?

— Book IV, 1952–56, pp. 36–7.

POETRY, PRAYER AND TRADE

Dr Johnson held that the range of possible subjects for poetry was limited and that it had both an upper and a lower limit. In his life of Milton he argues that the soul's communion with God in prayer is above the proper reach of poetry. It is not that a prayer cannot be put into the form of a poem, but that the artifice and composition required to form a good poem are inconsistent with that entire submission of the mind and the heart to the sole object of prayer which the art of prayer essentially demands. For the essence of prayer is not supplication, confession, acknowledgement of grace, praise or contrition, but *attention*, a conscious opening of the heart to what it is to receive, a holding of the will towards union with a higher will which no act of the human will can achieve, no proposition of the mind or imagination can set before it as an object. The attitude of prayer is a stillness. Kneeling or prostrate. But poetry is David dancing before the sacred Ark. Dr Johnson's objections which have not usually been taken very seriously have therefore a real point, not limited to his main contention that prayer is too sacred, an activity above the level or reach of profane powers; poetry is a secular occupation: the communion of Man with his God belongs to another realm altogether.

At the other end of the scale poetry has a natural limit too. The remarks of Johnson on the success of *The Fleece*, in his life of Dyer, show that in his opinion trade and commerce were below this limit. What Johnson seems to argue for here is a special range of 'poetic' subjects, but one might extract the essential point, again, by saying that there is no reason why a poem should not be written about practical affairs of any kind. Johnson says that poetry has done her best to elevate the subject of the wool-trade to the level of poetry and has laboured in vain. He speaks of the poet as using all the writer's art of delusion and so on. It might seem to us that Dyer was simply on the wrong task. Had he treated the wool-trade simply, truthfully and without trying to inflate his subject, perhaps he might have succeeded. But I think that Johnson may have seen deeper. Commerce is a practical activity concerned to promote practical ends. Poetry is a contemplative and creative activity concerned to bring into being a new order of nature and to maintain it. A poem has no *use* in the narrower sense of the word, though it has *use* in the sense that we would not be without it. Its use is in being what it is, not in being a means to something else. Poetry can deal with the manufacture and merchandise of woollens as it can with the growing of wool — but not in the terms of commerce. It has no concern with instructing the artisan or promoting sales and profits, any more than a poem about a war is concerned with teaching future Trojans military strategy or justifying Greek aggression. Johnson stands for the view that poetry is concerned with the human and great poetry with that which explores the metaphysical condition of man, and trade, mechanics, cosmetic art and skill at games of chance are examples of trivial occupations in this sense. They have no metaphysical importance and to take them as a field of poetry except in satire, is to vulgarize poetry, to make it either trivial, if it tries to preserve its proper nature, or mean and ridiculous if it accepts the values of the province it takes as its subject.

For our own day there are two points of importance in this. One may argue in various ways, more or less convincing, against Johnson's actual reasons for believing that neither religion nor trade are proper subjects for poetry. He may be right, however. But he is certainly right in the implied general arguments: that poetry has its own field, its own methods and cannot without destroying itself, go beyond them. In our own day, poetry has neglected this in two ways. It has tried to become a sort of magic of thaumaturgy, pretending to work by supernatural or non human means. On the other side it has aimed at a 'realism' of a peculiarly vulgarizing kind, the so-called Social Realism in which it became a means of political processes and ceased to be an end in itself.

— Book IV, 1952–56, pp. 42–5.

WHAT IS A MASTERPIECE?

A masterpiece is that sort of work by which we distinguish genius and therefore it has the characteristics that set genius apart from mere talent however great. There is an absolute difference in kind between a masterpiece and a work of the greatest talent, and it has a quality or character as distinctive and as immediately recognizable as the distinction in quality or character between the gray and black and white range and the range of colours. This is a useful analogy because there are degrees of genius as there are degrees of talent. Those things which appear black and white and gray in works of art, for example, may resemble very closely those in colour and we can have every gradation between the faintest monochrome tinting of a drawing and the full range of saturated colours. Yet if we can say that the drawing is coloured at all, we cannot maintain that this is simply an extension of the black and white quality. It is a new quality, however faint and immediately distinguishes itself from all essays in black and white.

This quality or character peculiar to masterpieces exhibits itself in three ways which we can call Greatness of Conception, Mastery of Execution and Fertility of Invention.

Fertility of Invention is usually the first sign of genius and is probably inborn. It does not mean mere prodigality or inexhaustible variety, thought this is often so. As mastery in execution develops, indeed, this prodigality may not appear in the work at all, having been a feature only of the composition as in Dryden's admirable description of his processes of composition, in old age. Fertility is what we recognize as the sign of a special 'gift' for a particular art, the ornate aptness and intuitive grasp as well as the natural flow of ideas and an untaught impetus to creation. But above all fertility is shown by that natural freshness of invention which we call originality, the power to generate living forms, to animate old forms even more than to originate new. For novelty of invention is by no means an essential part of originality.

Mastery is based on fertility but [it] is the result of will and conscious effort. Without the inborn gift there can only be a high degree of skill or expertise but mastery implies more than this. By constant thought, constant practice, constant awareness of the whole range of qualities and skills required and the need to make them fuse or work to a common end the artist may achieve the perfection of all individual controls. The process of learning and unlearning has been well described in *Zen in the Art of Archery* by Eugen Herrigel. One day the master says to him: Just then it shot — meaning that the pupil had achieved the level of perfect skill at which it begins to pass over into real mastery. When one can say 'it shoots' a new sort of insight is added; resources unknown and unpredictable appear, treasures of imagination reveal themselves, almost as a by-product of the selfless and continual effort to perfect skills and techniques. The latent genius is made available to the man and he 'becomes himself' in a way he could not have foreseen. Whatever he attempts henceforth will have the signature of higher powers.

Greatness of Conception has nothing to do essentially with largeness of plan or scale. It is the power to present the slightest detail, the most trivial subject with *mastery*, to achieve a new character or quality from the combination of even the simplest elements. The character of 'vision' or illumination which even the smallest masterpiece possesses.

One may illustrate the difference between a masterpiece and a work of great talent and skill by an analogy. Walking in the Honqua Valley in Victoria one moves among great hills impressive in their size and beauty but for all that enormous hills and no more, though they are called mountains. Coming round a bend of the river one sees Mt Buller at the top of the valley, of much the same shape, the same composition and only a few hundred feet higher than its neighbours. But those few hundred feet make all the difference: for they pass the snow line and there is the fantastic beauty of the snow-capped mountain, perhaps, as I saw it, with the sun shining on a snow storm near the summit. In those few hundred feet we had moved into another world. The masterpiece is like that. It may be of the same materials, technique, subject, ideas, language as a dozen works similar to it, but because of the 'mastery' it moves into another climate of the mind; it achieves a new integration of vision, consciousness, awareness, revelation, beauty or whatever you like to call it. It is for that reason that we speak of it as inspired and indeed it has something superhuman about it, if only in the sense that a man must be of special gift and achieve a special emancipation from himself to achieve it. But it is not necessarily supernatural or 'from elsewhere': it is a perfectly human use of human powers to achieve something beyond the human: or perhaps put in another way it is the justification for the assertions, in a previous note in this book, that genius is creative in a genuine sense, and that the masterpieces of art constitute in themselves a new order of nature.

It would follow from this that we may expect to find several well-defined types of inferior artist all of whom go to make up the ranks of 'talent', as opposed to genius. There will be corresponding types of inferior works of art though not so well-defined, since different deficiencies in the artist may make for similar defects in the work. All recognize the sort of artist who shows great taste, often enormous skill, judgement and intelligence but without the slightest touch of 'fertility' or the inborn gift. His works are often mistaken for masterpieces by popular taste. Hence the temporary vogue of works which puzzle later generations by their lack of vitality. Everyone is acquainted too with the work of 'promise', where real fertility and gift are evident but mastery is lacking either for lack of skill, as in the work of young poets and painters, or because the skills, however great, have never achieved that point of vision of which one can say not a 'Shot', but a 'It shot in me', that moment at which all the various powers and faculties of the man achieve a harmonious fusion so that they act as one power, and in consequence the artist finds himself conscious of a new power which is released and created by his other powers only in this peculiar combination.

— Book VI, 1958–59, pp. 73–8.

POETRY AS POWER

The cause of the people is indeed but little calculated as a subject for poetry: it admits of rhetoric, which goes into argument and explanation, but it presents no immediate or distinct images to the mind … The language of poetry naturally falls in with the language of power. The imagination is an exaggerating and exclusive faculty: it takes from one thing to add to another: it accumulates circumstances together to give the greatest possible effect to a favourite object. The understanding is a dividing and measuring faculty: it judges of things not according to their immediate impression on the mind, but according to their relations to one another. The one is a monopolizing faculty, which seeks the greatest quantity of present excitement by inequality and disproportion; the other is a distributive faculty which seeks the greatest quantity of ultimate good by justice and proportion. The one is an aristocratical, the other a republican faculty. The principle of poetry is a very anti-levelling principle. It aims at effect, it exists by contrast. It admits of no medium. It is everything by excess. It rises above the ordinary standard of sufferings and crimes. It presents a dazzling appearance. It shows its head turreted, crowned and crested. Its front is gilt and bloodstained. Before it 'it carries noise, and behind it leaves tears'. It has its altars and its victims, sacrifices, human sacrifices … It puts the individual for the species, the one above the infinite many, might before right.

Hazlitt: Characters of Shakespeare's Plays: Coriolanus.

Superficially what nonsense this is; and how deeply and seriously true!
— Book IV, 1954 [excerpts in this book not paginated].

THE TASK OF ART

The theory of 'natural orders' of beings or of creation. The world before the coming of the plants, bare, magnificent, sterile. Then the plants clothe it as in Milton's description. An absolute creation at a higher level of beauty. So a view of the world before and after man shows the creation of a new level of life. The social life of man without the arts is like the world before the coming of the plants. The task of the poets, the composers, etc., is to change the face of the world by filling it with a new and higher order of creation — Sidney's point about the 'golden world'.[8] The imitative view of art has obscured this truth for more than two thousand years. The truth was briefly perceived in the hundred years from Blake to Pater. Now it has begun to be obscured again by 'social', 'psychological' or 'amusement' theories of art. Fuddled by these false views the great work of covering the bare world goes badly.

— Book V, 1957–58, p. 88.

METAPHYSICAL & PHILOSOPHICAL POETRY

That poetry which expresses or embodies philosophical views I call properly philosophical poetry. The poet may, like Dante or Lucretius or Pope, be using and giving expression to an existing philosophy to which he subscribes. He may be bent on celebration of these views in themselves. He then writes a 'philosophical poem' in the usual sense of the word. Such [a] one [is] the De Rerum Natura by Lucretius; another is Pope's *An Essay on Man*. Or he may have some other purpose, to describe the world, or men, to tell a story or create a fable and to illuminate his picture and to organize and relate its detail by setting it with the frame of a philosophic system, such are *Paradise Lost*, *The Divine Comedy* and perhaps *The Metamorphoses* and *The Aeneid*. Or again, the philosophical system may be of his own making. Such would be the Prophetic Books of Blake, *The Prelude* and *Prometheus Unbound*. These are all properly speaking *philosophical poems*. They aim at a coherent theory of the world, already accessible in philosophic terms and capable of explanation as a philosophic *system*.

I distinguish from such poetry what I call *metaphysical* poems, which form the poetry not of explanation and application but the poetry of revelation and exploration. It is the difference between what Johnson calls 'sudden astonishment' and what he calls 'rational admiration', the two things that for him characterize the intellectual effects of the sublime in poetry. When the mind and the heart are led to grasp the view from Mount Meriah or from other great peaks, when they stand still in wonder at a new realm of experience which in itself is a challenge to the systems of belief and emulation within which they have been accustomed to live, when these orders of ideas are suddenly illuminated or given a deeper or another meaning when seen in the light of some extension of knowledge, or from the vantage point of some new range of power to see, then the poetry which embodies this illumination is properly speaking *metaphysical*. It is that aspect of poetry which acts as the forerunner and discoverer to philosophy proper, it is the explorer's journal where philosophy follows to make the maps.

In one sense all good poetry is metaphysical in this meaning of the word and the simplest poems may be intensely metaphysical, without being in the least philosophical. And conversely all the great philosophical poems in so far as they are poetry — in so far as they enlarge the world and raise the level of experience — are bound also to be metaphysical. And few discoverers can resist the impetus to systematize, and explain, so that many of the fundamentally metaphysical poems are in this sense philosophical: Blake and Wordsworth and Rilke.

— Book V, 1957–58, pp. 89–92.

ESTHETICS

The word *esthetic* denotes simply a relation of feeling. When our feelings are organized in some permanent way towards an object we have an 'esthetic system' or a system of esthetics.

The esthetics of beauty is only one among many possible, some actual and competing systems of esthetics. Appreciation of a collection like *The Stuffed Owl*[9] depends on an esthetics of ugliness or absurdity in which we are able to establish a scale of 'perfection' and in which the best examples are exquisite and perfect in their kind as the best examples of true poetry are. We enjoy an exquisite felicity of absurd or monstrous statement in which the slightest alteration of word or phrase would reduce the enjoyment.

In general any of the feelings can have its own esthetic. It is because so many of them — social feelings, moral feelings, fear, love, religious feelings, hate and greed — have in fact their own 'esthetic' that most questions of standard and value in art are so confusing and so complicated.

Nevertheless while all the arts can admit, in fact cannot exclude, these other esthetic systems, that of beauty remains the 'gold-standard', as it were. Modern poetry may be said largely to have gone off the gold-standard and this is its fundamental weakness.

— Book V, 1957–58, pp. 105–6.

KINDS OF POETRY

Nearly all modern criticism takes for granted that there is one sort of thing called poetry, one essence or 'quidditas poetica'. This only appears to vary as its total effect is varied by the accidents of subject mode, metre and style. At bottom most of the quarrels of critical theory arise from this unguarded assumption, and most of the modern heresies in practice arise from an attempt to refine poetry from its accidents and distil the pure essence. I believe that the truth is the other way about. There are a number of poetries each with its own essence-related *per species et differenties*[10] as a single genus, but the genus or family is not a thing in itself, it is a method of classification, as insects can be classified into species and genera each of which is actually existing, but the family of insects is not itself represented by a group of creatures which we can call 'pure insect'.

In the same way there is a common name of love which applies to men and to women because it is the same sort of thing in each case but there is no example of love pure and undifferentiated. Man's love for woman and woman's love for man are different sorts of love because they are directed to different objects and for different ends and because they arise from different sorts of creatures in each case. A man and a woman are both members of the human race but there are no examples of a 'common' human being in the world. There are only men and women. In the same way the notion of pure poetry is a delusion. There are only multiple species of poetry, each with its own character arising from its specific form, epic, lyric, dramatic and so forth. The characters of these poetries are like those of men's love and women's love, irreducible in kind.

— Book VI, 1960, pp. 97–8.

METAPHYSICS AND POETRY

A man who has continually before him the vision of the world as a whole, the variety, complexity and mystery of the whole world of man, the sense of the past, the future and the present as one process, and the metaphysical questions that the whole world-picture raises, a man continually obsessed with the passion for a synoptic view, cannot write the slightest of poems on the most particular of themes without reflecting this ruling passion, perhaps quite unconsciously — perhaps the better the less deliberately. It is this that gives poetry which in itself is [neither] metaphysical [nor] even reflective, its metaphysical force, its power of presenting things under the aspect of eternity — though eternity may never be mentioned. It is a light, itself unseen, by which one sees, the quality of love or hate, or comprehension or wonder, which implies all the rest.

— Book VII, 1961, p. 21.

LIMITS OF CLARITY

Ce que l'on conçoit bien s'énonce clairement[11]

Sure! But oh the raw unprocessed, un-conceived world which the well-conceived finds ineffable! One has to be one of those writers who perform only within the circle of language, who remain therefore unaware of the limitations of language, not to come constantly against the ineffable in experience. What cannot be said for lack of names, what cannot be said because of lack of definition in nuances of feeling, what cannot be said because of singularity of experience, a problem not confined to the mystics — what cannot be said because of the complexity of total impression, a complexity not to be rendered by enumeration of its parts seriatim.[12] And yet in this difficult edge of the realm, the writer may be more interested than in rendering what oft was thought but ne'er so well expressed.

— Book VIII, 1961, p. 25.

D. H. LAWRENCE AND HUMANISM

Somewhere inside there is a great chagrin and a growing discontent. The body is, in its spontaneous natural self, dead or paralysed. It has only the secondary life of a circus dog, acting up and showing off: and then collapsing.

What life could it have, of itself? The body's life is the life of sensations and emotions. The body feels real hunger, real thirst, real joy in the sun or the snow, real pleasure in the smell of roses or the look of a lilac bush; real anger, real sorrow, real love, real grief. All the emotions belong to the body and they are only recognized by the mind. We may hear the most sorrowful piece of news, and only feel a mental excitement. Then, hours after, perhaps in sleep, the awareness may reach the bodily centres, and true grief wrings the heart.

D. H. Lawrence

How true this is [in] one sense, as a description of a certain kind of dissociation that accompanies a certain kind of education. And yet what a sad and 'ironical confession'. For Lawrence obviously feels that he has escaped this, he is back in the real world and *Lady Chatterley's* is its scripture. Incidentally, a number of the writers who testified on behalf of the book in the court action gave themselves away just as Lawrence has here.

Yet one has only to reflect for an instant to see that Lawrence is hopelessly entangled in what he despises. What is this body that feels real emotions which the mind can only recognise and not share at all? What is this mind which lives only in a set of substitute feelings or simulacra of feelings, and which at times 'connives' at the profound emotion called 'belief' which is an emotion of the body? They are recognizable symptoms of a psychological dissociation of the one thing that should feel and think, into two impotent entities. Except in the realism of mental pathology, these entities of body and mind are fictions, convenient ways of talking about two aspects of one functioning creature which thinks and feels as one process, creative as responsive. It is kinder to Lawrence to imagine him incurably dissociated: the alternative is to place him among those who take this view of mind because they have not enough of it to know what mental life is really like.

— Book VII, 1961, pp. 95–6.

INTELLIGIBLE REFERENCE

One of the problems of writing is that of a common world of intelligible reference which one can share with the readers: the solidity of past literature is partly a result of its limited world, and partly of its coherently organized world. To take not merely the Western world but the English-speaking world today is to take a vast amorphous series of sub-societies in which few people can share the experiences that make reference valid and meaningful.

Teaching university students I have found that if Keats were writing the *Ode to the Nightingale* today he could not rely on his readers knowing what was meant by Bacchus and his pards, they often have not only not read the Bible but have even no idea who Ruth was and why her heart should be sad amid the alien corn.

The resources on which a poet can depend are becoming more and more impoverished and poetry that aims at any sort of general appeal is forced to be superficial. Faced with this dilemma I think there is nothing for a poet to do but to write with all the resources at his command — ignoring his actual readers. But he cannot afford to ignore all readers. In this direction lies the crankiness and sterility of solipsist art — the madman inventing his own language or giving way to the dictation of angels. The modern practice seems to be to write for an audience of other poets — this has its dangers too as has the alternative — writing for an academic audience whose interests are primarily critical and historical. Nor is it wise to invent an imaginary set of readers. They tend to be the stooges of the poet's wishes. One needs a *real* audience with a real reaction and a real and independent assessment, but an audience not professionally concerned with poetry. My own recourse is to write for a roughly selected group of literate people — the group is never consciously or specifically selected, and I often have different people in mind when writing different poems. But it is an awareness of a fairly large number of real people of widely differering tastes.

— Book VII, 1961, pp. 97–8.

PRIVATE AND PUBLIC POETRY

One often sees critical comments that imply that there are two distinct kinds of poetry, but there is no clear distinction and a man may write for himself alone, for an audience of one or two or three or for everyone. He may express his own feelings or ideas with the purpose of communicating them to others, he may write to express public views and sentiments for any number of persons, any group or his generation as a whole or he may simply create and express views which seem to him interesting or beautiful, or indeed repulsive or indifferent. And there may be any combination of these. He is under no obligations in such matters. He may write if he pleases at the invitation of angels like Blake or Rilke, though he does so at a risk. A poem does not necessarily speak for anyone; it speaks in the first instance for itself.

Nevertheless a poem to be intelligible must take into account the range of reference that its readers can be expected to take up from their experience and poetry may be regarded as more 'public' the wider the range of experience it assumes, as more personal or private, the fewer the number of persons who share in the experience called on in the poem. A purely private poem might be one which uses reference known only to the writer himself. He can make it public by explaining but he may treat it if he wishes as if everyone already shared his private associations and will then produce a perfectly lucid and coherent poem which is exactly the opposite in appearance.

Most love poetry for example is public poetry in the sense that it refers to parts of experience of love which are common to most lovers. One could write a love poem which was private in the sense that its frame of reference was to events and experiences shared only by the poet and the other party. If [Hanral Quais — semi-legible] for example instead of describing how he enjoyed his mistress through the wall of the tent while she suckled her baby, had referred to these peculiar circumstances, only she would have known what he was talking about but it would not have been a worse poem for that or a really obscure one. It would only have seemed so in the way that certain passages in poems of past ages or other civilisations may seem obscure until we look up the notes.

(If I were conducting a school for poets I would make my pupils at some stage write a purely private poem in this sense and then invite them to rewrite it as a public poem. In this way they could more easily come to know the limiting conditions of their craft.)

— Book VII, 1961, pp. 185–7.

ARISTOTLE'S TWO RACES

Men better or worse than they actually are: to represent them in one way or the other is the object of fiction, that is drama or narrative poetry. It soon becomes clear in the Poetics that this is a class distinction rather than a moral one. Those whose education has given them the opportunity to achieve the possibility of human development will be the better sort of men, fully human, in the full possession of their powers, intellect, and moral and social potential. The rest are the comic. Those in whom a lower grade of social education and natural surroundings together with the need to spend most of their time in toil, live unfitted and retarded. They remain distorted, incomplete, not fully human. (The *Politics* must be brought in to supplement the *Poetics* at this point.) Corresponding to these are two kinds of literature, Serious and Comic. There appears to be no kind of literature which represents men just as they are, that is of mixed kind on both sides of the social division of upper and lower classes. The convention is continued in literature for the next two thousand years or so, in spite of the Christian revolution which tries to look at all people as morally responsible and morally adult, and at the perfection of man's nature as out of this world.

The great gift of the novel was that it found a way of showing people as they actually are, capable of being serious and comic at once, though there is still an element of the two races in the novel tradition. On the other hand the novel for this very reason tends to exclude one sort of truth, a poetic truth which is realized in rare individuals. The novel has less metaphysical possibilities than poetry or poetic drama.

— Book VIII, 1964–65, p. 6.

BASENESS AND FORCE

Thinking of Fielding as a dramatist who found himself in the novel, I find myself also thinking that, looked at in another way, he could be regarded as a dramatist *manqué*. From this to a consideration of novelists like Henry James and Conrad who abuse the novelist's privilege of 'setting' by leaving no explanation and no interpretation un-suggested.

A play tells us less than a novel, whether it is the actor or the reader who has to deal with the text. There is dialogue and stage-direction and that is all. The dialogue first of all: what people say and the way they say it. From this we must get our notion of action, of situation, of character, of inner thoughts and inner life and we can do it very well. A good play abstracts the essentials of human nature and human action and is a more excellent esthetic device than a good novel.

But a good poem extracts the essence of this abstraction. It is metaphysical, where a play is a human abstract, and a novel by contrast is a mere psychological and social reconstruction.

— Book VIII, 1964–65, p. 18.

THE COMIC AND THE TRAGIC
(FURTHER THOUGHTS)

The distinction between comedy and tragedy which I have drawn in my essay on *All For Love*[13] is perhaps not a particularly important one for fiction or for drama, though it may be basic. For poetry however it is not only basic but essential. Without some such view of human affairs poetry is bound to be either confused or trivial.

For this reason verse drama by the very nature of its medium demands a tragic or a comic treatment.

The majority of great poetry inclines to the tragic view, ie., [it] finds significant only those aspects of human life and human nature in which the human at its height is put to supreme tests of its nature. The poet starts from the unspoken assumption of the most complete human nature, the noble outlook, the unquestioned acceptance of the highest values and the implicit offering of mind and heart to the ultimate tests. More than this he prefers the larger world opened by the tragic; in a phrase of Rilke's about Louise Labe 'elle lui prometterait la douleur comme un univers aggrandi'.[14]

— Book VIII, 1964, p. 41.

THE TWO BRAINS

A number of languages have two words for the specifically human ways of knowing, one as meaning to know something, the other to know about something, 'to know' and 'to know how'. This corresponds to a real division of function. There are already two sorts of education to train for these functions and perhaps two kinds of brain to carry them out. In the one set of activities the man must carry all he knows in his head. He is more efficient if he does and in some cases, as with a musician he cannot function till he can carry all he needs to know with him. In the other case the sheer amount of knowledge required is too much. It is the accumulation of the work of many brains and of many generations of brains. What the user needs is not knowledge in his head but the knowledge of where and how to look for it. Most of the actual knowledge is more profitibly stored somewhere else than in his head.

Brought to these reflections by the fact that I am so crippled, writing the simplest poem on a ship where there is no library except a few novels, I feel ashamed. A poet should carry it all in his head, otherwise his contrivances are suspect — cookery not conception!

— Book VIII, 1965, p. 56.

POETRY AND PROSE

Dryden spoke in his old age on a choice between expressing himself in verse or in the other harmony of prose, and no doubt he was right up to a point. Each has its own harmony — its peculiar structure, each is an art. But there is an essential difference, such that what can be done in one is peculiar to that medium and cannot be done in the other, and the superior effects, I like to believe belong to poetry.

Thinking of the essential difference I have come to conclude that it is not easily expressed though it is clear enough. I can best express it by the analogy of mineral and other substances which may exist in an amorphous or in a crystalline form. 'Amorphous' is not to be thought of as a sneer. It means that prose can be used and manipulated in many ways which the sharp metrical and syntactical form of verse will not allow. But if verse is more limited by its superior order it is capable, by virtue of that order of a brilliance and an impact that prose can never reach.

— Book VIII, 1964–65, p. 73.

SCULPTURE

A remark in a detective novel about a sculptor suddenly makes me think — I suppose I've thought of it before, but never as clearly — how little variety sculptors have in their material compared with the other arts. It is almost entirely confined to the human body and it depends very largely on the human face. In other words the sculptor *starts* with the knowledge that he has a few clichés from which he must find endless variety and originality. He is not even allowed to improvise very much or to modify past a certain point since he cannot afford to lose recognizable resemblance beyond a certain point. Whatever the cranks may say the thing about 'abstract' sculpture, significant form in itself, is that it does not signify anything much and cannot continue to satisfy. The sculptor is like a writer condemned to find variations on a single theme, a composer with a single air, and knowing that all the other writers or composers are in the same boat. The discipline of this must be tremendous, but the intensity of the esthetic impulse must be equally so. Imagine spending one's whole life writing poems on the same subject!

— Book VIII, 1965, p. 98.

LEONARDO'S TWO RACES, I

The classification of human types offers endless variety and pleasure. One is that which divides men into those who are only complete when alone — Leonardo's '*quando tu sei solo, tu sei tutto tuo*'[15] — and those who are only complete when in company with others — Bradley's theory that consciousness is a product of social life — I know a number of people who are restless, unhappy and even subject to neurotic terrors if forced to be alone for long. For such people the punishment of solitary confinement was destructive as the Goncourts argued in *La Fille Elisa* (?).[16] But for others, Leonardo or the man in the Cambridge scientific expedition who spent half a year alone and most of it in complete darkness under the ice, being alone has no terrors and in fact is a necessary thing. If I have to spend too long without being alone for long stretches of time, I become restless, feel myself disintegrating, aimless and in a sense no longer my own person.

As usual with men, each party tries to turn a natural fact into an obligation for which a morality is invented. For the gregarious there is the immorality of solitude; for the solitaries their contempt for the company addicts. In either case there is no justification: 'One law for the ox and the lion is oppression.'[17]

In terms of human ecology the two types are not completely distinct since it is rare to find even the most gregarious not enjoying a moment alone or the most solitary not feeling some need of pleasure which human company can supply. Moreover the two species have a complementary function each to the other in society, the gregarious happily performing those tasks which can be done only in company; the solitaries those which can only or best be done alone. There are many intermediate types between the extremes.

The conditions of primitive life suggest that the completely gregarious are the original type and that the solitary man has developed slowly, with difficulty and is still comparatively rare and not yet 'accepted' as a natural sub-species.

— Book VIII, 1965, pp. 121–8.

CAN IT HOLD?

In 1821 Thomas Love Peacock[18] said that poetry belonged to the barbarous ages of human society and that it was now maintaining a precarious hold in a world in which it had become obsolete except as a trivial amusement. It was an ominous pronouncement and had never been made in the world before, though Giambattista Vico[19] had hinted at it. Poetry in the past had been denounced as immoral or mischievous but no one had doubted that it was an important part of man's world.

In spite of Shelley's defence, Peacock seems more and more to have society on his side and as I try to write in verse I have more and more often the feeling that I am practicing an obsolete art like flint-knapping or water divining. Still it is the only thing I can do and all I really want to do.

— Book X, 1968, p. 73.

A SLOGAN FOR THE POETS

Unacknowledged legislators of the world unite! You have nothing to lose but your crystal balls!

— Book X, 1968, p. 11.

IMITATIONS AND EXPERIMENTS

Anything written in an older style or the manner of another age and place is apt to be treated either as parody or pastiche. But there is a clear and important difference between imitation in this sense and experiment such as a poet may choose to make in writing his own poem in another style than one habitual to him. The familiar topic of literary competition games such as those in the *New Statesman* — how Pope would have written *Come into the Garden, Maud* or *The Waste Land* — or even Pope's *Epistle to Augustus*, belong to one kind of imitation. Here the poet aims at writing not only in the manner of another but the sort of poem the other would have written. In the other sort of poem the writer wants to write his own poem from his own point of view, but wants to experiment with another style in doing so, because he feels it more appropriate to the theme or the feeling of his poem. The first is more like wearing historical costume to a fancy-dress ball, the second more like enlisting in the army of a foreign country and wearing its uniform. In the one you are pretending for the fun of it, in the other you are seriously trying to learn another language [other] than your own and to use it for a serious purpose. Writers are so commonly self-regarding that we have forgotten that a poem can be dramatic in the sense that an actor enters into his part. For the time being he will practice the art of being someone else. A bad actor will either be himself in the fancy dress of another personality or he will adapt that other personality to his own. A good actor will find in himself the true qualities and feelings to bring the part he plays to life. He neither abdicates nor adapts: he is at once himself and that other re-lived in himself. There is a kind of poetry that corresponds to this. The following two poems[20] are a sort of groping towards such a kind of *dramatic* poetry, which is also [as] sharply distinct from ordinary 'dramatic' poetry of the stage or

Browning's Dramatic Monologues as it is distinct from parody and pastiche.

I have decided to call them rôles or migrations.

— Book XII, 1971, pp. 58–60.

NOVELS

The reasons I read very few novels:
1. I might very well die before I got through all that conversation — then I should reproach myself for not having spent my time better.
2. I have more than enough conversation anyway — a reason, perhaps why I prefer older types of narrative where most of the story is in fact compact narrative.

Thrillers are different. I read a lot of them. They keep moving and the conversation is part of the action — as in the *Odyssey*.

Most novels are like a game of hide-and-seek: either the hiding places are too obvious and the game is a bore, or they are too difficult so that one loses interest in what is, after all, only a game.

— Book XIII, 1972, p. 70.

THE EMOTION OF POETS

There is a common delusion that poets are very emotional people — filled with powerful feelings which overflow in the passion and energy of their verses — Wordsworth's Damburst Theory of Poetry …

There is no substance in this; it is moreover a dangerous delusion that swamps many a young poet at the start. Poets do deal largely in emotion; they work in it as their material, or part of their material; they create new emotion in the sense that 'the emotions *in* the poem' — part of the material — are quite different from the 'emotions of the poem' — the esthetic effect.

For this reason [alone] they must remain rational men, not carried away by emotion but organizing and controlling it. The delight of creation and invention is their proper emotion and this must be in control of all the other feelings.

At the same time a poet is a man like other men subject to the same experiences and feelings and these are the sources of his material in the first instance. Emotion can only be observed by being felt and without the 'laboratory within', no poet can get to know his material. But this a very different thing from 'letting her rip' as Huck Finn says, and thinking the result is poetry.

It is a very common mistake of our own time and results in a great deal of emotional vomit published as poetry. This is not important *Canis rediritia vomiten suan*,[21] but if anyone else indulges in this perverse pleasure he at least knows that it is vomit. A more insidious result is the sort of book of poems which is mere reportage on emotions — the poet's or someone else's — what I call 'poetic journalism' — it is distinguished from real poetry by the fact that it reports feelings without eliciting their music, without making from this material a work of poetry capable of generating its own emotion.

As if hot on the heels of this, in a witless book on present day Brazilian poetry, I come on the translation of a poem by the poet whom a critic with the improbable name of Darcy Damasceno claims as the greatest of the Modernists — a stupid claim in any case since these Modernists go in for nonsense like

    Cie
        lo
            azul

— Book XIV, 1972, pp. 19–21.

ALEXANDER BLOK ON POETS

I recall that Alexander Blok said a poet should have a destiny, not a career.

    Alexander Toardovsky, reported in Pravda, May 12th, 1963

Get Blok's own words!

It is at any rate something everyone forgets today: the young poets expect to have a 'career' in poetry as though they were engineers or civil servants. And society, though grudgingly, approves and provides the hand-outs. As a result the jungle of mere talent has become so dense that genius is lost as it emerges — or worse, chooses a career, takes the path of promoting a talent and ends on a *fausse piste*[22] and necessarily so — because a 'career' implies a path already laid down and genius is stultified if it does not choose its own path. (This does not mean, as so many 'wild' artists think that genius does not have to learn to know the ordinary paths or that it must break with all tradition. 'Wild artists' are mostly small talents trying by mechanical means to simulate genius or turn themselves into geniuses.)

— Book XIV, 1972, pp. 63–4.

TWO VIEWS OF POETRY I

Rosemary [Dobson] has just called to see me with the preface to her new volume of 'Selected Poems'. I am surprised to see how different the writing of a poem is for her and for me. I had imagined we were rather alike in this respect. But she tells her readers:

> … there is always something that eludes one. I hope it will be perceived that the poems presented here are part of a search for something only fugitively glimpsed; a state of grace which one once knew, or imagined, or from which one was turned away. Surely everyone who writes poetry would agree that this is part of it — a doomed but urgent wish to express the inexpressible.[23]

Yes and no! And more *no* than *yes* in my own case. I am often aware of the ghost of the poem I tried to write or might have written, behind the one that ultimately stands on the paper. I am always running head on against the limitations of language and of imagination, but when a poem has emerged, has been struggled with and is now at last a finished object, it hardly ever seems to me to be an unachieved grasp at an unattainable or partly glimpsed idea. It is what it is: something new in the world, an achievement of something at one time, only half-glimpsed. 'Gesang ist Dasein!'[24]

It is curious that Rosemary whose poems are so clear, so realized and definite should think her readers might share her view of them as

Fallings from us, vanishings,
Blank misgivings of a creature
Moving about in worlds not realized,

in respect of the poem itself. Of course there are always 'unseen presences' but they are only there in virtue of a poem that is realized enough to make us aware of them.

— Book XV, 1973, pp. 31–2.

FISHHOOKS OF RHYME

In the process of a poem one is often at a stand for a rhyme and one will run over those that come to mind and even consult a rhyming dictionary, if that does not serve. But I have learned to take this slowly and mostly not always to take the first suitable rhyme that comes to hand. It is better to let them all dangle for a while baited with the general idea of what one wants to say and to see what fish will come to the hooks. It is often rewarding that the poem is enriched with unexpected treasure from the abyss.

This, as shrewd old Samuel Daniel saw, is one of the great advantages of Rhyme:

> And indeed I have wished there were not that multiplicite of rymes as is used by many in Sonnets, [including Sam himself] which yet we see in some so happily to succeed, and both been so farre from hindering their inventions, as hath begot conceit beyond expectation, and comparable to the best inventions of the world: For sure in an eminent spirit whome Nature hath fitted for that mysterie, Ryme is no impediment to his conceit, but rather gives him wings to mount, not out of his course, but as it were beyond his power to a farre happier flight.[25]

I should like to think that I was one of Sam's eminent spirits but at any rate I am sure that Nature has 'fitted me for that mystery' — what a poem in itself the phrase is! — and fishing for conceits is a greater pleasure to me than the sort carried on on riverbanks and shores. Of course both kinds of fishing sometimes end with 'a wet arse and no fish', as the enthusiasts of the sport put it.

— Book XV, 1974, pp.135–6.

DREAM-WORK AND POETRY

All the attention I have been giving lately to the process of dreaming rather than to the content of dreams, leads me to reflect on the difference of dream-work and poetic composition, though it is the more obvious resemblances that are usually noticed.

In the first place the dream-work is comparatively flimsy, however effective it may be in creating an illustration of reality — its mise en scène lacks coherence and continuity when examined by the waking mind. Its symbolism, as Freud noted, is often arcane and the connection between image and deeper meaning quite arbitrary and personal. Or on the other hand, as Jung noted, it tends to be tediously general, unimaginatively repeating a set of ancient clichés, which he dignified with the term 'archetypal images'. Like bad poetry it tends to putty the cracks in its construction with emotion out of proportion to the subject or even quite irrelevant to it.

Good poets vary in the amount of dream-work in their poems, but they always organise and re-work it. Bad poets give it to you raw, trusting the emotional confidence trick to get you to swallow it.

But the second thing is that poetry cannot come into being without using the dream-workers. Their contribution is the essential stuff of which poetry is fashioned even if they are not much good at fashioning it. Try to avoid them or despise them and you end up producing mechanical, flawless verse which is obviously no more than that.

Notes

1. Hope, Book IV, 1952–56, pp. 42–5.
2. Hope, Book VI, 1958–59, pp. 73–8.
3. Ibid., p. 75.
4. Hope, Book XIV, 1972, pp. 63–4.
5. Hope, Book VII, 1961, p. 21.
6. Hope, Book V, 1957–58, p. 91.
7. Hope, Book XV, 1973, pp. 31–2.
8. See Sidney, 'Defence of Poesie', p. 4, where Sidney, after having proclaimed that 'There is no art delivered unto mankind that hath not the works of nature for his principal object', and having explored how it fares in the hands of the astronomer, the geometrician, the musician, the lawyer, the historian, the physician and the metaphysic, declares: 'Only the poet, disclaiming to be tied to any such subjection, lifted up with the vigour of his own invention ... nature never set forth the earth in so rich tapestry as diverse poets have done; neither with so pleasant rivers, fruitful trees, sweet-smelling flowers, nor whatsoever else may make the too-much-loved earth more lovely; her world is brazen, the poets only deliver a golden.'
9. *The Stuffed Owl* is an anthology of bad verse selected by D. B. Wyndham Lewis and Charles Lee.
10. Translation of '*per species at differenties*': 'common and differentiating characteristics' (in logic as much as in botany).
11. Translation: What one conceives well expresses itself clearly.
12. Translation of '*seriatim*': 'point by point' or 'taking one item after another in a regular order'.
13. See Hope, *The Cave and the Spring*, pp. 144–63, where this article appears under the title 'All for Love, or Comedy as Tragedy'.
14. Translation of Rilke's comment: She would promise him sorrow on a grand scale.
15. Translation: 'When you are alone, then you are most yourself.'
16. The novel *La Fille Elisa* was written by Edmond Louis Antoine Huot de Goncourt in 1877 (translated Elisa, 1959). Hope seems to be under the impression that this book was written in concert with his brother Jules, but Jules died in 1870. Before, his death, he worked on a number of projects, including six books, four of which were novels of the naturalist school with his brother Edmond; their work is said to have paved the way for naturalism and impressionism.
17. See William Blake, *Visions of the Daughters of Albion*, Stanza 23: 'And is there not one / law for both the lion and the ox? / And is there not eternal fire, and eternal chains / To bind the phantoms of existence from eternal life?'
18. Thomas Love Peacock (1785–1866) was a novelist and poet. His novels were satirical romances and, although he published three volumes of verse, they are considered of less interest than his prose. He was an intimate friend of Shelley's and was his executor.
19. Vico Giambattista (1668–1744), Italian philosopher of cultural history and law, who is recognised today as a forerunner of cultural anthropology, or ethnology.

20 In the notebooks there are three poems, rather than the specified two Hope indicated, that follow this entry. They are (i) *Eyes and Tongues (Migration I)*; (ii) *Autolycus and Arsinfe (Migration II)* and (iii) *Friday's Child (Migration III)*.
21 Translation: The dog returns to its own vomit (so a fool returns to his folly).
22 Translation: False path.
23 See Rosemary Dobson, *Selected Poems*, 'Introduction', p. i.
24 Translation: Song of Being.
25 See Samuel Daniel, the 'Defense of Rhyme', 1662, in which he maintained, in reply to Thomas Campion's 'Art of English Poesy', the fitness of the English language for rhymed verse.

VI

SOURCE OF HIS POETRY

Hope seemed to be always on the lookout for a launching pad for his poetic vision, whether in letters from friends, newspaper articles or the odd quote he came across in his readings. The titles of his entries and the titles of his poems provided in the bibliography will demonstrate how often what began as an idea in the notebooks finally found itself expressed in a poem.

What is interesting is the diversity of these 'ideas'. A letter from a friend and fellow poet demanding reasons for Hope's silence elicits a poem from him offering not only the reasons requested but a satirical treatment of Australian literature. Readers will decide the extent to which Hope transgresses sensitive areas of race, class and gender. A discovery that the nightingale, pivotal for Keats' poem and for the tradition of European poetry, behaves other than the poets had supposed, gives Hope cause to demand a respect for 'truth'.[1] Receiving a letter from Rosemary Dobson that expressed her concern that her interest in Pausanias's descriptions was becoming an obsession, Hope responds with a poem. Noting that Auden wrote a poem attacking A. E. Housman in a vicious and personal way, Hope takes on Housman's persona and responds to the attack.[2] And reflecting on a display of modern art at the Guggenheim Museum in New York, Hope plans 'the judgment of Solomon Guggenheim' in verse; the works in question are presumably to be torn in two.

What do these excerpts tell us about Hope as an artist? Hope often writes about how poetry should 'create new being' and 'should create new values'.

It is evident that when Hope chooses to enter into an idea as an actor to test its assumptions, he does so with preconceived beliefs about the role of a creator. Consequently, he is preoccupied with the processes and methods of poetic composition. One becomes aware when reading the notebooks that he is laying down rules of conduct for the writer. Hope does see himself as an arbiter of taste and 'truth'.

He believes, for example, that when creating a symbolic world there should be a respect for 'facts' apparent in the external world. He will take writers to task if he decides they have behaved reprehensibly.

Hope tells us constantly that knowledge is provisional and that we cannot name the ultimate truth; nevertheless, he asserts that sources of truth and magic lie at the heart of biblical stories and ancient mythology. He surprises us, given his respect for rationality, when he says that supernatural events may not be discounted rationally. It is in this context of the irrational that he maintains that blind choices determine our destiny as much as those we make deliberately, and that dreams are a rich source of poetic vision and composition.

Hope's territory is one of paradox. If there is a problematic relationship between art and 'reality', between fact and fiction, between artistic licence and scientific fact, between choice and determinism, between artistic control and unconscious forces, Hope has it all ways.

EPISTLE TO V. B. ESQUIRE

My dear brother Vin,[3]
(Thus to begin
And hang a new pelt on
The bones of Skelton)
You wish to know why
I do not reply;
And I wish to declare —
Nay, more — I shall swear,
Under the eye of God,
I was not in quod;
Took no nasty poxes
From no dirty doxies
In my Equinoxes;
I was not too drunk

*And no wily monk
Lured me into La Trappe
Honi sori to the chap
Who thinks that sort of crap
Puts Hope off the map!
It was not, as you guess,
Any Idleness;
Nor was it the press
Of quorum and committee;
The Truth, more's the pity,
Is — let it be said —
The Bard was in Bed
With a pair of fat Muses
From whom I took bruises,
Contusions and whacks.
The Beast with Two Backs
Is a fine game to play;
But to roll in the hay
With two ladies at once —
— A pair of sweet c..ts
They undoubtedly were,
But a vigorous pair
And immortals to boot —
Well the root-a-toot-toot
Might keep any bard mute
(As I hope you agree)
Let alone me.
Still I wasn't too bad;
And a good time was had
By all; and they claim
That I died pretty game,
Which is more, they admit,
Than the rest of Aust. Lit.
Deserves said of it.*

*They say: 'We have tried
Local bards far and wide,
All crowing like roosters,
But bloody poor woosters.*

Such eunuchs and pansies
Are not what we fancies:
We like a Thing mansize.
Well, we started with Homer
And gave his a diploma.
All poets since then
Have been upstanding men;
Night and day they were at it;
While they raised half a fat, it
Was then Nature's Law, sir;
Not a bard could withdraw, sir!
From Homer to Chaucer,
From Chaucer to Browning,
They were upping and downing.
No Muse, on to Eliot
Ever lacked a great belly; it
Was downing and upping
And treading and tupping
And breeding and pupping;
All the bards did us over
And we were in Clover!

But here our research
On the rod, pole or perch
Of the bards of Australia
Has ended in failure.
Among these Dinkum Digs,
These Malthusian prigs,
These prim self-abusers,
These slip-rail seducers,
These marsupial prudes,
These epicene nudes,
These Didgery doosters,
These Marxian boosters,
'Have-beens' and 'Once-useters',
Not a Thing that will stand
In the whole Wide Brown Land!
Not a Muse up the spout!
We have proved, beyond doubt,

*And must state it perforce
(Though we hate to be coarse)
That the Aust. Lit. Prickle
Don't even tickle.
If it weren't for yourself
We'd be quite on the shelf,
And James P. McAuley
(A ram that taps brawly)
And last and most luckily
We found Vincent Buckeley.
Now there was a feast!
What a Bard! What a Beast!
One poet at least
Who will futter and utter
Not just fiddle and mutter*
....
*And our judgement will stand:
He has hair on his chest,
He is not like the rest
All flower and no root;
His stalk will bear fruit
When he started to stuff
We were soon up the duff,
And as soon, be it said,
We were both brought to bed
Of the best bloody book
Since Captain James Cook
Touched New Holland's strand.
For the rest of your land:
Let the Jindyworobaks
Chuck it back to the blacks!'*
    signed (sine dato)
    <u>Polyhymnia, Erato</u>

*And this, my dear Vin,
Is the god's truth — don't grin! —
For my long silent season
And also the reason
I refused Mr Pringle.*

As I sat in my ingle
Reviewing Young Vin,
These Muses came in,
Not wearing a stitch,
On tit, tail or snitch,
A-wagging their bums
And read my poor crumbs
Saying: 'This will not do;
We shall write the review.'

So I sent it to you.
Verbatim I quote it
As the goddesses wrote it.
....
Best of luck anyhow;
My regards to the boys;
Keep yourself in good voice;
Drink my health at the pub;
F… the Bread-and-Cheese Club
....
My respects to the Pope,
Vox vobiscum
yours

Hope.

(Part of a draft of Skeltonics sent to Vin. B. in 1955 as a reply to his pained inquiry why I had not agreed to review his book of poems in the *Sydney Morning Herald* and why I had not answered any of several letters he had written me. Keep this part of the letter as material for a hilarious attack on Australian Literature and all that parochial nonsense, when I have occasion for it.)
    August 1960

— Book VI, 1960, pp. 75–81.

GUGGENHEIM

I had heard a great deal about this controversial piece of architecture. When I saw it at last it seemed hardly to deserve so much discussion, a rather heavy commercial looking building in itself but an original idea for housing pictures. It obviously cost an immense amount of money. What I was not prepared for were the contents. Apart from a small loan exhibition of French impressionists, a collection of early Picassos, huddled in a sort of *vermi* form appendix to the main body, the whole immense shell was devoted to toys and scribbles of such triviality that I could hardly credit that it was a serious exhibition.

It will be interesting in a hundred years' time to hear critics explaining this gigantic hoax or auto-hallucination. Still, I came away very cheerful with the idea of a poem to be called: *The Judgement of Solomon Guggenheim*.

— New York, 1967
— Book IX, 1967, p. 65.

MORE HORSEPLAY

The Thelpousans call the goddess a Fury, and Antimachus (Author of the last epic *Thebais*) confirms this name in his poem on the *Argive* expedition against Thebes; the verse is: *at the Throne of Demeter the Fury* ... the goddess got her title of Fury because when Demeter was wandering in search of her child, they say Poseidon followed her lusting to couple with her, so she changed herself into a mare and grazed among the mares belonging to Apollo's son: But Poseidon saw how she tricked him and coupled with Demeter in the form of a stallion. At the time Demeter was very angry about what had happened though later she got over her wrath ...

Pausoniss Book 8

I wish I had read this before I wrote *The Countess of Pembroke's Dream*. It would have added another dimension again. Too late: the poem is actually printing at this moment. Actually it was in the past and arrived at breakfast next morning.

— 8 June, 1972
— Book XIII, 1972, p. 81.

PHILOMELA

I have just learned from the encyclopedia that the nightingale sings at any time of the day or night and only in the few weeks after its arrival from migration while mating, nest-building and egg-laying are going on. (In England from April on.) Furthermore it is only the cock who sings.

Alas for the tradition of European poetry! Virgil's bereft mother mourning for her stolen brood, and so on. Alas for the immortal bird pouring forth its deathless passion or singing of summer in full-throated ease. Alas for lone Daulis and the high Cephissian vale; the cock-bird is probably doing nothing more than defending his territory during the mating and nesting season, uttering defiance, 'whether the Muse or Love call thee his mate'.

(Use for Diamond-cut-diamond: The Nightingale replies to Mr Keats and co.)

— Book XV, 1973, p. 19.

BEYOND PHIGALIA

Rosemary [Dobson] sent me yesterday another poem from Pausanias[4] (Part 2, p. 471, n. 293 of Peter Levi's translation). The title is 'Phigalia' and she asks me whether I think this is getting to be too much:

> I've been wondering seriously if I should divorce myself from Pausanias. It's beginning to seem a bit obsessive.

The poem of course was delightful and partly to encourage her to go on till she has completed a series, which she should do, I sent her the following:

Beyond Phigalia

She was a woman possessed by an old book,
Even its footnotes were occasions of song.
One day she sent to the Oracle saying: 'Look
Into my case: tell me if I do wrong!'

'Should I divorce Pausanias, because
He is enchanted ground; because I fear
I may never return to be the woman I was,
Holding an old stone by a spring more dear?'

The Oracle answered: 'It is already too late.
Go on, go forward: it is all you can do.
She will greet you at nightfall by a ruined gate,
The woman who waited all these years to be you.'

— 8–IV–1973
— Book XV, 1973, pp. 20–1.

MORE ANSWERS: PROFESSOR A. E. HOUSMAN TO MR W. H. AUDEN

Time was, no man restored an
Old carcase to the sun;
But W. H. Auden,
He dug me up for fun.
A young ill-mannered poet,
He tore me from my shroud
And tossed my skull to show it
A-grinning to the crowd.

*When he was three and thirty
And I dead less than four,
He kept my heart like dirty
Postcards in his drawer.
He never wept, not Wystan;
His eye was sharp and dry;
They say he never missed an
Opening to pry.*

*But now his cruel winters
Drag to three score and ten,
Does he not feel the splinters
Of time like other men?
Has he no grief or canker
Heartache or damaged pride
No man alive would hanker
To publish far and wide?*

*Then may he not have readers
Like him who lie in wait
When ghouls and carrion feeders
Come jostling at his gate;
And may he hear no rabble
Of younger poets come
With graceless wit to scrabble
And wrench him from his tomb.*

1973

This may seem rather savage, seeing that Auden had the grace to withdraw the sonnet on Housman (*Another Time*, 1940) from later collections. But this may have been to save his own face. There was some forthright protest at the time of publication (*New Writing*, 1939). But there is no sign that Auden was ashamed of himself and in 1957 (*New Statesman*, 18th May) he wrote:

> The inner life of the neurotic is always projecting itself into external symptoms which are symbolic but decipherable confessions. The savagery of Housman's scholarly polemics, which included the composition of annihilating rebukes before he had

found the occasion and victim to deserve them, his obsession
with punctuation beyond the call of duty, are as revealing as if
he had written pornographic verse.

There had been no change of heart and no act of contrition; so have at him! Auden was surely not so unaware of the spirit of controversy in the field of classical scholarship in Housman's day, to think Housman unduly savage or to think that stockpiling a few insults in advance in this perpetual war need have indicated more than a grim sense of fun on Housman's part. As for 'punctuation beyond the call of duty'! What prigs psycho-analysis made of us all in those days! But Wystan surely led the van.

— 26–IV–1973
— Book XV, 1973, pp. 24–7.

MANDELSTRAM AND MAYAKOVSKY

It is recorded that Mandelstram made up his poems in his head before he put anything on paper and that he needed to move about when he was composing.

I remember that the same was true of Mayakovsky who somewhere or other talks of 'walking out a poem' or some such expression. Two poets more unlike each other in character or in the style of their poetry would be hard to find. I find this way of composing hard to imagine. I can get a general idea or compose fragments while standing or walking or lying down, but I have to get to a table and paper to put a poem together. There is an essential role for the bits scribbled down on paper. They 'hold' ideas or pieces of the growing poem that I would otherwise forget while working at the other parts and as the poem grows what is written serves as a point from which the rest takes shape. I can't hold it in my head and evaluate it. For that matter I cannot remember poems after I have written them or only very sketchily and imperfectly. I am quite unable to recite any of them without gaps here and there and changes of text. Both O. M. and V. M. seem to have been able to carry quite long poems in their heads and recite them word-perfect on the spur of the moment. Is there anything significant in this?

— Book XV, 1973, pp. 68–9.

GHOSTS OF ATLANTIS

> Evangelos Baikos of Akroteri had this comment on the excavation just concluded: 'This summer, my family could not work in the fields because of the ghosts. In the mountain that came from the sea. There are ghosts where now they make the excavations. I saw them. One morning when I went to collect the tomatoes and it was not yet sunrise, a big white light covered a great ghost covered with a shield. Then there were many, all in movement, yet they looked firm. They went towards the sea, in the opposite direction from the sunrise to escape the light which goes towards the west.'
>
> Ghosts are quite real on Thera ... there is unquestionably an atavistic feeling about this society, an unconscious awareness ... of the very ancient past. I came to wonder if it was because of this collective susceptibility that visual hallucinations [were] so common-place ... it is not at all surprising that from time to time they should react collectively in a way that betrays their amazing antiquity ... [etc., etc.]
>
> James W. Mavor Jr, *Voyage to Atlantis*, 1969, p. 254.

There is only one thing remarkable about James W. Mavor's account and that is that it never occurs to him for a moment that it is the people of Thera who see and himself who is blind. It would be nice to have the Theran point of view on the archeologists who crassly dig up the ancient graves unaware of the ghosts they disturb and which swarm around them.

A poem?

— Book XV, 1973 pp. 74–5.

THE NEW IMAGES

It is only about 50 years since Hubble and the 100 inch telescope on Mt Wilson began a revolution in cosmology almost as great as the Copernican one. In those few years 'science fiction' writers have familiarised us with the name Andromeda, which has begun to move in popular imagination from the name of the Constellation to that of M31, the Andromeda Nebula so closely resembling our own galaxy and its neighbour in space, one of a group journeying together. The Greater and Lesser Magellanic Clouds joined by tenuous gas and revolving round each other — our nearest neighbours among the galaxies are also members of the group.

Will these bodies in the next few hundred years not become as familiar as the sun and the moon have been in the past and as inexhaustible a source of images. To use them at present is difficult — they are just out of reach as it were, because so few people hold them in sight or in imagination. Yet I, with no more knowledge of astronomy than the next man, would know Andromeda if I saw her photograph in a line-up of galaxies. Soon her idea if not her image will be as familiar to everyone as the Moon's today. Just to treat them now on equal terms in a poem would involve the poet in too many footnotes.

(June 1973)

(A few days later I attempted such a poem. As a case in point, I doubt if the ordinary reader at present will recognise that the poem begins and ends with the techniques used respectively by astronomers and radio astronomers to remember the classification of stars by temperature. July 1973)

THE HELPERS

Last night an example of real co-operation. Before going to bed I was working at *Apollo and Daphne, II*, and, not very happy about the final stanzas, I decided to try again in the morning. I read for a while and went to sleep thinking again of the poem in which I had suddenly noticed a serious oversight in 'connection' — I decided the first thing would be to insert a new stanza ... Towards morning I woke aware that the dream workers were toiling at the end of the poem, choosing, rejecting and mending as I had been doing the night before, and that they had produced a new and delightful final stanza, correct in metre and rhyme scheme and consonant with what went before. At least I thought so till I woke right up when it became clear that the stanza, though a good one had nothing to do with the theme of *Apollo and Daphne* but was probably the end of a poem about Echo and Narcissus or perhaps Hylas and the Nymphs. While I was noticing this the first two lines of the stanza were withdrawn. But I kept the last two:

'The crystal plane absorbs them one by one
The pure element hides them from our view'

The dream workers were plainly disappointed at my rejection and pointed out how well the word 'absorbs' would echo the first word of the first stanza.

— Book XV, 1973, pp. 112–13.

APOLLO AND DAPHNE II

Wild with the intricate artifice of song
He wandered by the land in his own light
Flushed from the reeds she rose; yet, poised for flight,
She paused, as love unbidden loosed his tongue

And laughed and shook her head and turned and ran.
He thought: 'It is easy now; I have my cue;
Knowing beforehand what a woman will do,
A god may venture further than a man.'

So, letting her run, he followed at his ease.
She fled with such voluptuous grace, he thought
Her flight a game whose end was to be caught
Among those flowers ahead beneath the trees.

Her long thighs leaping seemed to glide on air;
Each sole behind kicked back a rosy kiss;
To watch her body in motion was such bliss
That, though he could have siezed her flying hair,

He followed, as in a dream, the dreamlike chase
Whose double rhythm seemed about to rehearse
The pulse and passion of his unfinished verse.
Will to hear it still, he slackened pace

But caught her at the entrance to the wood.
At his first touch she stopped and turned to wait
Masked in deep shade, so still, so cool, so straight.
Wild with desire, he leapt to where she stood,

But, even as he embraced his living goal,
Found all his baffled senses miss their mark:
Only two lips dissolving in the bark,
And two warm breasts fast hardening on the bole;

While all around a ghostly laughter stirred
Her leafy fronds that whispered on the bough:
'All you have won is tousel for your brow.'
'Love lost becomes a changeling for the word.'

'Sing, poet, sing that metamorphosis!
In this alone, men share in the divine;
In this alone, the gods their power resign;
The natural order triumphs alone in this.'

Wild with his grief, the god yet loosed his hold,
And turned, and, seated in the laurel shade,
Finished and sang the paean he had made
And found his triumph in this as he was told.
— Book XV, 1973, pp. 115–17.

EPIGRAPH OR THE NEW CRATYLUS

The design of the following treatise is to investigate the fundamental laws of those operations of the mind by which reasoning [poetry] is performed; to give expression to them in the language of [the imagination] a Calculus and upon this foundation to establish the science of logic [Poetics] and construct its method ...

This passage from George Booles introduction to the great works, *An Investigation of the Laws of Thought, on which are founded Mathematical Theories of Logic and Probabilities* (1854) [seems] to me, with the substitutions indicated by the words in square brackets, to sum up admirably what I have in mind in that slowly developing treatise, *The New Cratylus*, which I may yet live to write.

The whole of Boole's preface is stimulating particularly in the suggestion of the way arbitrary symbols can be used for precise thinking about precise thinking. Where Boole's first rule is that the symbols must always be used in a fixed sense which once determined one must never depart from in the same chain of reasoning, the investigation in the case of poetry will consider precisely that use of symbols in which the 'meaning of the word', may vary constantly in its various contexts while preserving a central fixed core of references.

But the nature of the investigations have this in common that each goes to the very root of the subject and all accepted views are tested and questioned.

As far as I know an investigation as radical as Boole's has never been undertaken for the language of poetry.

— Book XVIII, 1975, pp. 75–6.

LANDSCAPE AS MUSIC

The combination of a train and a great landscape presenting innumerable variations on its theme is the nearest thing I know to the great, extended work of music. Mahler comes to mind. All day I have been travelling along the shores of Lake Superior with its magnificent variations on its own theme of birch and spruce forest, shore and short lake ringed with islands and the great expanse of sky and fresh-water sea. Later this evening, after passing Thunder B. and turning North towards Winnipeg, there has been a 'third movement' of clear yellow and red twilight and smaller and magically still lakes full of the same sunset.

This theme could be thought out and made into something.

— Book XVIII, 1975, p. 77.

THE MAZE

> There remains another important aspect of the metaphor. This is the image of the Maze as the map of the journey through life into death and hence into resurrection … it hinges on the idea that one enters a maze at birth, guided only briefly by the umbilical cord which brought one forth from the maze in which one had dwelt *before* birth (the red thread of Ariadne, by which Theseus was guided through the Cretan Maze) …
>
> Michael Ayston: *A Meaning to the Maze*
> (7th Jackson Knight Lecture, 1973, p. 15.)

I know only Ayrton's etchings, the Archilochus series and the Minotaur series and I am deeply impressed by them. But this lecture is rambling and insubstantial. This passage is typical. The ancient maze patterns on tombstones, etc., were supposed to lead to the world of the dead and had no reference, as far as I know, to birth and entry into this life. The umbilical cord is not what leads us from the womb into the world but on the contrary what attaches the foetus to its mother's uterus. As for the red thread of Ariadne, it did not guide Theseus through the maze. He had to find his own way, which he did guided by the bellowing of the Minotaur. The thread was to guide him back again. *Out* of the maze. The whole essay displays this sloppy sort of argument.

Nevertheless the idea of the journey through life as a process of threading a maze is an arresting one. The character of a maze or labyrinth is that at each turn one is faced with one or several choices of direction only one of which will be successful. The choice is blind. Living is partly like that. Looking back one sees that comparatively trivial blind choices have often determined one's course and that the majority of people do end up in blind alleys. Use for a poem (?).

— Book XX, 1978, pp.137–8.

ADULTERY IN THE HEART

I have just begun to read Arberry's translation of Ibn Hazm's *The Ring of the Dove* (though I have had the book on my shelves for years — boredom with the whole subject of Courtly Love is probably the reason). Opening the book at random I came on the following which shows that Christ and Muhammed were at one on the subject of Adultery in the heart (Mathew, V, 28):

> The prophet of God said, 'Whoever looks upon a woman when he is fasting, so as to see the bulk of her bones, the same has broken his fast.'

Muhammed at least seems to have recognised the inevitability that desire would follow on the sight of the desirable shape in spite of any effort of will to stop it. Jesus seems to have been ignorant or innocent of this.

Muhammed probably took this view from the Christian one, though he was not nearly as strict on the definition of adultery as Christ who regards a second marriage with a divorced woman as adultery. Muhammed recognises divorce and remarriage.

I do not find the passage quoted in the *Koran*, if it is one of the *hadith* it maybe a later accretion to the faith, but equally likely to be of Christian origin.

(Use or remember for the poem on this subject.)

— Book XXI, 1980, pp. 113–14.

NATURE SLOWLY CREEPING UP …

Canberra Times, 18 October 1982

USSR
'Stone Age' family in Siberia

Moscow, Friday (AAP-AFP) Soviet geologists have discovered a family 'living in the Stone Age' in remote central Siberia.

The Likov family, so cut off in remote Siberia that it had never heard of Lenin, Stalin or Brezhnev, has become the most famous in the Soviet Union.

The modern world literally fell down on Miss Agafia Likova, 39, when three Soviet geologists landed near her home in central Siberia in a helicopter.

The *Komsomolskava Pravda* daily newspaper reported that one of them, Mr Nikolai Juravlov, described the family as 'people from the Stone Age'.

Their story is a weird one.

Generations of the Likov family have for centuries been opposed, for religious reasons, to the reforms brought in by Peter the Great in the 18th century.

They looked on him as irreligious and their 'personal enemy'.

All male members of the family, to show their opposition to Czar Peter, refused to carry out one of his main social reforms — cutting off long beards.

In 1942 Mr Likov senior, his wife and their three children journeyed into central Siberia and decided to stay away from other human beings.

He said at the time, 'We are withdrawing from the world — our religion orders us to do so.'

His children at the time were aged 16 and 6, besides newly born Agafia.

Agafia has lived all her life in the minuscule world of the five Likovs.

They rose at dawn and retired at dusk in their home-made log cabin surrounded by a potato patch. Radio, telephones and television were unknown to them.

Their only book was an old bible, blackened by the years, that they had brought with them.

There was no luxury, comfort or entertainment in their lives, but none of them has ever been ill despite the below-zero climate.
If this had come out five or six years ago I could have been suspected of having based *The People of the Pale* on it. But that poem was an elaboration of an actual dream in which I, in some future age and not

the girl narrator, actually visited a colony of tall white people in a fenced in compound and learned they were the last few survivors of the once dominant White Race. It would appear that Whistler's famous retort could apply here. These dreams set in the future occur from time to time. I have cited one in a previous notebook, I recall, but not as a separate activity of the Dream Team. They are usually extremely vivid and marked by unusual precision of visual detail and a distinct impression that I am looking into the future.

[Editor's note: *The People of the Pale* appears in Book XVIII, 1975, pp. 11–22.]

— Book XXII, 1982, pp. 107–8.

EXCERPT FROM POEM

White Giants, that was a shock! Indeed they reared
Over real men, more than two metres tall;
And their pale skins were ghastly — but really weird,
The most unnerving thing, the worst of all
Were their strange eyes — imagine they were blue!
Unlike the human eye's soft, lucid brown,
Their ice-blue glances seemed to pierce me through;
Blue lakes that drew me in and sucked my down …

Notes

1. See Hope, 'Keats and the Nightingale', in *A Book of Answers*, p. 34, where Hope, after pointing out an error re when the nightingale sings and why, and although accepting Keats' view that what the imagination seizes as beauty must be truth, he notes, 'But we turn our backs on the other sort of truths at our peril — at the peril of the integrity of poetry'. See also, ibid., p. 36, for Hope's 'answer' to Keats, *A Nightingale to Mr Keats (and to poets in general)*.
2. See Hope, *A Book of Answers*, pp. 93–5, for the background to the Housman/Auden/Hope controversy and for the published version of the poem that appears on the same topic in the notebooks (Book XV, 1973, pp. 24–7).
3. 'Vin' refers to Vincent Buckley (1925–88), Australian poet and critic and head of the English Department at Melbourne University. Hope and Buckley were colleagues at Melbourne University from 1945 until 1951 when Hope was appointed Professor of English at Canberra University College (later The Australian National University). Hope and Buckley maintained a lifelong correspondence.
4. Pausanias was a Greek traveller and geographer who wrote *Descriptions from Greece* in the second century AD. In his 10 books, he sketched the history and the topography of important cities; he described the surroundings of these cities, often including rituals and customs pertaining to the area. He was intrigued by places of worship and described in detail the nature of religious and historical remains. Rosemary Dobson shared a fascination for Pausanias's writings with Hope. See Rosemary Dobson, *Over the Frontier: Poems*, in which many of her 'Pausanias' poems were published.

VII

A SENSE OF DETACHMENT

Hope often emphasises that the special significance of a true work of art resides in the fact that it has 'escaped from the limitations of the personal and has soared beyond the personal concerns of its creator.' Poetry, he believes, is not so much a 'document' nor a communication but a 'performance' and a 'creation'. He is insistent that if it is used as a means to confess and exploit personal feelings of grief and loss as 'open wounds', it fails as great poetry. The confession of personal, immediate stories of suffering in a poem, he suggests, invokes a subtle form of fallacy in which the author, and not the poem, is attributed 'an ironical, cynical or satirical attitude to man and society'. The poems in these circumstances tend to be regarded as allegories and not as what Hope maintains they should be: creations of new being. Hope concurs with Keats: 'As to poetical character itself … it is not itself — it has no definition — is everything and nothing — It has no character as it enjoys light and shade; it lives in gusts, be it foul or fair, high or low, rich or poor, mean or elevated … A Poet is the most unpoetical of anything in existence; because it has no identity — he is continually informing and filling some other Body [Keats, Letters 93].'

As discussed at length in Chapter One, Hope's detachment is paradoxical and his flight from and embrace of his doppelgänger produces at times a unique kind of subjectivication. The necessary detachment that he demands of the poet relates more to the form of the poem, the mastery of a verse form, than it might to the content of the poems — if a poet invokes personal experience, the management of this, the crafting of it towards a musical enactment in verse form, distances the poet from the strictly personal. He concedes in another entry that 'one could imagine a whole life determined in the strangest way by a dream-life that the person knew nothing about'. If this is so there is bound to be, within any creation, elements of the self that are unmanageable. Nevertheless, in entering a poem as an actor and asking 'What if?' of a situation, creed or emotion, the formulation of this performance in verse form transforms the autobiographical emotions into something 'other', something outside normal understanding, and necessarily, something new.

Hope's last poems in *Orpheus* were selected by him with great care. It is clear that he wrote this book knowing that it would be his last. It contains poems that cover the 11 areas that I have chosen as chapter headings for this book. For example, there are specific poems that draw on mythology, legends and biblical stories (*Orpheus, Hymn to Saint Barbara, Mayan Books*), others invoking his interest in cosmology (*A Swallow in the House, Protest to Fred Hoyle*) and many poems on love and sexuality (*Teaser Rams, Love and Poetry, Post Coitum, The Oracle* and *The Female Principle*).

It fascinates me that in this volume, in which he bids farewell, Hope, contrary to most of his earlier work, invokes the 'I' of his persona, if not in a confessional manner, certainly in a way that confounds and belies the reader versed in his professed detachment. Hope accepts that he 'shall stand, looking rather out of place' when compared with his contemporaries (*Mermaid in the Zodiac*). *Memento Mori* and *Intimations of Mortality* express poignantly his alienation, fear and acceptance of the coming to the end of his creativity and his life. *Vistant* states clearly the end of his creative journey and is moving in its acquiescence to mortality and to his final somewhat querulous entreaty: 'To whom do I make my report?'

THE PHILOSOPHER AS HEALER

'Der Philosoph behandelt eine Frage; wie eine Krankheit' (Ludwig Wittgenstein)[1]

Is the philosopher doctor or patient? If the statement is true does this distinguish between two types of philosophers: the involved and the detached? But is it in any case more than a bit of conversational cleverness? In what sense is a philosophical question like a sickness in a healthy organism? Or in what sense is the way a philosopher treats his questions like a doctor treating a disease? These are two ways of looking at it. One assumes that a healthy mind or healthy organism does not raise philosophical questions. The other that philosophers take a clinical view of what are otherwise normal and healthy intellectual problems.

Of course some philosophies produce a sickness of the mind and some may be regarded as a sickness of the mind. But this has nothing to do with the point.

— Book VI, 1959, p. 41.

TYPES OF MEN: II

I should add to the note (in Notebook V, p. 7) on Yeats's lines:

The intellect of man is forced to choose
Perfection of the life or of the work.

Yeats[2]

Yeats was thinking about the poet and his work and it may be that this is particularly true of the poet. Perfection of the life in other fields of effort demands a consistent and integrated character; or, to put it another way, the gift or talent which has an end beyond itself, tends to be moulded and formed by the absorption of the man in the work. But the perfection of the poet's gift in his work may require him to remain chaotic as a character. Keats has expressed the heart of the matter:

> As to poetical character itself … it is not itself — it has no definition — is everything and nothing — It has no character — it enjoys light and shade; it lives in gusts, be it foul or fair, high or low, rich or poor, mean or elevated … A Poet is the most unpoetical of any thing in existence; because it has no identity — he is continually informing and filling some other Body.
>
> (Letters 93)

Perfection of the life in these circumstances is almost impossible in the ordinary sense. And yet as a life to live it is perfect.

— Book VI, 1960, p. 62.

THE UNKNOWN FACES AND FORCES

I have always felt strongly that, insofar as we base our views and our actions on experience, what happens to us in dreams is as much experience as what happens to us in waking life. When we remember what we experience in dreams we can treat it as part of the common store of experience and because we know it to be 'only a dream' its power to influence us is reduced. But the dreams we do not recall remain as independent agents and provocations. I dream that I meet the daughter of a friend who has gone away. This daughter was a schoolgirl when I last saw her but in the dream she is a young woman of twenty two or so, and in the course of this long dream we meet on several occasions, have many adventures together and fall in love. Had I not remembered and discounted the dream it might well have affected my attitude to this woman next time I met her and I should not have known why. Some sudden fears and aversions of an inexplicable kind may be of the same sort. One could imagine a whole life determined in the strangest way by a dream-life that the person knew nothing about.

— Book VI, 1960, p. 74.

THE TEXTURE OF POETRY

Nearly all the fashionable criticism of poetry nowadays is devoted to a close and minute verbal criticism and those poems which do not stand up to it are rejected. Thus Dr Leavis is able to prove that Milton is a bad poet and Marvell a much better one. It is as though they demanded that all paintings should be able to stand up to the scrutiny that a miniature will take. The looser or more open texture of long narrative or reflective poems demands a different sort of scrutiny from that to which we subject a short dense lyric.

The New Critics go on to worse excesses. They fragment and apply microscopic tests under which many good poems are bound to break down and in time the canon of acceptable poems becomes absurdly narrow. Good criticism demands close and careful scrutiny, but scrutiny of the natural eye at a proper distance. Use a microscope or even put your eye close against the painting and you will not see the painting at all. You will see only a meaningless surface of patches and blobs.

— Book VI, 1960, p. 101.

THE BIOGRAPHICAL CRITIC

John Middleton Murry's statement in his deplorable book on Keats, that poetry only has meaning to him in so far as it reveals the author's personality, is crude and absurd. But critics who think themselves free of the 'biographical fallacy' are always committing it in less crude forms. The commonest, as I have pointed out in 'The Sincerity of Poetry'[3] and 'The Practical Critic',[4] is to imagine that the poet is speaking in his own person or for himself as he might in a letter or a journal. This would lead to absurd results in many cases but the absurdity is not always apparent. There are obvious and less obvious manifestations.

For example if we were to take *Morning Meditation*[5] which I transcribed in this notebook a few pages back, the crudest interpretation, a sort often used with writers whose lives we know nothing about, would be to take it as a literally and factually true account of myself and my forebears and to criticize me and the poem accordingly. Absurd as this may sound, it is precisely what some critics do, let us say, to Shakespeare's *Sonnets* or Catullus's *Carmina*. Almost equally crude would be to criticise me and the poem because my grandfather though he had a beard did not have any of the habits I give the grandfather in the poem, my mother was not like the woman in the poem and my father did not cut his throat and so on; this is the sort of treatment critics have sometimes given to, say, Donne's *Anniversaries* or Pope's *Characters of Women*. But it would be hardly less crass for the critic to take the 'facts' of the poem as comic intention but to attribute to me a view in favour of the state of nature, or of longing for bold, bawdry and sexual licence. The Poet is taken to be expressing his view or his attitude, using the poem as a dramatic device. A more subtle and therefore a more dangerous form of the fallacy would be to attribute to the author and not to the poem an ironical, cynical or satirical attitude to man and society, or to regard it as an allegory.

I. A. Richards tended to suggest that the critic should avoid attitudes and presuppositions. This is impossible and the attempt to do so results in a peculiarly pallid or dishonest sort of criticism perhaps unfairly labelled 'academic'. If one could get people to see that a poem is neither a 'communication' nor a 'document' but a 'performance' and a 'creation', things would be easier. The trouble is, of course, that quite often poems do set out quite deliberately to be both personal communications or documents as explicit as diaries, and do make a special effort to be neither a performance nor the invention of a statement or point of view for its own sake. Because there is no means of telling which is which the critic's task is especially difficult if he tries to distinguish. He is safer if he treats all poems as though they had been written for the hell of it, as though the writer had said: 'Here's an interesting idea, let me see what would happen if I developed it.'

As far as I am concerned poems are like children: they are begotten as well as born, and they may as well bear the stamp of the circumstances that suggested them as of the poet who produced them, or a mixture of both; they may express views and ideas and feelings resembling those of the poet or views, ideas and feelings which interest him because they are totally unlike his own. They may be true confessions or complete inventions but in any case they are independent beings with a character not limited by or reducible to that of either parent. They are [Ding an sich].

— Book VIII, 1964–65, pp. 52–4.

AFTERTHOUGHTS — TO THE PRECEDING

In spite of the critic and the poet in such jolly agreement as in the preceding remarks, the reader in me says resolutely that he wouldn't be bothered with poems he couldn't take seriously; by this he means poems in which he 'seems' to hear a 'person' expressing *his* beliefs and *his* ideas. It is one thing he says to say we can set aside the question of whether we believe the theology of *Paradise Lost*, but what sort of a poem would it be if we felt that Milton had invented the theology in a spirit of 'as if'?

Similarly he says these roles are in a sense like an artist's sketchbook: it exists to catch the impression of an idea as it is observed, and to catch it fresh without trying to work it out or elaborate it or test it — it is not a record of *beliefs*. But would I be bothered to do it if I did not think they might be seriously entertained? So with poems.

— Book VIII, 1964–65, pp. 54.

THE INTENTIONAL FALLACY

There is obviously a need for caution in accepting an author's statement of what he meant to do or thought he was doing, but the whole popularity of the so-called 'intentional fallacy' in present day criticism appears to be derived from the fact that it allows critics to be irresponsible, to ignore the author's intentions altogether, as though his judgement were irrelevant and he were not entitled to a voice at all.

His voice is of course the poem itself. What he said he meant to do is interesting and may supply support, but it is evidence that cannot be accepted if the poem is plainly not what he intended it to be. But if the argument is in doubt then the critic must prove the author wrong. He cannot invoke the 'Intentional Fallacy' and ignore him. And he cannot, without the greatest difficulty, show that the intention is irrelevant even if it fails. Milton may not have been able to justify the ways of God to men, but if that is what he set out to do we cannot lightly ignore him and declare that he was of the Devil's party without knowing it. You must be able to prove it from the poem in any case.

— Book VIII, 1964–65, p.114.

THE CONQUEST OF TIME

It can be achieved in several ways, but each of them involves an enlargement of the mind. For example, standing looking at the stars at night one is simply in the presence of present lights, but to the astronomer who *knows*, who has made this knowledge part of his seeing, he is seeing now, events and aspects of things happening further back the further away they are; they are present at the same time, part of his 'now'.

Or again as I grow older and know more I lose more and more the sense of the past against the present. What Sappho sings or Socrates argues is as present as what my contemporaries sing or say, as relevant and as useful. I begin to lose my sense of 'now' as opposed to 'then' and, in anticipation, to see myself in the same time as what is to come, just as when I put down the dates of things to be done next week: they are already part of my life *now* which has to prepare for them *then*.

One has only to go on from either of these two experiences, and there are many others of a like kind, to see the real meaning of eternity, which at first appears a paradox. Eternity is not a state of things but a state of mind which contemplates all the moments of time as though they were present. It is not a mind contemplating a 'timeless world', which could only mean a world arrested in time like a single frame from cinema film.

If the astronomer could enlarge his vision to take in events from infinity, to see them as all happening at once but receding in time as well as in space, he would have reached the limit of the kind of mind we have, which is located in space. But if, at will or simultaneously, he could view these events from any or all possible locations, he would have a mind of another sort altogether: he would be God.

If one believes in a strict determinism the notion of eternity would take in all events to come as well as all past and present ones.

If one believes in a very limited determinism as I do, then the mind even of God will see only plans and blueprints of possible future states of the universe. For the future states of whole galaxies perhaps the fine detail will be there; but for future events of the actions of conscious beings only a few rather hazy blurs on the screen.

If one takes such a view and eternity does not imply the negation of time, eternity becomes something that grows in time and by means of time.

Was this what Blake meant when he said: 'Eternity is in love with the production of time'?

— Book XV, 1973, pp. 12–14.

ON THE ROAD TO XANADU AGAIN

On waking I seem to be either composing or discussing a poem in rough hexameters which fades rapidly but I am left with the last line:

'Bút isn't cóld catachrésis whát we are áctually séeking?'

Neither in the dream nor on waking have I any idea what catachresis is, except that it is a technical term in the theory of classical versification. On consulting the dictionary I find it means: Abuse of terms, tropes, metaphors, etc.; use of words in forced or unnatural senses. So that I was wrong even about this and the line is mere nonsense. But in the dream it had a mysterious sense of finality, of suggesting the solution of a teasing problem, of providing the key to a dilemma, etc.

— 24–III–1973
— Book XV, 1973, p. 15.

RUSKIN IN ITALY

I must dislike Ruskin more than I realized: coming on his *Poetry as Architecture* here, I was irritated by the harmless fact that he had rowed about Lake Como shortly before 1837 and had drawn and discussed the Villa Serbelloni (though he does not name it). As usual his description implies a serenity and beauty which his cold and graceless drawing denies. From his remarks it would appear that he was never inside the villa or its grounds and he seems unaware that, as it then stood and still is, it is a composite construction of many different periods — the earliest being the old church tower of the 12th century where I had my study. Ruskin discusses its design, together with that of the Villa Somma-Riva, also on the lake, as though they had both been placed where they are and designed by a single architect to fit into the natural scene of the background of lake and mountains. In particular he makes a point of the use of arches in these designs. As I remember, the grotto arches of the Villa Serbelloni, to which he gives great prominence in his drawing, were the afterthought of an 18th-century owner.

I am surprised by an extra feeling of antipathy that he should have been trailing his slime over any part of the world to which I am personally attached. The fact that it is all nonsense, makes the feeling all the more surprising.

— Eastern View, 1973
— Book XV, 1973, pp. 93–4.

FRANCIS WEBB

A week ago Rosemary [Dobson] rang me to say that Frank Webb,[6] whom I was about to visit in Rydalmere Mental Hospital, had suddenly died. He was sitting on a seat outside his ward, M9, waiting for the bus to go to mass, when he pitched forward and was dead when they picked him up.

This gentle, deranged man who prayed for me every day is much on my mind. My one visit cheered him and he began to write poems again — at least he finished one and sent it for publication.

Rosemary told me at the Seminar in Frank's memory organized at Sydney University a month or so later that a young wardsman at the hospital who befriended Frank claims that it was he who persuaded him to write his last poems. It may be so.

I had got him from the Literature Board a small grant of a hundred dollars — he would not take more — for his needs — tobacco, coffee at the cafeteria, fares to go to mass — and with the usual pace of government payments it took a couple of months to go through the machine. He had written to me rather anxiously about it over the last six weeks or so — he would not take money from me — and the day after I heard of his death the cheque arrived addressed to me as I was to deliver it personally. I don't suppose there is any smoking or causing to smoke in Heaven, but I should like to send him on some good rolling tobacco — he made his own cigarettes.

— Dec. 1973
— Book XV, 1973, pp. 97–8.

THE COFFIN SHAPE

The finest 'personal' image I recall is something in a letter of Lucy Heney's just after I had left for England in 1928 — Helen and Lucy had come down to Circular Quay to see the *Orama* off. I remember that shock of recognition of a phrase of genuine poetry: 'Alec with his coffin-shaped face'. It was absolutely accurate at the time and could have been no more than that, but I think I already knew the weight of death within those outlines — a weight it took me another forty years to get rid of. And I think Lucy with her extraordinary sensitiveness knew it.

— Book XV, 1974, p. 138.

THE FIRST-BORN

(An excerpt from the poem)

> 'Sanctify unto me àll the first-born, whatsoever openeth the womb among the Children of Israel, of man and beast, it is mine.' (Exodus 13, 1–2)

There is something different about them. Almost all
Voices of eldest children give them away.
 I know; I am one myself of the secret clan —,
They have listening faces; their stance, their steps recall
A guarded alertness from an earlier day
Far back in the dangerous history of man.

They cannot help it: it is a fear inbred
From times when the first-fruits were offered up
To ravenous gods. More precious than ram or goat
Was a first-born son on an altar dripping red;
And a first-born girl exposed on the mountain top
Felt the wolf's muzzle, hairy against her throat.

These cannot take life for granted as others do.
They shrink from kinship and kind; they have learned to greet
A kiss with caution, joy with a settled calm;
A celebration warns them they are taboo
And a caress reminds them that human meat
Torn at the summer solstice becomes a charm.

No matter what nonchalance he may command,
This one betrays at times the furtive eyes
Of a lost fugitive from some sacred grove;
This other, a still unsacrificed deodand,
Even in her rapture, a lover may surprise
Some anxious gesture at the climax of love.

Whatever opens the womb of men or beasts
Is sacred to Moloch's or Jahweh's holy writ:
Weak from her birth-pangs a girl-mother comes,
Milk still oozing from her swollen breasts,
And hurls her first-born into the fiery pit;
Its sole shriek drowned by the wild gongs and drums;

And, walking with joy in the clear mountain air,
A young boy laughing, the belov'd son,
Skipping and chattering at his father's side,
Touches the sacrifical knife: 'But where,
Where is the victim?' — Abraham, trudging on,
Groans out: 'God knows, my son, let God provide!'
— Book XV, 1974, pp. 160–2.

DANTE'S LOVE AND GRIEF

I perceive now why I have never been able to read the *Vita Nuova* without a sense of incredulity and boredom, despite the beauty and intensity of the tale of love and grief. The latter are genuine enough but Dante's innocence and youth made him spoil the effect by a display of poetic ingenuity. He is too much the busy author to convince with his picture of the ecstatic and the grief-stricken lover.

One is made too aware of his exploiting his bonanza of love and grief; his distributing, discussing and technical demonstration of the poems embodying his passion, his eager response to ladies who request him for more of the same, his seeking out audiences of sympathetic ladies to recite his sorrows to and share his tears with. A desperate lover with one eye on the publicity value of his despair is not a convincing object.

With what ingenuousness after his touching account of how he stood weeping for Beatrice in her grief for her father's death and heard the comments of her friends as they returned from mourning with her, on her sorrow and on the ravages that grief had made on Dante himself, he then goes straight on to exploit the situation:

> Ond' io poi pensando, proposi di dire parole, acciochè degnamente avea cagione di dire, nelle quali parole io conchiudessi tutto ciò che inteso avea da queste donne.[7]

This all too sudden replacement of wild and helpless grief by an enthusiastic attack of the *cacoethes scribend*[8] is a piece of ill-placed and unconscious comedy.

Yet how true it is to life! How exactly it catches the professional obsession of poets, their ineradicable detachment as writers, which leads them to look even on their moments of most ecstatic love and bitterest grief, as good copy for a future poem. It is what prompted Nietzsche's brutal remark about the shamelessness of poets in exploiting their own feelings. If Dante had been a more experienced writer he would not have given himself away so obviously — and incidentally have exposed the rest of us to ourselves.

I recollect on the same subject Lodge's[9] remark in his *Portraits of the English Worthies*:

> But the soul which is able to pour forth its sorrows in song, will have little trouble in recalling a desperate resolution.

Yeats, who should have known better, wrote that splendid verse on the academic critics who

> Edit and annotate the lines
> That young men tossing on their beds
> Rhymed out in love's despair
> To flatter beauty's ignorant ear.[10]

Yeats in his fifties was not so forgetful of his own sins as not to recall that a young man tossing on his bed writing verses to Maude Gonne and other beauties, could take time off from his despair to study the effects of his poem and arrange the esthetics of despair in suitably touching disarray.

— Book XVIII, 1975, pp. 23–6.

FLORBELA AND RIMBAUD

Rimbaud in his cheeky letter to Paul Demeny and his respectful one to Georges Izamband in 1871, when he was sixteen and a half, shares with them his discovery of the divided self necessary as he claims to being a poet.

> ... I recognise myself as a poet. This is not at all my fault. It is false to say 'I think'. One should say: it thinks me. Excuse me for the play on words. 'I' is an other. Too bad for the wood which finds itself a violin, etc: Because 'I' is an other. If the [illegible] ... wakes up — there is no fault that is obvious to me. I am assisting the disclosure of my thought ...

This had always seemed to me a profound HALF-truth. I do always have this sense of being present at the unfolding of my thought. But it unfolds to no purpose if I am simply an audience. There is work to be done and only the JE can do it. It is a sort of midwifery and at times the birth is more difficult than at others; sometimes more and sometimes less help is needed, sometimes, though rarely, hardly any at all. The value of the half-truth is that it is important that one should know that poetry is not a deliberate enterprise, a piece of engineering planned before and executed according to rule and recipe. The other and equally important half of the truth is that without conscious control and participation, the enterprise is likely to come to nothing or to be marred and flawed by verbal inadequacies and rhythmical lapses of the most amateur kind. The unconscious forces have the resources of imagination but they are weak on management, as my experience with the dream-workers has shown. Their taste is often appalling and their powers of integration nil. It was because he thought his half-truth the whole of the matter that Rimbaud later degenerated into the formless nonsense that spoils so much of *Les Illuminations and Un Saison en Enfer*.

Florbela de Almd Conceicao Espanca[11] seems, like Rimbaud, to have accepted the notion of the division of the self in the making of poetry. Like him she suffered in the process — *tant pis pour le bois* — and ultimately took the way out by suicide. But where Rimbaud accepts and finds the split person natural for a poet, Florbela Espanca revolts against it.

It is impossible to generalize from the two instances, especially two such odd personalities, but it occurs to me that there is a clue here to the limitations of women as poets. The poetry at its best is generally the poetry of the 'JE' disguised or used as a '*L'autre*': they rarely perform well when the forces have to be divided to obtain the 'impersonality' that great poetry demands.

This is a first thought; I suspect that when I have gone into it further I shall find that women are equally capable of great poetry but have in general been following a procedure not suited to their natures. They translate themselves into masculine terms and suffer from the mediocrity of most translation.

The great majority of *good* women poets have been personal and lyrical — the JE seems to be in undivided command. Here perhaps they are following their own natures. But for that reason perhaps they have not as a rule succeeded in producing poetry of the highest order. For that, 'JE doit être un autre'.

— Book XVIII, 1975, pp. 45–8.

THREE TYPES OF PEOPLE

Leafing through Vol. V of Byron's *Letters and Journals* to find the text of his controversy with Bowles about Pope, I come on a scrap of paper in my writing headed *Types of People*:

a. Those who centre the feelings in themselves: the blue of the hills, the music make me feel sad, etc.
b. Those who project themselves and their feelings into the objects that arouse them: the melancholy landscape of the hills, the sadness inherent in this music, etc.

What I had overlooked at the time — I think ten or more years ago — was that there is a third type of person who neither attributes his feelings to objects nor endows objects with the power of arousing the feelings in himself. This is the man who is inhabited by unattached feelings roving about in search of objects and subjects to justify and complete them. Some of these we call poets.

— Book XVIII, 1975, p. 53.

ANNE GODFREY-SMITH AND THE HONEY OF GENERATION

Odd that within a month the same ideas come to me from reading Lynne Strahan,[12] from answering a question at Woden Valley High School, from Anne[13] writing a letter about glove-puppets in a plane on her way from Brisbane to Darwin. The earlier note on Rimbaud and Florbela Espanca seems to be working towards the same idea. It is as though experience were conspiring to further an underground line of thought and bring it momentarily to the surface like a subterranean river.

At Woden Valley I was talking to a group of amiable children who have to 'do' my poems for the forthcoming Higher School Certificate and in reply to a question as to what I meant by a particular poem — I think *Imperial Adam* — I found myself explaining that most poems are a sort of co-operative effort between 'myself' as conscious controller, shaper and recorder and something I called the emerging idea of the poem which has its own direction and autonomous growth.

Anne's letter describes various puppeteers and puppet theatres she has seen in this year's tour of Australia for the Theatre Board of the Australia Council:

> I found a fascinating puppeteer on the coast at (Chevron Island?) — a woman called Kaye Nettler (?) who is a real artist … I am learning … about puppetry fast this year — I knew nothing about it before … Kaye is the first one I've seen and spoken to who really creates interesting and strange characters

and brings them to life in quite unnerving fashion. She won't use marionettes at all (puppets worked by strings) as she says they are too limiting. Her puppets are hand puppets — glove or rod puppets — I had a conversation with a glove puppet mouse called Charlie … Kaye was not using a mouse voice — it was her own — but the puppet came to life astonishingly, shrugging, explaining his dislike of cats in such a deprecating way, that my memory is of a conversation with Charlie, not of watching a puppet demonstrated … it's easy to make dolls, based on TV & cartoon characters & wriggle them round on strings, which is what most puppeteers do. But to create life out of bits of materials, some drapes over your hand is real art and immensely difficult. Oddly enough the more you try for realism in your puppets the less life they have — they have legs & arms & faces; but that only emphasizes the fact that they are dolls. But a head, with face and features suggested, placed on a rod, with a drape fitted round it and falling over your hand, so that with one hand you turn the head, with the other you slip the fingers into the drape & your hand becomes the puppet's hand — with these as your focus, you can, if you are an artist, create movement and gesture for the character that suggest life in a way that no lifeless, jointed limbs can do. Because your own life is now temporarily become the puppet's life — and your voice the voice of the character; and it's quite convincing. The puppeteer becomes the puppet during the performance. You know and use the idea of the puppet as something that is manipulated by some outside person or force & cannot dictate its own actions. This is not really the case, since the puppet dictates to the puppeteer, its actions and lines, through the very fact of its creation, by the puppeteer. A strange paradox — the poem writes the poet … What is this strange two-way relationship between the creation and the creator? The presence of the creation affects the creator and subjects him or her to certain courses of action. Is that what Milton had in the back of his mind when coping with his creation theme?

Anne here seems to me to be on to something very important. It is, of course, a two-way process. The poet and the poem work reciprocally. But the essential thing is for the poet to be receptive, malleable, adaptable to the needs of the growing and emerging poem. If he imposes recipes, this will not happen or the poem will be mutilated or stillborn.

The other side of the paradox of course is that touched on in the previous note about Rimbaud and Florbela. The poet as 're-created' by the poem must consciously shape and direct or the result will be flabby structure or messy shape.

There is also the problem of 'return', the change back in the poet, the 'JE', so that another poem can re-create him to his needs.

— 24–VIII–75
— Book XVIII, 1975, pp. 57–61.

WHY AND WHY NOT?

Why don't I write
As much as I might?
Other poets I know,
Always in full flow,
Burst up from underground,
Gush and abound.
It is different with me:
Like an old tree,
Closed in my bark,
I brood in the dark,
Till a chance claw,
Beak or knife score
Through to the wood.
Then, in slow flood,
Oozing their gum,
My poems come.

(13.II.1975)
— Book XVIII, 1975, p. 78.

THE ART OF THE TRIVIAL

Akhmatova put her finger exactly on what I object to in so much of the poetry of little personal experiences and reflections which is the other side of the portentously obscure in the writing of the last twenty-five years or so. She is reported by Lydia Chukovskaya who had asked her why she didn't like Stanislavsky's theatrical productions. A. A. A. did admit that he had found a method to bring out something in Chekhov's plays. But she had the same objection to Chekhov as to Stanislavsky: when S. tried to apply the same method to other sorts of drama, he ruined them. Stanislavsky himself (*My Life in Art*) points to the reason: 'What is important to me is not the truth outside myself, but the truth within myself ... the truth of my attitude towards anything on the stage, towards my partners who represent other characters in the play and towards their thoughts and feelings.'

It is this perversion of the principle of 'Man the measure of all things', to that of 'Man the measure by which all things are to be estimated', that lies at the root of the trouble. On the stage or in poetry, or in real life once you make the test, not what a thing is, but how important it is to you, you are on the path to the trivial and the trumped up.

— Book XX, 1977–79, pp. 31–3.

CLASSIFICATION OF MEN

Dichotomies are equally suspect; they divide groups into mutually exclusive kinds, whereas in real life there is more often an indefinite border-zone. It is the weakness of all syllogistic reasoning and indeed of most 'class of classes' logic. The logic is unarguable but it does not apply to the real world in any very useful way. Nevertheless it *is* useful as a method of *sorting out*, as a preliminary to analyzing actual states of affairs.

In a general way, among the many ways in which men can be sorted according to some single characteristics is that of the things that most attract their interests and to which they devote their main energies. The sort of person who devotes himself to objects and people is distinctively different, as a rule, from the sort of person who devotes himself to activities and processes. I can more easily imagine myself dying for a cause or giving up everything else for art and knowledge than for any person, however dear, or any possessions, however splendid or beautiful.

I think there is a deep and very important difference of types involved in this. There is, of course, no sharp dichotomy involved. Whether the difference is an innate one or not is hard to say, but it does seem to be connected with the two main attitudes to the world: that of the people who regard the world as a more or less fixed 'system', and that of those who regard it mainly as a continually changing 'process'. The world is, of course, always both a system and a process, but the one sort of man emphasizes the structure and regards its permanence as the important thing, the other emphasizes the process and tends to state his values in terms of it. This was my contention in arguing with McAuley about the European Tradition.

In terms of artists, the distinction is perhaps between, those whose interest is the production of 'art-objects' — paintings, sculpture, buildings, jewels, furniture and so on — and those intent on inventing art activities — music, dancing, poetry, story-telling, etc.

— Margaret River 1–X–77
— Book XX, 1977–79, pp. 39–41.

ERICA JONG

I met her at a poetry corroboree in Toronto the year before last and she earned my gratitude by reading a couple of acidulous short stories when I was suffering from a surfeit of mostly very indifferent poetry.

Now Anne has given me a copy of *The Fear of Flying*, which she clearly admires and thinks I should read. After dipping into it here and there it seems to me to consist of nothing but plastic wit about plastic people: why should I waste my time?

Besides it is full of people who get themselves psychoanalyzed as a way of life. I would as soon read a book about drug addicts. These people have stopped being people. They have destroyed themselves. Being funny about them seems a sort of perversion. Sylvia Plath all over again but worse.

— Colosseum Creek, Qld. 4–IX–1978

Other comparisons that occur to me are the dreary world of *The Happy Hooker* and that of the homosexual sub-society I was able to observe at first hand in Sydney in 1928 and 1931. Sex as a way of life, whether straight or queer is such an unmitigated bore.

— Book XX, 1978, p. 122.

MAKING LOVE

'What are you doing' he said.
They said: 'We are making love.'
'Is it made in the heart or the head,
And what do you make it of?'

'That is hard for us to say;
We make it up as we go
And it vanishes away
As soon as it's made, you know.'

'What instruments go to make
Such fleeting and fragile stuff?
'Two hearts that rejoice and ache
For each other are quite enough.'

'Is it easy to make?' 'O Yes,
Though there's no sure rule for it;
Each time we must gamble and guess
How this time the pieces fit.'

'But what when the joiners cease,
And the makers can make no more?'
'Then it leaves the spirit at peace,
But the heart, the heart sore.'

— Pebbly Beach 19–XI–79
— Book XXI, 1979, p. 38.

ARCHILOCHUS

'There is no dithyramb where there is no wine'

Homer? Homer to us is just a word;
His Iliad *tells us nothing of him at all;*
If possible The Odyssey *is worse.*
Archilochus, undeterred
By condition or shame, was wholly personal
Yet once was ranked with Homer for his verse.

The poems of Homer have survived entire,
But of Archilochus, unlucky dog,
Nothing but scraps and broken lines remain;

And yet they pulse with force and fire.
With him I hold amending dialogue
But labour to fix that savage spirit in vain.

'Archilochus, peerless poet of your age,
Singer of injuries, of neglect, of wrong,
Traducer alike of enemy and friend,
Dealer in excrement and rage,
Slanderer, poison-pen and scorpion-tongue,
Where did it get you, poet, in the end?'

'I was a spearman. For soldiers of the line
Life in my day was thankless, grim and hard.
Born out of wedlock — my mother was a slave —
My sole defence was the divine
Gift which the gods impartially award
To high or low: I used what gifts they gave.'

'You made a joke of throwing away your shield
Saying, I'll get another just as good,
And to the highest bidder sold our spear.'
'I ran, it is true, I did not yield
And till then fought as stoutly as I could.
Good sense may make men run as well as fear.'

'What of the old man driven to suicide?
Neobule and her sister in the noose
Choking to death for the unbearable shame
Spread by your spite?' 'I had my pride.
If satire overwhelmed their crude abuse,
I used it to protect my wounded name.'

'But worse, Archilochus, bastard, slave-girl's whelp,
Your drowned friends could not keep you from a feast,
All your companions washed up on the shore,
Cold sea fruit, piled like kelp.'
'I pledged them in wine; I made them a song at least.
They would have done the like for me, no more.'

'You valued pride, yet yours was not the pride
Of well-born men that brought great Hector low
And moved Achilles to honour a father's pleas.

'You boasted of what most men hide;
That high tradition it was your luck to know,
You mocked with the base scorn of Thersites.'

'I am a soldier; I am a poet; I am
A soldier's poet. That noble epic line
I too could master, but I chose instead
Plain facts — there is no dithyramb,
So said Cratinus, where there is no wine
— I drank and washed those heroes from my head.'

'Well, what does it avail you now? Your praise
Survives, but look and see what has become
Of all your poems: tags quoted from the past,
Tatters from dunghills, a chance phrase
On paper smeared by an Egyptian bum,
To this your life's whole work has come at last.'

'Garbage at Oxyrhyncus spared my page
Better than Athens or Alexandria could,
Or Constantinople that passed their learning on.
I cannot, I own, contain my rage
Knowing the blundering muse of Hesiod
Spared and my art swept to oblivion.

'Yet ruins of time, like the disasters of war,
We accept as rational men are bound to do.
To live, to be forgotten, each takes his chance.
It has happened to poets before;
You are a poet, it could happen to you
To perish by the blind malice of circumstance.'

'Surely the Fates punish insolence now and then?
Perhaps you incurred by the self-willed course you chose
Some god's displeasure, or the Muses' curse?'
'No, if the muse should judge like men,
What must we think of glorious Sappho whose
Fragments and tatters match those of my verse?'
'They say your mastery of the stinging word
Brings wasps to hover always round your tomb.'
'They do, yes, but the inference is wrong.
You have lived in Greece: you must have heard
That wasps will gather to the honey-comb
What draws then is the unfailing honey of song.'

And I recall, once in that house in Greece,
Breakfasting on our terrace in the sun,
On coffee and rolls and honey, how around.
The gold-striped wasps gave us no peace
But would not leave us till the meal was done.
I hear Archilochus laugh from underground.

— Pebbly Beach, November 1979
— Book XXI, 1979, pp. 40–5.

THE LANGUAGE OF LOVE

'He loved a wench well; and one time getting up one of the Mayds of Honour up against a tree in a Wood ('twas his first Lady) who seemed at first boarding to be something fearfull of her Honour, and modest, she cryed, 'Sweet Sir Walter, what doe you me ask? Will you undo me? Nay, sweet Sir Walter! Sweet Sir Walter! Sir Walter.' At last, as the danger and the pleasure at the same time grew higher, she cried in the ecstasy, 'Swisser Swatter, Swisser Swatter'.
— Aubrey: *Brief Lives*, Sir Walter Raleigh

Wicked Sir Walter with the maid of honour
Up against a tree in Windsor Great Park,
Pursuing his pleasure with a swift and even stroke,
She cried, 'Ah, sweet Sir Walter!' when first he fell upon her,
'Will you undo me?' But when he reached his mark,
'Swisser Swatter, swisser, swatter!' were all the words she spoke.

Love needs no language: the rhythms of heaven
In the mouths of great poets cannot compare
With that eloquent, ecstatic 'swisser, swisser Swatter!'
As it marked and matched that stroke so swift and so even.
Poets may pen gems sitting easy in a chair;
What they babble in bed can be quite another matter.
Some in exultant union may be able to utter
A whole world of vision, a new universe
In words that express and enchant and compel:
'Darling, darling, darling!' is all that we mutter.
It has the rhythm of love; it has the beat of verse;
It tells all and, after all, what else is there to tell.

— 30–XII–1979
— Book XXI, 1979, pp. 48–9.

RHETORIC

Leonie Kramer in the pamphlets she has recently published about me [*Australian Writers and their Work*, OUP 1979], mentions, I cannot tell whether with approval or disapproval, my habit of declamation and my rhetorical mannerisms [p. 40]. On the whole, I sense a deprecatory tone in what she says.

It is one of the oddities of modern criticism and probably a hangover from Wordsworth's insistence on 'the ordinary language of men', to put rhetoric and poetry at opposite poles of the use of language, to regard one as incompatible with the other. To maintain this we would have to dismiss much of the greatest poetry of past ages.

Leonie is very good, acute and just, but it strengthens my resolve *not* to read critical accounts of my work. It is intrusive, none of my business. I do what I have to do and what I *find* to do.

— 8–IV–1980
— Book XXI, 1980, p. 87.

PSYCHOANALYSIS AND POETRY

In order to do justice to a work of art, analytical psychology must rid itself entirely of medical prejudice; for a work of art is not a disease and consequently requires a different approach from a medical one. A doctor naturally has to seek out the cause of a disease in order to uproot it, but just as naturally the psychologist must adopt exactly the opposite attitude towards a work of art. Instead of investigating its typically human determinants, he will enquire first of all into its meaning, and will concern himself with its determinants only in so far as they enable him to understand it more fully. Personal causes have as much or as little to do with a work of art as the soil with the plant that springs from it. We can certainly learn to understand some of the plant's peculiarities by getting to know its habitat ... But nobody will maintain that everything essential has then been discovered about the plant itself. The personal orientation which the doctor needs when confronted with the question of aetiology in medicine is quite out of place in dealing with

a work of art, just because a work of art is not a human being, but is something supra-personal. It is a thing, not a personality, hence it cannot be judged by personal criteria. Indeed, the special significance of a true work of art resides in the fact that it has escaped from the limitations of the personal and has soared beyond the personal concerns of its creator.
>   C. G. Jung: 'On the Relation of Analytical Psychology to Poetry', *Collected Works of C. G. Jung*, Vol. 15, p. 71.

I came across this more or less by accident. It is the answer of course to Freud's crass reduction of works of art to their alleged underlying symbolized expression of repressed fears and desires, his fallacy of confusing results with their causes. But even more important is its recognition that a work of art is something complete in itself, as the plant is not explicable in terms only of its habitat, but a form explicable only in terms of the laws of its own nature inherent in the seed and that what is so explained in its turn is something else than the plant itself as [a] *thing in itself*, an individual entity different from every other plant of the same species grown in the same habitat.

I have never bothered much with Jung as I have, for example, studied Freud to disagree and refute. I know Jung mainly at second-hand and have always thought his theory of archetypal images as misleading as Freud's mumbo-jumbo that a work of art is no more than the underlying symbols to which he reduced it. In fact I have left them both behind me and think of their clashes of opinion as of no more importance than the battle of Tweedledum and Tweedledee.

I see now that I have probably underestimated Jung. I had better get to know him.

— 7–III–81
— Book XXI, 1981, pp. 176–9.

NIGHTMARES TO ORDER

The night before last in the course of a landscape dream of the most extensive and varied scenery I found myself on the shores of a lake at the foot of steep rocky slopes among huge and precipitous mountains. The scenery was magnificent and I was admiring it when the lake waters began to surge and rise driving me back up the precipice. This is an old and familiar nightmare. I began to climb and found myself very soon labouring and teetering on the verge of frightful abysses and bedevilled by vertigo. Immediately the fear got too much, the slope would even out or the actual cliff would bend gently away. This happened several times in succession, as though, in fact, I was controlling the nightmare. All the time fresh vistas of amazingly beautiful mountain scenery kept appearing as I climbed.

— 8–IV–1981
— Book XXII, 1981, p .6.

BURIDAN'S DONKEY

Interviewers often ask me about my religious beliefs (if any). I never know quite what to say. Boiled down to its essentials I suppose that my position is this: I find none of the evidence for the existence of God (or gods) at all convincing and the same is true of the so-called arguments to that effect. The evidence and the arguments to the contrary I find compelling.

Except for one thing: those people, and they are not few, who pay no attention to these things and rely on direct experience. As Jung in his memoirs records that the existence of God was the most obvious fact of his experience — it was self-evident. To such people the arguments against are like a colourblind man arguing against the existence of colour.

Between the two I am in the position of Buridan's Donkey.[14]

— 16–IV–1981
— Book XXII, 1981, p. 14.

INSIDE-OUTSIDE

I am sitting, lean forward, take my head in hands and shut my eyes. I am thinking about the poem I am working on and think to myself: 'It's all in there!' with a sense that I am outside and can't see in. Then I think: 'But if that is so where am I?' Surely I am in there too; where else could I be? But why am I not saying 'I am in *here*', rather than 'in there'? Are these just habits of mind, or conventions of language, or is there some real sense in which I am not 'in there', but participating in what goes on in there *from* the outside or at any rate from somewhere else?

— Book XXII, 1981, p. 45.

EXPLOITATION

Nietzsche somewhere remarks that poets are the most immoral of men, they live by exploiting their emotions: 'sie beuten sie auf'. I do not remember whether he appeared to be serious or [was] simply throwing off a half-serious provocative remark, a 'Witze'.[15]

It could have been merely a crack at the Romantic theory that poetry was the overflow of powerful feelings, the feelings of the poet himself. It could have gone deeper, a conviction that to exploit one's private feelings for gain or for the admiration of others was something to be ashamed of, a sort of prostitution. Nietzsche was not much of a poet. True poets know that they take their material where they find it. The source is irrelevant. But of course the basic mistake is to overlook the fact that whether the emotion in the poem is a personal one or not, the emotion of the poem, the emotion created by the poem is another matter entirely: it is not in any sense 'self-expression'.

— Book XXII, 1983, pp. 156–7.

Notes

1. Translation: the philosopher deals with a question as an illness.
2. See Yeats, 'The Choice', in *The Collected Poems of W. B. Yeats*, pp. 278–9.
3. See Hope, *The Cave and the Spring*, pp. 68–75.
4. Ibid., pp. 76–90.
5. See Hope, *Collected Poems, 1930–1965*, pp. 205–6. This poem is written in the first person; the narrator, while shaving, thinks of his father and grandfather, their shaving habits and some of their sexual habits. The narrator is represented as without wife and child and his father cuts his own throat. Hope chooses this poem as an example in which he could not be talking about himself, and argues how absurd the biographical critic might be.
6. Francis Webb (1925–73), Australian poet.
7. This quotation is taken from *La Vita Nuova*, Sec. XXII, Para. IV, which Hope incorporates in his commentary. In William Anderson's translation, the sentence reads as follows: 'Reflecting on this, I determined to write something — for I had sufficient worth saying — in which I would include everything I had learned from these ladies' (ladies attempting to comfort the mourning Beatrice).
8. Translation: writing itch.
9. Hope might have meant Thomas Fuller (1608–61) rather than Thomas Lodge. Fuller's *The History of the Worthies of England* appeared in 1663, a year after his death.
10. Yeats, 'The Scholars', in *The Collected Poems*, p. 158.
11. Florbela Espanca (1894–1930) was a Portuguese poet. One of Hope's unfinished projects, which he intended to call *Distaff and Lyre*, was to write a book on women poets stressing the ways in which they differ from their male contemporaries. Hope made a vast amount of notes to this end. Among these notes there exists a folder devoted to Florbela Espanca.
12. Lynne Strahane, an Australian feminist, edited with Patricia Grimshaw *The Half-Open Door* (1982), a collection of autobiographical essays which discuss the problems faced by women in their professional and personal lives.
13. Anne Godfrey-Smith, also known as Anne Edgeworth (1921–). Australian poet and author, based in Canberra since 1954 and author of *The Road to Leongatha* (1966), *Poems in Canberra* (1997) and *Turtles All the Way Down* (1999).
14. Hope sees himself as presented with two alternative views that have equal value and between which he cannot choose. The dilemma of a particular kind of moral choice between two evidently identical items is illustrated by the allegory of Buridan's Ass. Buridan (1300–58) was a moral philosopher. Buridan's Ass was hungry and thirsty and placed between a bundle of hay and a pail of water. It would die of hunger and thirst, having no way of deciding which way to move.
15. 'Sie beuten sie auf': one way or another. 'Witze': joke. The ideas attributed to Nietzsche have some bases of truth in Nietzsche's writings, though Hope is also correct in suspecting that Nietzsche's 'truths' are subverted by their author in that they are often delivered in a 'half-serious provocative remark'. See Nietzsche *Human, All Too Human*, pp. 82–3, in reference to the Greek poets: 'it was hard for them to desist from lies and deception in the course of everyday life — just as all potential people take a delight in lying, a delight that is moreover quite innocent.'

On p. 222, Nietzsche refers to the poet as a deceiver; see also *The Gay Science*, p. 140, where he notes: 'For as Homer says, "Many lies tell the poets"' and, further, p. 210, under the heading 'Poet and Liar', Nietzsche writes: 'The poet considers the liar a foster brother whom he did out of his milk. His brother remained weak and wretched and never even attained a good conscience.'

VIII

COSMOLOGY

'All time is now', Hope tells us, and yet he is aware of the complexity that occurs in the poetic imagination, fed by concepts of the past and the future from the perspective of an intangible present. Eternity is a paradox. Eternity is not a state of things but a state of mind which contemplates all the moments of time as though they were present. This is the case whether one is looking at a star whose light came into existence in times past, or whether one is, at this moment, thinking of a philosophy from antiquity or imagining a future possibility based on a present intuition.

Hope, trained as an empiricist, is wary of categorisation that separates matter, time and the spiritual. Values, social laws, moral precepts and scientific hypotheses are man-made and hence are precarious and reinvented as one scientific paradigm is usurped by another. Perhaps, he suggests, the mistake is to see ourselves as outside nature looking in rather than accepting that we are part of it. The idea that we are apart from nature and that our observations as a knower create knowledge also must mean, he argues, that self-scrutiny and self-consciousness are impossible.

Our knowledge, he shows, is beset by contradictions, and, although logic tells us we are blind to the complexity of our own age, we, nevertheless, go about creating knowledge as if we can predict and know the ramifications of this knowledge, as if our eyes are wide open. We assume, for example, that matter other than human has no consciousness; and what we cannot account for by 'scientific knowledge', we call mysticism, or coincidence, or superstition, when it might be the case that these areas will, as our knowledge increases, become comprehensible within a scientific context.

The meaning of the universe might not be found by looking for an order based on statistical probability but instead by chance, accident and coincidence. Chaos theory and complexity theory, in the 20th century, explored these areas. Nevertheless, when reading Hope's inquiries into the limitations on what we know, we do so through the imagination of a poet. The scientist, he pointed out in a lecture, 'works with daylight sight, reasoning from observed fact, while the poet works with a kind of night sight to extend the range of consciousness'.[1]

Hope's interest in cosmology stems from an interest that began in his childhood. One of his earliest childhood experiences responded to the knowledge that everything is composed of atoms and that these atoms are themselves composed of smaller particles arranged like the planets. He was haunted by the idea that each of these particles might be a universe reproducing the same sort of system and containing further universes ad infinitum, and then the other way, by imagining our visible universe as an infinitesimal particle in an atom of a larger universe and so on.[2]

This made him feel from an early age that a theology that posited a single God able to take notice of him was nonsense. On the other hand, Hope is rather amused at the way in which the scientist has traditionally believed that his or her view of the world is more acceptable than a religious one that cannot be tested with facts and experiments, at least not now, reminding us that we might be able to test such experiences in the future when we 'know' more.

Hope had flirted with the idea of studying science at university but felt that his lack of mathematical skills might prove a barrier. His interest, in particular in biophysics, never waned. His notebooks are testimony to this, giving particular attention to the ways in which the content of physics is determined by the technique which defines its boundaries. He reminds us, and the writers he argues with, that the framing of a hypothesis, the evolution of a new technique to test this hypothesis, is implicitly putting in what we expect to come out.

As a poet, Hope is excited by the limitations to our knowledge. He speaks of us as savages on an atoll trying to make a world picture on 'the basis of the flotsam and jetsam of the shoreline', and as 'fishermen', with our nets flung into 'the ocean of being' attempting, via our senses, which although enlarged by instruments are still only partly known, to know and contain what is currently unknowable. In his last book of poems, *Orpheus*, he enjoys taking on the scientist Hoyle when the latter notes that really efficient leaves, ones that trap sunlight, would be black, and that the green colour of leaves shows the light they are losing. Hope then asks:

> *But suppose the poets know things that scientists miss,*
> *Things we know in our bones. How we know none of us know*
> *If we trust what we see — though we know how deceptive it is.*
> *We accept what science demonstrates, but can it show*
> *There was not a good reason why chlorophyll failed your test?*
> *Could whoever made my world, if it was made at all,*
> *By any chance have listened to your protest*
> *And agreed so that everything afterwards went to the wall.*[3]

Hope would agree that science has provided us with many elegant systems to give us wings with which to soar through the dark. The ultimate answers, though, will, it seems, be met with further bafflement, no matter how swift and targeted our flight.

Hope is always keen to warn his readers when he enters areas of thought that are not those in which he can claim expertise; it is important to assess the extent to which his speculative theories carry weight from the perspective of those who are qualified in the area.

When selecting excerpts for the cosmology section, I approached the scientist Dr Mart Idnurm[4] and asked him to respond to a selection of Hope's cosmology from a scientific perspective. Idnurm, in response to *Mysticism of Matter*, notes that it 'contains a fascinating train of thought on the evolution of consciousness'. He concedes that the ideas seem very speculative, but he also insists that they are by no means absurd. He points out that these ideas are being pursued currently by the Transpersonal School of Psychology.[5] There appear to be Greek antecedents, such as Plotinus: 'Mankind is poised midway between the gods and beasts.' Reading *Plenum or Vacuum*, Idnurm agrees with Hope's 'argument for the universe as a plenum', noting that it would be vindicated by the discovery in the mid-1960s of the so-called cosmic background radiation, which fills space in at least one part of the universe (this radiation, incidentally, is regarded as a relic of the Big Bang).

Idnurm is excited by Hope's *Big-Little and Little-Big* excerpt. He writes:

> From the modern viewpoint A. D. Hope's ideas here are by no means completely fantastic. The idea that the sub-atomic particles may be universes in their own right is perhaps the furthest away from current thought, yet in a sense there is an entirely new world of Alice in Wonderland relationships displayed at the sub-microscopic level. On the large-scale the idea expressed by A. D. H. that our universe is but an atom, or part of, a still larger universe may not be so absurd. It seems quite possible at least that there exist sister universes akin to our own; still this is highly speculative.
>
> Closer [to] 'home' is the discussion about different laws seen at different scales. The important qualification, however, would be that the differences are only apparent. The same holds for all scales of existence, only for certain scales one can introduce approximations which simplify the laws and hence their application to practical problems, whether these be to the microchip, to the internal combustion engine or to the cosmos. So, Newtonian mechanics and the world (our everyday world) to which it applies is but one approximation to the general law that applies at other scales.
>
> Einstein's work is not a complete description of the system of all physical laws that govern the universe. He never assumed it to be more than the description of a facet of such a system, and continued his quest towards the next level of reality, the unified field theory, which utterly defeated him. Much development has taken place in that line of thought since Einstein died, and I believe that the solution may not be too far away. I understand too that Einstein's work is, like A. D. H. suggests, receding into history, though of course his systems, unlike that of Newton, still reign.

The notebooks provide many aspects of Hope's discourse with cosmology. The ideas he explores not only fertilise his poetic vision, they serve to open one's mind and spirit to the enigma of existence when we see ourselves as 'knowers'. The paradoxes that are met by Hope form, I think, the philosophical nexus of his 'creation of being'.

MYSTICISM OF MATTER

The starting point is that of ordinary materialism: that all agents known to us are material agents obeying invariable physical laws. But materialism really only recognises those characters and properties of matter which are universal. It therefore seeks to explain the characters of living bodies in terms of those of inanimate matter, in fact it is unhappy because it cannot reduce the first to the second. There seems a gap which cannot be passed. One could attack the problem from the other end: suppose that living bodies reveal certain universal properties and characters of matter which are latent in all matter (the hypotheses of J. C. 'Bhose' [illegible]).[6] This would involve us in no crude vitalism.

II

When we consider the ways in which energy is spent in Nature, we see everywhere in nature that the more primitive forces are crude and violent: the storms and floods and earthquakes, the cosmic conflagrations and cataclysms, and that these crudest and most primitive forces have a universal range; we see that organization of these forces both diminishes their violence and limits their range. The organization of living bodies exhibits this in its most advanced forms. The machines invented by man come somewhere in between the chemical compounds and the living bodies.

III

The General Picture:
1. Vast areas of the universe filled with simple, relativity, simple material substances, huge expenditure of energy and nothing but simple physical change as a result.

2. Small areas of the universe whose complex physical substances are built up. (The only area well known and studied is the Earth but there may be others and probably are many others at this level.)
3. In very limited areas, because the conditions merely 'recur' and the probability of this occurrence at all is very low indeed, matter shows still higher organization: the virus, the protein, molecules, etc. The inception of the 'open system' as independent and autonomous bodies. The open system, of course, is not in itself new — the stationary wave in a river, the growing crystal).
4. The single celled organism.
5. The *multicellular* organism
6. The animal conscious of its ends and purposes.
7. The self-conscious forms of matter.

These form a hierarchy, in each case more and more organized, giving release to latent possibilities of matter in the form of characters not possessed by the less organized forms and, in each case, more limited in range and location in the universe, but more capable of acting on the other forms of matter. The mistake has been to take this limitation as an indication that life, consciousness and self-consciousness are not universal, or necessary or implicit characters of matter; to regard them as something to be, if possible, reduced to simple physical and chemical properties of universal range.

IV

At the first two stages, bodies influence one another externally by attraction and repulsion. At the third and later stages they are organized to take up and transform the simpler bodies, to extend the amount of matter which has the higher organization. The history of life on the earth has been the history of the conquest of inanimate matter by animate. At the 6th stage (perhaps at the 5th), the development of a nervous system shows a special type of matter which is not only conscious, but conscious *for* the larger amount of unconscious matter within its own organization (the animal body) but the history of this stage has mainly been that of small parts of matter becoming conscious of a wider and wider range of things *external* to itself. In man this has reached the point where small parts of his own substance and a small part of the whole of matter, have become conscious of, or capable of being conscious of, the whole of the *rest*. This is the intellectual process of which modern science is an episode and perhaps the beginning of a new departure.

V

In man self-consciousness makes possible the free direction of energy, the early stages made possible the autonomy of energies of a material body. But there are signs that 'other consciousness', already existing within individual animal bodies is in [the] process of extension to bodies of which man is normally [illegible] conscious. Mystics appear to possess this power. If this 8th stage, which at present appears only under limited conditions, erratically and sporadically became general, we should have parts of the material universe capable of being conscious *for* the rest, as they are now capable of being conscious *of* it. We should have a conscious world perhaps, perhaps in the end a conscious universe, and ultimately a self-conscious, autonomous universe and the adventure of biology would be complete. It is not absurd but it is incomprehensible except as a general idea. No conception of the sort of organization that would be required is possible to us any more than any conception of self-conscious and other-conscious matter would be in terms of the characters and organization of unicellular animals. But its advent need not be infinitely remote in time. The lower the organization in the past, the slower has been the period of development, the more it has depended on the chance occurrence of natural but unlikely conditions. By the standards of former stages that of the conscious and self-conscious stages has been incredibly swift. The 'sporadic' stage of the occurrence of mystics once passed, the progress may be very rapid indeed.

VII

There are constant occurrences of events within nature which are called 'miraculous' or 'supernatural' and a persistent tradition of and belief in divine beings. The attitude of science is to treat these as delusions or mistakes as some of them demonstrably are. The attitude of religions has been more and more to treat such events as outside the order of Nature because they cannot be explained in terms of natural science. But life, consciousness, self-consciousness are characters of a limited range of material bodies each inexplicable in terms of the preceding stage — each only explicable in terms of a kind of organization unknown at the earlier stage. Just as various types of man-like creatures appeared and most of them disappeared and one survived, so it may be that forms of material organization unrecognizable except in their effects to our own more primitive organization, have occurred sporadically and disappeared. We may call these 'gods'. Divine characters are, judging from their effects, precisely what we should expect on the analogy of earlier stages and on the direction indicated by the progression — vital > conscious > self-conscious > other-conscious:

(a) They occur so rarely that we doubt their occurrence at all, just as a committee of unicellular creatures inhabiting the whole surface of the earth would rightly doubt rumours of the first multicellular animals and would say there was an obvious 'scientific' explanation, ie., that these were simply colonies of unicellular individuals pooling their resources. The 'supernatural' powers due to specialization of function in the higher type of animal would be incomprehensible to the unicellular animals and their effects which would be evident *would* be discounted as 'superstition'. In the same way the first few creatures capable of colour vision would be dismissed by the colourblind majority as 'mystics'.

(b) The divine characteristics, unknown and possibly unknowable to us, show by their effects that they have powers over matter unknown to us — the so called miracles. Ability to think would be a miracle to a polypus or an earthworm; ability to propose and criticise ends to a lower vertebrate; consciousness of the structure of the universe or of one's own motives to an anthropoid ape; ability to reproduce and transform inorganic matter, to stars and meteors. Miracles indicate a type of organization able to operate in ways which indicate a superior control over matter to our own.

(c) The effects indicate vaguely an extension of the range of other-consciousness or perhaps an adaptation of this to an entirely new type of power. At all the earlier stages the 'new' power has always been an adaptation of some power already existing in matter to a new sort of function.

(d) A constant attribute of divinity has been that of 'creation'. What this means at the higher stage the mystics hint at but cannot tell us. But it may be something as extraordinary to us as reproduction or enzyme building would be to a stone or a Mozart symphony to a lobster.

— Canberra Community Hospital (1953)
— Book IV, 1953, pp. 1–9.

THE INSTANT VIEW FALLACY I

MORE ASTRONOMICAL CONFUSION

Here it is again! A useful book by two scientists, *Astronomy: Fundamentals and Frontiers* (Robert Jastrow and Malcolm Thompson, 1972), shows the careless reference which often appears to bedevil cosmological argument in support of various 'models' of the universe. In the same paragraph I read:

> If a supernova happens to occur nearby in our Galaxy, it appears as a new star in the sky … The last supernova that exploded in our Galaxy was seen in Europe in 1604, and caused a sensation. One of the earliest reported supernovas was a brilliant explosion recorded by Chinese astronomers in AD 1054.[7]

So far, so good. The event referred to is the date at which the explosions were observed on earth. But the next sentence reads:

> At the position of the supernova there is today a great cloud of gas known as the Crab Nebula, expanding outward at a speed of 1,000 miles per second, which contains the remains of the star *that exploded 900 years ago.*[8]

Professors Jastrow and Thompson are, of course, perfectly aware that the phrase underlined is completely false and should read *whose explosion was observed 900 years ago*, but forget that they are writing a book for use by liberal-arts college students who may take it literally. But it is not the only case in which this sort of thinking appears to muddle an argument by treating the evidence as though light was transmitted instantaneously from all parts of the universe.

For example, it is not at all clear that Jastrow and Thompson do not mean their readers to take quite literally the sentence: 'At the position of this supernova *there is today* a great cloud of gas ...', etc. We have in fact no evidence at all of what is there today.

— Book XXI, 1979, pp. 7–8.

PLENUM OR VACUUM?

We are accustomed to think of the universe as consisting largely of empty space with matter very sparsely and unevenly distributed in it. This must partly be the effect of the scale of the viewer; creatures of the size of sub-atomic particles would take the same view of what Hamlet calls this too, too solid flesh. It would be hard or impossible for them to conceive [of] me as a 'solid' body, coordinated and organized to act as a whole. But the view of the universe as empty is due also to our habit of thinking of matter as the only form of 'filling' and discounting the electro-magnetic waves of various kinds. Not only is the distribution of 'matter' in the form of particles and dust much more general thoughout the empty space of the universe than was formerly supposed, but the whole of this space is full of motions. Now that the boundaries between matter and energy are no longer as sharply drawn as they used to be we could easily come to think of the universe as a plenum: Zero with a difference!

— Book VII, 1961, p. 1.

THE HISTORICAL SENSE II

What chiefly marks our lack of an Historical Sense, as distict from a Sense of History, is the fact that we are so well aware of the false views of the world on which past ages have depended for the world pictures they have constructed for themselves: the Copernican concept of the cosmos for example, affects every view of man held before its appearance and must considerably modify the view of God, if it does not call it [into] question altogether. The Darwinian hypothesis has a similar, though less thorough-going tendency to upset the assumptions on which man's view of himself and his society, and the whole world picture, must rest. Some of the implications of earlier theories are only now beginning to have general affect. Those of Einstein, of Marx and Freud are perhaps still to be felt. What is clear in studying the history of previous fundamental revolutions in ideas, revolutions which question and then destroy something so obvious that no one would question it, something apparent yet false, is that the revolution itself proceeds by degrees. It is usually as with Copernicus or Darwin, incompletely or falsely formulated at first, it does not realise its own implications and its founders are usually anxious to make the theory conform to parts of the world-view that the new theory actually makes absurd or meaningless. Before one set of implications is fully grasped, before a new world-view becomes generally accepted, another may be on its way, made possible by the first which it is destined to over-set.

All this we know; our sense of what has happened in history and is quite likely to happen again is excellent. What we lack is a sense of the precariousness of our present world picture in the face of history. There is no general view that *our* general view is as likely to be over set in the future, as [were] the general views of the past. We tend to think of ourselves as living in a 'scientific' age, such that no new discovery or radically new idea could over-set the general world picture. Yet this has precisely been the blindness of past ages. In a previous note I suggested that over-reliance on the general, the common, neglect of the individual, the unusual, the unique is characteristic of our notion of the scientific attitude, and that when we become aware of this the whole world picture may change and the present one appear as out-moded as the medieval cosmos elaborated from Ptolomy, and the implications for man and society may be as profoundly revolutionary. A new conception of matter, a new conception of life, of consciousness, of other-consciousness, of the limitations of the human to grasp the nature of things — any of these at any time now may render our world picture as a whole archaic and absurd. And there may be thousands of others not even guessed at.

Without at least an inkling of the probable fragility of our own world-view we cannot in fact be said to have an historical sense even of the history of other world-views.

It may be that too well developed an historical sense is a disadvantage and can never be common. Belief and disbelief are easy. To live and act satisfactorarily in a world in which all the basic things are no more than probable and most of them hypothetical, is not possible to most of us. To act on *as if* is harder than on *est* and *non est*.

— Book VIII, 1964–65, pp. 47–49.

THE THING CONCEPT

Our way of thinking about the world is basically that of things related to and interacting with other things. Our languages presuppose this in their very structures, our logic and science are constructed on this assumption and of course it works well enough for the ordinary world around us. Any other way of thinking would seem to be 'unthinkable', though physics has lately been forced to question it in dealing with the bases of the material world, and philosophy has been trying to invent 'logics' not tied to this assumption, and philosophical linguistics has been busy purging language of false or merely verbal *things* and ghost substantives. If we scrutinize our notion of 'things' over the whole range of our knowledge we shall find a range of objects capable of holding and altering relations without themselves being changed, capable of moving as a whole in space, capable of moving other objects or influencing them where the status and nature of the *thing* is clear enough.

A stone, [a] star, a drop of water, a bubble of gas in a liquid is each a thing. Their parts cohere; they move and are moved as a whole. But is a cloud, a mountain, a wind or a wave a 'thing' in quite the same sense? The objects mentioned are complex bodies composed of things, molecules and atoms which themselves move and are moved as a whole and are distinct from their surroundings. But are the 'particles' which compose the atoms things in the same sense? Present views in physics would suggest that they are not and that below a certain level the concepts of the macrocosmic world are simply inappropriate and its language misleading.

It is natural for us to regard the chain of being as if it were a sort of hierarchy:

Atoms
Molecules

> Loose aggregations of molecules
> Chemical continuations of molecules
> Self-contained 'pieces' of the foregoing [illegible]
> Organisms
> Consciously self-directing organisms.

It is natural enough in this simple and largely unconscious mythology to regard ourselves as the 'thing' par excellence, the sole and final example of a fully autonomous 'body' and to build on this, equally unconsciously a view of a homo-centric universe, just as Ptolomoic cosmology led to the view of a geocentric universe and supported a homocentric view of man's position in it.

Suppose that we had now reached a stage in human history where this sort of thinking was about to become as obsolete as Ptolomoic concepts of the cosmos! Not the least obstacle to the Copernican type of view was the vested interest which human vanity had in the other view — the microcosm, that core and rationale of man's existence seemed to be lost if the earth was no longer the centre of the material world and man the top of the material creation.

Suppose the vanity of being the highest organization of matter, the most thingy of Things turned out to be equally an illusion! Suppose the next age of science were to prove a revolution profounder than any previous one, a revolution in which man was forced to see himself a mere part or 'cell' in higher organizations of which he had had till then no more conception than he had previously of the system of the heavens or the structure of the atom.

All his previous world-views would then seem to him to have been like the views of an intelligent cell in an animal body trying to give an account of that body in terms of combinations of individual cells alone and their interactions, singly and as organizations, without any inkling of the body itself as a *Ding an Sich*, with its own total organization, its own purposes and procedures. The single-cell scientist or the single-cell philosopher would no doubt evolve remarkably clever and to some extent plausible accounts, but they would be as ingeniously false as the most subtle refinements of the attempts to explain the motions of the sun, moon and planets and the system of the fixed stars in terms of a universe with the earth at the centre and the other bodies revolving around it.

Such a cell might be able to grasp dimly the nature of a multi-cellular, conscious and autonomous being, but it would probably not get very far since its thinking would be limited to cell-to-cell experience. It would not be possible to conceive the real nature of the higher entelechy. And this would be the most likely obstacle to the human conception of the higher entelechy of a super-individual, whatever it was.

(Very possibly this way of thinking in terms of a super individual is just what would stand in the way of our realizing the possibility of an organization to which, as in the sub-atomic world, such concepts would be inappropriate, temporal and spatial relations being of a sort not applicable in the intermediate cosmos of 'things'. Sept. 1968.) A direct attack would be useless, results in a sort of theology or anthropomorphic concept of the sort we are already used to in religious and science fiction.

Yet there is a possible way out. The mere idea of an 'intelligent' cell is contradictory since intelligence is the character only of a higher organization of a multicellular body. A higher than human entelechy might and probably would have the characters of the lower ones, but it might have other powers as inconceivable to us because we lack it, as intelligence is impossible to a single cell. Nevertheless the great difference in the rising scale is the point where intelligence becomes possible. Something analogous to the Browning method might at least give us a clue. What the nervous system has achieved for the multicellular body, may [as an] analogy, be the sort of thing that intelligent beings can voluntarily do for the understanding of or even the evolution of higher sorts of entity.

But the Browning method needs a note to itself and must wait till I get back to my books and papers.

— Off Guardafui, Indian Ocean, Dec. 1965.
— Book VIII, 1965, pp. 169–74.

BIG-LITTLE AND LITTLE-BIG

From the time that I learned as a child that everything is composed of atoms with a great deal of space between and that these atoms are themselves composed of smaller particles arranged like planets around the sun with vast spaces between relative to size of the particles, I was seized, indeed haunted by the idea that each of these particles might be a universe reproducing the same sort of system as our macrocosmic universe and containing further universes ad infinitum. From there it was an easy thing to go the other way and imagine our visible universe as an infinitesimal particle in an atom of a larger universe and so on ad infinitum and this seemed to make nonsense of a theology that posited a single creator able to take cognisance of me.

From the time I could count, the 'folie de l'infinité'[9] has been with me in the form of trying to make the infinite an imaginable, siezable image. First came the notion of counting to the end of the series of integers. Later with the calculus the notion of the infinitesimal, an infinite enclosed in a definite. I wrestled with Socrates' argument [illegible] in the Phaedo and later with the paradoxes of Zeno. The discovery of particles of brief duration introduced me to the idea of something with a definite nature and structure which yet exists only for an infinitesimal time. And this in turn introduced me to the idea of time scales of a relative sort: the notion that there might be lives lived on a time scale such that our own was like that of a transitory sub-atomic particle by comparison, and which might in turn be infinitesimal in comparison with others, far beyond the

> A thousand ages in Thy sight
> Are as an evening gone

of the Old Hundred. So that it might be perfectly possible that just as the cells which make up the body — or some of them — grow old and are replaced, we might ourselves be passing elements in the organization of other living beings imperceptible to us on account of their vastly greater time-scales and yet, unknown to us, influenced and subject to direction and control by the whole macro-being. Or that the same space might be occupied by other macro-societies of which we were as unaware as the micro-organisms living in and on and around us to whom we are simply 'environment', indeed that the Biosphere might itself be such a creature and the *Anima Mundi* more than Plato's dream.

Another set of such possibilities has arisen to haunt my imagination from the consideration of incommensurable quantities, and yet another from the speculations of some phycisists, in recent years, on the possibility of an 'anti-matter' parallel to the matter of our perceived world — or again from the possibility that the relations of time, space and energy which hold in this universe are not continued beyond the organization at atomic or sub-atomic level but are 'local' to a certain range and that below this range other laws hold and other concepts are necessary (accounting for the apparent logical problems and discrepancies encountered by physicists trying to account for the behaviour of subatomic particles). And this raises the question [of] whether there might not be an upper limit in this sense as well as a lower. There would not, therefore, be an infinite series of worlds each continuous with and homogeneous with the others, but a series of worlds connected only by unknown laws and other logics, each strictly incommensurable and incomparable with the others.

Such ways of thinking are probably very naive and simple-minded but they are so habitual to me that all my thinking is permeated and coloured by them. Any theory of the world based on what we know, any system of belief has for me, a provisional quality, an 'unfinished' aspect when viewed in the light of what we do not know. The actual seems always something held in suspense between all the forms of the possible, the definite ready in a moment to dissolve into the ocean of the unlimited. And I live my life in local space and time with a premonition that the human mind is already on the brink of a metaphysical revolution more profound than that by which the Ptolemaic cosmos was replaced by the Copernican and Newtonian. Einstein may one day look like the last of an old line — comparable to those astronomers before Copernicus who in the light of growing awareness of discrepancies in the old system, tried to solve them by refinement of theory, more and more elaborate systems of epicycles, and so on. His apparent breakthrough in theory may in time be seen to be no such thing, but an ingenious fiddle with time, space and energy in order to preserve an old world-view — a fiddling mainly valuable in taking a further step towards proving it inadequate and opening the way to another sort of thinking. If so, he would be pleased, I imagine.

— Atlantic off Morocco, 1971
— Book XII, 1971, pp. 24–9.

THE BOOT STRAP TRICK I

The biochemical world we have until now been describing is a static one. It is a world of things rather than of events ... In order to obtain this picture, we have had deliberately to destroy the living tissue at some arbitrary time and systematically to fragment it into its component chemicals. Yet by doing so we have ignored just those characteristics which make life different from death. The proteins, nucleic acids, lipids, carbohydrates, of a living animal are to all intents and purposes identical with those of one just dead. But no one would mistake the one for the other ... where has the life gone? Can we describe the difference that we know exists between life and non-life in chemical form?

Of course, we can. But to do so we must shift the perspective from which we have been studying the chemistry of the cell. We must no longer ask what they are made of but, rather, how are they kept in existence? For the highly organized molecules we have been describing all have one most important characteristic in common: By comparison with more elementary chemicals, they are all highly unstable. They readily begin to break down as soon as their environment alters beyond certain well-defined limits of pH and temperature ...

The second characteristic implicit in the macromolecules is that they are all extremely *unlikely* substances. Those materials which life produces in such abundances still defeat the synthetic techniques of the chemist. In the living cell they cannot arise purely by random chemical reactions; they must be synthesized according to precisely planned pathways which can achieve a specificity far beyond that of the chemist. There must be mechanisms within the cell which can distinguish between even such close relatives as the d- and l-isomers of amino acids, or between sugars such as glucose and galactose.

This second problem would not perhaps be so overwhelming if the synthesis were, so to speak, a once-for-all job, if the lipid, protein and carbo-hydrate molecules had only to be made in the desired quantities, laid down in the appropriate structure, and then were able to go on functioning indefinitely until 'fair-wear-and-tear' demanded their replacement. But such is not the case ... Throughout the body the molecule which survives for more than a few days without undergoing change was found to be the exception rather than the rule. The discovery of the prodigality of this constant flux of molecules ...

> revolutionized bio-chemical thinking. It became clear that one, perhaps *the* major function of the living cell, was the constant re-creation of itself from within.
> — Steven Rose: *The Chemistry of Life*, 1968, pp. 77–78

It becomes clear that the discovery of some of the simpler 'organic' molecules in the clouds of interstellar space, which has been hailed as evidence of the 'automatic' evolution of life in the universe by chance interaction is largely a bit of nonsense, like the similar and earlier dream of the evolution, by lightning strikes on a primitive warm 'soup' of simpler chemical formations in the primordial oceans. Chance collision and chance chemical bonding has no more likelihood of achieving the precise chains of reactions required by wholly *unlikely* living substances than the 400 monkeys of legend striking the keys at random [have] at some point of time any chance of producing a play by Shakespeare or the motes in the Brownian movement in a glass of water [have] of ever arranging themselves in the shape of a lion or even of a simple crystal lattice. The random effects concerned do not form a closed series such that each possible combination given enough time must be achieved, including that of the text of the play. They form an infinite series even if the number of letters involved is finite in much the same way that the value of π is an infinite series though only ten digits are involved. Random combination of letters can never achieve the result of a selective, purposeful and creative imagination using those letters in the form of words even though only a few thousand words are in question. In the same way random association can never achieve the planned, purposeful and orderly structure of a single cell.

Vitalism in its ancient crude form may be as discredited as the 'phlogiston' theory, but it is by no means extinct and will not be until someone can explain and even demonstrate how a living cell can arise from random collisions of non-living chemicals. Every scientific advance increases the mystery of life and of consciousness.

Human beings represent, as far as we know, the only chemical structures able to investigate and reflect on themselves; but they represent the only conscious or sentient creatures able to investigate the chemical bases of thought, feeling, sensation and will.

These are not in Mr Rose's brief, but it is part of his bio-chemists' faith that, like life itself, they will ultimately be shown to be based on chemical structure and reactions.

So they probably will. It is the 'reductive' theory so common in modern science that worries me, the theory that reduces all chemical characters to their physical substrates, all vital character to their chemical substrates and all conscious characters likewise. At each stage matter emerges into a new mode of being which possesses character not possessed by its constituent parts and *not* reducible to the character of those parts. And it is precisely these emergences of new, irreducible characters that pose a logical problem — which can be put in the form of a riddle: What is it, composed only of A and B, which gives rise to C?
— Book XXI, 1979, pp. 13–19.

THE INSTANT VIEW FALLACY II:
ACCORDING TO HOYLE

Here is Fred Hoyle, for whom I have the greatest admiration apparently committing what I call the Instant View Fallacy, that is the mistake of treating the whole visible universe as though what we see at any one instant were happening simultaneously instead of the view he has just stressed that the further away we look the more remote are the events in the past that we see. The theory that the universe is uniformly expanding rests on the fallacy which in turn rests on the increasing shift towards the *red* end of the spectrum as we view events farther and farther away.

'The relationship of the polygons* is determined by the relative motions of the galaxies. If the larger polygon occurs *later* in time, the galaxies are moving away from each other. If the larger polygon is *earlier*, the galaxies would approach each other as time went on. In the first case the universe would be expanding, in the second, contracting.' (*Ten Faces of the Universe*, p. 99.)

The assumption here is that the polygon in question is observed as at one time. But this is obviously impossible. If we view the polygon 'face-on', all the galaxies will be equi-distant from us in time and space. The observed red-shift would tell us nothing but the fact that this set of galaxies was once receding at the same rate. We are to suppose that each galaxy is at a different distance from us so that we view the system end-on and in perspective. If we take a set of galaxies which includes M15 the nearest large one and others at the limit of observation, there is a time difference between what we see in the case of M15 (2 million light years approx.) and the farthest galaxy (5,000 million light years approx.) of 4,995 million light years. Since the age of the universe is at present calculated to be between 12 and 15 billion years (Hoyle appears to use the American billion), all we can say is that literally as far as we can see, 5,000 million years ago objects at that limit were receding from us in every direction at very high speeds, and that at intermediate periods nearer objects were receding at lesser speeds. What they are now doing is unknown. M15 five million years ago seems indeed to have been slowly approaching. But again what it is now doing is unknown. Hoyle at any rate, once a steady-state man, recognizes that the universe could now be contracting on itself (p. 100). But the polygons on which his earlier argument is based can never *at any time* have actually existed. You cannot draw a 'line' between objects in space and moving rapidly when their positions are only known at different times.

* Of a set of galaxies formed by joining the set (in this case 5) by lines on a plane though in actuality the figure would be three dimensional; one polygon is represented as smaller than the other, though the relative shape is the same.

— Book XXI, 1980, pp. 141–3.

THE INSTANT VIEW FALLACY III: ACCORDING TO KAUFFMAN

Here it is again in its crudest and most careless form. W. J. Kauffmann III, according to his book *Black Holes and Warped Space-Time* (1979), is a leading US astronomer, physicist and cosmologist. He certainly knows better, yet on p. 57, I find the following:

> The fastest pulsar, called the Crab Pulsar, is located at the center of the Crab Nebula in the constellation of Taurus … This dramatic nebula is the remnant of a supernova that erupted on July 4, 1054, as recorded by the ancient Chinese historian Toktaga … The neutron star at the center of this nebula is *therefore only nine hundred years old.*

Four pages back under a photograph of [the] Crab Nebula as it appears today I read:

> The nebula, located in the constellation of Taurus, is 6,500 light years away and measures 8 light years in diameter.

The Crab Nebula appears from photographs to be roughly elliptical in shape with one of the diameters facing about twice as long as the other; the third diameter from front to rear is probably not measurable but if the nebula is really ovoid in form [it] could be about the same as the top-to-bottom diameter (the smaller).

Clearly the proper figure for the age of the nebula as we see it at present should be 6,500 + 900 years + an undefined time for the exploding star to reach the dimensions of the 'two inches' against the night sky recorded by the Chinese observers before it shrank to its present proportions, as they record it did after more than a year. If we assume that the explosion took about a year to reach its peak we have an age of 7,401 years.

Sir Fred Hoyle in a recent book, *Life Cloud*, written in collaboration with N. C. Wickramasinghe, makes the same slip as Kauffmann.

> Since 1968 scores of pulsars have been discovered. They all 'pulse' with almost clockwork regularity and with periods typically of about one second, significantly larger than the period of the Crab pulsar [33 milliseconds]. The pulse period is thought to lengthen slowly as a pulsar ages, *so that the Crab is a particularly young example being less than a thousand years old.* (p. 57, my italics.)

— Book XXI, 1980, pp. 146–8.

THE BOOT-STRAP TRICK II

Further to Steven Rose's *The Chemistry of Life*:

> For many years the principle of spontaneous generation of everything from barnacles to micro-organisms was implicitly believed by the vast bulk of mankind [except that 'the vast bulk of

mankind' never even considered these possibilities any more than the rest of their animal species did — or could. A nice example of the tendency of scientists to think in terms of their own specialties, as though their concerns were matters of common knowledge.] It was the rigorous investigations of Pasteur in the middle of the nineteenth century that conclusively demonstrated that life as we now know it could not have arisen spontaneously from non-living matter. Every living thing, said Pasteur, has arisen from another living thing. Nor should this surprise us, for even the simplest of present-day living organisms are highly complex, highly improbable molecular structures, whose chance assembly from their elements would involve odds of such astronomical unlikelihood that we may regard it, for practical purposes, as impossible. The chemicals which compose present life forms require to be synthesized by specifically catalysed reactions, and these specific catalysts are themselves the product of the living organism and cannot arise spontaneously. If we are to seek for the origins of the complex of attributes that we regard as life today, we must assume that these attributes evolved only slowly over the thousands of millions of years of blank history that separate the origin of the earth from even the earliest living form whose fossilized traces we can now observe. (p. 248)[10]

This is fair enough. But he still clings to the possibility of such an evolution. I must take advice from the mathematicians and the experts on the theory of probability on my argument in BS' theory I that the crucial point is the difference between the predictability of the combinations possible in a limited series and those in an unlimited series, particularly of those mathematical series in which it is possible to generate an infinite series from a finite series of integers of which language appears to be a member.

In any case, until I am proved wrong, my impulse is to say, 'this is my case: *j' y suis, j'y reste.*'

Some form of Vitalism remains a possibility — even if we do not know how or in what terms it can be formulated. It remains possible because in the present state of our knowledge, no other alternative can be suggested. It remains *faute de mieux*, but it does remain.

— 12–VIII–79
— Book XXI, 1979, pp. 21–3.

A BOY THINKING

Another point just met in Sagan's *Broca's Brain* (p. 176). In his discussion of the better examples of Science Fiction he remarks:

> *He Who Shrank*, by Harry Hasse, presents an entrancing cosmological speculation which is being seriously revived today, the idea of an infinite regress of universes — in which each of our elementary particles is a universe one level down, and in which we are an elementary particle in the next universe up.

By 'seriously revived' he means, of course revived as an hypothesis by serious scientists as an explanatory notion in a systematic schema in cosmology. That it is an old idea revived, I did not know though from the first formulation of the atomic theory by Leukkippos and Demokritos it must have occurred independently to many minds. I recall that it occurred to mine when I was a small boy, about ten years old if I recall correctly. It arose from reading some popular scientific account of the atomic theory of the period in which complex atoms consisting of a nucleus and rings of electrons figured (but not the sub-atomic particles of today).

My notion arose from childish consideration of Olbers' famous paradox[11] — though I had never heard of Olbers — why is the sky dark at night? In an infinite universe, I reasoned, there should be an infinite amount of light — I think some theological ideas intruded here vaguely: the notion of God as the source of light — but I went on: suppose *this* universe is inside another in much the same way that an atom may be enclosed in a collection of molecules in a solid — suppose we are part of an atom-universe which is inside the leg of a super-chair composed of other atom-universes — then our universe would be dark, except for the light it could produce inside itself. I recall very clearly the particular chair-leg I was looking at as I worked this out.

From here it was an easy step to ask why, if this were so, there could not be an infinite regress in both directions of universes within universes; indeed it seemed a logical conclusion since I had had to abandon the theory that this particular universe was infinite in space and time. I had tried without success to imagine a finite or closed universe with 'nothing outside it', though at the time I knew nothing of this idea as a scientific theory deriving from Einstein's theories. I had simply found a comfortable way of resolving an uncomfortable clash of ideas involved in the notion of a limited universe.

Later in reading D. W. Sciama's account of Olbers and his paradox, I learned that C. V. L. Charlier in 1922 had proposed to solve the paradox by something like an infinite regress of galaxies, clusters of galaxies and clusters of such clusters and so on to a point where the distances between clusters accounts for the darkness of the night sky through the inverse square law. I doubt if I should have been impressed since I had fallen in love with my own 'metaphysical' theory and was as fascinated by the thought of 'our' atoms as possible universes containing others as by the macrocosmic model. Charlier's theory makes no provision for this.

The only advance on this early theorising occurred to me on a train-journey from Western Australia. The idea that by a revolutionary theory of time and space the two ends of the regress might be joined and the series of universes be shown to be re-entrant on one another. There the mind boggled and rested in its bogglement.

— Book XXII, 1981, pp. 19–22.

Notes

1. Hope, 'Address to Australian College of Ophthalmologists', A. D. Hope Papers.
2. Hope, Book XII, 1971, p. 24.
3. Hope, 'Protest to Fred Hoyle', in *Orpheus*, p . 5 7 .
4. I approached Dr Idnurm as I needed the response of a scientist who was well read in literary and philosophical areas. Mart Idnurm is a visiting fellow at the Research School of Earth Sciences, ANU, and is widely published in his discipline. These notes were made in Canberra in 1996 where, over several days, I consulted with Dr Idnurm.
5. Hope wrote the entries in 1953; Dr Idnurm is commenting on them in 1996.
6. The hypotheses of 'J. C. Bhose' has not been traceable. The name itself has been written in the notebook in a scrawl. It is now assumed that the name is incorrect.
7. Jastrow & Thompson, *Astronomy: Fundamentals and Frontiers*.
8. Ibid.
9. Translation of 'folie de l'infinité': The foolishness of infinity.
10. Rose, *The Chemistry of Life*, p. 248.
11. See Encylopaedia Britannica, 1994–98. This paradox was discussed in 1823 by the German astronomer Heinrich Olbers, and its discovery is widely attributed to him. In cosmology, the paradox related to the problem of why the sky is dark at night. If the universe is endless and uniformly populated with luminous stars, then every line of sight must eventually terminate at the surface of a star. Hence, contrary to observation, this argument implies that the night sky should everywhere be bright, with no dark spaces between the stars. The answer is that the stars do not live infinitely long, so there is not enough starlight to fill the universe. A wrong answer, frequently given, is that the expansion of the universe weakens the starlight.

IX

WINE, WOMEN AND INSECTUAL SONG

Hope's concern with sex in general and with his own sexuality is one of the sources of strength in his poetry. His attempt to understand female sexuality is recorded throughout the notebooks, as is his awareness of his exclusion from understanding. He felt that an understanding of the differences between men and women was the key to constructing a new metaphysical world view. Hope maintains that as long as our knowledge of these differences is left untapped, our metaphysical view of the human condition will remain limited. The excerpts Hope has chosen from the Kinsey Report are important in regards to Hope's interest in itemising perceived differences between the sexes. To a large extent, they confirm Hope's views that men and women are organised differently and possess unique perceptions and separate aims. Hope believes that man has done his best 'to minimize, if not to destroy, the only independent source of knowledge existing, that between men and women'.[1]

The sexuality of Hope's sexual imagery makes the quotations he has chosen on insect and animal sexual behaviour quite fascinating. He does not, of course, argue that human beings are insects or animals; but analogy, he argues, 'is not to be despised. It has no demonstrative force, but it can suggest unsuspected types of structure, unguessed forces and overlooked points of view which can then be tested by the usual methods. It is perhaps the element of analogy in the argument which has always made "inductive argument" refractory to logical demonstration.'

Contemporary feminists will find much to argue with in Hope's attitudes; but many will also see the value of exploring a male mind on these issues. It is essential, though, to recognise Hope's detachment. To take the content of the poems as representing Hope's experiences of or beliefs about sexuality is to ignore Hope's insistence that he enters a poem as an actor and not as himself. Nevertheless, given Hope's views that men and women have 'quite different organizations, ranges of perception, and ends and aims', it is reasonable in terms of Hope's own arguments to recognise that these are the compositions of a male, and are therefore specific to one of the 'two species of intelligent beings on earth'.[2]

Hope's view that men and women are organised differently does not include a subscription to biologism and essentialism. Indeed his argument, penned in 1952, that the differences between men and women are metaphysical, is prophetic of Julia Kristeva's words in the early 1980s: 'the very dichotomy man/woman as an opposition between two rival entities may be understood as belonging to metaphysics. What can "identity", even "sexual identity", mean in a new theoretical and scientific space where the very notion of identity is challenged?'[3] Hope's plea for the metaphysical basis of possible new knowledge from the sexes is made on the basis that the metaphysical categories set up by the patriarchy are limited and destructive.

Hope had been a hero of the anti-puritan brigade from the 1940s to the mid-1960s, having dared to use explicit sexual references in his poetry. His bawdy, sensual poetry, whether satirising an aspect of life or exploring the enigma of the sexual act itself, was celebrated by men and women alike. The advent of women's liberation in the early 1970s, involving women as radical feminists, rejected the male symbolic order in the name of difference and extolled femininity.[4] This must have been very confusing for men of Hope's generation — not to mention the generation that followed. The women's movement had an extensive agenda and one of the issues concerned the manner in which women were represented in the media and literature as primarily the objects of male desire. There was a sudden onslaught of criticism of Hope's poems as degrading to women. Hope felt that it was from some quarters unreasonable and ill-informed in relation to his perceptions, aims and ends. John Docker's article on the subject exemplifies the nature of the critique. Hope's women, he argues, are depersonalised, non-intellectual and non-rational; they are invariably beautiful, and their ultimate purpose is a channel of contact 'with the universal process by men'.[5] It is true that all these points can be found in Hope's poems; it is, however, also the case that the opposite point of view is also present in Hope's work. Poems such as *Advice to Young Ladies*,[6] *Botany Bay or The Rights of Women*[7] and *Orpheus*,[8] to mention but a few, contain more complex representations of the feminine than Docker allows. Nevertheless, Docker's position offers a challenge of a kind that warrants a response.[9]

It is the case that I could scrounge through Hope's poetry and find examples that would support Docker's critique. I would, however, be taking them out of context, eliminating their satiric purpose and failing to place them alongside other examples that present contrary ideas. Playing devil's advocate, I searched the notebooks for the most damning example. This little poem is called *On a Fine Day in Summer*:

> *The sun doth shine*
> *The world is mine*
> *My bones are full of marrow*
> *O for a wench*
> *That has a trench*
> *Where I may push my barrow!*
>
> *Big tits and little wits*
> *Do often go together,*
> *But who would want*
> *A talking cunt*
> *In such fine fucking weather.*

The context of this is that it is a response to Rosamond Tuve's book on Elizabethan and metaphysical imagery:[10] if it objectifies one particular woman and argues for the preference of a mindless one on such a fine day, any female would-be executioner of the poet/narrator might first ask of herself has she ever felt the same towards a male on a fine day.[11] Would a poem expressing a similar attitude and written in a similar style by a woman be received with animosity by some men? Would they wish to censor it on either pornographic or ideological grounds? Hope, I suspect, would argue that women, in their difference, would be less interested in representing their sexuality in this manner. His selections from the Kinsey

Reports on human sexual behaviour represent his views on this point. Hope believed that females were rarely engaged in the production of sexually explicit material that did not have as its basis 'more general emotional situations, affectional relationships and love', and that 'These things do not bring specifically erotic responses from males, and we cannot discover that they bring more than minimal responses from females'.[12] Furthermore, Hope in a later entry in the Notebooks came to recognise that the 'Kinsey investigators were swayed [in their conclusions] by the nature of the male response'.[13] He concluded that 'The imagination of women seems to me as powerful as that of men in sexual matters but its images are different and they arouse sexual responses of surprising force and urgency by means that to a male would arouse interest or admiration but not desire'.[14] Whether Hope's insights are correct or not is not the point here. Instead, the fact that this is his view is of interest as it is one that, when brought to his erotic poetry, assists in the reading of it.

I have read dozens of Hope's sexually explicit poems; it is also the case that very few of them have been included in the notebooks. I confess that there are some poems of Hope's I do not particularly like. These tend to be ones that present the male spectator viewing the female body as if it contains no essence or personality. She is idealised as a beautiful object while being dehumanised. Some of his bawdy poems might well be funny, and do involve the men as much as the women as butts of the joke, but despite their wit, lucidity, form and humour, these poems are not ones that I would return to; they do not create being, add to life's experiences, or illuminate human experience for me. If these are the only poems that people read then it perhaps becomes understandable why Hope is termed sexist and narrow in his perception of male and female relations. However, there are many poems that do illuminate the world for me. They might present a male view of life, and this does seem to involve seeing a woman in 'her parts', but they have something to tell us from that perspective about the human condition that has a validity that should not be censored.[15]

A substantial number of Hope's poems involve women. The narrators in Hope's poems might be doing one of the following: utilising the experiences of the woman's physical beauty as a gateway to new perception, treating women as enigmatic beings that are to be feared, reducing the woman to parts when highlighting her animal nature above her human one, or characterising the female as someone who might offer the answers to questions of beauty, philosophy and other 'truths' but who will exact a price. The female character will appear often as the object of male love and/or desire, but she will also be seen in her animal nature pervaded by passions that men can never satisfy. Although the woman personae will be seen as in tune with nature, in their procreative role they will alienate men. Feminist criticism often refers to the binary logic in which male/female is contrasted with culture/nature and to the way nature is treated as an inferior order of existence. It is important to realise that Hope does not have this view at all. His poems might not be about the way women see themselves; they are essentially about how men have seen and do see women.[16]

If one accepts that the metaphysical world views of men and women are different, the cultural context in which a dialogue takes place must allow for honesty. To put this another way, if it is (as it is) the case that women have been imprisoned in male-language for centuries, do we, because of this, now want an intellectual environment in which male writers are imprisoned, albeit that some might argue, liberated, in female contexts and language? Hope would argue, I suspect, that the latter is impossible; he has said 'they wouldn't get it right'. Nevertheless, what men and women can be imprisoned by is a need to reneg on what they truly feel and wish to write because they fear that the expression of these thoughts or emotions might be considered unsound. Is our ultimate aim a kind of bisexual literary perception, to be taken on by men and women equally? Given the fruits of the latter, would such a perception exclude other sources of human experience?[17]

Alec Hope once had to cut an interview with me short, as he had been asked to attend a women's studies seminar and be accountable for such poems as *One Fine Day in Summer*. I told him not to expect any mercy and asked him how he was going to cope when he was besieged by criticism. His eyes glinted in amusement and he said, 'I'll just check out their legs.' At the time, I laughed spontaneously but later became confused as to why I had found it funny. It would not be amusing if Hope did do this. Neither is it remotely possible that he would behave in such a gauche manner. The humour, in fact, resides in Hope's iconoclastic response to any rigid stance that did not allow for difference, irony and debate. Hope's irreverent comment represents his objection to any critic who might proclaim that his view of women is that they are reducible to 'a pair of legs'. The comment draws attention to the fact that sexual attraction is often left out of feminist discourse, and also how such a dramatisation of male sexuality might be seen as sexist when it might simply be male. Additionally, Hope makes it a point of honour not be subdued by the rules, protocols and visions of ideological correctness of others.

Hope might, on a more serious note, point out, as he so often does in the notebooks, that the voice in a poem is not necessarily his. Hope will, as an actor, enter many different kinds of male 'minds' in his poems, showing the extent to which men have accepted social and cultural constructs of women that have been based on biologism and essentialism. He has, however, dealt with sexuality in other ways. For example, in *Orpheus*, his poem *Teaser Rams*[18] explores the plight of a woman who is not satisfied sexually by her husband, who, like a 'teaser ram', took her to a realm of expectation that he was unable to meet. She is eventually satisfied by a chance encounter with an itinerant farm labourer. The poem came from the experiences of a young man who attended a class taught by Hope in the Trade School. Nevertheless, Hope manages the material; the female character is not depersonalised and the mood of the poem, although at times humorous, is also sad and empathetic. *Intimations of Mortality*[19] expresses his dread of death. It plays with the idea that he now must be protected from his desire of women; but he, in almost the same instant, changes his mind: 'I'd like some snatch before I die.' As he thinks of women and his great need of them, he equally thinks of the texts he leaves behind and prays to man and God that their meaning will be protected.

IV
...
Rather in Man and God I trust
That both in this world and the next
They guard my meaning and my text.

V
A man must do the best he can.
That's his test of being a man.
But what he fails to do at best,
That is still the acid test

VI
...
Here's the rubbish left behind
By careless love and reckless wit.

Burrow in and what you find
May God give you joy of it
...

Finally he leaves us on his most serious note:

VI
If those with whom I shared a bed
Love me a little when I'm dead
And it don't make them weep but laugh,
That will be my best epitaph.

The voice here is unmistakably Hope's.

Hope has never intruded into the privacy of those he loved by writing explicitly about them; it is not surprising that the notebooks do not provide any such material. Instead, what one discovers are sources of imagery and a metaphysical vision that might feed his poetry. Sex, like laughter, is, in Hope's poems, a very serious business, and engages emotions that range from fun, play and passion to grief and alienation. They might be written in a satirical mode and directed at other questions; they miggt be emulations of earlier styles of love poetry and they might be exploratory, querying the enigma of love that offers the deepest grief and the highest joys.

ΗΑΟδ ΟΡΟΜ

Men without women are said to drink a great deal. It is a commonplace of psychology that alcoholism is often due to the frustration of other passions or to the fear of other desires. Could not the opposite also be true? A puerile and obsessive lubricity in certain people deprived of alcohol or ashamed to be known to desire the satisfaction of cruelty, forced to repress anger or a lust to dominate, or having no natural outlet for spite or greed. Is the Mohammedan paradise perhaps the compensating dream for men whose religion forbids them to get drunk?

— Book V, 1957–58, p. 9.

THE BASIS OF METAPHYSICS

Metaphysics is an attempt to give a whole view to the world and, as the presumption is that no human being can do this, to indicate as far as possible the gaps and failures of any system or view. We can ask significant questions to which we cannot give answers. The sum of such questions indicates the limits of knowledge. The panoptic science is bound in ways to be the most incomplete of the sciences, for it depends on an attempt to give a coherent and systematic view of the whole range of knowledge and is based on particular sciences themselves incomplete and on other sources of knowledge some of them not subject to scientific disciplines.

The sources of knowledge are of various kinds.

(a) There is the whole range of objects of experience and their [illegible] which are the subject of the specific analytic sciences (physics, biology, psychology, sociology etc);

(b) all of the sources of knowledge which deal with facts as aggregates (making experience, history, the arts as contemplative activities;

(c) there are the studies that consider the discipline of knowledge itself, (logic, mathematics and grammar in its widest sense);

(d) there is the study of values, and the individual value studies, ethics, which economics draws on;

(e) there is the study of the sources of knowledge, including metaphysics, and including the claims of other possible worlds of knowledge: illumination, mysticism, divine revelation, types of perception other than those already recognised.

One metaphysical view will differ from another and any metaphysical picture will be limited by a number of factors: (a) The range of established facts available to the picture maker and his power of assessing them critically. The sciences now present a range of systematized knowledge so great and requiring specialist knowledge as recondite for their assessment, that [it] is beyond the powers of any one metaphysician to deal with them all. So certain sciences tend to bias the picture; Physics more than Biology for example. This bias and distortion is increased by the fact that some sciences are more advanced than others. By certain assumptions, such as that of uniformity of nature, which is interpreted to mean that evidence from other sources, to be accepted as or taken seriously, must conform to the world picture presented by the experimental sciences, other sources of knowledge are treated as secondary — not standing in their own right or constituting a *criticism* of the experimental sciences. Even among the latter, physics and chemistry assume a priority over the biological sciences. Thus metaphysics has tended to take sides, to be apologist for some departments or sources of knowledge against others. Its proper function has been neglected and it has fallen into disrepute. People like Ayre can argue more or less plausibly that it has no function. Its proper function, of course, is that of the synoptic science: the consideration of the frame of things as a whole, neglecting none of the claims of any of the sources of knowledge as having necessary priority or authority. Its primary concern is with a *consistent* theory of the world and therefore with criticism of the theories based on partial views of the world. Its method is to apply the findings of each source of knowledge to those of all the other sources, to illuminate dark places, to suggest new ways of looking at established facts, to take bold steps into the unknown and suggest methods of testing wider theories than any single science can frame.

The limitation of metaphysics, which is concerned with the limitations of all sources of knowledge is the limitation of human beings as knowers. Two species of intelligent beings on the earth, with quite different organizations, ranges of perception, and ends and aims would be a great advantage, provided they were able to communicate their knowledge and to criticize the findings based on these sources of knowledge. Man is unfortunately extremely homogeneous. He has moreover done his best to minimize, if not to destroy the only independent source of knowledge existing, that between men and women. Most people would laugh if it were suggested that this was important. Truth knows the difference of sex. Intelligence is not specifically male or female. This may be true enough and it is important that it should be true. For the coherence of communication depends on it. But it is beside the point. The point is that men and women are differently organized beings, that they have sorts of experiences peculiar to each in virtue of this organization and that however trivial these differences may be, they *do* represent distinct bases for a metaphysical view.

I am inclined to think, moreover that these differences are by no means trivial. They only seem so because they have never been seriously explored. The history of knowledge in general and the history of metaphysics in particular, have shown how profound a difference in theory, how great an advance, often follows an apparently trivial shift in point of view about some fundamentally simple bit of evidence. How different our view of the world might have been had colour sense not developed, had we developed X-ray vision, or had all had the mystic endowment.

— Book IV, 1952–56, pp. 27–31.

THE COURTSHIP OF DROSOPHILA SUBOBSCORA

The typical sequence of events after placing a virgin female with an outbred male is as follows. After a few minutes in the same container, the male appears to catch sight of the female; he turns and approaches her, giving a series of rapid flicks with his wings. After tapping her with his front legs, he circles round so as to stand facing her head to head, with his proboscis [an elongated part of the mouth of some insects, used for sucking things] extended towards her. The female then executes a rapid side-stepping dance, moving first to one side and then to the other, the male side-stepping as well so as to keep facing her. The female then stands still, and the male circles round rapidly and mounts. The whole process, from the first approach ... to the actual mounting, may take only a few seconds.

Sometimes, however, the female may break off in the middle of the sidestepping dance, and turn her back on the male, or fly away, in which case the male will again approach her head to head if opportunity arises. Now if a male is an outbred one, mating usually takes place after one or after relatively few dances. With an inbred male, on the other hand, a whole series of dances may take place, after each of which the female moves away without mating. After such a series of rebuffs, a male may approach a female from the side or from behind and attempt to mount, without the preliminary dance, but such attempts are never successful ... The difference is probably this: the movements of a dancing female are very rapid, but an outbred male will usually manage to maintain his position facing the female. Inbred males on the other hand often lag behind ...

The difference between the two kinds of males probably arises because of the greater athletic ability of out-bred males. This difference is only detected by the female because she dances; dancing is a fly's way of being 'hard to get'.

If this interpretation is correct, a female is not selecting a male because he is fertile, but because he can co-ordinate his movements with hers during the dance.

John Maynard Smith: *The Theory of Evolution*, pp. 149–50, Penguin Books, 1958.

— Book VI, 1957, pp. 88–9.

COMMENTS ON: A BLASON[20]

A. A. The details are right but the point of view wrong, and the feeling is too. For a woman the chief feeling is: now he is here. He is touching me. The concentration on external details is more like a man and so is the concentration on localized feelings and sensations. For a woman it is all happening inside her, all through her, all over her — yes, a rising and a swelling tide. Her feelings are directed to herself and not to her lover. And for her it is the continuing feeling after the climax that is more important. A woman's tragedy is that just when she turns from herself to her lover, he turns away; for him it is all over.

J. F. You have caught it perfectly. That is just the way it is … Of course it is from a man's point of view — but a man's view of what *is* a woman's point of view.

C. M. *It is not like that at all.* Not for a woman. For a girl there is a modicum of truth in your poem — an intelligent girl who has discovered that frank enumerations have a certain cachet — but even in that case there is one thing that makes it bizarre. Your creature is a mirror to the man, and that is all wrong, wrong wrong … Even a half-baked girl never stops *seeing herself*; it would be quite impossible for her to celebrate him only so that she can celebrate herself … The divine joke is that no man is magnificent in bed to any woman. She can admire him truly, deeply for his bravery in say, war, his beautiful gift of the gab, his acumen, his life — without — women, that life she has no part in. But once he comes to her he lays aside his indifference, his independence, and she loves him, because she must, and she despises him, because she must ... Only with our children do we put subterfuge away. Go back to your old pisspot and fiddle fart your way through your fairy tale but don't delude yourself that you know any part of the beautiful ritual. Masturbation, that's what your poem is.

— Book VI, 1959, pp. 30–1.

SUBURBAN DOGS

I think from time to time of the condition of dogs in the suburbs of one of our cities. People usually keep dogs, because bitches go on heat and are a nuisance. So comparatively few bitches survive. Dogs are both sociable and free. They get about and make their own arrangements and they visit and form canine clubs, which, I suppose, are the civilized form of the primitive hunting pack. But as these dogs are leisured animals who do not have to work for a living, the club is loose and shifting in its membership and purely social and for diversion. When a bitch comes on heat in the neighborhood they all attend and, while there is some incidental quarrelling over precedence, there is rarely any attempt at monopoly. They take turns and share the common opportunity. Among wild dogs, I believe, mating involves pairing.

It is interesting to speculate what would happen in a human society where men outnumbered women to the same extent — quite a possible state of affairs when one thinks of the practice of the Arabs in the [illegible]. Would mutual love become an antisocial sort of behaviour — a disruption of the manners and morals of the club? Would the strong establish a monopoly so that sexual life was* recognized and approved but divided by a rigid caste system: the homosexual and the heterosexual classes? Or might it even be possible that women would form an aristocracy of power in virtue of their monopoly of the rare and precious goods they could provide if the old conventions of Courtly Love become an economic and social reality? Would society be able to resist the forces of tension and disruption that might be set up? Would the practice of emasculating the majority of males at birth, as we do with our flocks, not be forced on such a society as a way of preserving itself?

The reverse of the situation in which the males were as greatly outnumbered by the females is easier to imagine for the solution is easier. The ultimate sexual purpose of women is children and they could all achieve this purpose with a little organization. But mutual love would still be a problem and might well come to be treated as wicked and antisocial.

— The privilege of the few and a kind of capitalism? Would there be two classes?

— Book VI, 1959, pp. 33–4.

THE REVENGE OF APHRODITE

An even more lively and sardonic speculation could arise from the idea of a society in which the sexual life of men and women was in any case of the same pattern as the sexual life of dogs or that of deer: either a common season of rut and a common season of child-bearing — or a world in which each woman periodically went on heat and irresistibly attracted all the males in her orbit. In the second case we could either imagine the quite different constitution of society necessary to meet the case or — what would be more amusing — imagine a playful deity, female no doubt, ordaining the change and imposing it on our present society without warning — perhaps as a punishment for being flouted by a human lover who remained faithful to his human love in spite of her blandishments.

— Book VI, 1959, p. 33a.

THE NOMADS

There are those who have a standing need of the other sex, those for whom this need takes the form of a permanent passion and attachment, who in a very real sense only live when they live together. Everything else Croce said of Ariosto, that love was not to his purpose but that he had a continual 'Bisogna di Femminita',[21] an atmosphere as necessary to his work as the smell of rotting apples was to Schiller.

But there are also those to whom the other sex is like the Fertile

Crescent to the desert Arabs. They could not imagine a worse fate than to be compelled to live in the cities and the fat farmlands. The desert is their home, their element, their way of life. For them love is a raid on the settled lands, from which they withdrew again to the desert; and this is the way of it, whether they raid the same city each time or plunder in various places.

— Book VI, 1959, p. 40.

CONVENTIONS OF FICTION

The most important of these are the conventions of ignoring actual and normal occurrences. *Lolita* I suppose caused such a stir because there is a convention to ignore in fiction the fact that little girls are often sexually precocious and that elderly men often feel like Tom Carew[22] about little girls.

It is a curious convention of fiction that a woman is promiscuous or a female rake if she is capable of loving more than one man at a time or having sexual relations with them. There is nothing odd about her having several children and loving them all more or less equally at the same time and there [are] many women who find themselves in the same position with more than one man at the same time. They may have difficulty in a practical way because men in love are apt to be possessive but it causes them no trouble as a situation in itself and their love for one no more conflicts with their love for another than their love for one child conflicts with that for another. But fiction assumes that it is bound to conflict.

— Book VI, 1960, p. 84.

FACE TO FACE

Man must be almost the only animal race that mates with the male and female face to face and able to look into each other's eyes. Seals, I believe also mate in this way but the bull seal is so much larger than the female that he must quite over lie her.

Alas for romantic notions which might see in this another

specifically 'human' trait like laughter, another distinction between human love and animal appetite! The partners in this congress, if they keep their powers of observation, observe not the tender or loving face of the other, but as the climax approaches, a strange and even a terrifying mask, an emptying of the person and the emergence of an unknown, impersonal spirit. The pupils dilate (a curious remote stare in the woman, a ferocious glare in the man), the lines of beauty, character and personality disappear and the muscles of the face change and generalize the human mask, and often the mouth is strained to a strange grimace or frenzied rictus.

To the romantic this must be disappointing, but to those who see it aright this *is* right and profoundly moving too. For in that moment the great forces, greater than ourselves, take over and we put on their anonymity and this is actually a visible change — we can see it happen and have assurance that it is not merely an imagined communion or an intellectual fancy.

— Book VIII, 1964–65, pp. 163–4.

LOVE AMONG THE COCKROACHES

Nauphoeta cinerea [cockroaches], a widespread species ... in their warm, damp, dark environment, vision plays a smaller part [than among butterflies]. Sexually mature males are highly active and touch antennae with any other cockroach they meet. The antennae of virgin females secrete a substance which excites the male to further antennal stimulation. After this preliminary, the male poses in a standard position, sometimes for as long as a minute, with raised wings and lowered abdomen. The female takes the opportunity to nibble at the secretions of glands on the male's back. The secretions contain a substance which attracts the female and makes her keep still during coitus. This substance has been named seducin. During coitus the male grasps the female with his claspers, which are at the rear end; insemination takes place with the pair in a straight line facing opposite ways.

J. A. Barnett: *'Instinct' and 'Intelligence'*, p. 93.

— Book XII, 1979, p. 49.

THE IMAGINATION OF WOMEN

From *Sexual Behavior in the Human Female*, Kinsey, Martin, Paneroy et al. (W. B. Saunders & Co., Philadelphia & London' 1953).

(Masturbation)

The masturbation fantasies were usually in accord with the overt experience of the individual. Males not infrequently have fantasies of unfulfilled or repressed desires, but the fantasies among the females had less often concerned activities of a sort which they had not had: if kissing had been the limit of the female's petting experience, it was the limit of her fantasies; it was only after the petting had included genital manipulations that the fantasies went that [sic] far. The fantasies had rarely included coitus unless the female had had coital experience. On the other hand many of the females who had had overt sexual contacts had never fantasized about them while they were masturbating.

The data on the fantasies were essentially alike in all of the age groups and in all of the educational levels represented by the sample. In the male the maximum amount of fantasy is found among the better educated groups, but education does not seem to increase the female's inclination to fantasy.

Most males' fantasy is in connection with most of their masturbation. Fantasies, as a matter of fact, often provide the stimulus which initiates the male's masturbation. Memories of past experience, the anticipation of renewed experience and the contemplation of new types of activity are such significant factors in his arousal that it is usually difficult for a male to reach orgasm in masturbation without the aid of some sort of fantasy. Consequently the female's ability to achieve orgasm without fantasy emphasizes her greater dependence upon physical and physiological sources of erotic arousal [pp. 164–5; or perhaps a deficiency of a certain sort of imagination].

('Wet' Dreams)

Among both females and males, nocturnal sex dreams, more than any other type of sexual outlet, appear to have their origins in what are primarily psychologic stimuli ... one of the most characteristic aspects of the orgasms which occur while an individual sleeps is the fact that they are almost always accompanied by dreams, even among females who are rarely or never given to sexual fantasy while they masturbate or engage in any other type of daytime sexual activity ... We are inclined to agree with most psychologists and psychiatrists in believing that the dreams are not only necessary factors in the great majority of cases, but the prime precipitating factors of most nocturnal orgasms, but the physiology of the matter is still not understood ... [pp. 193–4]

In the available sample, there seems to have been no correlation between the educational background of the female and the [accumulative?] or active incidence of her nocturnal sex dreams, or the frequency with which she had such dreams and the point of orgasm ... The educational background of the male does seem to have a direct effect on the frequencies of his nocturnal emissions. The males who go furthest in their educational careers appear to have better developed imaginative capacities, and this seems to have an effect upon the development of their psychosexual responses. [p. 201]

(What they dream about)

The sexual partners in these dreams were usually obscure or unidentifiable — an epitomization of some general type of person; and even the actor in the dream was not always the dreamer but a person who combined the capacities of an observer and the participant in the activity. More precise data are needed on this matter. Many of the heterosexual dreams had an indefinitely affectionate or generally social content which did not include overtly physical contacts. While such dreams may in actuality be sexual in significance they are quite different from the overtly sexual dreams which males usually have ... Sex dreams whether they occur in the female or the male, are often a reflection of experience which the individual has actually had. On the other hand, some 13% of the females in the sample (Negro and White), who had ever dreamed, had sex dreams that went beyond their actual experience. [p. 213]

(Art and Image)

Photographs of female nudes and magazines exhibiting nude or near-nude females are produced primarily for the consumption of males. There are, however, photographs and magazines portraying nude and near-nude males — but these are also produced for the consumption of males. There are almost no male or female nudes which are produced for the consumption of females. The failure of nearly all females to find erotic arousal in such portrayals is so well-known to the distributors of nude photography and nude magazines that they have considered that it would not be profitable to produce such material for a primarily female audience. [p. 653]

... a very high proportion of the male artists who portray the human form, either male or female, do so in a fashion which suggests an erotic interest in that form ... in some years of searching, we have been able to find only eight instances of important female artists who have drawn the human figure, female or male in a fashion which qualified artists, female or male, judge to be erotic. [p. 654]

Most heterosexual males are aroused by observing the female breasts or legs or some other part of the female body. They are usually aroused when they see the female genitalia ... Many females are surprised to learn that there is anyone who finds the observation of male genitalia erotically stimulating. Many females consider that the male genitalia are ugly and repulsive in appearance and the observation of the male genitalia may actually inhibit their erotic responses ... Among the infra-human species of mammals there seems to be something of the same difference between the reactions of females and males to the genitalia of the opposite sex ... A great many of the males in the sample had been aroused by observing their own genitalia ... Few of the females in the sample had found any erotic stimulation in looking at their own genitalia. [pp. 656–8]

... the females found [erotic situations in] moving pictures erotically stimulating somewhat more often than the males. [p. 666]

Practically all males who are not exclusively homosexual may be erotically aroused by thinking of certain females, or of females in general. Fewer males of the lower educational levels are aroused by such fantasies, and older males sometimes lose their capacity to be stimulated by fantasies, and males who are exclusively homosexual may not fantasy concerning females. But most males in our sample (84%) indicated that they were at least sometimes and in most instances often aroused by thinking of sexual relations with females ... A smaller proportion (69%) of the females in the sample reported that they had ever had erotic fantasies about males and nearly 31% insisted that they had never been aroused by thinking about males or of sexual relations with them ... even some of the females who were most responsive in physical relationships had never been aroused by fantasies about males. [pp. 665–6]

Sexual arousal from fantasies about other males ... is as frequent among homosexual males as heterosexual fantasies are among heterosexual males. Such erotic fantasies are less frequent among homosexual females, but they do occur in as high or higher percentage of homosexual females (74%) as heterosexual fantasies occur among heterosexual females. [pp. 666–7]

Erotic responses while reading novels, essays, poetry or other literary materials may depend upon the general emotional content of the work, upon specifically romantic material in it, upon sexual vocabulary ... or upon its more specific descriptions of sexual activity ... The reactions of females and males in our sample were as follows:

	Females	Males
Definite or frequent	16%	21%
Some response	44%	38%
Never	40%	41%

It will be noted that the females and males in the sample had responded erotically in nearly the same numbers ... Twice as many of the females in the sample had responded to literary materials as had ever responded to the observation of the portrayal of sexual action, and five times as many as had responded to photographs or other portrayals of nude human figures. At this point we do not clearly understand why this should be so. [pp. 669–70]

What is commonly identified as pornography is literature or drawing which has the erotic arousal of the reader or observer as its deliberate and primary or sole objective ... In every modern language the amount of deliberately pornographic material that has been produced is beyond ready calculation ... Similarly there is an unlimited amount of pornographic drawing and painting which has been produced by artists of some ability in every part of the world, and there is no end to the amateur portrayals of sexual action.

But in all this quantity of pornographic production it is exceedingly difficult to find any material that has been produced by females ... Females produce another more extensive literature which is called erotic, and do drawings which are called erotic; but most of these deal with more general emotional situations, afectional relationships and love. These things do not bring specifically erotic responses from males, and we cannot discover that they bring more than minimal responses from females. [pp. 671–2]

HAIL, HOLY LIGHT! I

The physical means of uniting the male and the female sex cells is extremely varied in animals ... in aquatic forms there is a whole gamut of methods ... In some hydroids, for instance, there is a simple simultaneous squirting of the eggs into the water, and the timing is governed by the light. Hydractinia ... is such a form, and after almost exactly one hour in light preceded by a longer period of total obscurity, both the sperm and the eggs are shed; it is a beautiful and dramatic sight to watch in the laboratory as the round green eggs float free in the water and the [myriad] white sperm squirt out like wisps of smoke.

Cells and Societies by John Tyler Bonner, Princeton University Press, p. 196.

The sight may be beautiful but the idea is even more so. This might make the basis of a poem. Cf. Ophrys and Andrena.

— Book VIII, 1964, p. 9.

HAIL, HOLY LIGHT! II

... the common firefly *Lampyris* glows softly in the dark ...The female firefly perched on a leaf-tip can summon a passing mate by flashing at the correct time interval after he has broadcast a luminous message. With his extra large eyes, he sees her signal. He turns in his flight, and comes in for a landing beside her.

Occasionally the flash from a leaf tip [from the winkable tail-lights of the female] invites the flying male to a female that is not of his own kind. She has winked too soon or too late [siren behaviour], and in this way trespassed on the communication band of another species. Usually the ardent male pays for her mistake with his life [if it is a mistake why should she not feel like supper as well as love?], for a firefly that cannot become a suitor is merely a meal for her.

... firefly males in Burma have evolved a more fool-proof system. Night after night, on the leaf-tips of jungle trees, they flash in unison. The whole forest pulsates ... and it is up to the females to approach if they are willing, sexually acceptable and physically fit. Their night vision is as important as that of the flashing suitors. Indeed, they have equally large eyes.

(As previous note, pp. 262–3.)
— Book VIII, 1964, pp. 108–9.

HAIL, HOLY LIGHT! III

... the fireworms which swarm at night in waters off [the coast of] Bermuda. Female fireworms propel themselves on [an] upward slanting course from the coral reefs among which they reached maturity. As they rise, loaded with ripe eggs, they light up like passenger trains ascending a long grade through dark mountains. Smaller males cavort like comets, writing little streaks and dashes of luminescence just below the surface until they meet a mate. Then comes one matching flare of light, and both parents fade into the black waters, while the fertilized eggs ... cascade gently towards the bottom.

(Ibid., p. 263.)
— Book VIII, 1964, pp. 108–9.

INTOXICATION, HEAVENLY MAID, DESCEND

> The most famous example of sex differences in detection of odours was discovered by … Henri Fabre while watching Chinese silkworm moths. Females of this insect are completely insensitive to the scent lure with which they summon mates. Yet marked males of the silkworm moth have been known to fly upwind seven miles to a fragrant female of their kind. The chemical compound with which a female silkworm moth attracts its mates is highly specific; no other species seem[s] aware of it. In 1959, the Nobel Laureate Adolph Butenandt of the Max Planck Institute for Biochemistry in Munich succeeded in analyzing it. He found it to be an alcohol with sixteen carbon atoms per molecule, a 'yellowish greasy material from which the human nose gains only a slight pleasant odour suggesting that of leather.'
>
> Lotus & Margery Milne:
> *The Senses of Animals and Men*, Penguin, p. 142.

An Alcohol!

— Book VIII, 1964.

WHY DID KING LEAR HAVE DAUGHTERS

First answer: because Shakespeare found three daughters in his sources who in turn found that in Geoffrey of Monmouth. All the same, it is curious in an age in which kings have sons to succeed them and the legend could just as well have been told of three sons. The play is much concerned with disruptions of the order of nature causing evil and disaster. Edmund is wicked and destructive because he is a bastard; Goneril and Regan are wicked and unnatural because they oppose and break the sacred natural obligations of children to their parents and of subjects to their King. It is this unnatural act which turns them into monsters. But is not Lear's 'unnatural' act in giving away his kingdom to women, the first cause and root of all the disasters that follow? We are too apt to give the events of the play a psychological or a practical interpretation which it will not bear.

Such dire events do not spring from such trivial causes alone, but in the first instance from the upsetting of the order of nature. It is a metaphysical not a psychological tragedy. It is scarcely even a moral tragedy. No one is very much to blame. Gloucester in his youth had fallen in love and begotten a bastard son (a sin — but what nobleman hadn't?). Lear in his old age wishes to retire and hand over the government. By an accident of nature he has only daughters to receive it. The order of nature is broken and, by a sort of inevitable chain reaction, it leads to other unnatural acts. Son against father, daughters against father, subject against prince and female against male authority, and so on. Cordelia is as much to blame as anyone if one is going to hand out moral 'credits'. And Lear himself is led to the most awful and impious act of all, the prayer to Nature to destroy her own divine order: 'all germens spill at once.'

And, as with natural disasters in general, the good and the bad suffer alike. It is a complete mistake to view the play as an essay in moral and poetic justice as some 19th-century critics have tried to do; it is even more of a mistake to see it as an essay in psychology exhibiting the results of arbitrary behaviour, favouritism, greed and ambition as modern critics sometimes do.

Yet the elements are there. We are only wrong in making them the motive force and the creative intention of the play.

— Book XIII, 1971, pp. 16–18.

ANOTHER HERO OF OUR TIME

Antechinus stuartii, a marsupial ... about the size of a mouse and ... lives on the eastern coastal strip and in Victoria in sclerophyll forest and evidently makes solitary nests in undergrowth. It also climbs trees. Antechinus is a predator and lives on insects and earthworms. It is a quick-moving nocturnal animal ... The female gives birth in September and the males live less than a year. In June and July they become intolerant of other members of their species. In the ACT they mate during the second half of August [and die]. The only males that remain alive after that are embryos in utero ... whereas rodents copulate frequently for a few seconds at a time, Antechinus males may take about five hours over a single act of coitus, before moving on to another female but there is no reason to think that the strenuous mating causes the males sudden death. But it has been found that if males are castrated they do not die after copulation.

(ANU Reporter, 24–XI–72)

There is a splendid full-page portrait of the hero in the *Report of the Committee on the National Estate* by E. Slater, p. 48. He is eating a Bogong Moth.

Eheu, fugaces, Postume, Postume, Labuntur mores!²³ I am reminded of the famous Arabian tribe of which it was said that its men loved only the once and then died.

Unlike the salmon in which *both* sexes die after spawning.

Keep in mind for *The Bestiary of Venus*.

— Book XIV, 1972, pp. 59–60.

FIG-LEAF DEMOCRACY

Women have always depended on their powers of attraction and the strongest of these powers is in their appearance to the eye. It follows that the wearing of clothes, especially of voluminous clothing that obscures their sexually exciting contours is a disadvantage, in the contest for notice, to the most attractive women and a compensation to those who are physically less attractive. It reduces all women to a common field of rivalry — the face, hands, gestures, voice — and a restricted one where the less physically favoured girl can compete on more equal terms with the beauties. Clothing is first of all a levelling device: it is, in terms of the power system of the female world, a kind of democracy.

But like other forms of democracy it is no sooner established than its devotees set about to defeat its operation. For the attractive and the ill-favoured alike clothes are next designed to act as secondary sexual lures. For the attractive to display and emphasise their best features, for the unattractive to create an illusion designed to divert attention from blemishes or to suggest what is not the case. In the last twenty years the ill-favoured have been fighting a losing battle. As female clothing becomes more exiguous and more revealing the unhappy fat, lumpy, skinny or knock-kneed girl is forced to reveal these damaging facts for she dare not go against fashion. Indeed she is often convinced that to be in the fashion will itself bring her the powers of attraction that nature has denied her.

— Book XV, 1973, pp. 9–10.

SECOND THOUGHTS ON THE KINSEY REPORT

Re-reading the extracts I made from the Kinsey Report on the differences between the imaginations of men and women in dreams, sexual fantasies and day-dreaming and in their response to the opposite sex and depiction of sexual acts in art and in literature, it occurred to me how very much the Kinsey investigators were swayed by the nature of the male response.

Clearly they took this as the norm and so concluded that the female of the species has only vague imaginative responses to sex in contrast to the vivid and specific imagination characteristic of the male.

I did not notice it at the time, though the argument as a whole seemed to me inconclusive, but as I consider material for D. J.'s Notebooks,[24] the fallacy in their reasoning is suddenly quite clear: they had not considered the many forms that quite specific images may take.

I think it probable that in the first instance, they totally neglected to consider what I have elsewhere called 'the tyranny of the eye'; all their examples are drawn from visual responses. Men tend to respond mechanically to the shapes and signs of the female body — it is their primary and powerful stimulus and urge and the Kinsey team [was] probably right in finding this, in general, weak as a stimulus in female response — though they failed to take training into account and overlooked the fact I have observed that some women at least are endowed with all the male susceptibility to shape and to signs of sexual promise.

But what the K. Team [seems] to have overlooked is that if women respond poorly to visual stimuli they respond fiercely and fully to Tactual stimuli — much more so than men — I am in bed with X and ravished by her shape and texture and say so and she replies equally responsive: 'I love the way you handle me.' It is natural enough that in making love women, on the whole, attend to what is done to them rather than to what they are doing. But it goes further than this. A man making love is always intensely conscious of the object of his passionate endeavours; indeed he feels that it is an endeavour on his part, and to come to the right true end of love he keeps his mind on the object: in that lies all that inflames desire, mounts and consummates it. But I have questioned many women about this and most of them say: in order to reach climax I have to concentrate on myself: as soon as the motion towards orgasm begins I go away, I look inward; my contribution to mutual fruition is to keep myself moving up the ladder of inner expectation. (Whereas the male usually has to keep his responses in check if he wants to make it a mutual climax.)

All this would fit in with the greater importance for the female of cuddling, of close and prolonged contact — a faculty which is carried over into motherhood and has a very important role to play in rearing the young. The Kinsey team on the whole neglected to check on the amount of sensory (in the tactile, etc., sense) imagination in the human female and to compose it with the same elements in male imagination, where they might well have found the latter ineffective and inferior. One of the traps into which they fell was the fact that art can readily reproduce visual sexual stimuli, but, short of Aldous Huxley's 'Feelies', it cannot produce a similar braille for the tactile and inner bodily responses.

But at the other end of the scale they are even more crass. In actual fucking a man is aware of his own energies and rejoices in them, their arousal and élan have little to do with the personality of the other party, much more with her body, her physical responses, her liveliness and vigour. Women's sexual response seems to be aroused more by personality, by prestige, by achievement and expertise and deftness. (Mona Levi throwing her arms around Cocky when he caught a big fish! I said, 'I didn't know you felt that way about him' and she answered, 'I don't but I feel that way about his catching the fish.')

What is crass about the Kinsey Report is that they knew all this but in a sense discounted it. The imagination of women seems to me as powerful as that of men in sexual matters but its images are different and they arouse sexual responses of surprising force and urgency by means that to the male would arouse interest or admiration but not desire.

— Book XVI, 1974, pp. 9–12.

DONNE'S DOPPELGÄNGER

> ... marriage should have no beginning before marriage, no half-marriage, no lending away of the body in unchaste wantonnesse before. The body is the temple of the Holy Ghost; and when two bodies, by marriage are to be made one temple, the wife is not the chancell reserv'd and shut up, and the man that walks below, indifferent and at liberty for every passenger.
>
> J. Donne: *Sermon at a Marriage*, May 30, 1621

What a double-take this sermon must have been! How the commentary of his earlier life, both 'all his profane mistresses', and his seduction of Ann More must have risen like ghosts to preach another sermon on another text, taken perhaps from that greatest of counter-gospels, *The Extasy*: Did the Dean of St Paul's manage wholly to preach down Jack Donne? I doubt it.

Donne was then 49. The famous effigy in his shroud, eyes closed and lips drawn back a little as though beginning to smile is undoubtedly meant to portray the expression of a man who has made a good end and had a foretaste of bliss. But it could equally be the expression of a cat who has been at the cream and got away with it satisfactorily.

(See Plate vii in Bahd's *Life*.)

— Book XVIII, 1975, p. 30.

LYNNE STRAHAN AND THE HONEY OF GENERATION

Writing to Lynne about her poems which she has sent me for an opinion, I comment on the remarkable imagery of several poems dealing with the experience — and indeed the metaphysics — of pregnancy in the series *Green Cycle*, and add an idea springing from this: that perhaps the usual image for creation of a poem — a child shaping in the womb — is in fact quite wrong; the opposite should be the case. What is peculiar about the poet is that he — or she in the case of Lynne — enters the womb of the poem and generates a pregnancy waiting to be activated. The poet is reborn each time from the womb of the poem and this is what Yeats may have meant when he said that in reading the poem he has not added to his knowledge but to his *being*. The reader relives the rebirth and emerges fire-new. Perhaps here is another image which might serve to distinguish the male from the female poet. If both act according [to] their natures, the process would be different in each case. The male analogy would be as described; the female would be that of the egg descending into the womb of the poem and waiting to be fertilized.

This is wild nonsense but the logic of analogy is not to be despised. It has no demonstrative force, but it can suggest unsuspected types of structure, unguessed forces and overlooked points of view which can then be tested by the usual methods.

It is perhaps the element of analogy in the argument which has always made 'inductive argument' refractory to logical demonstration.

— 29–VII–1975

— Book XVIII, 1975, pp. 49–50.

WIND AND SEA

'To remember the sound of the wind — the peculiar wretchedness one can feel while the wind blows ... Walking along the Thorndon Esplanade when the wind carries the sea over ... [Katherine Mansfield, *Journal*].' How strange, how completely alien this is to me! I find the wind exhilarating, exciting, uplifting and the noise of the sea so necessary to the life of the spirit that I have to renew the experience at intervals. (But Katherine Mansfield felt as I do about the sea: 'Oh, I have such a longing for the sea ... To stand on the shore long enough to feel the land behind one withdrawn into silence and the loud tumbling of the waves rise and break over one's whole being' [*Letters*, 1917].) This seems to be one of the things that divides the human race down the middle into two incompatible parties. I remember that my mother was nearly driven mad by the equinoctial gales of autumn and spring in Tasmania, and that she was in despair when my father, who like me loved the sound of the sea chose for his retirement a piece of land high on the headland at Bungan Head.

It is not, as far as I can tell, a sex-difference though more women than men have confessed that the sound of wind makes them restless, uneasy, miserable or neurotic — and so with the sea — but it does suggest that here is something to be followed up. What other experiences of a quite simple sensory kind evoke opposite reactions? How deep do they go? How many are 'natural' reactions; how many the result of habit or social conditioning?

The irony of two lovers in each other's arms, the one luxuriating [in] the noise of wind and rain and the thunder of the sea outside and the other fighting to keep tense nerves and 'hysterica passio' from destroying the magic of the moment.

—VIII–75
— Book XVIII, 1975, pp. 51–2.

RENEWING VIRGINITY

I have recorded elsewhere my visit to the Aghia Moue outside Nauplia, site of the Zoodokhos Pighi anciently known as the spring Kanathos which must surely be cognate with Kanasso = to make a gurgling sound. I have been irritated by the fact that I could find it nowhere in Pausanias as I wanted to make it the subject of one of the *Poems from Pausanias* in the broadcast programme of that title which Rosemary and I are preparing. However I have found it there at last by looking up the index to Frazer's edition of Pausanias, together with quite a lot of interesting information about Hera from Pauly-Wissowa.

The main question I find no answer to among the scholars — they do not seem to want to concern themselves with it — is: why should Hera have wanted to renew her virginity annually? The Greeks had a number of virgin goddesses, Artemis, Athene, etc., who stayed that way in spite of being, like Hera, fertility deities among their other attributes. Others, like Persephone lost their virginities and stayed that way too.

The annual renewal suggests that in the Argolid it may have had functions similar to those of Demeter at Eleusis — Pausanias' remark that his story about Kanathos is taken from a mystery cult of Hera at Argot. Like the probable rites of Eleusis in that mystery that at Argos may have continued on annual divine marriage, and Hera, like

Demeter, may have had originally the character of a triple goddess, combining in alternation the character of virgin, mother, and hag. Or again as Hera, Athene, Artemis and Persephone appear not to be Greek names at all; Hera like the others may have originally been a virgin earth-goddess of Minoan or earlier times whom the invading Greeks made the wife of their sky-god Zeus. Since the early Greek mysteries may have been kept secret — they apparently contained no secret doctrines like those of the later mystery-cults — as a woman's religion surviving against opposition from earlier times, the annual secret restoration of Hera's virginity may have been directed against Zeus the Ravisher. Greek legend in general represents the marriage as a very uneasy one. In the *Argolid* Zeus was reputed to have ambushed and overpowered Hera in the form of a cuckoo and the famous Heraeun, not far from Mycenae, [a] cult statue in Hera's temple [has] Zeus represented as a cuckoo sitting on the end of her scepter, which may well be a satirical touch. The cuckoo of course had association with Hera before her association with Zeus and this according to Pausanias was his reason for adopting this disguise: 'in one hand she holds a sceptre, in the other a pomegranate. As the story of the pomegranate is rather secret, I shall omit it; but they say the cuckoo sits on her sceptre because, when Zeus first became enamored of the virgin Hera, he changed into this bird and she hunted him for a pet' (Pausanias, II, 17.4).[25]

This certainly suggests not that Hera wanted a pet-bird but that she engaged in an annual cuckoo hunt, like the hunting of the wren in northern Europe. The time would have been spring. The pomegranate again suggests that as a virgin spring goddess Hera may have been originally a double of Persephone.

But there are other enchanting possibilities. The virginity of Artemis seems to have been connected with her original character as mistress of wild animals and to have been important because of a mysterious and terrible force residing in virginity itself — a force that makes the taking of virginity a very dangerous business in the eyes of many primitive peoples. One thinks of Hera's contest with Poseidon for the land of Argolis and the fact that she won. It parallels the contest of Poseidon and Athene for the land of Attica and the fact that the virgin goddess won there too. It looks like the same myth in another setting and it is to be presumed that in the original form it was the virgin goddess, Hera, not the wife of Poseidon's brother, who won the contest.

What a pity that Pausanias was so scrupulous about the pomegranate, it might have answered a number of questions.

What a happy man Sir James George Frazer must have been, taking this vast world for his province and able to spend so much of his life exploring it.

But I can only visit it: I have other fish to fry.

— 4-1-1976
— Book XVIII, 1976, pp. 105–10.

EFFECTS OF LOVE

O'amor espiritualisa o homem — e materialisa a mulher?[26]
(Eça de Queiroz)

This is the theory on which so much of European literature is based. Such poems as *Troilus and Criseyde*, Spenser's *Four Hymns* and Tennyson's *Idylls of the King* illustrate various aspects of it. It is to be doubted whether it has much substance. Both sexes appear to be equally eager to enjoy the pleasures of the flesh and there appears to be no difference in their desire to enjoy each other on a more romantic plane. Eça de Queiroz' story is an ironical picture of what goes wrong when people adopt the view expressed above.

— Book XXI, 1981, p. 188.

MARTHA

(A Continuation of Luke 10, 38)

'Now it came to pass, as they went, that he entered into a certain village: and a certain woman named Martha received him into her house.

And she had a sister called Mary, which also sat at Jesus' feet, and heard his word.

But Martha was cumbered about much serving, and came to him, and said, Lord, dost thou not care that my sister hath left me to serve alone? Bid her therefore that she help me.

And Jesus answered and said unto her, Martha, thou art careful and troubled about many things.

But one thing is needful: and Mary hath chosen that good part, which shall not be taken away from her. Nevertheless be of good cheer, for I am mindful of thy need also, and I myself shall be thy help.

And Martha's wrath was appeased, for she said in her heart, though none helped me in the serving of meat, yet the Lord himself will help me with the washing up.

But when they were risen from meat, Jesus returned again to his chair, and Mary likewise sat as before at his feet.

Then was Martha much grieved, and she followed them to where they sat with the rest and said, Lord, hast thou then forgotten thy promise to help me? For the dishes that remain are yet to be made clean.

And he answered and said, Nay, Martha, hast thou so little faith? Chide not, but go and see, for it is already done. And she went and lo, all the pots were scoured and the cups and dishes sided away.

But Martha murmured and said to herself, Behold I asked for the help of his fellowship, but his fellowship he hath granted to my sister and my brother, and me he hath put off only with miracles.'

I have always felt that Martha got a shabby deal on this occasion and I am not moved by St Thomas Aquinas explaining that the incident was meant to symbolise the difference between the Active and the Contemplative Life.

As for Lazarus no one even considered that he might have set a table or wielded a dishcloth.

— 13–I–1982
— Book XXII, 1982, pp. 78–80.

Notes

1. Hope, Book IV, 1952–56, pp. 27–31.
2. Ibid.
3. Julia Kristeva, 'Women's time', pp. 33–4.
4. See Toril Moi, *Sexual/Textual Politics*, p. 12, where she presents Julia Kristeva's view that the feminist struggle must be seen historically and politically as a three-tiered one, which can be schematically summarised as follows: 1. Women demand equal access to the male symbolic order. Liberal feminism. Equality; 2. Women reject the male symbolic order in the name of difference. Radical feminism. Femininity extolled; and 3. Women reject the dichotomy between masculine and feminine as metaphysical.
5. See John Docker, 'The Image of Woman in A. D. Hope's Poetry', pp. 42–58.
6. Hope, *Collected Poems, 1930–1965*, pp. 207–8.
7. Hope, *The Age of Reason*, pp. 115–38.
8. Hope, *Orpheus*, p. 1.
9. See Ann McCulloch, 'A Lecture', pp. 11–30, for a detailed response to Docker's arguments.
10. See Tuve, *Elizabethan and Metaphysical Imagery: Renaissance Poetic and Twentieth Century Critics.*
11. McCulloch, 'A Lecture', *Security of Allusion*, p. 26.
12. See Kinsey Report, pp. 671–2.
13. Hope, Book XV, 1974, p. 12.
14. Ibid.
15. See McCulloch, 'Landing A. D. Hope', p. 268, where I draw on these same points when discussing the difficulties involved in 'Landing A. D. Hope'; that is, in determining his 'use' of and attitude towards women in his poetry.
16. See ibid., p. 266, where I have drawn on these ideas when discussing Hope's interest in male mythology (Faust, Odysseus and Don Juan).
17. See ibid., p. 267, where this argument is contextualised within a larger argument concerning the difficulties in categorising Hope's erotic poetry.
18. Hope, *Orpheus*, p. 26.
19. Ibid., pp. 15–16.
20. See Hope, *Collected Works*, p. 153, for the poem *A Blason*, which this excerpt is commenting on.
21. Translation: need for the feminine.
22. Thomas Carew (1598–1639) was a poet and disciple of Ben Jonson. It is possible that Hope is referring to Carew's poem *A Rapture*, which has been said to 'turn Donne's ode to nakedness into a risquè tour of Celia's nether parts'. See *The New Princeton Handbook of Poetic Terms*, p. 167. See also Nixon, 'Carew's Response to Jonson and Donne', p. 91, where he draws attention to the image of the bee in *A Rapture*, which is 'plundering Celia's body, selecting and exploring the possibilities of sensual poetry'.
23. Translation: 'Eheu fugaces labuntur anni' forms the first two lines of Horace's *Odes* (ii. xii), meaning 'Alas, the fleeting years slip away', which Hope switches into bemoaning the loss of custom and convention ('mores').

24 D.J.'s Notebooks refers to a project Hope was working on called 'The Don Juan Notebooks'. Hope had begun a critical history of the Don Juan legend but abandoned it. He retrieved the idea later when he became interested in the successive metamorphoses of the legend from the original Burlador de Seville to the 19th-century romantic Don Juan as he appears in *Tales of Hoffman* and in Pushkin's play. In the 20th century (in Hope's rendition), he appears as a scientist, pursuing that most boring of subjects, sexology. He gets his comeuppance from the emergence of a lady who is his female counterpart (Letter to Ann McCulloch, July 1986). Hope wanted this book to be a send-up of modern psychology of sex — especially 'our old pals Sigmund and Carl (better known as Jung) who had made such a "brou-ha-ha" on the subject in our age'. Hope's intentions were, in a humorous vein, to do to Freud and Jung what Aristophanes did to Socrates in *The Clouds*.

25 The references to Hera's annual washing to renew her virginity at the Kanathos spring is mentioned in Pausanias, *Book* IX, 39.3–4; Hera, the pomegranate and the cuckoo, in Pausanias, *Book* II, 17.4.

26 Translation: Does spiritual and human love have multiple manifestations?.

X

A SENSE OF DESTINY

This chapter examines the way that the poet views his pathway and its pitfalls, and also its seductive powers, which prevented him from following any other road.

In terms of public acclaim, A. D. Hope was a modest man. Literary awards meant less to him than the moment that followed the completion of a poem. From the age of eight, when he wrote his mother a poem, he knew that it was his destiny to spend his life writing poetry. His academic profession was in many ways experienced by him as a disruption and interruption to his calling. He conceded, however, that it was a necessary interruption. It also gave to his readers much distinguished critical writing and contributed in no small way to the establishment of Australian literature as an academic area of study. In exploring the question of Hope's 'sense of destiny', it is appropriate to give an overview of his achievements as a published writer.

Hope's first book of poetry, *The Wandering Islands*, was published in 1955 and won the Grace Leven Prize. In 1960, *Poems* was published followed three years later by *Selected Poems*. In 1969, A. D. Hope published his award-winning *New Poems 1965–1969*. Having retired from his position as head of the English Department in 1967 and being elected Professor Emeritus, Hope was free to pursue his vocation as a poet full-time. The years ahead were to prove rewarding; Hope remained engaged in his role as educator and consultant in Australian literature. In 1970, *A Midsummer Eve's Dream* and a revised edition of *Dunciad Minor* were published, and in that same year Hope taught at Sweet Briar College, Virginia, in the United States.

Returning to Australia in 1972, Hope joined the Commonwealth Literary Fund Advisory Board, contributing his voice to the encouragement of Australian writers. *Collected Poems 1930–1965* was reprinted as the first Australian paperback edition (1972), and again in 1975 in an Angus and Robertson 'Classics' series with the addition of poems from *New Poems 1965–1969* and with revised notes to Book V of Dunciad Minor. Hope's contribution to poetry was recognised by an award of OBE and an honorary degree from the ANU. Hope's growing popularity as a poet is evident with the publication of *Selected Poems* (1973), which was reprinted in 1974 and 1975. *Henry Kendall*, containing an introduction by A. D. Hope and poems and prose by Kendall by Leonie Kramer, was also published in 1973. In that year, Hope became a member of the Literature Board of the Australia Council (1973–74) and received an honorary degree from the University of New England. The next year saw a second edition of The Cave and the Spring and the publication of *Native Companions* (1974). This latter book is a mixture of reviews often slightly revised or augmented with later comments, three articles that Hope termed 'more or less autobiographical' and revised texts of lectures he gave in the course of his academic teaching. Hope decided to give up reviewing in 1966, due to its being time-consuming and poorly paid. The reviews he chose to include in this book he saw as 'having some critical theory involved or some general critical attitude beyond the particular work under review'.[1]

In 1975, *Judith Wright and A Late Picking, 1965–1974* were published. In writing about Judith Wright, a dear friend as well as a fellow poet, Hope decided that given that there was an abundance of material being written about her poetry he would focus in this study on her intellectual development and its importance as a background to her poetry rather than as a commentary on the poetry itself. All of the poems in *A Late Picking* first appeared in literary journals and magazines in Australia, the US and Canada. Within a year of the publication of these two texts, Hope received the Robert Frost Award for Poetry and an honorary degree from Monash University.

In 1978, Hope again published two texts, one critical prose, The Pack of Autolycus, and the other, a new collection of poetry, *A Book of*

Answers. *The Pack of Autolycus* consisted of what Hope selected to be the best lectures he had given during his academic career. *A Book of Answers* consists of poems in which Hope 'answers back' to poets across time who have affected him. The poems of his 'old favourites' are reconsidered: Donne, Marvell, Milton, Dryden, Pope, Byron, Keats, Tennyson, Browning and Hopkins. Hope also speaks back to the poems of Europeans such as Heine, Tolstoy and Baudelaire; he takes on some contemporaries: Yeats, Graves, T. S. Eliot; and finally plays havoc with his friends: James McAuley, Judith Wright, Gwen Harwood, Rosemary Dobson and David Campbell. In 1979, Hope's *New Cratylus* was published. This was Hope's attempt to argue his case for what he thought great poetry must entail and what he believed was wrong with contemporary criticism, in particular New Criticism and Leavism. He attacks poets such as T. S. Eliot, extolling the charms and musical superiority of traditional forms and damning Free Verse as being formless and unmusical.

In 1981, Hope was made Companion of the Order of Australia. The next year was an important one for Alec Hope in that *The Tragical History of Faustus*, begun 50 years earlier when he returned from Oxford, finally saw the light of day. Two years later a selection of Hope's poetry was translated by him into Italian: *Tre Volti Dell' Amore*. In 1985, *The Age of Reason* was published — a collection of poems that David Brookes contextualises in *The Double Looking Glass* as poems 'not on reason itself but the gaps, the not-reason within and about it'. It is, as Brooks notes, about 'reason's contexts, about its ineluctable relations with such things, its sometimes clearly unsovereign place amongst them'.[2]

Hope's second adventure with play-writing was rewarded with the publication of *Ladies from the Sea*, an amusing and instructive play that examines how Odysseus, having returned home to his loyal wife, behaves when he is visited by the lovers (Calypso, Circe, Nausica) he met on his 20-year journey home.

In 1989, Hope was made an honorary member of the American Academy and Institute of Arts and Letters. The National Library holds manuscripts that outline eight further projects Hope had planned but which he thought in 1986 he would 'probably never live to complete'. Hope had prepared for his death for a long time. His last book of poetry (*Orpheus*, 1991) was written consciously as his last offering. In *Intimations of Mortality* he makes a plea to his readers:

Share the carcass, spare the soul;
Leave my laurels, sere or green.
Maggot, buzzard, critic, ghoul
Pick my bones but pick them clean

Despite his apparent lack of interest in public acclaim, he could not help but be aware that he was achieving fame and occasionally notoriety in the literary world. When discussing his own sense of destiny, Hope had definite ideas. After a lengthy interview with him one afternoon, he wrote me a letter on the subject:

> A vocation is different from an ambition though one can add ambition to it. The ambitious man sets himself a definite and tangible goal of success, the goal of a vocation is a response to something the man called is unable to define, it is a continual adventure into the unknown. I don't want to be too solemn about this. I recall Alexander Blok's wise remark: 'A poet,' he said, 'does not have a career, he has only a destiny.' I would like to say that this was my view but I was never conscious of having a destiny either, simply a sense that poetry was my business in this world and that nothing else really mattered. For all that I have been extraordinarily dilatory about setting about my business — often writing nothing or even attempting to for months or years at a time and when I returned to it as a result of a nagging in my mind, taking it up again with something like repulsion, until by middle-age it gradually grew on me and drew me on. Even so I did not publish or attempt to publish until quite late in life. I cannot claim anything like a single-minded devotion to my vocation and I am not aware of ever having made any real sacrifices to pursue it.
>
> As a result, now that I have overcome my former disinclination to look backwards, as I review the experiences of my life, the course I have chosen in relating it does seem to me the only possible one, because I can perceive no shape, no main trend, no coherent pattern in it — apart from a vague and probably illusory sense of having been 'guided'.

Hope notes that his Calvinist conscience kept muttering that he had largely wasted his life and talents, but that he was comforted by the fact that on the whole he had enjoyed it. In this letter Hope repeats what he said to me numerous times: that if there were a guiding principle or force anywhere in his affairs it was 'simply a constant impulse to preserve and foster negative capability'.[3]

This chapter, nevertheless, shows how Hope responded to praise and criticism throughout his life. It also seeks to illustrate, in a more personal way, how he saw himself. At times, his comments show the man behind the mask. Feelings of self-consciousness and of being an outsider sit alongside those of a man always prepared to see the humour in any situation.

THE PROGRESS OF POESY

The poet, when his heart is young
And pure the stream and bland the words,
The Milky Muses from his tongue
Dispense insipid whey and curds.
But with the years the curds mature;
Grown rotten ripe, his talents please.
With gusto now the epicure
Cuts deep into his stinking cheese.

— Book VI, 1959, p. 28.

THE THREE POEMS

There are nearly always three poems involved in the writing of one. There is the poem I first see in my mind often in considerable detail and with all its tone, metre, shape, and so on fairly well defined. There is the poem I actually write, often quite different and nearly always emerging with a different 'tone' from that I first saw for it. And then there is the ghost of another possible poem on the same subject which nearly always suggests itself at some stage of the writing. But the poem actually written stands in the way and makes it impossible to realise this third poem at all.

Why is it that poets so rarely use the devise of 'variations on a theme' so usual with composers?

— Book VI, 1959, p. 35.

PERSONAL ODDITIES

One is so used to oneself that real oddities often pass unnoticed. I have very little visual imagination. When I dream the details are usually vague. I cannot recall even the best-known faces except in a schematic, half-notional way; if I invent scenes, places or people I cannot imagine them in any detail or with particular vividness. Yet if I shut my eyes, there often occurs the most vivid, detailed and extraordinary scenes, faces of endless series of unknown people all animated and changing in a way I could never by an effort of will summon to imagination. At other times a succession of patterns and formalized shapes and intricate arabesques occur complete and excitingly beautiful. Yet I can never achieve more than the crudest doodling if I try to invent patterns — I might add that if light falls on my closed lids I usually see a cunt in vivid detail, a very animated and provoking little snitch it is too, but nothing more, except a hint of the curve of thigh or loin. Rather like Alice's Cheshire Cat at the point when only the smile remained. Yet my visual memory is unable to manage much more than the schoolboy's diagrammatic travesty of this charming feature of the human landscape.

It is much the same with music. I could not compose a tune and have the poorest memory for music I hear, yet from an early age have involuntarily sung or whistled quite long pieces of music often with themes developed in a complex way, without in the least foreseeing how it is to develop or knowing where it comes from. It is just as though I put on an unknown recording and was myself the gramophone.

With words nothing of the sort occurs. I compose consciously and deliberately and with control and foresight of my imagination and hardly any automation or spontaneous flow of inspiration.

Merely trying not to be bad is much more difficult than simply trying to be good.

— Book VI, 1960, pp. 95–6.

LIVING TO MUSIC

This has always been my feeling about the world and in the last few years has acquired the force of a conviction: that there is a sort of music, a rhythm, energy, and melody to which one lives very much as a dancer moves to music. This is the 'real life' and is distinguished from the rest by the fact that these are only the 'noises' of life in this other part of experience, without a guiding rhythm or sense of a developing melody.

When I was a child I used to listen to the music and sing bits of it to myself. I suppose I made it up. I still do from time to time but mostly it is replaced by fragments of the well-known composers. (No twentieth-century music, of course.) I remember old Mr Frazer listening to me singing when I was about eight and asking: 'What was that?' I said 'Nothing, I thought of it myself, it came into my head.' He said: 'You ought to get someone to write it down.'

— Book X, 1967, p. 112.

SACRED RELICS

I am sitting in a lecture at the third Nichol Smith Seminar in eighteenth-century studies. James Clifford, that great and humane scholar, is discussing the unknown fate of Johnson's original letters to Boswell:

'... Boswell could hardly have destroyed those priceless treasures.' Of course he was speaking for Boswell, for whom any letter of Johnson's would have been a 'priceless treasure', but the tone of his voice showed that he was speaking for himself as well, the yearning of a man who has devoted great powers and insight, a whole life, to the life of another man in whose worth his own worth must find its guarantee.

Suddenly it all seems false, a kind of worship of idols. The letters of Johnson are not priceless treasures, though they are good enough letters of their kind. Johnson's worth would not be diminished if they had all perished as Shakespeare's have — I suspect that Shakespeare, the good manager, wrote home regularly ...

But chiefly I think of the false air that would breathe from letters written in the knowledge that anything a man scribbled to a friend would become a 'priceless treasure'. How could it help infecting the result? One eye on the recipient and both eyes on posterity! There is a side to scholarship which goes beyond service to the text and becomes the worship of the miraculously resurrected turd!

— Book XV, 1973, pp. 72–3.

W. H. AUDEN

Yesterday a newspaper reporter rang me up to tell me that W. H. Auden had died the day before. I was shocked but not grieved — mainly shocked, I suspect, because he was born in the same year as I (21–II–1907) and it was a sort of memento mori to know that he was dead.

The reporter, who was plainly not a reader of poetry, said he had been told that my own poetry was like Auden's and had been influenced by it. I remember that earlier, after I came back from Oxford, which he left before I arrived, I used to think so and to console myself with the fact that I had at any rate invented my kind of verse quite independently. I don't know why I bothered, since now I cannot see any likeness at all, at any age. He was in any case much cleverer, more intellectually agile and verbally inventive than I could ever hope to be. I admired him a great deal and in many ways, but I never liked him much. I suppose I still have to give up the idea of publishing my Housman piece in Diamond-cut-diamond now he is dead. It would be poetic justice but would be as bad mannered as he was to the dead Housman.[4]

— 1–X–73

In spite of the fact that I can see no likeness in our poetry, I have always felt in an odd sort of doppelgänger relation to him as though we were opposite sides of the same coin so to speak. I feel as though my twin brother had died — no grief but a real gap in nature.

— Book XV, 1973, pp. 87–8.

THE THEORY OF THE MASK

Yeats was onto something — there is no doubt about that, but his theory of the mask is unsatisfactory and rather repellent. Like his magic spells, at once too simple and too mechanical. I have just found this description of the actor making up (from Baudelaire) which comes closer to what Yeats, I think, was trying to say:

> Et quand le grand acteur, nourri de son rôle, habillé, grimé, se troove en face de son miroir, horrible au charmant, seduisant au

répulsif, et qu'il y contemple cette nouvelle personalité qui doit devenir la sienne pendant quelques heures, il tire de cette analyse un nouveau parachèvement. Un espèce de magnétisme de récurrence. Alors l'operation magique est terminée, le miracle de l'objectivité est accompli, et l'artists peu [t] prononcer son Eureka. Type d'amour eu d'horreur il peut entrer en scène.
L'Art Romantique. Philbert Rouvière[5]

This could well be an image of the poet in those relationships with himself and his poem which Yeats was trying to express in his theory of the mask. Joyce was possibly expressing something of the kind in his theory of the three types of composition: the lyric, the epic and the dramatic. But this again is unsatisfactory, for the highest 'grade' is too godlike (paring his fingernails). What Baudelaire has caught is what is lacking in Yeats and Joyce. The artist is completely involved, he is fully conscious of himself and the 'persona'; for the time being he undergoes a metamorphosis which is total and is what B. calls the 'miracle of objectivity'.

There is still something missing but perhaps it cannot be said at all; it can only be experienced; those who have, sometimes call it 'inspiration'. It eludes description, but it is the 'tertium quid' which the theatrical images of the make-up and the mask ignore and by this lack prove unsatisfying.

— Book XV, 1973, pp. 99–100.

WILLIAM DOBELL

A very great portrait painter! So I have been shocked today to see in the Adelaide gallery, what is obviously a late, perhaps a very late self-portrait — a kind of good-natured old ghost peering out of a lot of painterish ectoplasm — an electrifying and disturbing death-mask. But what was most disturbing was that it looked rather like me.

(On the train between Adelaide and Port Augusta — 2–V–1975.)
— Book XVIII, 1975, p. 29.

A WARNING BEACON

On more than one occasion lately I have been seduced into commenting on my own poems — usually after giving a reading of them. I have not succumbed yet to the abyss: lecturing on myself though I have got perilously close to it. I have always thought it a quite disgusting thing to do, though I am aware it is a common enough thing nowadays.

So I am delighted this morning to come across Disraeli's remark at a public banquet in Scotland:

'An author who speaks about his own books is almost as bad as a mother who talks about her own children.' (1873)

True enough but what mother or what author has ever been able to resist such talk? Emily Bronte is the only one I can think of.

— Book XX, 1977, p. 1.

PRESIDENT OF NEPHELOCOCCYGIA[6]

Geoffrey Dutton, who is a very nice man but always a bit of a galah, has just said in public that I would make a suitable president for the Republic of Australia that he wants to come into being. It looks as though my contemporaries don't know what to do with me, and elevation of a poetical Struldbrugg[7] to Cloud-Cuckoo head of state is their desperate solution to a problem that will settle itself soon enough without their help.

— 27–VIII–77
— Book XX, 1977, p. 26.

UNDERSTANDING MUSIC

Maria got to her feet. 'I'll go,' she said. She remembered Loiseau once saying that Mozart was the only person who understood him.
Len Deighton, *An Expensive Place to Die*, pp. 101–2.

Len Deighton is a talented writer of thrillers and no hack, but this is a surprising remark to find in *An Expensive Place to Die*, by no means one of his best. And it is out of character for the tough, sentimental and not very imaginative policeman Loiseau.

For all that it is a gem in itself. It is this feeling about the greatest works of music — indeed of all the arts that they understand me whereas with lesser works I feel that I understand them, which is the dividing line between the two, between the masterpieces and even the greatest productions of mere talent. Remember this!

— 4–V–1979
— Book XXI, 1979, p. 10.

POETS AT THE HELM

Philip Martin[8] has just presented me with the poems of Karol Wojtyla, the present Pope, and I am led to the odd reflection that the only other world-leader who was also a poet in my time was Chairman Mao Tse Tung. What would Plato, who thought only philosophers should be kings and that poets should be expelled from the commonwealth, have said about this, I wonder?

Don't tell me, I can guess. Plato is sometimes deliberately enigmatic, but he is rarely mysterious. His Socrates is nearly always predictable. You can see him coming. He was not a poet. But Plato was. There is surely a fine irony in the section of the *Republic* in which Socrates bans poetry from the ideal state.

— 5–VI–1979
— Book XXI, 1979, p. 20.

ARABIA FELIX!

Two surprising bits of news within a few days of each other: Mrs Fernandez, the cultural secretary at the Mexican Embassy, tells me that her sister, who is teaching English in Bahrein, has been reading my poems to her classes. Leonie Kramer showed me a literary critical magazine issued by the university of Sana'a in South [Yemen] containing an article on the same product. My, O my! Next thing they'll be hanging up my mu'allaqat[9] in the Kasbah.

— Book XXI, 1979, p. 39.

ET WORDSWORTH FELIX!

A university colleague whom I met outside the theatre last night while talking to John Passmore remarked:

'I was in London recently and went to a Conference at which Max Black talked about the language of poetry. He used as examples only two poems, one by Wordsworth and one by *you*.'

I said: 'Well it's only fair. In Canberra I talked to *him* about the language of mathematics.'

I was tempted to add: 'Anyway it's nice to find Wordsworth in good company for once." Seeing my friend had meant it the other way about [Ed's note: Additional comment added at a later date by Hope: I could not recall, when I wrote this, who the friend was. It was Jack Smart,[10] the philosopher. Jack is a bit of a flat earth man: he does not understand irony. I don't know about John Passmore.[11] He has a sense of fun but, I suspect, too literal in the long run. But I refrained because they might have taken me seriously.] the words could have been repeated, moreover, without the intonation and become a legend of crass self-esteem. I have to be careful nowadays, thought mostly I forget to be.

— 14–1–1980
— Book XXI, 1980, p. 50.

MEN OF ACHIEVEMENT

Like everyone else I am pestered by publications of the *Who's Who?* type. I usually fill in the requisite information and post it on. But there is a sort of self-advertising, lick-spittle request which I invariably throw into the waste-paper basket. One of these entitled *Men of Achievement* has just solicited me for the last time, I hope. This time I returned their wheedling screed with a note:

> Dear Mr Kay,
> Good wine needs no Bush!
> yours
> A. D. Hope

I hope it stops him but I doubt it.

— Book XXI, 1980, p. 57.

A PROPHET IN HIS OWN COUNTRY

This is the kind of letter I most treasure:

> 14 March 1980
>
> My family has always understood how much I love your poetry, and they were sweet when A *Late Picking* came out. We had been burnt out early in the year, losing about 3500 sheep and miles and miles of fencing, and there seemed so many more priorities than a book of poems. But they all said, get it, and I did. I know a fire is nothing compared with real troubles, but that book did so much to cheer me at the time.
>
> Mrs Sue Kelly

Literary commendations these days come in thick and fast, but I read them saying to myself: 'Who now reads Cowley?' But Sue Kelly's letter written from what she describes as her country neighbours ('My Philistine friends' — no top-lofty criticism implied. I remember David Campbell's remarks in the same vein about his neighbours — the accent is on the words 'friends' and, humorously only, on 'Philistine') — is a mark on the wall: — Hope was here! Long after I have been swept aside by the new trends of this and future times, I may live on in the memory of country folk and artisans who otherwise would in no sense have regarded themselves as 'literary'. It is a nice thought.

— 21–III–1980
— Book XXI, 1980, pp. 79–80.

SPREADING THE VIRUS

Pleasing piece of news! At the Brennan Society meeting in Sydney last week, a very beautiful Irish girl asked to have a word with me: 'I thought I would like to tell you that I found two Irish poets in Dublin where I was a week or so ago both unknown to the other reading your *New Cratylus*.' She could not recall the name of one but the other was Seamus Heaney, whom I met in Toronto. I did not expect the book to have much impact outside Australia, but it appears that the virus is quietly spreading. I should like to think that I contributed to the death of free verse and the other heresies the book attacks.

— 29–III–1980
— Book XXI, 1980, p.81.

SEASONS OF SACRED LUST

I have just, at her request entertained the Japanese poet, Kazuko Shiraishi to dinner. She presented me with a copy of translations of her poems into English with the title above. She used the title page to write an inscription which, incorporating the printed title, reads:

> Dedicated to
> A. D. HOPE
> SEASONS OF SACRED LUST
> which I dream
> to see you.
> 'Poetry is my
> country,
> my passport'
>
> Kazuko Shiraishi

It left me wondering if it means what it seems to mean (if so she comes too late). Her English is odd but quite adequate, as she grew up in Vancouver.

— Book XXI, 1980, p. 82.

SINGING IN THE EARS

Working for the last few days at home in almost total silence I keep noticing the very loud and continuous 'singing', or 'ringing', in my ears, maintained at a constant pitch and with a fairly regular rhythm. I have always had this sensation when in a silent room or in stillness out-of-doors. It seems to be a sort of carrier wave for apprehension of real sound, comparable to the vague light patterns one sees in complete darkness. It occurs to me that perhaps dreaming is a similar maintaining of imagination at a more or less incoherent level when the mind is shut off from contact with the consciously apprehended world. Even in the absence of external stimulation the senses and the mind do not relax completely, but maintain a waiting tension ready for instant response when the external world impinges. Follow this up.

— 18-1-1980
— Book XXI, 1980, p. 91.

DER UNTERSCHIED

I came across this in Goethe this morning over breakfast:

Bin so in Lieb zu ihr versunken
Als hatt ich von ihren Blut getrunken.[12]

And reflecting that my poem *The Cannibal to his Love* is generally condemned, while Goethe's distich has been selected in the anthology I was reading. I wrote this:

If I had written such a line
All would cry: 'Out, revolting swine!'
If Goethe says it, it's divine.

But German it is! How basically Teutonic.

— Book XXI, 1980, p. 110.

LIKE — UNLIKE?

Reading again with delighted and indulgent wonder Butler's *The Authoress of the Odyssey*,[13] I am suddenly struck with its similarity of approach to that of my own book on Dunbar's poem *The Two Married Women and the Widow*. In both books there is the spectacle of the amateur taking what he wants for his argument from sciences and fields of knowledge in which he has no specialized training; in both there is the tendency to be convinced by evidence that favours and to ignore considerations that go against the theory; both go in for elaborate but flimsy geographical and mythological networks of support and rest as much on our ignorance of social systems in the past as on our interpretation of fragments of evidence that have survived. It is interesting that scholars have largely ignored both books. Butler of course has all the marks of the amateur and the crank — what about me?

— Book XXI, 1980, p. 111.

CORRECTING THE RECORD

Manning Clark has just published in the *University Recorder* some reminiscences of the early days of his appointment in Canberra University College, in the course of which he recalls a high occasion, when Alec Hope walked into the Blue Room at the Hotel Canberra the day after the publication of *The Wandering Islands*.

The book as I recall, made no immediate impression and could not possibly have done so the day after publication; Manning Clark does not say what the 'sensation' was that my entrance was supposed to have caused.

People like Manning and Douglas Stewart, as they get older tend to live in the golden light of a period in their past in which all the geese were swans and the swans themselves archangels six-winged.

— June 1980
— Book XXI, 1980, p. 112.

GOD'S LAST EFFORT

I notice that several of the worst deserts, hot or cold, and other miserable or un-salubrious parts of the world, are commonly referred to as 'The Last Place God Made'.

This seems to imply that God had come to the end of his resources and had to make do with bits and leftovers or that he had deteriorated as a creator. Otherwise with increasing practice one would have expected the last work of the Deity to be his masterpiece.

— 14–VII–1980
— Book XXI, 1980, p. 119.

WANDERING FAUSTUS

My poor *Faustus*, first of all my books [to] have to beg for lodgings, has been from one publisher to another without success and from one producer to another without any recognition of what I was trying to do.

The publishers are quite straight-forward. They fear the book would have too narrow an appeal: they would lose money. The producers just prefer the mangled version. Here is a reply to Tim Cunow[14] from the Director of the Sydney Theatre Company:

> Here is *The Tragical History of Dr Faustus* as amended by A. D. Hope. I regret to say it is too much for us. This seems to be a gargantuan task. It seems to be a competently done job but is not theatrically convincing. In other words it feels more like a theoretical exercise. Also it seems to fall half-way between two stools. While the amendments made by the anonymous hack are interpolations, they do or can work well on stage. Either one accepts them or perhaps does a totally new adaptation rather than a 'purging' as here.

What is distressing is that he is probably right. But I would contest the view that my version is no more than a 'purging': it is a restoration, or an attempt at it. But he is possibly right in his implication that it is not as good theatre as the knock-about farce it replaces —

and it is possible that the same was true of the original Marlowe they replace, and indeed, that this is what prompted the replacements.

I wonder, will it ever see the stage?

— 3rd–IX–1980
— Book XXI, 1980, pp. 133–4.

THE TERRORS OF DEATH

The recent deaths of James McAuley and David Campbell and the rush to assess, explain or chronicle them in print recalls Dr Arbuthnot's remark made about Edmund Curll's score or so of 'Lives': 'Curll is one of the new terrors of Death.'[15]

Peter Coleman's *The Heart of James McAuley*, just published, is not in the Curll class but worries me. Most of what it has to say seems true enough but it is a bit too neat and tidy to be convincing. Things I know about Jim escape in all directions from the packaging. He was more amorphous than this, more untidy in the structure of his living.

No doubt someone will try to do the like for me. Philip Martin is presumably on the job already. In the conversations I had with him last year, I continually felt that involuntary attempt to get me into a neat package and even while I felt that the intellectual cage was quite just and perceptive, I was tempted at every step to revolt, to cry: I am Proteus: let me out of here!

— 7th–XII–1980
— Book XXI, 1980, pp. 144–5.

INTERNATIONAL PROFILES

Today I received in the mail another invitation to Vanity Publishing from Ernest Kay of the International Biographical Centre in Cambridge, U.K. This project invites me to compose a full page biography of myself accompanied with a photograph for a publication entitled 'International Register of Profiles'. The appeal to vanity has a sharp edge: 'We can include only 1000 biographical entries in this unique work.'

I wonder who falls for this nonsense. It would be interesting to see a copy of this and their 'Men of Achievement' volume to see if any real celebrities take it on.

Into the WPB, Dr Kay!

— 12th–III–1981
— Book XXI, 1981, p. 180.

MATHEMATICS AND POETRY

Some time ago Leonie Kramer asked me if she could show my *Three Songs from Pythagoras* to an eminent mathematician and physicist — they had not at that time appeared in print. I never heard more of this till last week when she revealed at lunch that, when she asked the great man what he thought, he had commented unfavourably. 'Weren't the mathematics correct?' she asked. 'O the mathematics were fine,' he said, 'but I thought the poetry was awful!'

Well, well! Ne Sutor ultra crepidam! Or is it: Ne supra crepidam sutor indicaret?[16]

I forget my Latin but I seem to have heard both versions.

But who is the shoemaker in this case? I am afraid it is only too clear.

— John James Hospital, Deakin
— Book XXII, 1981, p. 4.

WALKING WESTWARD

(Reflections on my 74th birthday)

My next year's birthday gift will be
Three quarters of a century
Of rhyme and reason, cunt and can.
Enough, indeed, for any man.

— July 1981
— Book XXII, July 1981, p. 26.

THE LANGUAGE OF POETS

> George [Pavlopoulos] spoke of Seferis, of how Seferis had deeply understood Solomos, the Greek Byron, and the Cretan Erotokritos and the folk songs, and brought all these things together in a living speech that had not lost the mighty force of its origins.
> Peter Levi, *The Hill of Kronos*, p. 67

I should like to think that those last twenty words might one day be applied to the language of my poems.
— Book XXII, 1982, p. 69.

AUTOBIOGRAPHY

'But what's an autobiography? Surely it's a romance of which one is oneself the hero.' These words spoken by a character in Robertson Davies' novel, *World of Wonders*, hit me hard as I am hesitatingly and rather ashamedly jotting down a few reminiscences with the intention of leaving them to be read after my death. The sentence I have quoted is of course not a definition. There can be many other sorts of autobiographies. The suggestion that all people who tell the story of their own life, deliberately manipulate it to show themselves in an attractive light is of course absurd. Though even St Augustine cannot resist telling God what an important sinner he has to deal with. The tone is meant to be confessional but it hardly succeeds. Augustine cannot resist dramatizing his sins. Yet, by any standard of comparison, he must appear a pretty mediocre specimen of naughtiness.

The sting lies in the alternative idea that one cannot help romancing about oneself. Whether one is pleased with oneself or deeply dissatisfied or anything in between, one cannot help giving a *partial* account since an impartial account would have to see the subject equally from within and from without and to take into account motives and aims which are actually hidden from us. No-one can help some unconscious 'editing' just as no-one can help presenting a more rounded and coherent view of his own life than the facts probably warrant. What we omit may distort things as much as what we assemble and arrange for telling; and who can omit nothing when everything is relevant, or tell all without putting the emphasis on some things more than on others.

None of this is a reason for not writing an autobiography, since it presents an important, sometimes an essential part of a jigsaw that can never in any case be complete.

— 4–VI–1982
— Book XXII, 1982, pp. 76–7.

GOOD NEWS FOR POETS

From Joseph Hone's *Life of W. B. Yeats*: 'at Cannes … Yeats was twice assailed by influenza. He was told the real trouble was exhaustion from the overwork of years. The doctors advised him to withdraw from public life … and one of them said that he must walk slowly, even move his head slowly, that his thoughts might become slow also. The same man added: "If I had met you when this [his nervous breakdown and lung disease] was beginning, five years ago, I could have saved you it all by sending you off on a bout of dissipation — all the great creators of the past were devils. Drink and women have saved many men from death and madness."'

Well, as far as the precautions go, I can claim to be preserved already for a very ripe old age — and I am steadily keeping up the treatment from day to day. I am reminded of a sprightly old lady just turned a hundred whose picture I saw in the papers lately with a glass of champagne in her hand. She attributed her longevity to life-long recourse to the same medicine. But I have two elixirs to her one. What Fun!

— 18–IX–1983
— Book XXII, 1983, pp. 160–1.

Notes

1. Interview with Ann McCulloch, March, 1990.
2. Brooks, *The Double-Looking Glass*, p. 275.
3. Hope, Letter to Ann McCulloch, July 1988.
4. In fact, in 1978, Hope changed his mind and published his 'Housman piece' in *A Book of Answers*, pp. 93–5, noting that his decision to publish it was determined by the fact that his attack, unlike Auden's on Housman, 'does not refer to his private life, of which I know nothing'. In this instance, I assume that Hope no longer saw his actions as being similar, and therefore no longer 'Diamond-cut-diamond'. See Room (ed.), *Brewer's Dictionary of Phrase and Fable*, p. 339, where a 'Diamond-cut-diamond' situation is one, for example, where there is meeting or match between two equally able people.
5. This passage was taken from the second volume of Baudelaire's collected essays. Translation: And when the great actor, brought forth by his role, costumed, made up, finds himself opposite his mirror, hideous or charming, seductive or repulsive, and while he contemplates there this new personality which must become his own for several hours, he draws from this analysis a new completeness, a kind of magnetism of recurrence. Then, the magical operation is ended, the miracle of objectivity is accomplished, and the artist can utter his 'Eureka' as a symbol of love or horror, he can move onto the stage.
6. Translation: President of Cloud Cuckoo Land.
7. The Struldbruggs were a race of immortals unique to the island of Luggnagg in Jonathan Swift's *Gulliver's Travels*. They had a special mark that characterised them as having insight on how kingdoms should operate. Hope's reference to the term personifies himself satirically as one so deemed.
8. The poet Philip Martin was educated at Melbourne University and taught in the English Department at Monash University. Philip Martin was working on a book on Hope before Martin's illness and he spent a great deal of time consulting with Hope.
9. The mu'allaqat refers to a style of poetry from pre-Islamic Arabia, samples of which were allowed to remain after the Muslim order was established in 622 CE. The name translates as 'hanged poems', and refers to the fact that the poems were hung on the walls of the ka'aba, the cubic temple in Mecca. A characteristic of the poetry is that each line is polished to perfection with the overall structure being less important. Hence they are known by the description 'a string of pearls'.
10. Jack Smart (1920–) was Professor of Philosophy at the Institute of Advanced Studies at the Australian National University.
11. John Passmore (1914–2004) was also Professor of Philosophy at the Institute of Advanced Studies, the Australian National University. He was a visiting fellow in history there in 1995.
12. Translation: 'I am so deeply in love with her / As if I had drunk her blood.'
13. Samuel Butler (1835–1902) was known primarily as a satirist. Butler's *The Authoress of the Odyssey* was published in 1897; it presented the theory that the *Odyssey* was written by a woman, due to the many descriptions of domesticity in the book.

14 Tim Cunow is Hope's literary agent.
15 Edmund Curll (1675–1747), was a bookseller and pamphleteer and was known for being involved in literary frauds and publications of a controversial nature.
16 Translation: 'Ne sutor ultra crepidam' and 'Ne supra crepidam sutor indiracet' translates as 'the cobbler must not go beyond the sandal' and 'let the cobbler not judge beyond the sandal', both of which imply that one should not criticise beyond one's sphere of knowledge.

XI

THE DREAM-TEAM

Hope refers to Freud's theory of dreams as 'mumbo jumbo', and he records his own theory of dreams along with copious dreams of his own. It might be the case that Hope's antagonism to Freud is based on his protectiveness towards his own work; he did not want his readers to reduce his poems to their sexual basis alone. Of course, along with Freud, he accepts the existence of an unconscious, but for him it was not composed of repressed desires; it housed his dream-team.

Hope's dream-team is composed of 'revellers' and 'roisterers', who invent whole scenarios for his imagination to claim as he sleeps; they are 'the back-room boys' who call to his attention moments of cowardice displayed by him in his daylight writings; they have at times terrible taste and absolutely no idea of management. It is from his dreams that Hope is able 'To tap creative energy from a host / of clues he is forbidden to meet below / Levels of consciousness he is master of' (*On the Night Shift*).

Hope was meticulous in his recording of his dreams; and the dream-team is conversant with every area of thought that interested him.

MORE TROUBLE FOR DESCARTES

Descartes could find no sure test to prove that when he was dreaming the world of his waking experience was more the real world than the world of his dreams — no test based on the evidence provided by either world, that is. I dream that I am sitting in a crowded railway carriage, facing back and watching a crowd of people trying to board the train. A drunken young man pushes his head in the door and shouts abuse and nonsense at the passengers while his wife and friends try to drag him back. At this moment the train starts with a jerk and the man is knocked down as the friends drag him clear and then pull him to his feet. As the train pulls out the crowd [moves] along the platform jostling, shouting and talking to one another. I see all their faces and the details of their clothes, a momentary glimpse of twenty or more people with individual differences down to the fine detail which I would be incapable when awake of imagining in as many hours as there are seconds in the experience. Where do they come from? How can I instantaneously come to 'create' so many human beings unknown to me; and, even if that is what I do, how do they manage, if they are no more than the creation of my dreaming mind, to carry on their activities so various and inexplicable to me, in the same autonomous and unpredictable way that people behave in waking life? Moreover in my dream I am present myself taking part in these activities which are not the activities of my waking life. I have 'created myself too. Indeed I have no evidence to refute the suggestion which might be made to me that I am not part of the dream of the angry man who shouts at me and that he is not relying as I or Descartes might do on his 'cogito ergo sum'. How do I know indeed that every person on the train and on the platform is not doing the same thing and convinced that he is the dreamer and all the others are part of the dream. Of course it is unlikely that they do any more than I-in-the-dream do. In the dream neither I nor any of the others have any reason to raise the question for no-one knows that he is dreaming.

This notion of the corporate dream in which each participant supports the dream for the others is in fact not a mere ingenious fancy. It is precisely the nature of what we call a civilization or a culture, a nation, an institution, a group or a family. Only rare individuals at rare moments wake for a while and know that what they took for obvious reality is in fact a corporate dream.

— Book VI, 1960, pp. 64–5

'DU, DOPPELGÄNGER, DU BLEICHE GESELLE

> And it seemed to Torless that he was glad of this. At this moment he had no liking for human beings — for all who were adults. He never liked them when it was dark. He was in the habit then of cancelling them out of his thoughts. After that the world seemed to him like a somber, empty house, and in his breast there was a sense of awe and horror, as though he must now search room after room — dark rooms where he did not know what the corners might conceal — groping his way across the thresholds that no human foot would ever step on again, until — until in one room the doors would suddenly slam behind him and before him and he would stand confronting the mistress of the black hordes herself. And at the same instant the locks would snap shut in all doors through which he had come; and only far beyond, outside the walls, would the shades of darkness stand on guard like black eunuchs, warding off any human approach.[1]

This strikes me particularly as an extremely vivid description of the dream I had more than once as a child at Kirklands.[2] It must have been between the ages of five and eight or nine but probably earlier rather than later so that there is little chance of its having been suggested by books or talk. In the dream I went into the room upstairs which was unfurnished except for my father's photographic equipment. In the dream it would be quite empty as when I first saw it, with bare boards. The only difference was that I saw a door at the opposite end of the room to the left of the dormer window and, surprised that I had not noticed it before, I opened it and found it opened on another room with another door leading to a stair. All the rooms were perfectly empty and I continued to go from one to the next impelled by a sort of terrified fascination because I knew that some dreadful and menacing being was waiting for me behind one of the doors. Only I never got there. I always woke up in terror as I put my hand on the door-knob. The only difference between my dream and Törless's is that the creature waiting for me had no specific sex and was only possibly human. It was its unknown nature that was so terrifying. I cannot help feeling that Musil could not have invented this 'metaphor', but that he had

had the same dream as I had. *Die Vermining des Zoglings* <u>Torless</u> was published in 1906 when Musil was 26. I was born in 1907. When I was thirty or so I wrote *Ascent into Hell*[3] which briefly described my childhood nightmares including this one.

I suppose there is nothing much in all this. It is not an improbable coincidence; there is no need to talk of archetypal dreams, though I have met someone who once described almost the identical dream he or she had had as [a] child.

But the impression is exciting and disturbing — as if I knew inside me that the obvious and the conventional explanations were not the real one and something much more mysterious had surfaced and been glimpsed for a moment. Perhaps it is only the still powerful memory of my dream that causes this.

— Book IX, 1966, pp. 129–31.

A DREAM

Last night sleeping in a tent on this beach and two days after talking with R. D. Fitzgerald about our Irish ancestors I have a dream, most of it now forgotten, in which at the end I am standing before a man who is kneeling at my feet. He is imploring his life, he has blue eyes, the typical Celtic face seen in the crude stone heads of ancient Gaul and Ireland and as I look at him I see that he is myself. I am not ill-disposed to him but he is an enemy and I am on the point of deciding that I shall take his head when I wake up. Then I remember that I had a similar dream as a boy in which I met my enemy outside the nursery window at Kirklands and killed him — shot him, I think — at the moment I recognized him as myself and tried to stop but it was too late. As far as I can recall I have had this dream at long intervals all my life. Sometimes it is distressing, sometimes not, but it is always rather exciting to meet myself as another person and not a matter of surprise or shock as it is in Heine's poem. It seems quite natural and a welcome discovery, in most cases, for the confrontation is not usually hostile. [Possibly] this is the real motive for The *Journals of Joseph Trinidad* which I have planned to write if I last.

— Seven Mile Beach, Berry, 1968

On the other hand it is not exciting but slightly repulsive to meet several simulacra of myself in a tailor's cabinet or fitting room. They are too much the autocratic apes and too much touched with the faint sense of parody which an exact mirror image has. The dream images are independent persons and only in a metaphysical way myself.

I have gone naked here for two days. On this beach is a great grey log inscribed: FUCKERS' LOG. NOW IS THE TIME FOR FUCK. This pleases me and feeling as I do with all this sea and sun and sleep and the great stretch of empty sand, I cannot help agreeing with the sentiments. Among the graffiti is the wonderful word FUCKWIT!

— Book X, 1968, pp. 14–15.

DREAM! A VISIT FROM THE DEAD

Last night a very vivid dream of a group of people in a house, not an actual one, but in the country in New South Wales. Of those present I now remember only Dorothy Auchterlonie and David Campbell who was the owner of the house.[4] David brought home W. B. Yeats. I did not meet him beyond the usual introduction but at one point in the evening after some amused remark of mine to my neighbour he stood up, like Don Quixote on Arms and Letters at the inn, and addressed us in simple and noble eloquence. I have already forgotten but I think I was laughing at the gullibility of poets and his speech was in defence of it.

— Forest Hill, Victoria, 1968
— Book X, 1968, p. 48.

THE FACES

All my life, like many other people I know I have been apt to see faces in the patterns of damp on walls, the clouds or the silhouettes of trees at night against the sky. But in the last ten years or so the thing has begun to get out of hand. Everywhere any chance pattern of rumpled clothes, foliage, shadow or texture resolves itself in vivid faces often of fine modelling and lively and dramatic expression. It is as though they were there independently and the physical basis were only a means or pretext for showing themselves. If I shut my eyes they crowd onto the dark screen and become mobile sometimes in crowds, more often dissolving one into and after the other. But why always and only human faces? And why always of unknown people? Where do these strangers come from? Where do they live when I am not looking at them?

— Book X, 1968, p. 186.

A DREAM THEORY

I wake here from a busy sleep in which I have been working out a theory of the nature of sleep: sleep is still something of a mystery, both as to its biological function and as to what actually occurs when we sleep. My sleeping mind comes up with a new explanation which pleases my waking mind and is as follows:

'Sleep is primarily a repayment of Time. Human consciousness is only possible because it borrows from past and present and future to form what is called the "false present". But the debts of nature must be repaid. One never gets anything for nothing. What we borrow in the waking life must be repaid by periods of unconsciousness — periods out of time in which the brain runs "wild", out of any organized sequence. Consciousness is essentially an animal device to "borrow" time, but if the animal defaults it becomes bankrupt: the bankrupt mind, in terms of time, is what we call insanity, a state of permanent dreaming.'

When I woke I was still in my dream, explaining this theory to a second person — possibly myself — I was on the point of saying that the idea was metaphysical and not psychological.

It is the sort of thing that happens in dreams, seems logical at the time but appears absurd on waking. But I wonder if it may not be a clue to something sensible.

Think about it!

— Edinburgh 1971
— Book XII, 1971, pp. 20–1.

DAS AFFENSCHIFF

A curious dream at the moment of waking such that the idea and the impulse come from the dream side but one continues half-awake to elaborate it, manipulate and edit it. The original is a verbal dream in which I am reciting a translation of a short poem or epigram after Robert (or Gerald, I cannot remember which came first) of Antioch. The concluding lines are to the effect:

'Thus it is with religion among men. It is a wretched craft but if they do not cling to it, they perish.' At the same time I see a page on which I am translating the final lines into Latin elegiacs but [I am] baffled because I cannot recall the quantities correctly and have no dictionary at hand. Also simultaneously with these impressions I see the poem as an 'illustration' like those to Renaissance Emblem Books: three or four apes sitting side by side, clinging with their feet to a log drifting on a stormy sea. As I lie there still half asleep I catch myself 'editing' the dream — rejecting Robert or Gerald of Antioch as unlikely names for Byzantine poets and seeking for a more probable substitute; filling in the first part of the epigram by deliberate composition to fit the last lines, rejecting the three apes on a log as too close to the banal three wise monkeys of India, dear to tourists, and substituting an emblem picture of a great tree trunk with branches attached and some leaves flying in the wind; the tree wallows realistically in the waves, the spray continually breaks over a crowd of bedraggled ape-like figures who climb and scramble up the higher branches and, of course, make them top-heavy so that as they roll and dip under the water, other branches are brought to the top and the scramble is renewed. The whole 'dream' is in [the] process of transformation, but if I had not caught myself in the act, I would later have had no suspicion that I had not dreamed it so.

— 17–V–71
— Book XII, 1971, pp. 69–70.

OS TEREBINTHII

A voice in last night's dream explains to me that *Os terebinthii* is the name of the principle of initiation and explanation. For instance, in a great mosaic — at once a vast mosaic appears visually before me, made up of little square tiles — in a mosaic such as this which contains a pattern, too complex to be taken in by the eye, one must find the tile which is the *os terebinthii* from which the whole pattern proceeds and, following the sequence from there, the pattern will become visible — the tiles were in various shades of red and dull orange so that they were confusing like the more difficult Ishihafa colour tests. In the same way, to understand the way a cell or any living system works one must find the nucleolus in it from which its 'process' is initiated — it may be a single molecule — this is the *os terebinthii*. The voice, as in the last dream, kept urging me to wake and write it down before the wealth of examples it gave were forgotten. But I resisted this and have now forgotten most of this very elaborate theory. From where did my sleeping mind dredge up the terebinth, the turpentine tree, in this adjectival form? And what is its significance? I would suppose, from the Bible; but neither Isaiah 6.13 nor Hosea 4.13 are particularly relevant. As far as I know I have never read the references in Virgil (*Aeneid* x. 136) or in *Propertius* (III.7.49) which are in any case even less relevant. I had never, as far as I know, met the verb 'terebro' or its related forms, which might have been relevant in the queer way dreams confuse and amalgamate works. Yet at the time and even now, some time later, the phrase — os terebinthii — seems to be charged with an arcane meaning.

— 1971
— Book XII, 1971, pp. 82–3.

ANOTHER WITNESS

A. L. Burns[5] tonight recounted that just after his father died — about twenty years ago — he dreamed that he saw his mother entering a shop and that while she was standing at the counter she suddenly keeled over and fell to the floor. 'I saw, at least I couldn't see it but I know that she was bleeding' — he named an internal complaint and described the symptoms. 'I was so impressed with the dream that next day I rang the family doctor, told him details and asked whether it was likely. He said that he had known such things (prophetic or clairvoyant experiences) before and advised me to ring up, which I did.

And it turned out to have been exactly as I dreamed it: she *was* in a shop, she did fall to the ground and it was a case of — [naming the complaint] — she was with my aunts who at first were very cagey, till I gave them the details. "But how did you know?" I answered that I just knew.'

— 21–IX–1971
— Book XII, 1971, p. 126.

ANOTHER DREAM WORLD

… I wake tonight from a dream in which I am reading a North American epic of the early 19th century called *Gertrude of Wyoming* — no relation to Thomas Campbell's poem except in name; the poem which is of a remarkably low level of theme and language breaks off at a couplet beginning:

> *I came among men of low or common or*
> *… of an Indian summer*

and I wake with a contemporary critic's feeling of contempt for the sort of verse that passed for poetry on the country across the Atlantic. But why? Why should my sleeping mind traduce the then late American colonies and Byron's friend? Not that Campbell's poem is much chop; but it is at least literate in a *dull way*.

— 6–VI–72
— Book XIII, 1972, p. 80.

DREAMS OF THE DEAD

I can understand why the ancients and people in the past took these so seriously. There is something about these dreams that seems 'uncontrolled' by the imagination, the desires and fears of the dreamer — a real intrusion of another personality, as it were.

At long intervals I have dreams about my mother who is always between forty and fifty — she died in her sixties. This last night for example a long confused dream in which I am explaining to a foreigner how much I enjoy staying in a hotel near Central Station in Sydney — because fifty or sixty steam engines are usually sounding off at night — is followed by a short coherent dream that I am talking to my mother who is in bed in the next room, through the door between — she is in some distress which I cannot understand till she tells me she is going to have a baby — I get out of bed and go in, put my arms around her and say: 'But darling why didn't you tell me before. It's nothing to worry about.' Yet all the time I am aware that she is a 'revenante'.

I remember my father saying in his last years that she was with him all the time and talked to him every day. Every time I have a dream about her I wake with a first reaction: 'But this is absurd, she has been dead all these years!' And this is accompanied by the distinct feeling that I have had a visit — something more than a figment of my dream, a real presence.

— 27–VI–72
— Book XIII, 1972, pp. 91–2.

THE BEST OF BOTH WORLDS

The Controller of Dreams not only shows an increasing tendency to solve difficult problems, boring worries and terror situations by saying, 'You don't have to put up with this: Wake up!', he also can encourage me to take advantage of them.

The night before last, for example, in a dream I was in some other city on a public occasion, expected to announce and distribute the prizes for some competition the nature of which was not very clear to me. It was a festive occasion with people moving about and talking and champagne was circulating freely. But I was exasperated and embarrassed by the fact that the moment for the speech and the announcements was coming close and I could not get anyone to tell me the nature of the competition, of the winning entries or even the names of the prize-winners beyond three names written on a sheet of yellow paper in mustard-coloured ink, which were in any case illegible. I had had a couple of glasses of excellent champagne and was about to voice my exasperation, when the familiar voice of the Controller suggested that I should simply wake up which would save me from an embarrassing fiasco and punish the promoters for their carelessness and bad manners, because I would not be there when called on. I was about to agree when, with a surprising cunning, he suggested I put off waking and have another glass of champagne while I could. So I did and enjoyed it immensely as an added revenge.

This is the first time I remember the C. of D. being really immoral. Usually he simply shows common sense in getting me out of stupid situations. But it seems to be a comic sort of immorality — a game we play together.

— 23–IV–1973
— Book XV, 1973, pp. 22–3.

FOMELHAUT

The dream-team [likes] to keep up with current interests. I have just waked from a dream in which I am told that Fomelhaut is my star and I see a 'negative' photograph of a very bright star in the right of the picture accompanied by a group of very faint stars in the left. I am raising the question as to whether Fomelhaut may not turn out, when a really big telescope is turned on it, to resolve into a whole galaxy but the unseen informant tells it is indeed a star and part of our own galaxy. I am convinced that I am in some undefined way identified with it.

This nonsense is clearly the result of my attempts in the past few days to catch up on cosmological theory since Fred Hoyle wrote *Galaxie, Nuclei and Quasars*.

— 29–VI–73

(Looking it up, I discover [a] that it is spelt Fomalhaut and does exist, is one of the brightest stars, is in the Constellation Pisces Australis at a distance of 23 light years and is therefore one of our closest neighbours in space. Finally that its name is Arabic and means Mouth of the Fish. As my dream workers presumably knew nothing of this except that the word was Arabic — that was 'in' the dream — they were plainly working by the light of Nature — or should we say, the moonlight of Nature?)

— Book XV, 1973, p. 48.

THE HELPERS

Observation of Voznesensky's poems and their rhythmical structure in the past week or so, led me to wonder whether I might not find here a solution to the problem of a rhythmical structure for *The Battle of Junin*. It was a vague thought. But apparently my dream-workers got busy on the idea and two days ago just as I was waking up they presented me with several lines, just as a model, which I could both hear and see on the page. It was 'stepped' verse of the kind made fashionable by Mayakovsky and often used by Voznesensky. 'Well what do you think of *that*?' they asked with obvious satisfaction; and it really did seem like a solution to the problem. But as soon as I woke I recognized it as the metre of the Irish ballad, *Finnegan's Wake*: just the sort of unvarying thump I wanted to avoid.

— Book XIV, 1973, p. 72.

DREAM WITHIN DREAM

In the dream I recognize the fact that what I am witnessing has been the subject of other dreams in the past though there is always one constant and several variable elements so that it is like an algebraic formula. I am on the shore of a sea, lake or wide river and a boat full of people is rowed quickly past, stops and turns back.

The constant element is that it is in [the] charge of an oriental, either Japanese or Chinese who falls into the water and drowns. The other people in the boat and on the shore are real. The drowning oriental is a ghost, presumably of someone who did drown there in time past. As the boat turns and rows back, his head can be seen in the water a distance from the bows and as if moving with the boat, but gradually dissolving to a blur of shadow on the water. In the dream I am convinced that I have had this dream many times before though in many different forms. On waking I cannot recall any other instance, though the conviction is still a strong one. The phantom of the Japanese boatman is particularly clear, the other persons [are] not clearly defined, though one, a woman who stands in the boat reminds me of Susan Eade.[6]

— 5–III–1974

— Book XV, 1974, pp. 158–9.

THE DREAM PHILOSOPHER

At the end of what seems to have been a rambling, not very serious academic discussion including such topics as: whether 'Philosophy's claim that it is so complex a subject that it should have a separate handbook setting out its curriculum or not', there comes the interesting statement flatly enunciated by one of the interlocutors: 'Goethe remained a sort of mystical positivist to the end of his life.'

As I know practically nothing about positivism except that it is associated with the name of Auguste Comte, and as I know also very little about Goethe's ideas, I wonder what on earth the dream-team thought this meant — or have they been reading things behind my back?

— Book XV, 1974, p. 163.

MORE BACK-ROOM NONSENSE

I have just waked from a strenuous dream in which I seemed to [be] working hard at the composition of a poem in Russian in which the image of the poem was an elegant red motor-car of about 1910 vintage and there was to be some equally elegant word-play with the nouns [illegible]. It was to be in the metre of Pushkin's poem about the drowned man, though not in the same stanza form. This ambitious scheme was coupled with a translation into English in the form of a sonnet which had already been completed before the composition of the original. As I woke up I was convinced that the sonnet was written out and should be transcribed into this notebook. After I had assured myself that this was not so, I went back to sleep and the dream-team set to work on the Russian version with renewed enthusiasm and equal lack of success. They *will* overreach themselves.

— Book XV, 1974, p. 164.

DREAM-TEAM EDUCATIONAL

Tonight they introduced a familiar routine: I have left my academic post (or retired) and have taken one as a senior English master in a country or Sydney suburban High School and am going through the uncomfortable experience of my first day. Usually in these dreams I am doing it for the money and so it was tonight. This time Paul McEwen[7] of the Canberra Boys' Grammar School had persuaded me to join the staff and invited me to attend an informal session of senior pupils in which they gave short papers on subjects of their own choosing. As I entered the classroom a pupil of about 17, obviously dismayed by my entry was giving a critique of a poem by A. D. Hope, which he was treating very severely and, analyzing it, coming to the conclusion that my main fault was intellectual arrogance. I tried to look encouraging without much success.

— Book XIX, 1976, pp. 1–2.

DREAM POEM

I wake in the night with a line of an inchoate or imagined poem, — the image in fact forming around the line.

'It cuts the heart out of my breast to see those children grow.'

Almost in the few seconds of waking there is added to this the idea of one woman envying another who married the man she been in love with; the poem is all about the children of the other woman. Possibilities in this (?).

(My Dream poems are sometimes entire, though never remembered in their entirety; more often like this one they are in a process of crystallizing round individual lines or fragments and the setting or idea follows these, rather than generating them.)

— Wangaratta 21–V–1976
— Book XIX, 1976, p. 53.

MORE DREAM ASTRONOMY

I am listening to three astronomers from different observatories who have just met to compare notes on a remarkable new discovery. They show me photographs of a star, the first is simply a bright star of apparently first or second magnitude. This they indicate is the way it had appeared until recently. The second photograph is apparently of a higher magnification and shows a bright perimeter enclosing a central black disk. The third picture is a blow-up of the second and shows the black disk as an irregular patchwork of dark and light, though all black towards the centre. I gather from the conversation of the three that they have the first ocular evidence of the way a black hole develops in a collapsing giant star, and that there are unexpected features such as the patchiness from which they are able to develop a new theory that helps resolve the paradox of infinite compression of matter which the present theory seem[s] to imply.

Just as I wake I learn that the star is quite a well-known one and is called The Companion of Betelgeuse.

(Looking up the facts I find that Alpha Orionis [Betelgeuse] does not have a companion though Rigel [Beta Orionis] does. I may have read these facts and the fact that Betelgeuse is a star of the first magnitude, indeed a supergiant and a pulsating star, but I am sure that my waking mind was unaware of them. The Dream-team apparently had a clue but not much more than that.)

— Book XIX, 1976, pp. 107–8.

PIANO CONCERTO

The Dream-team was over-ambitious last night. They tried to produce me as the author of a full scale piano concerto. I was immensely pleased and turned over the printed score and admired the elaborate cover. I even sat down confidently to the piano a few minutes before the concert was to begin. On the seat beside me was my mother somewhat larger than life whom, as she had trained to be a concert pianist, I expected to be the actual performer. But she said, 'Why don't you play it yourself?' I gazed hopelessly at the score as she went on encouraging me and I struck some notes at random, but realized I could not even read the score I was supposed to have written and composed — and yet the theme of the first movement was in my mind. I said: 'No, I couldn't do it. I haven't played the piano in years.' Actually apart from a few lessons when I was fourteen or so, I have never played it at all. And so my mother consented to play. But then we were told that some other item in the concert had replaced us as the first item and this was the beginning of a series of delays and frustrations culminating in the news that the orchestra had failed to arrive and we would have to be content with presenting the piano part of which we were presented a transposed score with piano parts for the orchestral bits. Finally it became clear that in fact there would be no performance at all.

On waking I realized that all this had been the result of someone in the team realizing that in spite of the elaborate score, there was in fact no concerto and the dream-team [was] as unable to present the actual music as I was to read it.

— Book XXI, 1979, pp. 32–3.

LITERARY REMINISCENCES

Another new venture for the Dream-team. In the dream I am partly listening to an account of minor literary characters, partly reading notes, jotted down on sheets of lined writing paper, of their meetings in the nineties of the last century. They appeared to meet in some sparsely furnished room in Sydney where they drank and chatted. When I woke no actual details of their persons or their talk and sometimes boisterous fun remained — only the impression, the feel of it.

— Book XXI, 1979, p. 34.

DREAM STONE

I woke suddenly about midnight on the night of an almost full moon from a dream about Avebury and the 'divinity' of the great stones. In the dream I have been contemplating a poem of which I am able to salvage two lines:

> And how shall flesh not own
> The power of stark stone?

— Book XXI, 1980, p. 83.

A LECTURE ON CHEKHOV

Last night I dreamed that I was invited to a class conducted by Nina Christesen on Chekhov. The class was noisy and inattentive and Nina seemed irresolute and put out by their behaviour. So I made a loud noise saying: 'Shut up all of you. I am going to talk to you.' There was immediate silence and I realized at the same moment that I could not recall any single play or story by Chekhov. The Dream-Team had either over-reached themselves or were setting me up to appear ridiculous. However I recollected two passages, one in Chekhov's letter to his brother in which he describes the romantic and 'literary' method of describing moonlight on the water and his own realistic description of the light glinting off a broken bottle stuck in the mud. The other passage was the remark of Anna Akhmatova to Lydia Chukovskaya about how boring she found Chekhov's famous naturalism. Armed with these I began to talk impromptu and quite easily about Chekhov's 'naturalism' and about 19th-century theories of realism in general. But I was aware that I would have to illustrate my remarks by reference to at least *one* of Chekhov's works. I could only recall the titles of two of the plays, *Uncle Vanya* and *The Cherry Orchard* and nothing precise about their contents. At this point the Dream Workers let me off the hook and I woke up. But by then, I was determined to go on since as soon as I woke my memory improved, and for several minutes I continued to compose my lecture, even breaking into dog-Russian for good measure.

— Book XXI, 1980, pp. 84–5.

DREAM-SAGA

The Dream-team the night before last attempted to mount an Icelandic saga but could not cope in the end. The plot was simple and saga-like, the pursuit of a man who knew too much of events touching the honour of his friend, and who without actually revealing the disgraceful facts, had talked too freely of his knowing them. The pursuit occurred over brown and black rocks, an old lava flow either into the sea, or forming a peninsula to the mainland. The revenge was accomplished when the pursuer overtook his victim among the rocks and with typical Icelandic brevity apologized to him as he killed him — rather as Hrafnkell apologizes to the shepherd boy. Only in this case the victim, who at this point seemed to be me, was finished off with a long knife not as in Hrafnkell's case an axe. Rather un-Icelandic were the thoughts and feelings of the victim during the chase: his remorse at having injured his friend, his shame at the running away and his feeling that it would be better to turn round and face the killer. All this was delivered needless to say in English or acted out as in a film. The Team met their Waterloo as the killer, having returned to the settlement, went to the Club House (the setting had changed to modern Iceland) and proceeded to pin or nail a notice to the bulletin-board announcing the fact of his vengeance. In the dream I seemed to be standing behind him. The notice purported to be Icelandic but I could not read any of it and obviously neither could the Dream-team.

— Book XXI, 1980, p. 89.

DREAM-TEAM HISTORY

The boys excelled themselves last night. I woke from a dream in which I had been persuaded by a now shadowy interlocutor — though I recall that I had a definite and vigorous discussion with him — to look at some students' essays on seventeenth century religious polemics. This had apparently led on to his inviting me to take up the subject myself, which I had reluctantly agreed to do — or rather, had allowed myself step by step to become involved in. I had made the point that sixteenth-century religious controversy between Protestants and Catholics had mainly been polemical and abusive, but that in the seventeenth century the better minds on both sides had recognized the worth and standing of the intellectual opposition and the need to stop finding political rationalizations disguised as philosophical or theological arguments. The opponents could no longer be treated as corrupt and dishonest. The basis of the controversy had to be broadened to one of serious philosophical and theological systems. Agreed on this, we then went on to say that I would be involved in the serious controversies within both Catholic and Protestant parties and in the new problems raised by seventeenth-century science and epistemology. I woke in a sort of stupor at the magnitude of the task I had committed myself to, and with a great sense of relief that I had escaped the whole thing.

The odd thing about this was that although the thesis was in general a correct one, the Dream-team had in the main no detailed knowledge of the subject at all — much less than I have when awake. In the dream they had me and the other person mentioning names of leaders of important movements. The reference to sixteenth-century philosophy was devoid of the great names and their theories, the controversy of the Lettres Provincials was touched on but Pascal was not — and so on. It was a rather an ingenious attempt to give me something to worry about.

— Book XXI, 1980, pp. 123–4.

DREAM ABILITIES

… My invariable dream experience is that I am unable to read. I can recognize, for example, a stop sign by its colour and its octagonal shape, but I cannot read the word STOP, although I know it is there. I have the impression of understanding the meaning of a page of type, but not of reading it word by word or sentence by sentence. I cannot reliably perform even simple arithmetic operations in the dream-state. I make a variety of verbal confusions of no apparent symbolic significance, like mixing up Schumann and Schubert, I am a little aphasic and entirely alexic.

Carl Sagan: *The Dragons of Eden*, p. 144

This bears out most of my own observations of the limitations of the Dream-team. Not that I am entirely 'alexic':* I can often read a few lines of print — but never for long. In continuous reading, I appear to be reading the words but in fact rarely read the print; I follow the narrative by 'learning' the words. As for Sagan's confusions of words of 'no apparent symbolic significance' (he is a mildly convinced Freudian), he has no notion apparently of the rich word-play that goes on in my dreams, the sort of plays on words, purely because they are alike in sound, that fascinate young children learning their language and that form one of the substrates of poetry.

It appears from Sagan's remark about Stop Signs that he dreams in colours which I rarely do and almost never in the literary or intellectual contexts of most of the dreams I have recorded in these notebooks. This would fit in with his evolutionary thesis: that dreaming is both a very ancient practice and like the physiology of the infant, tends to reflect earlier stages of mammalian and human history. Colour sight would seem to have developed later than black and white vision in mammals. But he cannot for this reason comment on the intense euphoria of my occasional colour dreams, nor their usual perfectly clear transfusion with a generalized and 'innocent', sexual pleasure.

What he, perhaps, misses in the description of reading difficulties (and in my case, lack of precise imagery of places, at times) is the way our senses and our minds tend to 'fill in' the missing details in ordinary waking life. We work on 'patterns', some unlearned and some acquired which are 'corrected' by the actual situation. In dreams we lack an actual corrective experience but the Dream-team works on the assumption that there is, that we will fill in the raw details not actually supplied. So a 'rough approximation' will give us the illusion of a precisely detailed situation.

There is much else in this book, especially on dreams, that I must return to, though Sagan** is to be treated as a stimulator rather than as an authority. If one forgets this, one tends to recall what he calls 'scientific myths' as though they were established theories — though god knows, the borderline between the two is vague enough.

— Alice Springs 22–VIII–1980

* I wrote 'Alexic' — perhaps one of those amusing 'confusions' in which Sagan can find no 'symbolic' significance. He forgets that someone called Alec and frequently called Alex (or in Russia, Alexei) might be tripped for the fun of it by the Dream-team, by the phrase: 'I am entirely Alexic.' Sagan seems to know his own Dream-team only vaguely. They, at any rate, do not tease him good-humouredly as mine do me. A lot goes on at an ordinary level without [the] benefit of Freudian Symbolism.

** Carl Sagan is apparently a well-known astronomer. Odd how many astronomers in recent years have take[n] up one or more aspects of biology.

— Book XXI, 1980, pp. 125–8.

DREAMS AS PLAY

[Editor's Note: Hope on reading Novalis on dreams, records his disappointment that his own theory of dreams was not original.]

I have for so long believed I had discovered this view of dreams, that I was disappointed to find that Novalis had anticipated me by 180 years or so. I wish now I had finished the poem I began on the subject, *On the Night Shift*, before I found out.

— 3–1–1981
— Book XXI, 1981, pp. 154.

PHASELLUS ILLE

Last night I was talking with some friend who was urging me to join with him in a series of poems attacking someone responsible for the death of a pet bird of a lady known to us both. He showed me fragments of a Latin poem he was composing. I could not read the text but at once began to recollect fragments of Catallus's two hendecasyllabic poems on the subject and the rhythm of hendecasyllabic verse was running in my head. However bird, lady and my indignant friend soon vanished from the dream and it became evident that they were part of a ploy by the dream-team to get me to return to a poem started some years ago called *A Joke with Catallus* and based on a parody of

> *Phasellus ille quem*
> *videtis, hospites* …[8]

I became so involved that on waking I rose and found my Catallus and looked up the structure of the metre with the conviction that I was about to compose *in Latin*. It only came to me gradually that the whole enterprise was ridiculous. But the Dream-team had succeeded in sending me back to consider the English imitation. Since I published a translation of the original in the Bathurst High School magazine when I was about 15, there may be reasons for this odd dream of which I am unaware.

— 14–1–1981
— Book XXI, 1981, pp. 159–60.

JOHN FIELD (1782–1837)

The Dream-team [does] not usually shine at musical composition but last night was an exception. I and some others were present at a final rehearsal by a small amateur group of musicians who seemed to be vaguely connected with the Websters. I had letters from Hilary and Camilla the day before. They seated themselves in a bare room, some on chairs others squatting or sitting on the floor. Some produced sheets of music from small cases which turned into music stands. But no-one, as far as I could see, looked at the score. They were led by a handsome, young man but most of the others were girls. The audience sat at the side and in front of them was a sort of day bed spread with old lace.

At a sign from the leader who played a curious woodwind sort [of] instrument of a type I had not seen before, they burst into a lively and beautiful first movement of a sonata for flutes and woodwind instruments *molto con brio*[9] and played for several minutes until the leader stopped them to discuss some point of execution. The discussion then became a general one about the composition. I spoke up and asked who the composer was and was told that it was a work by Field and at the same time saw the name printed in bold type on the top corner of one of the scores. I started to say: Oh Field the best English composer after Purcell, but did not manage to be heard.

Actually it was not very like anything by Field that I have heard — my mother used to play his Nocturnes when I was a boy — more like Cimarosa or 'English Bach' if one can imagine a combination of the two styles with a touch of Vivaldi at his most energetic. After that the dream changed to the following morning when I was helping two elderly servants scrub out the concert room and hose it down using the long-handled scrubbing brushes used by sailors swabbing the decks.

I knew practically nothing about Field except that he anticipated or, as I thought my mother had told me, was influenced by Chopin. In the dream I thought his name was Andrew Field (rather than John)* and that he had lived most of his life in England rather than on the Continent. Certainly the delightful sonata of which I heard most of the first movement bore not the slightest resemblance either to the style of Field or of Chopin.

PS. I noticed when the music stopped that the audience had been given copies of a printed poem of some pages in length on which the music was supposed to be based. But I did not manage to read any of the poem and did not identify its author.

Andrew Field, Professor of Biography at Griffith University in Queensland and a friend of mine is probably the reason for this mistake.

— Book XXI, 1981, pp. 156–8.

READING IN DREAMS

In spite of my general agreement with Carl Sagan on this point, I do occasionally have a clear visual perception of actual words on paper, as in the dream about John Field's music a few days ago. Last night I found myself entered for a training course in marine navigation, with a vague implication of naval service. The recruits after their initial briefing were to be taken to their training centre on the coast and we were giving a series of simple exercises connected with this expedition by ship. The first was a position reading 5N 35.79W, which we were to locate on a large-scale chart of a complex coastline with many islands and deep bays and estuaries. The map was covered with place names. Working by the bearings given I quickly located the spot which turned out to be the site of the training centre — a small town on a deep bay — and I distinctly saw and read its name: 'Penzance.' The bearings themselves of course were nonsense. The Dream-team was unable to cope with real ones, but the chart or map was at least in conformity with the bearings given so that one could find them by the usual method of indications of longitude and latitude. Apart from Penzance, however, all the other map names were unreadable. I could *see* them but not decipher them.

— Book XX, 1981, pp. 169–70.

DREAM-TEST BY DREAM

I get bored with the endless changes of Dream-Team invention but here is an odd one. I was on a sea coast somewhere in Portugal and throughout the dream everyone was speaking Portuguese which

I could not understand but tried to speak a few words of, recalling in my dream that I had been reading a story in Portuguese before I fell asleep. I was carrying a cheap cardboard suitcase which contained my vestments as altar-boy to a priest — but when I showed him a crimson elaborately embroidered and fringed cassock he signed to me to put it away. We entered a small church where he said a brief mass to a congregation of one and I sat on a side-seat. But from there I could see at a little distance a large cathedral whose main doors kept opening to give me glimpses of the interior which seemed splendidly ornate. After the service in the little chapel I walked to the cathedral and entered. A woman came up to me and talked to me for a minute in Portuguese — 'sirn' and 'não' so that all I could do was nod and smile as if I understood and interject an occasional Portuguese word — the only Portuguese words I could recall in the dream. The woman soon went away and I was able to look around me. The interior was decorated in red and gold, the apse extremely high and covered by a barrel vault, and the walls richly decorated in squares within squares of deep ochre framed in lighter red. Then came the curious part of the dream in which it occurred to me, since this was a dream, that I could test whether one could see sharp and precise detail in a dream or whether in fact this was an illusion and that, in fact, one saw only blurred and very general impressions. At once the high wall I had been looking at swung back in position and I verified that I was indeed seeing it in as sharp detail as in waking sight. The odd thing is that I was quite satisfied that in this way I had tested Carl Sagan's theory that one cannot read the actual letters in a dream script. The architecture of the cathedral bore no resemblance to any style I had actually seen in Portugal. The story I had been reading was *José Mathias* by Eça de Queiroz. It could have no connection with the dream except to influence its setting in Portugal.

— Book XXI, 1981, pp. 185–7.

A CONFLATION OF BARDS

Tonight I woke from a dream of a quarrel between two poets. At first the dream was of the arrival of a family party including a number of friends in a pantechnicen from the coast. They had loaded it that morning and were now to unload it and I went to get some cans of beer for them before they started as it was a hot day. I was particularly anxious to give one to the friend who had driven the van and could not see him anywhere so I asked one of the women if she had seen him. She said he had left and it was clear from her manner that she had had a quarrel with him. I asked where he had gone and she pointed to a big main highway past the house saying he had decided to catch a bus on to the city. At this point the identity of neither party was clear. They were both vaguely 'friends'.

I crossed the highway carrying the two cans of beer and saw my friend waiting at a stop at the bottom of the hill and as I made my way towards him saw that it was the poet David Rowbotham[10] whom I know slightly. As I caught up with him I could see he was in a rage and he swung away from me as I approached. I said, 'David, I'm terribly sorry that this has happened'. He replied, 'A. L., the stupid bitch! What a stupid thing to object to.' 'What words?' I asked — 'Oh, objecting because someone says "For chrissake."' 'Who said for chrissake?' He said, 'You did.' He waved away the can of beer and I said, 'Look, David, you know how I love and admire you', and he seemed mollified but still angry. At that moment I saw a bus stopping at the bottom of the hill and left him to it.

The odd thing is, only clear to me when I woke, that the woman was the poet Anne Lloyd[11] whom I know well and correspond with. But David Rowbotham in the dream had the voice and appearance of a farmer or someone who lives out of doors. I realise that in the dream he was conflated with David Campbell and that Anne Lloyd was also a double character, conflated, I think, with Jennifer Maiden,[12] who has just sent me her latest book of poems. None of the four poets is, as far as I know, acquainted with any of the others. David Rowbotham has recently written to me and rung me up to protest about being omitted from Leonie Kramer's *Oxford History of Australian Literature* which made him very angry. The warm feelings I expressed and the distress I felt at the quarrel were not appropriate to him but would have been to David Campbell. Altogether a very odd mix-up by the ingenious but I fear not always ingenious Dream-team. What are they playing at?

— 26–VII–1981
— Book XXII, 1981, pp. 23–5.

A NEW DREAM-TEAM VENTURE

The D. T. have not produced any notable variation on their ordinary pranks for some time apart from inflicting some agonising nightmares and withholding the usual licence to wake myself up if it gets unbearable. But last night they moved into quite new territory. In the part of the dream which I can recall, just before waking I was another actual person, a man who died as I discovered on waking in 1926, the etcher and writer Joseph Pennell.[13] I was aware of my dream identity and quite unaware that I had a different waking identity or indeed that I was dreaming. In the dream I was engaged in talking to someone unidentified — possibly a student or an interviewer — about the technique of pen-drawing and demonstrating it at the same time. In one exercise I was taking, as an illustration, one of my own drawings of a beech tree and making a rapid sketch as I talked of the bottom of the bole and the thickening of the root system at ground level explaining how the structure gave a sense of firm and powerful fixation in the ground. In a second illustration I was explaining how I indicated by successive short pen strokes, the sense of a shimmering path of light, say from the moon, across a stretch of water and as I did was conscious of doing this on the shore of a stretch of water with a city skyline on the other side.

As far as I know I have never had any particular interest in Pennell's work as an artist, of which I have seen a few examples, mainly etchings or reproductions of them. I woke thinking the Dream-team had got things wrong in introducing pen-drawings but was surprised on checking with the Encyclopaedia Britannica to find that he had in fact published a book on the subject, *Pen Drawing and Pen Draughtsmen* (1889).

Very Odd!

— 27–VIII–1981
— Book XXII, 1981, pp. 31–3.

BLACK HOLE FAILURE

This time the Dream-team had launched a nightmare scenario. In it mankind had solved the problem of an unlimited power supply and the whole apparatus was housed in a large cupboard which had a seat for the Controller before it. I was to replace him in a few minutes. The controller in question was my young friend Jeremy Slocombe who had presented me, in real life, with the little goat, a piece of harness-ornament from Harappa. I was tired and the script of the events called for me to fall asleep in the control chair and to wake finding the whole very dangerous apparatus loose from its siting and rushing about out of control. I recall remarking that the door was not kept locked and that this was very dangerous. Unfortunately instead of falling asleep as the script required I really woke up and said to myself: How absurd! What means could they possibly imagine to provide all that energy from so small an apparatus. And immediately the answer came: 'Harness a Black Hole!' I have no doubt that this is what the Team intended but I would be surprised if they could present the idea in such a way as to make it at all plausible, let alone convincing, even as a device to run a nightmare on.

— Book XXII, 1982, pp. 90–1.

DREAM-TEAM PROPHETS?

Last night I dreamed I had had a moderately severe stroke while travelling in Portugal or Italy. In the beginning of the dream I was in a country restaurant from which we were due to return by car to the town where we were lodging. It began with my cleaning my coat and shirt from something splashed over it which it appeared I had done in falling. I gathered this from the waiter who was helping me clean myself. I did not recollect the fall, nor, when I returned to the table after the stroke which had occurred earlier. But I had lost control over my arms and legs and had trouble in articulating. Penelope and Emily were at the table and were apprehensive and upset. The restaurant manager was leaning over me and then squatting beside my chair trying to explain that I must not think of returning to town and that he had reserved rooms in the establishment for the night. I had difficulty in understanding — partly his broken English and partly my own condition — but I rejected the idea thinking to myself the wounded animal has only one thought: to get back to its lair. I tried to say 'We will catch a bus or train. The car can stay here.' Emily was talking in her high rapid voice — she had, of course, been dead for some years as in this and other dreams — when she is excited and I could not follow. Later while we waited for tickets at the station my father was there too, saying nothing and walking gloomily up and down. I had no idea in the dream that they were both dead long ago. My own mind was obsessed with the thought that now I could never finish *The Age of Reason* which I am working on at present. The dream may have been partly prompted by the fact that earlier in the night I had been reading Florbela Espanca's *Diário de ultimo ano* in the facsimile edition which Isabel Moutinho[14] has just sent me. That would account for Portugal and the sense of approaching death, since Florbela knew she was dying in the last year of her life. But the whole thing was both unnerving and grotesque. The whole thing too ended with the reappearance of the sleek, smiling manager of the restaurant at the barrier of the station tendering his bill, which somebody else paid. I remember thinking: well anyway I don't have to worry about money any more and somebody else will pay for my funeral. In travel dreams I am always worrying about money or finding I haven't nearly enough for fares and hotels.

The Dream-team [was] clearly having a bit of fun with me — earlier that night they had me at a reception in Italy which was to announce my engagement to a nice Italian girl.

Isabel has just suggested I make a translation of Camoens' best-known sonnets. I have consented provided she will help by making the selection and commenting on the drafts.

I have just talked with Isabel about the project and she gave me the ideal towards which I must work: 'You must translate in such a way that I can say to myself, that is how Camoens would have written if his native language had been English instead of Portuguese.' I thought of Amanda Haight's[15] comment on hearing me read one of my translations from Akhmatova.

— 5–IX–1982
— Book XXII, 1983, pp. 121–3.

Notes

1. Musil, *Young Torless*, p. 38.
2. 'Kirklands', situated on the Macquarie River 11 kilometres from Campbell Town, in Tasmania, was the Hope home from 1910–20.
3. Hope's *Ascent into Hell*, was first published in *Melbourne University Magazine*, 1947, pp. 34–5.
4. Dorothy Auchterlonie and David Campbell were both close friends of Hope. Auchterlonie (married name Green) was a colleague of Hope's in the English Department at the ANU. Her expertise was in Australian Literature. She wrote a biography of Henry Handel Richardson, *Ulysses Bound* (1973), two collections of poems under her family name and a collection of her critical essays have been published. David Campbell was a fellow poet who has published more than 10 collections of poetry as well as two collections of short stories.
5. A. L. Burns was the father of Andrew Hope's partner Sarah Burns. He was a long-term friend of the family and during his work-life was an academic in the History Department at ANU. Andrew Hope is Hope's son.
6. Susan Eade, at the time Hope made this entry, was a doctoral student in the History Department at ANU. In 1975, she, along with Ann Curthoys and Peter Spearite, edited *Women at Work*. Susan Eade teaches women's studies at Flinders University, Adelaide.
7. Paul McEwen was the headmaster of Canberra Boys' Grammar from 1959–85.
8. The parody mentioned alludes to Catullus, *Carmem IV*; the opening line cited being roughly translatable in 11 syllables as: 'This boat tells us that it has been observed, friends …'
9. Translation: with great vivacity.
10. David Rowbotham: an award-winning Australian poet. He has published eight collections of poems. His earlier work dealt primarily with the Queensland landscape and his later work moved towards a 'more idiosyncratic vision that resists categorisation'. He has been viewed as among those Australian poets 'who have been involved in a radical redefinition of Australian poetry'. See *The Oxford Companion to Australian Literature*, p. 601.
11. Anne Lloyd: an Australian poet, whose poems, along with those of Kate Llewellyn, Joyce Lee and Susan Hampton were published in Rosemary Dobson's edition, *Sister Poets, 1* in 1979.
12. Jennifer Maiden: an Australian writer known primarily for her poetry; she has also written short stories and novels.
13. Joseph Pennell: a 19th-century American artist (lithographer) and writer.
14. Isabel Moutinho, who teaches Spanish and Portuguese at Latrobe University, had been working with Hope on a project involving the translation of the lyrics of Camoens.
15. Amanda Haight is the author of *Anna Akhmatova: A Poetic Pilgrimage* (1976). The work is a critical biography analysing the relation of the poet's life to her poetry.

XII

ARGUMENT BY ANALOGY

Hope's poems often take the form of an argument about some philosophical question; but the argument is usually couched in analogy. Hope uses comparisons because he sees them as the only means of saying what cannot be said by any form of direct statement and of extending the limits of experience and feeling beyond what they are capable of by other means.

Analogy, Hope concedes, might be poor argument and it might break under the test of logic, but it is, he argues, 'the perpetual source of discovery, insight, illumination, the marriage of disparate experiences drawn together by a natural desire and impelled by a mutual delight for the ends of [the] procreation of ideas'.

And so in this section the menu I have constructed, by my selections, will give you the verbal taste of dishes drawn from diverse foods for thought encompassing astrology, agricultural science, biochemistry, ecology, mathematics, animal husbandry, botany, physics, myth, legend and folklore, physics, sexuality and theories of the supernatural.

PARAMECIA

[Sonneborn] discovered that certain strains of *Paramecia Aurelia*, which he called 'killers', liberate into the medium in which they live a poison which kills other strains of Paramecium which he called 'sensitives'. The 'killers' are resistant to their own poison, which has been called paramecia. Killing takes place slowly, the 'sensitives' taking about two days to die.

Though 'killers' are found in nature, it is not known whether they are at an advantage over 'sensitives' under natural conditions ... Because of the slowness with which killing takes place, it is possible to get conjugation between 'killers' and 'sensitives'. If each ex-conjugant is cultured separately, the 'killer' is found to give rise to 'killer' cultures, the 'sensitive' to 'sensitive' cultures, and there is usually no exchange of 'killer' properties. Occasionally, when the males have remained in contact for a very long time, the 'sensitive' ex-conjugant may also produce a 'killer' culture ... 'Killers' remain 'killers' only so long as they reproduce slowly, when cultures are fed abundantly and multiply rapidly, the capacity to kill is gradually lost ... In some stocks, paramecia leads to a complete paralysis of the locomotory and feeding systems, and the animals die of starvation; in others they become full of vacuoles, swell and burst.

Famous Animals 4: Paramecium
by C. H. Brock: New Biology II

How similar the state of affairs among human beings! Most of us I suppose could be called 'indifferents'. But the 'sensitives' and the 'killers' are not at all rare. All sensitives know the 'killers' and avoid them if they can, though it is often difficult, for they rarely show any outward signs, are often charming and lively and kind and sociable. One only finds out by living with them and finding all one's creative forces growing feeble and dying. Then one must escape at all costs and at once. The worst cases are those in which the victim does not realise that he has chosen a killer until he or she is committed for what this Brock politely calls 'prolonged conjugation'. The fate of a sensitive married to a 'killer' and attached to the killer by love and admiration is usually desperate.

Apart from the creative faculties, something very similar occurs in the realm of personality among men and women. What I have just referred to is an unconscious, innate and natural power to blight and destroy imagination; it is not a power the possessor can exercise as he wills. It is simply there and operates on sensitives quite automatically. It is not a defect of quality but a positive quality of rare persons just as the power of creative imagination itself is in other rare persons. In the field of personality, however, 'killers' and 'sensitives' also occur. Here the 'killer' is usually unaware of his lethal power but the sensitive observes it at once and if he cannot escape, he may actually die after a time. When a 'killer' and a sensitive fall in love as they may do, it leads to the death of the sensitive who loses his or her will to escape. But if the will or the instinct of preservation triumphs it is the killer who is made wretched and unhappy. He cannot understand why and feels that he has been treated unjustly.

In the long association of Wordsworth and Coleridge there was, I feel such a fatal conjugation of 'killer' and 'sensitive'. Coleridge finally rebelled just in time to save his life and sanity, but his creative powers were quite ruined and his imagination irrecoverably enfeebled. Within Hayley there seems to have been a 'killer'. At least Blake found him so and describes the effect very vividly. Lives of men of genius and records of divorce, etc., should provide many cases.

— Book V, 1957–58, pp. 78–81.

REFLECTIONS ON FUCKING

Analogy may be poor argument and break under the test of logic, but it is the perpetual source of discovery, insight, illumination, the marriage of disparate experiences drawn together by a natural desire and impelled by a mutual delight for the ends of [the] procreation of ideas.

Chemistry and biology supply endless material for reflection leading to this end, which I cannot help feeling to be the natural end and cause of poetry. Stendhal's analogy of love and crystallisation was a good one but not quite good enough, for in the depositing of crystals there is no change of the elements analogous to what happens in love. A chemical rather than a mechanical change might make a better analogy and a biochemical analogy would be better still.

The hard-headed and the tough-minded and the sentimentalist alike are apt to come to the conclusion that love is nonsense and that the only real element in it is the pleasure of fucking, a fine pleasure but not to be overrated, momentary and in itself no more important one way or another than that of eating and drinking. This is like a man reasoning that it is absurd to make a fuss about a spark or a match and to talk in terms of conflagrations and explosions. He will strike all the matches in the box one after another to show that they do not add up to more than a chain of pretty little flares. What happens when the barrel of gunpowder or the summer forest are combined with the match, he dismisses as moonshine and imagination. All the aspects and forms of love which have analogies in the explosion, the conflagration, the steady flame, escape a mind whose experience is limited to the momentary but essential spark.

But *essential*!

— Book V, 1957, pp. 85–6.

TEASER RAMS

Vasectomized rams used as teasers … help to concentrate the lambing into a short period, and so saved time, labour and mortalities. This was one of the main points of an address by Dr. J. C. Potter, Adviser in Animal Husbandry at the recent … conference … The vasectomized ram is one that is entire, except that a slight operation has removed his ability to produce lambs. He is used as a 'teaser', helping to bring the ewes on heat, so that drop of the lambs shall be better grouped. Ewes remained on heat for about 24 hours and the period between heats was 17 days. The teaser rams were removed after 14 days and the working rams immediately joined.

— The Adelaide *Chronicle*, 20–VI–57

One's first impression is a sort of comic horror at the ingenuity of one's own species: the second the more sinister feeling aroused by the thought of what might happen in a human society run on scientific eugenic lines: one of the possible worlds of the future. But in the third instance one begins to reflect on a society as it is and wonder whether the ingenious authors of the scheme might not have taken a hint from actual experience. There is an anology to the 'teaser ram' and the 'teaser ewe' in human society; their function is to arouse, to excite, to set the passions going and they are forever deluded — often tragically — into thinking themselves the *objects* of passions which they have only kindled for another to profit by. Yet they are fortunate if they escape: their worst fate is to marry and to find that they are impotent to bring a passion to its full maturity and that they, who are often themselves passionate, are despised or become objects of irritation. Among the more obscure causes of despair, suicide and spiritual death this must be a not infrequent one.

— Book V, 1958, pp. 14–15.[1]

THE FRUGALITY OF NATURE

The anatomy of man as we know it instructs us to look for analogous forms and processes in his mental life, his passions and his society. Nature sometimes develops new organs for new powers and functions. But often she adapts or transfers structures already existing for quite other functions. A good example is to be found in the organs of speech and hearing. The tongue and the lips and the respiratory system are concerned with fuelling the organism, the intake of air and food and drink. The larynx and glottis originally served to protect the lower respiratory organs from the intrusion of food and drink. The ear develops from an organ concerned primarily with balance and posture. In all these cases the original function continues. Other parts of the structure have lost their original function altogether. The pharyngeal [illegible] in embryos of lower vertebrates develop into gills, inter alia, but in land animals into a variety of structures, for example, the malleus and the incus in the middle ear are structures adapted from what were originally parts of the skeleton of gill arches and bones involved in the mechanism of the jaws in lower vertebrates. From this collection of 'second-hand' and superfluous structures man has organised the marvellous machinery of speech and hearing. All this is well known. But we can perhaps see the same sort of process carried a step further and in the same way. The human brain and human consciousness which make language possible represent perhaps another line of adaptation of development of the same sort. What began as a development of the cerebral cortex with the function of developing a more adaptable and effective, *instructive* animal, led to the development of a new kind of animal in whom the instinct patterns remained generalised and primitive; the new animal was able to reflect and choose its ends. It was conscious and self-conscious. And in the end it was capable of free contemplation and creative activity no longer tied to the specific biological ends of self-preservation, maintenance and reproduction. Biologically useful curiosity became free inquiry; primitive fear, submission and sociable obedience became worship, primitive playfulness and manipulation and display became art. To identify these things with their origins is to commit the same sort of error as to confuse speaking with eating and breathing. They are something entirely new and different, though they use old mechanisms and structures. Nobody would make so gross an error in the second case, yet it is commonly made in the first.

But we perhaps tend to make exactly the same sort of error when we regard poetry as a form of social communication. We ought to recognise that on the basis of language developed for practical social communication, man has built up an entirely new set of activities and functions — something as different from the primitive functions and nature of language as speaking is different from eating and breathing. What we fail to recognise is the emergence of a new order of nature.

It might be argued in the same way that the sexual mechanisms and drives with a purely reproductive function produce in man a new order of nature which we call love. Past generations were perhaps more aware of this than our own, which has laboured to confound love with sexual urge and impetus. But the view that love is something different in kind and on a different natural 'level' would still get many to support it. What would cause more doubt is the view that from love itself there has emerged a new and higher order of natural powers which we vaguely refer to as 'visionary', a new mode or order of comprehension differing as much from ordinary perception as Newton's contemplation of the universe differs from the dog's awareness of his meaty bone. When I speak of poetry as metaphysical or as concerned with the metaphysical image of man, I intend the use of language in the service of this faculty.

I feel drawn to this area. It strikes with an inner conviction of its possible truth, but I should hesitate to make it an article of faith.

What is still emerging cannot be clearly seen and is bound to be seen in the confusion of the sort of experience to which we are still largely limited. Poetry is still creating the order of experience necessary to comprehend what poetry really is, as man when first evolving language must have been limited in his power to understand what he was evolving. The development of language is itself necessary before we can undertake an investigation of the nature of language.

— Cambridge 1958
— Book V, 1958, pp. 51–5.

FOOD AND LITERATURE

Just as inanimate matter enters the body and becomes its fuel and some part of it becomes the body itself — it comes to life and is able to feel and think — so the inanimate thoughts and feelings of other people stored in books enter the mind and become part of the mind — become what the inanimate matter feels and thinks. But whereas the original substances of food and air and drink are broken down by enzyme and other action and rebuilt into authentic materials of the body, the ingested thoughts and feelings remain much as they were, with their own structure and organisation; they come to life while we read, recall or recite, and they take colour and a new interpretation, different from those they had in the original mind in which they lived and grew, but the life they now lead is parasitic. They are like the figures of Helen and Alexander the Great to which Faustus gave temporary body and life, demonic life under control of the magician animating the proper and essential forms of persons long dead. To read a poem by Blake or by Pushkin is to bring something of Blake or Pushkin to life. Creation of the living poem in a living mind is something that *that* mind itself is incapable of producing, and the life given is that of an inferior demon. So on a wild and inferior stock one may graft a branch of a cultivated and perfected fruit which buds and flowers and fruits long after the tree that alone could produce it has been cut down and burned.

II

Just as some of what we take in by our mouths is merely fuel, or mainly fuel and has only a temporary vivification, while some is built into the structure of the body in a more permanent way, so we can distinguish literature which is mainly of use to energise and activate the mind and literature which is nutrient and built into the structure of the mind. And in both spheres there are drugs and intoxicants. Mind, like body, willingly acts as host to substances that pay for brief vivification, by producing for us anaesthesia, hyperesthesia, delirium or dream.

— Book VI, 1959, pp. 7–8.

REFLECTION ON GENESIS XX 17 (1)

There is an analogy to be drawn between the history of food-getting and the history of other processes and activities. Up to this century the numbers of men on the earth has been such that the traditional methods of producing food have sufficed and the foods themselves have sufficed. Now the individual farmer and pastoralist cannot feed us all and will be less able to feed us all in the future. Scientific mass-farming more and more replaces individual crop growing. New methods of producing fats and proteins by synthesis, new types of foods become important for the survival of the human race. Meat may disappear as a staple and become a rare luxury, wheat and rice may give way to the soya bean or to protein extracted from grass and leaves and algae. In a thousand years from now the art of cookery may be lost or replaced by an art based on products unknown in the past 100,000 years of human culture. But the same sort of thing is already happening to education, to art, and perhaps may happen to love, to morals, to the mores of society. The mere problem of keeping the increasing mass of men fed, organised and alive may destroy the 'natural' process, the traditional forms of society are slowly evolving and modified on the basis of primitive needs and resources. The twentieth century may be seen as the point of departure, the point at which radical invention replaced mere tinkering and modification. The replacement of wood or wool by synthetic substances never before [seen] in nature may be only a symptom of an equally necessary replacement of the arts and social institutions we know by synthetic substitutes, as the old staples are shown to be incapable of production in sufficient quantity to go round or as the new organization forced on human society destroys the means by which they grew or the conditions which made them possible in older forms of society. When all the ground is necessary for growing soya beans to give everyone enough to eat, the human race may not be able to afford beef or wine. And for the same sort of reason they may not be able to afford Bach or Titian or Shakespeare.

— Book VI, 1960, pp. 43–4.

PISSING AGAINST THE WALL

For in very deed, as the Lord God of Israel liveth … except thou hadst hasted and come to meet me, surely there had not been left unto Nabal by the morning light any that pisseth against the wall.

(I, Sam, 25; 34.)

This delightful phrase occurs seven times in Samuel and Kings, always in connection with the destruction of all the males of a tribe or family. What delights me is not the savage formula itself, though that is fine enough, but the sense of the continuity of civilization in small things. For civilisation begins with a wall, and pissing against a wall is the habit of the dweller within walls from the first wall to the present day.

Savages squat or piss into a bush; women squat and piss into a hole — civilised men have this little ceremony and the Bible preserves the memory of its antiquity and universality.

I Sam, 25: 22, 34.
I Kings, 14: 10; 16: 11; 21: 21.
II Kings, 9: 8.

— Book VI, 1960, p. 73.

FURTHER REFLECTIONS ON GENESIS XX. 17.

One could continue the previous note on this topic by pointing out that this has already begun to happen in the 'advanced' societies which have begun to arise in our lives in answer to the pressure of population and the problem raised by societies of hundreds of millions of people — societies so big that they must be more and more closely organized to retain coherence. These are the so-called totalitarian states: Nazi Germany, Fascist Italy, Soviet Russia, Soviet China and so on. The literature they have produced is negligible in quality and while they may require more time to prove the point, they already seem to demonstrate that total planned control must take in literature and that the sort of control necessary is inimical to the appearance of works of genius. They breed their own standardized literature for mass consumption, which compares with the old 'wild' forms of literature as synthetic proteins compare with beef-steak and venison.

Nor is it necessary that the artificial control should be political. The great academic machine in the United States is having a like effect. The need to produce hundreds of thousands of research theses on a small body of literature forces the universities to extend their field to take in current writers. The growth of mass amusement and the production of a huge sub-literature for the merely literate, from which publishers make their money, forces the serious writers more and more to write with the academic audience in mind and forces them into the universities to earn their livings by lecturing in literature. Creative writing courses help the process. Above all the fact that research on such a scale exhausts its material, turns the thesis industry more and more to criticism and critical theories proliferate and become fashionable not in proportion to their value but in proportion to the demand for new grounds of reassessment, so that as Malcolm Cowley points out writers tend more and more to write to theory. The academic machine begins to 'take over' literature and to control its sources of raw material and the result is equally inimical to the production of works of genius.

— Book VI, 1960, pp. 85–6.

STATISTICAL MORALITY

In small tribes and societies what every individual does is important and is under constant scrutiny and assessment. Moral judgement is absolute and individual; the standard is set high and failure to reach the standard carries inexorable sanctions. A single act of immorality will brand a man or woman for life.

In large societies while certain acts are punishable by law, the standard of morality tends to be statistical rather than individual, an average norm of acceptable behaviour, and a competitive scale is discouraged.

— Book VI, 1960, p. 88.

TRAFFIC LAWS AND MORAL LAWS

A comparison of the two might be fruitful. Both have as a practical end to make the way people behave among themselves workable. Both have a formal and conventional aspect, eg., keeping to the left, turning the other cheek, which could be achieved in some other way; keeping to the right, returning good for evil. Each has to admit exceptions, eg., in two- or three-lane one-way roads, or where one is bound to defend someone else.

But the main value of such a comparison would to be sort out, in the case of morals or ethics, the real moral issues from the conventional ones. Thus there is nothing intrinsically better or worse in driving on one side of the road than on the other. But there is something intrinsically wrong in killing and injuring others ... and for this reason there must be a rule, and the rule of keeping to the left receives moral force and sanction in this way. It is then immoral to drive on the wrong side of the road. Though it would not be so if you knew the road was empty. There is nothing immoral in driving on the wrong side of the road for a while on a long stretch of country road which you can see is clear for example, though you are technically breaking the law. This is because the act in itself has no moral significance, whereas the act of killing or injuring other people on the road has: it is intrinsically wrong and bad.

What is so clear in the case of traffic laws is not nearly so clear in the case let us say of sexual morals. There [is] clearly a set of convenient, useful and necessary rules in each society and these differ from society to society just as some keep to the right on the roads and some keep to the left. But the sanctions must be stronger since the consequences of infringement are not so obviously fatal or deleterious in many cases and there is no possibility of proper policing on the regulations or application of penalties by suspending the licence to fuck or imposing fines for irregular sexual behaviour. Society gets over this by making the convention itself *intrinsically* right and condemning those who treat the convention as a mere convention, even when they are doing no harm to anyone.

— Book VII, 1961, pp. 7–8.

NOTES FOR A FLOWER PIECE

The cultivation and display of sexual characteristics is a constant and continuing bent in human nature. It is probably instinctive and innate. Yet in most societies the sexual organs themselves are not publicly displayed or made part of the rituals of courting. There are some exceptions to this, enough to suggest that they could be so cultivated but for the taboos which almost always impose concealment and lead to the emphasising of secondary sexual characters.

By a curious irony the human race cultivates and displays not its own sexual organs but those of plants, and if they were conscious of this fact horticulture might rank among the major sexual perversions. But of course the breeding and enjoyment of flowers is the most innocent of occupations.

An imaginary society comes to mind, a perfectly possible one in the vast range of social types known to exist, in which not only was display and cultivation of the sexual organs accepted and encouraged, but all the resources of selection, breeding and hybridisation practiced in horticulture, had their parallel in human affairs. Just as the exotic and luxuriant blooms to be seen at a flower show are the result of selection and development of often insignificant wild blooms, so this society had produced varieties as beautiful, exotic and curious as the human sexual organs — true flowers in their power to attract the opposite sex by their brilliance of colour, sweetness of smell and extravagant variety of form and movement.

Such a society would have to impose controls on love even stronger than those in existing societies, but they would be based on esthetic preferences rather than on moral or religious taboos. It would have an elaborate and complex class-system or caste system based on the maintenance of the approved 'flower-types'.

— Book V, 1957–58, pp. 1–2.

SIGHT

It is probably a commonplace of observation but it had never struck me until today that sight is the only sense which we can exercise and shut off at will. We are always tasting, feeling, smelling, hearing and so on as long as there is anything to taste, smell, feel or hear, stimulating the organs of these senses. We can stop our ears, paralyse our taste buds or [torture?] other senses with drugs, but nature provides us with no method of closing our ears or our noses or our tactile organs, similar to the provision we have for closing our eyes. The biological reason for this may simply be that the eye is so delicate and so exposed by its nature that it must be continually moistened and cleaned and protected during sleep from dust and damage. But the primary purpose and function of an organ may be and often is less important than the secondary functions it acquires. It may be foolish, but I can't help feeling that this distinction of sight from the other senses is very important, though I can't quite think why.

— Book VIII, 1964, p. 22.

BOUND FEET

I have seen pictures of the horribly distorted feet of Chinese beauties in former times and these [illegible] the elongated heads of some South Americans produced by binding the baby's skull. The distorted ribs of some Victorian beauties, produced by corseting, came somewhere between the two and they may stand for a whole series of physical distortions and maimings produced by odd social standards of beauty or elegance, moral beliefs or mere token distortions that run from mere variations on nature, eg., fattening women to gross proportions to make them more desirable, shaving the facial hair of men, etc, through those that interfere with natural function, eg., lip-discs, circumcision, to those which maim the body and cripple natural function, eg., foot-binding, castration and the artificially induced paralysis and degradation of limbs produced by some Indian fakirs through keeping them rigid and immobile.

Alongside these one may set the training of limbs and organs to produce results impossible by mere natural use, and the strengthening and repair of naturally occurring distortions, defects and distorting malfunctions which are also common features of human societies.

I wonder if there has been any study of the mind which looked at things in this way, observing distortions and crippling loss of function produced by custom and education till the socially admired result is a mind as useless as a Chinese girl's bound foot, or as grotesque as the duck-lipped woman of some African tribes. One can easily fall into a silly sort of romantic Rousseauism here if one fails to distinguish this sort of thing from training or education which can produce exceptional powers, or which is simply useful and beneficial.

Suppose a literature, an art of fiction which simply looked at its characters from this point of view instead of from that of personal preference or social or moral codes, a literature which saw human beings and affairs from a naturalist's point of view. Swift was moving in this direction, but the people in G. T.ii are seen from outside. Tolstoy is full of moral bias and social taboo. The literature I am thinking of treats men and women as if the author were one himself and their society as if he belonged to another species.

— Book VIII, 1964, pp. 50–1.

PLANT SUCCESSION OR THE ECOLOGY OF POETRY RECONSIDERED

There are many plant species throughout the world for which fire plays an important role in preparing suitable seedbed conditions and in eliminating the more shade-tolerant plants that compete with them and impair their early growth. Parts of the story of *Sequoia gigantea* have already been told ... The story concerns a process known as plant succession, the continual change of the plant communities. As groups of plants change the soil's nature by the addition of their remains, other species respond to the new conditions, invade the area and gradually crowd out the other plants. Each invading species of plants is usually better for growth in reduced sunlight and soil moisture than were the plants of each previous group. In turn as these plants change the environment, still others invade and crowd them out. Changes continue until a long enduring community of shade-tolerant plant species is established that can reseed successfully in full competition with itself. This stage, in which the soil depth becomes static, is known as the climax stage of plant succession ... The climax is reached only through the absence of disturbance factors, such as fire, blowdowns, insect and fungus epidemics, logging or other interference by man. The presence of any one of these factors arrests normal progression and usually returns plant communities to an earlier stage. Then plant invasion begins again and proceeds once more towards the climax. In temperate climates, where soil moisture is adequate throughout the growing season, later stages of succession are generally typified by trees. The sequioa story is one of repeated disturbances that have set back the succession of other plants and have favoured the reproduction of the sequoia, a tree of intermediate position in plant succession. Fire is the most important disturbance factor in this story ... Fossil sequoias from Nevada date back to the Miocene and Pliocene epochs (from about 12 to 25 million years ago) ... Abundant evidence reveals that fires were frequent in the sequoia groves before the advent of Western civilisation. Sequoias five feet or more in diameter without large fire scars on the trunks are scarce, if not non-existent, so it is inferred that the species indeed developed with fire as an accomplice.

     R. E. Hartsveldt: 'Fire Ecology of the Giant Sequoias',
     Natural History, Vol. LXXIII, Dec. 1964, No. 10.

This is an ironical comment on my article 'The Ecology of Poetry' which took the analogy of the destruction of a stable forest ecology in the plant world and applied it to poetry since the seventeenth century. In suggesting that the novel drove out as well as replaced the epic, there is nothing at variance with ecological facts, but what I failed to take into account, because I did not know of it, was Plant Succession. On this analogy the replacement of the epic might have seemed a natural process rather than one, as I suggested, of interference with natural balance. And the epic, most naturally comparable to the giant sequoia, would on this analogy be the least fitting comparison, since the epic would then seem both to be an 'intermediate form' and one which successfully maintained itself at the expense of the lesser forms, and that by the destructive incursion of fire, by destruction of the ecology of the forest from without.

A good illustration of the danger and of the limits of argument or illustration from analogy — and of that dangerous thing: a little knowledge.

— Book VIII, 1965, pp. 63–5.

NOTE FROM GIDE (THE SOUL)

In his last journal André Gide says that he believes in the existence of the soul, but as something tied and perishing with the body, produced by the body. This is my feeling too, but I cannot think of this soul as an epiphenomenon. A symphony is not a mere epiphenomenon of an orchestra and a concert hall. It is a real and independently existing thing. A poem is not contained in the ink in the ink pot. The whole controversy as to whether 'immaterial' bodies or spiritual beings exist, whether souls are products of bodies or independent existences, is probably as wrong-headed as a controversy as to whether symphonies can exist without orchestras or are produced by orchestras. No orchestra can create a symphony and no symphony can have actual musical existence without an orchestra.

Suppose an orchestra under the control of a symphony conscious of its own score and able to perform, to score new movements, and invent variations on itself, and to direct the orchestra, and you would have something like a soul.

Souls are in general divided into those which perform variations on a traditional theme and those which improvise and create themselves.

— Book VIII, 1965, p. 148.

ECONOMICS OF SPACE AND TIME

Whatever we possess is, in virtue of our possession, an economic asset, over and above any other value we may put on it, and whether we use it or not. Whatever we use for our ends is in a sense a possession whether we own it, borrow it, or pick it up by the way. In a general way our economic assets can be divided in terms of space and time.

But the value systems of these two economies differ radically one from the other. In space we begin with practically nothing and in theory what we may acquire is practically unlimited. We may die paupers or multi-millionaires, whether our possessions are counted in goods, in power, in knowledge or in anything else that may be accumulated under our control.

But there is a limitation on this power of acquisition and the limitation is always a function of the economics of time. The economics of time are quite different. Some of us have more expectation of life than others, but on an average it runs to a common capital of something over sixty years for Western European men and slightly more for European women. None of us, given the maximum expectation, can increase his capital much over a hundred years by any exercise of will and energy, by any fortunate disposition of birth, intelligence, education or genius. The economics of space produces a capitalist society, if given free rein; the economics of time a roughly egalitarian society. Any man of imagination can suppose and desire an almost indefinite extension of his time capital. But there is no way of achieving it. As far as time is concerned he is on a fixed income and it is an income not to be earned by merit, effort or luck, but paid out of a limited and steadily diminishing capital. Except in a metaphorical way, he cannot sell or buy time. He cannot even waste or destroy it in any real sense because if he does nothing with it, he still has the same 'time on his hands'.

All economic theories appear to concern themselves almost entirely with the economics of space and to ignore the modification of their value-systems imposed by the fact that the economics of time affect those of space and follow different laws. Where some notice is taken of time it is treated as a mere part of the economics of space and subject to the same laws, instead of constituting a separate value system.

A man can sell all his goods and give them to the poor. His capital in time is not disposable in this way: it is doled out to him a piece at a time like weekly pocket-money to a schoolboy. One reason why economics pays so little attention to time is naturally that time is not disposable, it cannot be used as a medium of exchange. It has therefore no social value, and conventional economics deals exclusively in social values. The valuer is a unitary figure; he exists only as a member of a group competing for something they wish to acquire; and idiosyncratic or personal values do not exist except insofar as what is unique in them can be excluded and the residue of shared desires turned into units of value that can be summed and equated with others. The economics of time, by the very fact that time cannot be exchanged, is radically different. It deals in personal individual and unique values. Its units, if there can be a statistical unit in such matters, are basically incommensurable with the units of other individuals; they can only be expressed in terms of individual preference. If I choose to lose the whole world and save my soul there is ultimately no arguing with this value system. The minutes of time that make up a life are a sort of coinage, quite neutral in value themselves or only, theoretically, of equal value as 'living time' until the person in question decides to mint his own coinage, so to speak. For me, every moment of poetry is worth a hundred of pushpin; for the next man it may be the reverse.[3] The economics of time, as a pure theory is therefore very difficult to formulate and is only susceptible to statistical formulation insofar as the individual shares his values with others — that is to say partially and incompletely. Is what is true of the economics of time, also true of the morals and the esthetics of time?

— London 1971
— Book XII, 1971, p. 8–12.

ELECTIVE AFFINITIES

What then are antibodies? They are protein molecules present in the serum which have the capacity to unite with, and bind firmly to, an antigenic determinant on an antigen molecule. Moreover, they are highly specific molecules. For each antigen there is a corresponding different antibody. As with locks and keys, only certain pairs fit.

G. J. V. Nossal: *Antibodies and Immunity*, p. 22

It is pleasing to see the theory of elective affinities justified at last, if only at the molecular level in biology. And as in the original notion of the *Wahlverwandtschaften*,[4] it is an aristocratic process, only occurring in the vertebrates and, in its more sophisticated forms, only in the higher vertebrates.

But one could turn the analogy the other way about and view marriage as nature's way of managing the disrupting and socially dangerous forces of love and the violent self released sexual energy. These forces have to be very powerful to ensure the continuation of the species. If only the energy actually required, to attract the male and female together, were provided, the other forces of life and other interests, distractions and fears would make mating too precarious a business. The forces of love and sexual drive must be present when needed to a degree sufficient to master all rival forces. But nature must then provide a mechanism to prevent this vital energy from disrupting the whole social body, breaking down the hierarchy of controls and relationships of a culture, and producing the sort of social anarchy observed by [the zoo-keeper] when he introduced a number of females into a monkey cage at the London Zoo, inhabited only by a group of males before. In their natural state of social intercourse these animals have a hierarchy of controls and specific inter-personal relationships which prevents what happened at the zoo: all the males began fighting among themselves for possession of a female. The usual dominance-submission relations between individuals [were] swept away, civil war and anarchy resulted and the unfortunate females were torn to pieces and the males themselves badly damaged in the conflict.

We could view the institution of marriage as the outward or formal manifestation of something similar to what Nossal calls 'specific complementarity between antigenic determinants and antibody combining sites'. Like the molecules in question men and women are complex in their reactions. The sexual urge is powerful and not specific. Any female or any male will do, and if none are available some substitute will be found. But love operates in the opposite way: it is specific and responds only to its own elective affinity. Moreover once this has been found and the two have 'locked', the dangerous drive in all directions is sealed into one object. If one regards the male as the antigen,* then he is rendered harmless to society, he has been immunized.

One could amuse oneself by elaborating the analogy. There are cells, phagocytes (a more primitive immunological system), which are stimulated by antigen simply to absorb and digest antibodies. There are some types of female in society whose function seems to be similar in respect of the males who cannot be immunised or have resisted the process, and so on.

* 'Some antibody molecules are extremely well fitted to their corresponding antigens and bind very firmly with it; others still bind but much less strongly. The strength of binding can be measured quite accurately and is called the *avidity* of the antibody' (Ibid., p. 84)

It is noteworthy that the avidity increases with the passage of time. Not only is more antibody made but it is of better quality.

— Book XIII, 1971, pp. 21–4.

BEINGS IN TIME, ONCE MORE

One may follow a river from its source to the sea. At each point in the journey one may imagine oneself (and it may actually be possible to realise this idea) accompanying the same 'piece of water' on its way. This stretch of the stream is the equivalent of the river 'now' in time. Above this point is the 'future' river, below, the 'past' river. Or looked at in another way in respect of the part of the river one is accompanying, the stretches of the bank still to come are its future, those already passed, its past. But if one goes up high enough one may view the whole river from beginning to end and the river's now, its past and its future exist only in time. From the point of view of the first observer the river is a being in space and does not exist as a whole at any one moment. From the point of view of the second observer it is a being in time. (Analogy only).

— Book XII, 1971, p. 45.

POETS ANONYMOUS

Since we frequently meet in the past year or so, David Campbell, Rosemary Dobson, Bob Brissenden and I, I have proposed to form them into a society on the lines of Alcoholics Anonymous. They seem rather shocked at the joke, even when I explain that its purpose is to keep down the incredible proliferation of poetasters — Pope's point — to cure them or help them cure themselves of this dangerous addiction — and so, to leave only the incorrigible addicts like ourselves.

Worthy persons are always trying to encourage poetry, as though it were in danger of dying out, like a rare animal species, unless protected and fostered. In fact, it has become a sort of pest and cries out for control.

— March 1973

(Reflections after sitting for two days on the Literary Committee of the Council for the Arts.)

— Book XV, 1973, p. 11.

WORLDS NOT REALISED

I have a constant sense of them and a feeling that the next stage in science will be to take them seriously.

What will be needed is team-work between physiologists, physicists and psychologists to map the course. For example, to answer questions like the following:

1. If two worlds were to occupy the same space in the way that the Post Office can send a number of messages simultaneously over the same wire, what would be the differences in rate, frequency and time scale necessary for them to operate independently and without being aware of each other?
2. What sensory apparatus do we lack (on the analogy of the gaps in our power to respond to the electromagnetic series)?
3. What corporeal and time scales would we need for one system to be able to operate in and pass through the matter of the other system without interference?
4. Assuming that the same matter as well as the same space is used by both systems:
   a. What so-far unrealised super-systems (or micro-systems) could there be on, say, the analogy of human consciousness of which

the individual cells are unaware and would probably be unaware even if they could be aware of themselves and one another?

b. What higher kinds of mind could we envisage on such analogies?

5. What possibilities lie in such theories as that of matter and anti-matter? Could there be two neutral systems as well as two mutually destructive systems?

6. What is the nature of aberrant events which seem to occur as *Lusus naturae*? Is our tendency to explain them away justified? Is their rarity of occurrence anything against them or is there a possibility that on a different scale of observation they would be seen to have their own regularities and 'laws'?

And so on ...

— Book XV, 1974, pp. 173–4.

TIME AND ETERNITY

It is obvious that we need both concepts — Time, for practical reasons and Eternity to swallow the logical problems and contradictions involved by any attempt to give a coherent account of time.

The connection between the two concepts is improbable and is best left vague if we are to find each useful in its own area of thought; but of course we cannot help trying to relate one to the other.

Thinking in physiological terms I come up with a series of metaphors: 'Time is the arsehole of Eternity.'

But it could equally be: 'Eternity is the womb of Time.'

(And one remembers Blake's splendid 'proverb of Hell': 'Eternity is in love with the productions of Time'.

— Book XX, 1977, pp. 46.

Notes

1. See Hope, 'Teaser Rams', in *Orpheus*, Melbourne: Harper Collins Publishers, 1991, pp. 26–9, where the resultant poem from Hope's speculations was first published.
2. G.T. refers to *Gulliver's Travels*
3. Pushpin is a child's game involving players attempting to cross their pins. Hope is referring to Jeremy Bentham's argument in *The Rationale of Reward* (Book Three, Chapter One) that 'Prejudice apart, the game of push-pin is of equal value with the arts and sciences of music and poetry. If the game of push-pin furnish more pleasure, it is more valuable than either. Everybody can play at push-pin: poetry and music are relished only by a few. The game of push-pin is always innocent … If poetry and music deserve to be preferred before a game of push-pin, it must be because they are calculated to gratify those individuals who are most difficult to be pleased.' Robert Herrick's poem *Love's Play at Push-Pin*, with the implication that the game has the potential to cause pain for the competitors, adds complexity to Hope's allusion:

   > LOVE and myself, believe me, on a day
   > At childish push-pin, for our sport, did play;
   > I put, he pushed, and, heedless of my skin,
   > Love pricked my finger with a golden pin;
   > Since which it festers so that I can prove
   > 'Twas but a trick to poison me with love:
   > Little the wound was, greater was the smart,
   > The finger bled, but burnt was all my heart.

4. *Wahlverwandtschaften* is a title of a novel by Goethe (1809) and translates as 'Elective Affinities'.

BIBLIOGRAPHY

Works by A. D. Hope

Books of Poetry

Hope, A. D., *The Wandering Islands*, Edwards and Shaw, Sydney, 1955.
— *Poems,* Hamish Hamilton, London, 1960.
— *Selected Poems*, Angus and Robertson, Sydney, 1963.
— *New Poems: 1930–1969*, Angus and Robertson, Sydney, 1972.
— *Dunciad Minor: An heroick poem*, Melbourne University Press, Melbourne, 1970.
— *A Book of Answers*, Angus and Robertson, Sydney, 1978.
— *Antechinas*, Angus and Robertson, Sydney, 1981.
— *The Age of Reason*, Melbourne University Press, Melbourne, 1985.
— *Orpheus*, Angus and Robertson, Sydney, 1991.

Plays

Hope, A. D.,*The Tragical History of Doctor Faustus: By Christopher Marlowe, purged and amended by A. D. Hope*, Australian National University Press, Canberra, 1982.
— *Ladies from the Sea*, Melbourne University Press, Melbourne, 1987.

Books of Criticism

Hope, A. D.,*The Structure of Verse and Prose*, Australasian Medical Publishing Co., Sydney, 1963.
— *Australian Literature 1950–1962*, Melbourne University Press, Melbourne, 1963.
— *The Literary Influence of Academies*, lecture delivered to the Australian Academy of the Humanities, First Annual General Meeting, Canberra, 9 May 1970, Sydney University Press, Sydney, 1970.
— *A Midsummer Eve's Dream: Variations on a Theme by William Dunbar*, Viking Press, New York, 1970.
— *Henry Kendall: A Dialogue with the Past*, the first Herbert Blaiklock Memorial Lecture, delivered at the University of Sydney on 14 July 1971, Wentworth Press, Surrey Hills, 1972.

— *Henry Kendall*, (ed. with Leonie Kramer), Sun Books, Melbourne, 1973.
— *Native Companions: Essays and Comments on Australian Literature 1936–1966*, Angus and Robertson, Sydney, 1974.
— *The Cave and the Spring: Essays in Poetry*, 2nd ed., Sydney University Press, Sydney, 1974.
— *Judith Wright*, Oxford University Press, Melbourne, 1975.
— *The Pack of Autolycus*, Australian National University Press, Canberra, 1978.
— *The New Cratylus: Notes on the Craft of Poetry*, Oxford University Press, Melbourne, 1979.
— *Directions in Australian Poetry*, Foundation for Australian Literary Studies, Townsville, 1984.
— *Chance Encounters*, Melbourne University Press, Melbourne, 1992.

Selected Articles and Chapters

Hope, A. D., 'The Meaning of Good,' *Australasian Journal of Psychology and Philosophy*, Vol. 21, No. 1, 1943.
— 'The Esthetic Theory of James Joyce,' *Australasian Journal of Psychology and Philosophy*, Vol. 21, No. 1, 1943.
— 'The Study of English,' *Melbourne Graduate*, Vol. 4, No. 1, 1953, pp. 10–19.
— 'Australian Literature and the Universities,' *Meanjin*, Vol. 13, No. 1954.
— 'The Poet's Use of Language,' *Technology: The Journal of the University of New South Wales*, Vol. 21, No. 2, 1962.
— 'Standards in Australian Literature,' in Graham Johnston (ed.), *Australian Literary Criticism*, Oxford University Press, Melbourne, 1962.
— 'Pushkin's Don Juan,' *Melbourne Slavonic Studies*, Vol. 1, 1967.
— 'Presidential Address,' *English in Australia*, No. 5, 1967.
— 'The Frontiers of Literature,' *Quarterly Journal of the Library of Congress*, Vol. 27, No. 2, 1970.
— 'Dostoyevsky and Nietzsche,' *Melbourne Slavonic Studies*, Vol. 4, 1970.
— 'The Reputation of Karoline von Gündernode,' in *Australian Academy of the Humanities: Proceedings*, Sydney University Press, Sydney, 1972.
— 'Voznesensky's "Lament for Two Unborn Poems",' *Melbourne Slavonic Studies*, 1972.
— 'Randolph Stow and the Tourmaline Affair,' in W. S. Ramson (ed.), *The Australian Experience: Critical Essays on Australian Novels*, Australian National University Press, Canberra, 1974.
— 'The Blind Swallow: Some Parleyings with Mandelstam,' *Melbourne Slavonic Studies*, 1975.
— 'Poetry as Journalism,' *Westerly*, Vol. 3, 1975.
— 'Talking to God: The Poetry of Francis Webb,' *Poetry Australia*, Vol. 56, 1975.

— 'Introduction,' *Siren and Satyr: The Persona; Philosophy of Norman Lindsay*, Sun Books, Melbourne, 1976.

Bibliography

Hooton, Joy W., *A. D. Hope*, Oxford University Press, Melbourne, 1979.

Critical References on Hope

Abraham, Lyndy, 'A. D. Hope and the Poetry of Allusion,' *Australian Literary Studies*, Vol. 9, No. 2, 1979.

Ali-Shah, Omah, *Rub-a-iy-at English*, Penguin, Harmondsworth, 1972.

Argyle, Barry, 'The Poetry of A. D. Hope,' *Journal of Commonwealth Literature*, Vol. 3, 1967.

Barnes, John, 'A Question of Standards,' *Meanjin*, Vol. 16, No. 3, 1957.

Brissenden, R. F., 'Hope Without Bawd' (review of *Collected Poems 1930–1965* by A. D. Hope), *Comment*, Vol. 1, No. 2, 1966.

— 'A. D. Hope's New Poems,' *Southerly*, Vol. 30, No. 2, 1970.

— 'A. D. Hope's "The Double Looking Glass": A Reading,' *Australian Literary Studies*, Vol. 6, No. 4, 1974.

Brooks, David, 'Orpheus and the Age of Reason', *Redoubt*, Vol. 13, 1992.

— *The Double Looking Glass: New and Classic Essays on the Poetry of A. D. Hope*, University of Queensland Press, St Lucia, 2000.

Buckley, Vincent, 'A. D. Hope: The Unknown Poet,' *Essays in Poetry: Mainly Australian*, Melbourne University Press, Melbourne, 1957.

— 'Utopianism and Vitalism in Australian Literature,' *Quadrant*, Vol. 3, No. 2, 1959.

— 'Towards an Australian Literature,' *Meanjin*, Vol. 16, No. 3, 1957.

— *Cutting Green Hay: Friendships, Movements and Cultural Conflicts in Australia's Great Decades*, Penguin, Ringwood, 1983.

Campbell, David, 'The Brutal Mouth of Song' (review of *The Wandering Islands* by A. D. Hope), *Southerly*, Vol. 17, No. 2, 1956.

Davie, Donald, 'Australians and Others' (review of *Poems* by A. D. Hope), *Spectator*, 24 March 1974.

Docker, John, 'Sex and Nature in Modern Poetry', *Arena*, 22, 1970.

— 'The Image of Woman in A. D. Hope's Poetry,' in John Docker, *Australian Cultural Elites: Intellectual Traditions in Sydney and Melbourne*, Angus and Robertson, Sydney, 1974.

Dutton, Geoffrey, 'Intellectualised Pornography: "Imperial Adam" and Kenneth Slessor,' *Southerly*, Vol. 49, No. 3, 1989.

Dutton, Geoffrey (ed.), *The Literature of Australia*, Penguin, Ringwood, 1976.

Fuller, Roy, 'A. D. Hope's *Collected Poems*,' *Meanjin*, Vol. 25, No. 2, 1966.

Goldberg, S. L, 'The Poet as Hero: A. D. Hope's *The Wandering Islands*,' *Meanjin*, Vol. 16, No. 2, 1957.

Graham, Suzanne, 'Myth and the Poetry of A. D. Hope,' *Australian Literary Studies*, Vol. 7, No. 12, 1955.
Harris, Max, 'A. D. Hope: Sensuous Excitement — or Monotonous Imagery?,' *Voice*, Vol. 4, No. 12, 1955.
Harrison, James, 'Hope's "Agony Column",' *Explicator*, Vol. 47, No. 3, 1987.
Hart, Kevin, 'A. D. Hope,' in the *Oxford Australian Writers Series*, Oxford University Press, Melbourne, 1992.
Hergenhan, Laurie et al. (eds), *The Penguin New Literary History of Australia*, Penguin, Ringwood, 1988.
Heseltine, H. P., 'Paradise Within: A. D. Hope's *New Poems*,' *Meanjin*, Vol. 29, No. 4, 1970.
— 'From Dim Surmise to Final Lucid Speech: The Late Poetry of A. D. Hope,' in D. John Hollander, 'Review of *New Poems: 1965–1969* by A. D. Hope,' *Harper's Magazine*, September 1970.
Jones, Evan, 'Three Conservatives,' *Bulletin*, 21 October 1961.
— 'The Poet in The University,' *Australian Author*, Vol. 1, No. 4, 1969.
Kermode, Frank, 'Poetry in Australia,' *Manchester Guardian*, 17 March 1961.
King, Bruce, 'A. D. Hope and Australian Poetry,' *Sewanee Review*, Vol. 87, No. 1, 1979.
Kuch, Peter and Kavanagh, Paul, 'Daytime Thoughts about the Night Shift: Alec Hope talks to Peter Kuch and Paul Kavanagh,' *Southerly*, Vol. 47, No. 2, 1956.
Macainsh, Noel 'A. D. Hope's Malthusian Muse: Lubricious Disaster,' *Quadrant*, Vol. 29, No. 3, 1986.
— 'The Suburban Aristocrat: A. D. Hope and Classicism,' *Meridian*, Vol. 4, No. 1, 1985.
— 'Fine Wine and Triumphant Music — A. D. Hope's Poetic,' *Westerly*, Vol. 31, No. 3, 1986.
Malouf, David, 'A. D. Hope's *New Cratylus*,' *Meanjin*, Vol. 39, No. 2, 1980.
Martin, Philip, 'A. D. Hope, Nonconformist,' *Journal of Popular Culture*, Vol. 23, No. 2, 1989.
McAuley, James, 'The Pyramid in the Waste: An Introduction to A. D. Hope's Poetry,' *Quadrant*, Vol. 5, No. 4, 1961.
— 'A. D. Hope,' in James McAuley, *A Map of Australian Verse: The Twentieth Century*, Oxford University Press, Melbourne, 1975.
McCulloch, Ann, 'A Lecture: Given on the Eve of A. D. Hope's Eightieth Birthday,' in David Brooks (ed.), *Security of Allusion*, The Phoenix Review/Bistro Editions, Faculty of Arts, Australian National University, Canberra, 1992.
— *A. D. Hope: The Dance of Language: An Annotated Chronology, His Life, His Work, His Views*, Monograph, Deakin University Press, Geelong, 1995.

— 'A. D. Hope: An Annotated Chronology,' in David Brooks (ed.), *The Double Looking Glass: New and Classic Essays on the Poetry of A. D. Hope*, University of Queensland Press, St Lucia, 2000.

— 'Landing A. D. Hope,' in David Brooks (ed.), *The Double Looking Glass: New and Classic Essays on the Poetry of A. D. Hope*, University of Queensland Press, St Lucia, 2000.

McLeod, A. L, 'Maturity in Australian Satire: The Poetry of A. D. Hope,' *Modern Language Studies*, Vol. 10, No. 2, 1980.

Metzger, Ross, 'Alienation and Prophecy: The Grotesque in the Poetry of A. D. Hope,' *Southerly*, Vol. 36, No. 3, 1976.

Moore, Susan, 'A. D. Hope's Three Faces of Love,' *Australian Literary Studies*, Vol. 10, No. 3, 1982.

Morse, Ruth, 'Editing A. D. Hope,' *Australian Literary Studies*, Vol. 12, No. 4, 1986.

— 'Security of Allusion: Andre Chenier and the Poetry of A. D. Hope,', *Quadrant*, Vol. 32, 1988.

Narasimhaiah, C. D, 'A. D. Hope: Poetry of Shocked Sensibility,' *ACLAS Bulletin*, Vol. 4, No. 4, 1976.

Robertson, Davies, *World of Wonders*, Viking Press, New York, 1975.

Royston, Clowes, *The Structure of Life*, Penguin, Baltimore, 1967.

Roper, Sheila L., 'An Exhumation: A Missing Link in Modern Australian Poetry,' *Southerly*, Vol. 47, No. 1, 1972.

Smith, William Jay, 'A. D. Hope and the Comic Vision: Four Recent Contributions,' *Hollins Critic*, Vol. 9, No. 2, 1972.

Strauss, Jennifer, 'Vision that keeps the night and saves the day: Whose is the task defined in "An Epistle from Holofernes"?', in David Brooks (ed.) *The Double Looking Glass*, University of Queensland Press, St Lucia, 2000.

Suchting, W. A, 'The Poetry of A. D. Hope: A Frame of Reference,' *Meanjin*, Vol. 21, No. 2, 1962.

Steele, Peter,'Contemporary Australian poetry,' *Spirit*, Vol. 36, No. 4, 1970.

Taylor, Andrew, 'A. D. Hope: The Double Tongue of Harmony,' in Taylor, *Reading Australian Poetry*, University of Queensland Press, St Lucia, 1987.

Tennant, Gaye, 'A. D. Hope: Sensuous Excitement — or Monotonous Imagery?', *Voice*, Vol. 4, No. 12, 1955.

Wallace-Crabbe, Chris, 'Three Faces of Hope,' in Wallace-Crabbe, *Melbourne or the Bush: Essays on Australian Literature and Society*, Angus and Robertson, Sydney, 1974.

— 'True Tales and False Alike Work by Suggestion,' *Australian Literary Studies*, Vol. 14, No. 4, 1991.

Walsh, William, 'A. D. Hope,' in Walsh *A Manifold Voice: Studies in Commonwealth Literature*, Chatto and Windus, London, 1970.

Webb, Edwin, 'Dualities and their Resolution in the Poetry of A. D. Hope,' *Southerly*, Vol. 32, No. 3, 1972.
Wieland, James, '" Eater of Time": Poetry and History in A. D. Hope,' *Journal of English Sana'a University*, Vol. 6, 1979.
— 'A. D. Hope's Latter-Day Ulysses: "The End of A Journey" and the Literary Background,' *Australian Literary Studies*, Vol. 10, No. 4, 1982.
Wilkes, G. A., 'The Poetry of A. D. Hope,' *Australian Quarterly*, Vol. 36, No. 1, 1964.
— 'Going Over the Terrain in a Different Way: An Alternative View of Australian Literary History,' *Southerly*, Vol. 35, No. 2, 1975.
Zwicky, Fay, 'Another Side of Paradise: A. D. Hope and Judith Wright,' *Southerly*, Vol. 48, No. 1, 1988.

Papers

The National Library of Australia (Canberra) holds manuscripts, letters, notebooks, lectures and substantial amounts of other Hope materials. The Menzies Library at the Australian National University; the Fryer Memorial Library, Brisbane; Latrobe Library, Melbourne; Mitchell Library, Sydney; Baillieu Library, Melbourne University, Melbourne, also hold materials. Broadcasting material is held by Australian Broadcasting Commission, Archives Department, Melbourne. Further material remains in possession of the family of A. D. Hope.

Filmed Documentaries/Videos (includes interviews with Hope)

McCulloch, Ann, *Programme One: Biography: a. Childhood; b. Wine, Women and Song; c. Academic Career* (100 minutes), (Deakin University, Melbourne, 1995).

Programme Two: Theories: a. Hope and Freud; b. Hope and Women; c. Negative Capability; d. The A. D. Hope and Patrick White Controversy; e. A. D. Hope: Anti-Modernist with a Post-Modernist Sensibility; f. Cosmology; g. Hope's 'Theory of Dreams' (120 minutes), (Deakin University, Melbourne, 1995).

Programme Three: A. D. Hope and Australian Letters: a. Australian Literature, Its Inception in University Courses; b. A. D. Hope: An Australian Poet?; c. Other Australian Poets; d. European Influences on Australian Poetry; e. The Ern Malley Hoax; f. Political Beliefs; g. A. D. Hope: Anti-Modernist; h. A. D. Hope and Literary Criticism (130 minutes), (Deakin University, Melbourne, 1995).

Programme Four: Sexuality: a. Mating Behaviour; b. Women as Subject, Muse and Metaphor; c. Erotic Poetry; d. Women as Poets; e. Penelope (110 minutes), (Deakin University, Melbourne, 1995).

Programme Five: a. A. D. Hope, The Work: a. Performance of the Poetry;
b. Two Scenes from A. D. Hope's Ladies from the Sea: A theatrical Workshop through Camera (Directors, Ann McCulloch and Adrian Barker, 60 minutes), (Deakin University, Melbourne, 1995).
Programme Six: Tributes, Other Writers Respond (40 minutes), (Deakin University, Melbourne, 1995).

Works Consulted by Hope

Adamson, Jane, *Othello as Tragedy: Some Problems of Judgement and Feeling*, Cambridge University Press, New York, 1980.
Arnold, M. (ed.), *Six Chief Lives from Johnson's Lives of the English Poets*, P. Dodsley, London, 1938.
Aubrey, J., *Brief Lives*, 2 vols, edited from the original manuscript and with an introduction by Oliver Lawson Dick, Secker and Warburg, London, 1958.
Ayrton, Michael, *The Maze Maker, 1921–1975*, London, Langmans, 1967.
Barnett, S. A., *Instinct and Intelligence: The Behaviour of Animals and Man*, Penguin, Harmondsworth, 1970.
Bentham, Jeremy, *The Rationale of Reward*, London, 1825.
Bernard, Oliver (ed.), *Rimbaud*, Penguin, Hammondsworth, 1968.
Blake, William, *Letters from William Blake to Thomas Butts*, Oxford University Press, Oxford, 1926.
Bonner, Tyler, *Cells and Societies*, Princeton University Press, Princeton, 1961.
Boole, George, *An Investigation of the Laws of Thought on which are Founded the Mathematical Theories of Logic and Probabilities*, Dover, New York, 1958.
Coleman, Peter, *The Heart of James McAuley: Life and Work of the Australian Poet*, Wildcat Press, Sydney, 1980.
Dante, Alighieri, *Vita Nuova*, Penguin Books, Hammondsworth, 1971.
de Montherland, Henry, *Le Chaos et La Nuit*, Gallimard, Paris, 1963.
Dobson, Rosemary, *Selected Poems*, Angus and Robertson, Sydney, 1973.
— *Sister Poets I*, Sisters Publishing, Carlton, 1976.
— *Over the Frontier Poems*, Angus and Robertson, Sydney, 1978.
Donne, J., *Sermons*, G. R. Potter and E. M. Simpson (eds), (10 Vols), Clarendon Press, Oxford, 1953.
Elweil-Sutton, L. P., *In Search of Omar Khayyam*, a translation of Ali Dashti's *Dar Jostoju-ye Khayyam*, Columbia University Press, New York, 1971.
Foreman, M. B. (ed.), *Letters of John Keats*, Oxford University Press, New York, 1935.
Furphy, Joseph, *The Buln-Buln and the Brolga*, Angus and Robertson, Sydney, 1948.
Gray, Thomas, *Elegy in a Country Church Yard*, 1716–71, (reprinted 1927).
Harvey, Paul (ed.), *Oxford Companion to English Literature*, Clarendon Press, Oxford, 1933.

Hardy, Thomas, 1840–1928, *Satires of Circumstances: Lyrics and Reveries; with Miscellaneous Verses by Thomas Hardy*, Oxford University Press, Oxford, 1982.

Herrigel, Eugene, *Zen and the Art of Archery*, R. F. C Hull (trans), Routledge & Kegan Paul, London, 1982.

Hazlitt, William, *Lectures on the Literature of the Age of Elizabeth, and Characters of Shakespear's Plays*, G. Bell & Sons, London, 1884.

Hoyle, Fred, *Lifecloud: the Origin of Life in the Universe*, J. M. Dent, London, 1978.

— *Ten Faces of the Universe*, Heinemann, London, 1977.

— *Galaxies, Nuclei and Quasars*, Heinemann, London, 1966.

Hartsveldt, R. E., 'Fire-Ecology of the Giant Sequoias', *Natural History*, Vol. LXXIII, No. 10, December 1964.

Jastrow, Robert & Thompson, Malcolm, *Astronomy: Fundamental and Frontiers*, Wiley, New York, 1972.

Jong, Erica, *Fear of Flying*, Graffton Books, London, 1974.

Jung, C. G., 'On the Relation of Analytical Psychology to Poetry,' in *The Spirit in Man, Art and Literature*, Princeton University Press, New Jersey, 1972.

Keats, John, *Correspondence Selections*, Robert Gittings (ed.), Armstrong, Scribner, New York, 1878.

Koestler, Arthur, *The Roots of Coincidence*, Vintage, New York, 1973.

Kramer, Leonie, *A. D. Hope*, Oxford University Press, Melbourne, 1979.

Lewis, D. B. Wyndham and Charles Lee, *The Stuffed Owl: An Anthology of Bad Verse*, Dent, London, 1924.

Lorus J. and M. Milne, *The Senses of Animals and Men*, Harmondsworth, Penguin, 1965.

Mansfield, Katherine, *Journal of Katherine Mansfield*, John Middleton Murry (ed.), Knoph, New York, 1927.

Mathews, P. T., *The Nuclear Apple: Recent Discoveries in Fundamental Physics*, St Martin Press, New York, 1971.

Maynor, James Watt, *Voyage to Atlantis*, Fontana, London, 1973.

Middleton Murry, John, *Keats*, Jonothan Cape, London, 1955.

Milton, John, *Paradise Lost*, Christopher Rils (ed.), Harmondsworth, Penguin Books, 1974.

Moorehead, Alan, *Darwin and the Beagle*, England, Penguin, 1971.

Musil, Robert, *Die Vermining des Zöglings Torless*, Eithne Wilkins and Ernest Kaiser (trans), Panther Books, London, 1971.

Newton, Isaac, 'Philosophiae naturalis principia mathematica,' *Principia*, London, Jussu Societatis Regiae, ac typis, Josephi Streater, 1687.

— 'Celestial Mechanics,' *Principia*, 1687.

Nossal, G. J. V., *Antibodies and Immunity*, Nelson, Melbourne, 1969.

Pope, Alexander, *Epistles to Several Persons, Epistle IV, To Richard Boyle, Earl of Burlingon*, D. F. Theall and I. Lancshire (eds), Department of English, University of Toronto, University of Toronto Press, 1997.

Pausanias, *Descriptions of Greece*, Peter Levi (trans), Hammondsworth, Penguin, 1971.

Rose, Steven, *The Chemistry of Life*, Penguin, Hammondsworth, 1968.

Ruskin, John, *The Poetry of Architecture*, AMS Press, New York, 1971.

Sagan, Carl, *The Dragons of Eden: Speculations on the Evolution of Human Intelligence*, Random House, New York, 1977.

— *Roca's Bain: Reflections on the Romance of Science*, Random House, New York, 1979.

St Augustine, *Confessions*, Vernon J. Bourke (trans), Catholic University of America Press, Wahington, 1966.

Saint-Pierre, Jaques and Henri de Bernardin, *Paul and Virginie*, John Donovan (trans), P. Owen, London, 1982.

Salter, E., *Report of the Committee in the Natural Estate*.

Schmidt, Albert-Marie, *La litterature symboliste 1870–1900*, Presses universitaires de France, Paris, 1960.

Sidney, Philip, *Defence of Poetry*, J. A. van-Dorsten (ed.), Oxford University Press, Oxford, 1973.

Smart, Christopher, *The Poetical Works of Christopher Smart, Vol. 3, A translation of the Psalms of David*, Marcus Walsh (ed.), Clarendon, Oxford, nd.

Smith, John Maynard, *The Theory of Evolution*, Penguin, Hammondsworth, 1958.

Stewart, Douglas (ed.), *Selected Pen Dawings*, Foreword by Norman Lindsay, Angus and Robertson, Sydney, 1968.

Stanislavsky, Konstantin, *My Life in Art*, J. J. Robbins (trans), Geoffrey Bles, London, 1948.

Steele, Peter, Jonathan Swift: Preacher and Jester. Unpublished Phd thesis. 1975.

Stow, Randolph, *Act One: Poems*, MacDonald, London, 1957.

Swinburne, Algernon Charles, *Atlanta in Calydon*, 1864, Chatto & Windus, London, 1917.

Swift, Jonathan, *Gulliver's Travels*, Signet Classics, New York, 1960.

Tuve, Rosamond, *Elizabethan and Metaphysical Imagery: Renaissance Poetic and Twentieth Century Critics*, University of Chicago Press, Chicago, 1947.

Wallace-Crabbe, Chris, 'The Experimental Artist' in *Toil and Spin: Two Directions in Modern Poetry*, Hutchison, Richmond, 1979.

Wittengenstein, L., *The Philosopher Doctor or Patient*.

Wordsworth, W., *Prelude*.

Xaviera, *The Happy Hooker*, Warner Books, New York, 1973.

Yeats, W. B., *The Collected Poems of W. B. Yeats*, Macmillian & Co. Ltd, London, 1961.

Selected Bibliography

Allott, Miriam, *John Keats*, Ian Scott-Kilvert (ed.), Longman Group Ltd, London, 1976.

Brohan, T. V. F. (ed.), *The New Princeton Handbook of Poetic Terms*, Princeton University Press, New Jersey, 1994.

Clemens, Justin and Dominic Pettman, *Avoiding the Subject: Media, Culture and the Object*, Amsterdam University Press, Amsterdam, 2004.

Cook, Elizabeth (ed.), *The Oxford Authors: John Keats*, Oxford University Press, Oxford, 1990.

Cumberlege, Geoffrey, *Letters of John Keats, Selected by Frederick Page*, Oxford University Press, London, 1954.

De Almeida, Hermione, *Romantic Medicine and John Keats*, Oxford University Press, Oxford, 1991.

Deleuze, G. and F. Guattari, *A Thousand Plateaus: Capitalism & Schizophrenia*, B. Massumi (trans), University of Minnesota Press, Minneapolis. 1994.

— *On the Line*, John Johnston (trans), Columbia University Press, New York, 1983.

The Hutcheson Dictionary of Ideas, Helicon Publishing Ltd, London, 1995.

Gittings, Robert (ed.), *Letters of John Keats*, Oxford University Press, Oxford, 1992.

Graves, Robert, *TheWhite Goddess: A Historical Grammar of Poetic Myth*, Faber & Faber, London, 1948.

Greenberg, Clement, 'Modernist Painting', in C. Harrison and P. Wood (eds), *Art in Theory 1900–1990*, Blackwell, Oxford, 1992.

Grosz, E., *Space, Time and Perversion*, Routledge, New York. 1995.

Guattari, F., *Chaosmosis: an ethico-aesthetic paradigm*, Paul Barrins and Julian Pefanis (trans), Power Publications, Sydney, 1992.

Hooton, Joy (ed.), *Rosemary Dobson: A Celebration*, Friends of the National Library of Australia, Canberra, 2000.

Kelley, Mary (ed.), *The Portable Margaret Fuller*, Penguin, Middlesex, 1994.

Nietzsche, Friedrich, *Human, All Too Human*, Cambridge University Press, London, 1986.

— *The Gay Science*, Vintage Books, New York, 1974.

Nixon, Scott, 'Baren's Response to Jonson and Donne,' *Studies in English Literature — 1500–1900*, Vol. 39, No. 1, 1999.

Wilde, William H., J. Hooton and B. Andrews, *The Oxford Companion to Australian Literature*, Oxford University Press, Melbourne, 1985.

Wright, E., *Psychoanalytical Criticism: Theory in Practice*, Routledge, New York, 1989.

PANDANUS BOOKS

Pandanus Books was established in 2001 within the Research School of Pacific and Asian Studies (RSPAS) at The Australian National University. Concentrating on Asia and the Pacific, Pandanus Books embraces a variety of genres and has particular strength in the areas of biography, memoir, fiction and poetry. As a result of Pandanus' position within the Research School of Pacific and Asian Studies, the list includes high-quality scholarly texts, several of which are aimed at a general readership. Since its inception, Pandanus Books has developed into an editorially independent publishing enterprise with an imaginative list of titles and high-quality production values.

THE SULLIVAN'S CREEK SERIES

The Sullivan's Creek Series is a developing initiative of Pandanus Books seeking to explore Australia through the work of new writers. Publishing history, biography, memoir, scholarly texts, fiction and poetry, the imprint complements the Asia and Pacific focus of Pandanus Books.

www.ingramcontent.com/pod-product-compliance
Lightning Source LLC
Chambersburg PA
CBHW061752290426
44108CB00029B/2970